DATE			

The Course of French History

The Course of French History

PIERRE GOUBERT

Translated by
Maarten Ultee

1988 Franklin Watts *New York / Toronto*

A GROLIER COMPANY

Library of Congress Cataloging-in-Publication Data

Goubert, Pierre.
The course of French history.

Translation of: Initiation a l'histoire de la France.
Includes index.
1. France—History. I. Title.
DC38.G6813   1987   944   87-13285
ISBN 0-531-15054-2

First published in France in 1984 by Fayard/Tallandier.
English translation copyright © 1988 by Franklin Watts, Inc.
Translator's preface copyright © 1988 by Maarten Ultee
"From the Great War to the Near Present" (Chapter Eighteen)
copyright © 1988 by Franklin Watts, Inc.
First United States publication 1988 by
Franklin Watts, Inc., 387 Park Avenue South,
New York, N.Y. 10016.
All rights reserved
6   5   4   3   2   1

A la mémoire de
Fernand Braudel

Additional historical studies by
Pierre Goubert available in English

Louis the Fourteenth and the Twenty Million Frenchmen
The Ancien Régime: French Society 1600–1750
The French Peasantry in the Seventeenth Century

TABLE
OF
CONTENTS

———

LIST
OF
GENEALOGIES

═══

LIST
OF
MAPS

═══

TRANSLATOR'S INTRODUCTION

To the uninitiated reader, Pierre Goubert's view of the history of France may seem highly individual, iconoclastic, and even paradoxical. The great events and personalities of French history from the founding of the monarchy to the present day appear in a new light. Goubert balances his mention of the triumphs of Joan of Arc, Louis XI, Louis XIV, Napoleon, and Charles de Gaulle with accounts of their failures. He finds much to admire and to criticize in the revolutions and near-revolutions of 1789, 1830, 1848, 1871 and 1968—and he makes pointed remarks about the political figures of the Third, Fourth, and Fifth Republics.

All this we might expect from any new history of France, but Pierre Goubert presents this history from a popular point of view. He is most concerned with how events influenced the lives of ordinary people. As a social and economic historian of the seventeenth century, Goubert studied records of births, marriages, and deaths among the people of the northern French city of Beauvais. He had been sent there as a school-teacher in 1941, in the midst of a war that had devastated the heart of the old city. Since he was not a native of the area, Goubert tried to rediscover the past of Beauvais by talking with old people, making use of their memories along with whatever could be salvaged from the damaged archives. Often he used parish registers and private sources that other historians and archivists had overlooked. He systematically traced families over generations and related their individual struggles to the larger trends in French economy and society. How *did* ordinary people respond to poor harvests, epidemics, wars, and economic depressions? For Goubert, the answer to this question was history, just as important and valid as the activity of kings and generals, Renaissance men and enlightened writers.

Goubert's emphasis on the common people of Beauvais and the surrounding countryside may be seen as a labor of love, paying homage to his own peasant ancestors and his adopted city. His great work of historical reconstitution ran parallel to the economic reconstruction of France after World War II; both were largely completed during the much-maligned Fourth Republic. The fruit of Goubert's research was a massive thesis published in 1960, a year after his shorter study of three merchant families. The thesis contained dozens of tables, maps, and graphs as well as warm descriptions of the countryside. It was immediately hailed by French reviewers as a "masterpiece," "the work of a great historian," and "the most important work of the French historical school on the seventeenth century in a long time." The author, then aged 45, was appointed professor at the University of Paris and there influenced a generation of academic historians.

Goubert has also realized his desire to be an historian of the people, and to write history for the people. In 1966, he published *Louis XIV and Twenty Million Frenchmen,* a biography that openly declared its unconventional emphasis. Goubert saw a need for scholars to communicate their ideas to the general public, even if the historical figure of Louis XIV should appear less great when set in relation to his kingdom and his age. The book was a popular bestseller in France and was translated into English in 1970. In 1968, Goubert had published an abridged paperback edition of the Beauvais thesis, omitting the scholarly apparatus. The following year he produced a collection of documents on the Ancien Régime— "a testament written before its time"—an immensely useful handbook for students. As a result, Goubert the scholar has been widely read; he has composed this history of France for the general public.

In all of his works Pierre Goubert has rejected theorizing and systematizing. He is neither a dogmatic Marxist nor an abstract philosopher of history. Indeed, his work on the Ancien Regime suggested that most theories and systems are "the very negation of historical endeavor and even of intelligence." Thus Goubert is very much aware of the dangers of over-emphasizing the importance of intellectual trends. His histories are richly detailed accounts of past societies that go far beyond the anecdotes of kings and philosophers. In his biography of Louis XIV, Goubert admitted paying little attention to the "miniscule elite" of intellectual figures because they presented no threat to the kingdom and had practically no immediate impact. Yet in the French edition of this present book he regrets the deliberate omission of "civilization" in the traditional sense of arts and letters, and reports that certain choices had to be made. As Robert Harding has noted, "Goubert is a materialist by temperament, not by creed." He recognizes the importance of ideas, but prefers "direct knowledge obtained from archival or published sources"—reliable, concrete information about the past.

In this history of France, Pierre Goubert presents a popular introduction and interpretation. He acknowledges that "the essence of history may be economic (railways), epidemiological (the Black Death), or purely political, dependent on the unconscious fantasy of a monarch." Human beings are often less than glorious, and their vanity has led to destructive wars. The historian's task is to render justice—to appreciate the motives of men and women of the past, to place them in social perspective, and to restore the reputation of unjustly condemned or forgotten figures.

For Goubert, to render justice is not the same as to render judgments, which he declares is *not* the responsibility of a professional historian. Instead he presents evidence and invites readers to judge for themselves. It may be argued that Goubert's deliberate choice of subjects and evidence does represent his forming of judgments. Naturally, he wants readers to accept his point of view. After all, he does not conceal his sympathy for the poor and oppressed, or his enthusiastic republican sentiments. The English-speaking public should understand that Goubert is engaged in dialogue both with his readers and with the tradition of general histories of France. Too often these histories have been highly romantic, obsessed with national glories, insensitive to the role of the people. In France, histories are political statements.

We might well accept Pierre Goubert as a genial guide to the France of before the world wars. Indeed, the French edition of this book stopped in 1914. For the peasants as for the urban bourgeoisie of that vanished age, the ownership of land and the majestic stability of the gold *franc* ruled for nearly two centuries. When industrial revolution and war came, many lives and landscapes were irrevocably altered. To the vast majority of French people, these economic and social facts were more important than the plumage of kings and queens, or the speculations of philosophers and priests. But the author has tried to strike a balance: hence his references to political events and personalities that affected the nation as a whole.

For this English edition, Pierre Goubert has written a concluding chapter to bring the history down to the present day. His insights into our own century make rewarding reading: reviewers have noted his "irony-etched portraits" and irrepressible humor. When he mentions a person or movement fleetingly, it is often to deliver an aside to the audience, not to introduce new themes. He is as candid and forthright as a good teacher who intends to provoke comments. These are the virtues and delights of his book.

Chapter One

FRANCE UNDER THE EARLY CAPETIANS: 987–1180

THE EARLY CAPETIANS

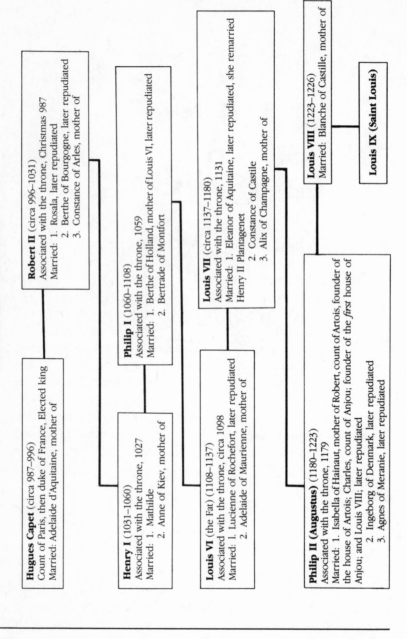

Hugues Capet (circa 987–996)
Count of Paris, then duke of France, Elected king
Married: Adelaide d'Aquitaine, mother of

Robert II (circa 996–1031)
Associated with the throne, Christmas 987
Married: 1. Rosala, later repudiated
        2. Berthe of Bourgogne, later repudiated
        3. Constance of Arles, mother of

Henry I (1031–1060)
Associated with the throne, 1027
Married: 1. Mathilde
        2. Anne of Kiev, mother of

Philip I (1060–1108)
Associated with the throne, 1059
Married: 1. Berthe of Holland, mother of Louis VI, later repudiated
        2. Bertrade of Montfort

Louis VI (the Fat) (1108–1137)
Associated with the throne, circa 1098
Married: 1. Lucienne of Rochefort, later repudiated
        2. Adelaide of Maurienne, mother of

Louis VII (circa 1137–1180)
Associated with the throne, 1131
Married: 1. Eleanor of Aquitaine, later repudiated, she remarried
           Henry II Plantagenet
        2. Constance of Castile
        3. Alix of Champagne, mother of

Philip II (Augustus) (1180–1223)
Associated with the throne, 1179
Married: 1. Isabella of Hainaut, mother of Robert, count of Artois, founder of
           the house of Artois; Charles, count of Anjou; founder of the *first* house of
           Anjou; and Louis VIII; later repudiated
        2. Ingeborg of Denmark, later repudiated
        3. Agnes of Meranie, later repudiated

Louis VIII (1223–1226)
Married: Blanche of Castille, mother of

Louis IX (Saint Louis)

The last thousand years of French history began in July 987, at Noyon. This ancient town, located in a prosperous grain-growing region of northern France, had been the site of a bishopric for four centuries. Charlemagne had been crowned king of Neustria there in 768. But in 987 Noyon did not yet have its gothic cathedral, so plainly visible today from express trains rushing along the main railway line between Brussels and Paris. Noyon in the tenth century was little more than a village, a meeting place for a dozen of the most important counts and dukes of Western Francia, a remnant of Charlemagne's once-great empire. These men spent several weeks bargaining; then, encouraged by Archbishop Adalbero of Reims, they chose one of their number king. The honor fell to Hugh Capet, first of the Capetian kings; from this obscure event arose the kingdom of France.

KING HUGH

Hugh came from a powerful family of counts of Paris and dukes of France. They had fought the Norman invaders, disputed the rule of the last descendants of Charlemagne, and even displaced them on two occasions. From time to time these lords possessed or at least dominated vast forests, lands, and strongholds from the Aisne River in the north down to the Loire. Hugh, perhaps called "Capet" because he wore the *cappa* as lay abbot of Saint-Martin of Tours, was the bearer of a great name and enjoyed the support of the Church. His personal domains were scattered from Compiègne to Orléans, a distance of 120 miles. Yet at times, bandit-vassals obstructed his passage, and he found it difficult to travel through his own lands. Actually this weakness may have been to his advantage in establishing the monarchy, for at first other rulers took little notice of him. Hugh acted wisely in having himself crowned and becoming "the Lord's anointed," a quasi-religious figure. Six months later, he ordered another ceremony "associating" his son Robert with the crown. Robert was also duly anointed and recognized by all the great nobles, and he was able to succeed to the royal title on his father's death. So began the rule of a dynasty that lasted for more than eight centuries. But in the beginning no one could foresee that it would preside over one of the richest and most powerful countries in Europe.

What was the meaning of that term France, or *Francia*? It was evidently derived from the Franks, a Germanic tribe who had invaded and occupied Romanized Gaul five hundred years before. *Francia* did have at least three specific meanings. In its most restricted sense, it referred to the small area of woods and rich farmland between Paris and the great forests surrounding the old town of Senlis. These fine grain-growing lands had been settled and worked for centuries. *France* has long remained part of place names in this region, such as Belloy-en-France; Roissy-en-France, site of the Charles de Gaulle international airport; and the Parisian suburb of Saint-Denis-en-France, burial place of the kings.

France also had a larger sense in the expression "Ile-de-France"—a duchy once controlled by Hugh Capet's predecessors—Robert the Strong, Eudes, and Hugh the Great. At one time this duchy extended from the borders of Normandy in the west to Champagne in the east, and as far north as the

Aisne. This Ile-de-France was more a discontinuous military zone than a territorial domain.

Finally, there was the area soon known as the kingdom of France, the *Francia Occidentalis* where Hugh Capet and his descendants reigned as king of the Franks. It had been defined as precisely as possible by the Treaty of Verdun signed in 843.

WESTERN FRANCIA

When Charlemagne died in 814, he was succeeded by his sole surviving son, Louis the Pious. But by 840 the succession after Louis was complicated by the struggles of his three sons. Frankish custom suggested that the immense Carolingian empire be divided among them equally, just like any other inheritance. Of course only one heir could have the prestigious "Holy" and "Roman" imperial crown, which became the prized possession of the kings of Germania. There it stayed, although French kings right down to Louis XIV had their imperial dreams for centuries.

To settle continuing disputes over the lands, a group of 120 experts came together at Metz in October 842. The lands to be divided included the valleys of the Rhine, Moselle, and Meuse rivers—the very heart of the Carolingian empire. These experts were apparently familiar with a fragment of Aristotle's *Politics,* which recommended that a state be self-sufficient in natural resources in order to survive. Thus they proposed rough dividing lines running north/south. Each prince received a strip of northern coast rich in fish, salt-marshes, and pastures. Then came a band of alluvial plain for growing wheat and planting vineyards, as well as mountains and forests filled with chestnuts and oaks where pigs could forage. Finally there was the Mediterranean coast, quite different in its agriculture patterns and vibrant Roman culture. The southern coasts of Frankish Europe stood in sharp contrast to the Mediterranean, with its insatiable pirates and its two brilliant, competing civilizations, Byzantium and Islam.

11

Western Francia, our subject, was readily defined by the Mediterranean Sea and four great rivers. In the popular imagination, these were long considered the natural frontiers of France. By setting the boundary at the Scheldt, France could lay claim to the entire county of Flanders, even north of Bruges. These claims proved quite important in the later middle ages. Toward the northeast, French territory rarely extended as far as the Meuse; more often the Argonne forest was a barrier. The Saône up to Dijon in Burgundy and finally the Rhône in the southeast completed the whole. These traditional boundaries were slow to disappear. As late as the nineteenth century, boatmen along the Rhône still called the left bank "empi" (for empire) and the right bank "riau" (for *royaume,* kingdom). Over the centuries these territorial limits would shift back and forth, provoking endless disputes over sovereignty.

This curiously elongated France retained the county of Barcelona for three centuries and the county of Flanders for nearly seven centuries—at least in law. Not until King Francis I was taken prisoner in 1525 did Emperor Charles V incorporate Flanders into The Netherlands, pushing the French frontier much farther south. And in the seventeenth century, Louis XIII reasserted French claims to Barcelona.

Francia was thus filled with dukes and counts—of Artois, Champagne, Burgundy, Auvergne, Périgord, Aquitaine, Gascony, and Anjou. Normandy was given to the capable administration of Rollo and his Vikings in 911. In addition there were hundreds of petty feudal vassals, armed men who increased their wealth by pillage and did not hesitate to provoke quarrels with their sworn lord and king. No nation could have been more irregular and changeable than this puzzle of seigneuries and fiefs, the French countryside.

THE COUNTRYSIDE
AROUND A.D. 1000

For five centuries previously, since the fall of the Roman Empire, barbarians from the east and the north had swept across

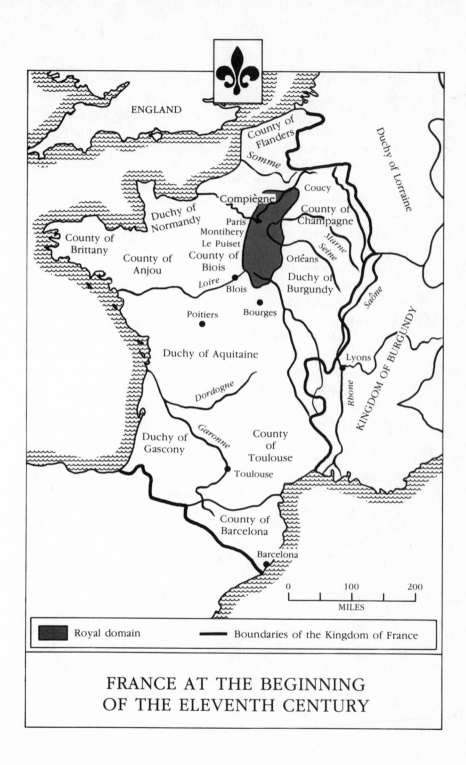

ENGLAND

County of
Flanders

Somme

Coucy

Compiègne

County of
Champagne

Duchy of
Normandy

Paris

Montihery

Le Puiset

Marne

Seine

County of
Brittany

County of
Anjou

County of
Biois

Orléans

Duchy of
Burgundy

Loire

Blois

Saône

Poitiers

Bourges

Duchy of Aquitaine

Lyons

Rhône

KINGDOM OF BURGUNDY

Duchy of Lorraine

Dordogne

Garonne

Duchy of
Gascony

County
of
Toulouse

Toulouse

County of
Barcelona

Barcelona

| 0 | | 100 | | 200 |

MILES

Royal domain   Boundaries of the Kingdom of France

FRANCE AT THE BEGINNING
OF THE ELEVENTH CENTURY

Europe, even to the western frontiers of Roman Gaul. The last and most terrible wave of invaders, the Normans and the Magyars, had settled down by the first half of the tenth century. During the prolonged struggles, most former Gallo-Roman towns had been seriously damaged or destroyed. Among the ruins only a few hundred people survived, typically fewer than two thousand in each city. They scavenged the old stones for building materials and haphazardly repaired once sturdy city walls. These hardy souls included the bishop and canons of the local church, other clerics, servants and slaves, a few merchants, and artisans. In these towns and in the Cluniac monasteries, they saved civilization from dying out completely.

With the exception of these small urban islands, France was an immense forest. In some places the forest was dense and dark; in others it had been reduced to smaller woods, interrupted here and there by primitive fields. Traveling bands of workers used slash-and-burn techniques to clear the barely tamed landscape. What little transport and communication there was took place on water, or along narrow tracks and lanes. Some of these routes followed the traces of Roman roads, popularly attributed to Julius Caesar or Brunehaut, the wife of Sigebert, king of Austrasia in the sixth century. Pockets of human settlement were dispersed widely across the land, often near protective forts. Most of these early defenses were not made of stone—instead they consisted of wooden palisades, sharpened stakes, and deep ditches. At night the inhabitants took shelter behind the walls; during the daytime they worked the land as peasants, hunters, gatherers, herders, and foresters. And almost all their work was done under the watchful eyes and heavy hands of rich warriors, gradually known as *seigneurs* or lords.

The forest was dense and frightening, and it may be hard for us to understand how important it was to the medieval economy. In the forest, hunters found abundant game, powerful and dangerous animals that provided meat for the lord's table. Woodcutters obtained the basic material for houses and fortifications, household furniture and tools. Wood was the primary fuel for forges, and cooking fires were often kept burning outside houses that lacked hearths and chimneys.

To feed the people and their livestock, the forest provided mushrooms, berries, chestnuts, and undomesticated fruits. Our ancestors sought out beehives for their wax and honey. People respected and feared those who lived deep in the woods— they might be religious hermits, lumberjacks, bark-strippers, charcoal-burners and herdsmen. For many months of the year, cattle and horses, sheep and goats were allowed to roam freely regardless of the danger of their young. Also within the forest were the lairs of huge black hogs, half-wild beasts that rooted out acorns. These animals wandered about or were penned providing smoked and salted meat, the basis of a hearty diet.

In the rare clearings, irregularly located and unequally inhabited, there were often enclosed villages containing one or two dozen huts. Generally a place was set aside for cattle and a still larger one for the hemp field and the heavily fertilized and handworked garden, growing mostly beans, peas, and onions. Outside this village zone, this little world of *manse,* or group of family manses, began the arable domain, the bordering agricultural land that would be well laid out in the future. A few vines grew there so that the rich and the priests would have their wine, the beverage for the nobility and for the Catholic mass.

In the damp lowlands that people endeavored to drain, they prepared hay fields to feed the cattle, more and more needed for haulage and transportation. Most of the work, though, was devoted to the production of *bled,* cereal grain used to make bread of varied nature and color, from millet to rye and wheat as well as many mixtures. These lands were poorly fertilized and were barely scratched by plowshares, which were still too light, or by plows, often devoid of wheels or moldboards, containing little iron; at best they were made of fire-hardened wood.

The grains were usually eaten in the form of gruel since bread seemed to have been reserved for the rich. The harvest produced three bushels of grain for one bushel of seed. This ratio was achieved every other year at most, because biennial rotation required leaving fields fallow. People had not yet given up the old practice of scraping the surface and burning the vegetation; itinerant slash-and-burn practices would persist locally for centuries. On rich lands, however, spring barley and oats could be planted in March, or during Lent, a first timid attempt at triennial crop rotation. Of course, oats were in great demand for the war-horses of the knights.

THE CONDITION OF THE PEASANTS

While the rich gorged themselves on venison, smoked ham, bacon, and wines that were often resinated or spiced, the peasantry had to be content with porridge and peas. In winter they huddled in their heatless hovels, probably dressed in the hides of wild beasts. Their survival depended on the weather: the few monks whose chronicles have reached us evoke in terrible detail the famines that decimated the people and tell us that they were often reduced to cannibalism. They did not all die, of course; we now know that the population was no longer declining and would soon increase. At least at the beginning of the millennium, while the diseases caused by malnutrition and rye ergot were well known, the plague had long been forgotten and would return only much later.

The condition of these rough-looking peasants varied from slavery to freedom. Slaves were still a significant minority, living in groups of ten or twenty in noble houses and devoting their time to personal service, crafts, and agriculture, especially in the gardens; a very few rich farmers and petty lords held several slave couples. As had been the custom in Roman times, slaves were sold, bought, or stolen like mere objects. Subject to permanent *corvée* or forced and unpaid labor, they owned nothing and left nothing behind. They could not marry without their masters' permission, but to the credit of the Church they could become clerics after having been freed. Their number was declining, though they did not disappear.

At the same time, the relatively old system of seigneurial landholding, or rural lordship, was set in place for centuries, to become gradually less strict until its abolition in 1791. Rural lordship was based on parceling out the domain between the lord's reserve land, which was quite large, and land ceded to the peasants in exchange for payments of all kinds—work, grain, small cash sums. These lands were called tenures, or censives, because the *cens,* a fundamental rent, signified and recognized the ultimate property rights of the lord. The peasant's harshest duty was to cultivate the lands of the reserve for no other compensation than a food allowance—a *corvée* usually requiring three days out of six.

Even so, the condition of peasants varied. The most disadvantaged were the then quite numerous serfs: they paid the lord a kind of personal tallage, remained obligated to compulsory labor under variable conditions, could not marry outside the lands of the lord without paying a right of *formariage,* and could not transmit pieces of furniture or land to their children unless the latter lived with them, and even then the lord would still take part of their inheritance, often a cow. Significant traces of these conditions survived to the eighteenth century, when Voltaire denounced them.

Other peasants who were simple villeins enjoyed less constraining conditions, while continuing to honor the lord with some of their work and a variable portion of their harvest. They were the remote ancestors of the peasants of the seventeenth century.

In the south, especially on the vast lands of Aquitaine, for a long time there survived groups of peasants who were more or less free and who cultivated lands that truly belonged to them; they were the allodials or landowners not under the authority of a lord. Later, the number of these owners sharply declined, but some could still be found in the middle of the seventeenth century in Auvergne as well as in Burgundy.

We may suppose that the peasantry must have bred many children, lost half of them, and survived despite rickets and intestinal problems stemming from malnutrition—their food was at times heavy, at times horrid, and often minimal. They must have lived in constant fear of plagues, wars, famines, and epidemics, or resigned themselves to believe in the stars, the forces of nature, and hidden demons, while finding their ultimate recourse, after the protection of their lord, in the fervor and wonderful hopes offered by the clergy. Besides hermits and monks, there was a priest in every village, and the first chancels, chapels, and oratories of bonded and cut stone were beginning to be built.

THE POWERFUL: WARRIORS AND LORDS

For a long time, the thin cultured elite of the clerics had set itself far above lay society. They also drew a ready distinction between warriors and peasants, rich and poor, nobles and villeins. In this fashion the theory of the three orders came about, which with a smattering of Latin and as much arrogance as ignorance sums up—quite abruptly—the composition of society as *oratores* (those who pray), *bellatores* (those who fight), and *laboratores* (those who work), the last group being despised by the others and working themselves to death so that their betters could pray and wage war.

Whether they descended from the Carolingian nobility of dukes, counts, and the occasional marquis, or imposed themselves by sheer might, these powerful laymen who dominated Francia in the year 1000 were all large landowners and thus also landholding lords. They were all warriors, therefore all knights in the first sense of the term, as one who fights on horseback (in French, *chevalier,* one who fights on a *cheval*); and in the second sense as well, as one who has entered by "dubbing" into a kind of order reserved to initiates. Lastly, they were part of a fabric of ancient origins that vertically bound mounted warriors, great landowners, and nobles in the feudal system.

Feudalism in the strict sense of the term means those links between man and man, going down from the suzerain of suzerains (formerly the emperor, now the king) to the very last of the vassals, often called *vavasors* by the Normans. In this hierarchy, on this scale, only knights and nobles were included; commoners and villeins always remained outsiders, although clerics might have rank.

The ceremony of homage, later called faith and homage, comprised three customary rituals: first the kneeling vassal putting his hands in those of the lord, then the oath of fidelity on the Bible or on relics, often accompanied by a kiss on the mouth as if two breaths of life were exchanged. These two acts were generally followed by a symbolic gift from the lord: a glove, a stick, a ring, a lump of earth, or a twig. This was the actual investiture of a vassal and above all his infeudation, the lord's grant to the vassal of a fief, fittingly symbolized by earth or leaves.

The fief was at first given only for the lifetime of the vassal, but it quickly became hereditary. The recipients themselves fell into the habit of parceling it out among their sons, which increased feudal fragmentation and caused a certain impoverishment of some of the petty lords who had to dream of seeking their fortune elsewhere, notably by going on Crusades.

The duties of the lord consisted of protecting his vassals in times of war and peace, and of supporting them, most often in his residence, where the vassal could become a kind of "domestic," in the favorable sense of companion and kindred spirit in the home (*domus*).

Besides fidelity, the duties of the vassal were defined in two words: *consilium* and *auxilium*. The first means participation in the court and council of the sovereign, thus in his justice. The second entailed military aid, joining the host— from the Latin *hostis,* or army—of the lord whenever he requested it, though the obligation was quickly limited to forty days. Auxilium also entailed financial aid in the so-called "four cases": the ransom of a captured lord, the wedding of his eldest daughter, the knighting of his eldest son, and the lord's departure on a Crusade.

These bonds of vassalage could become more complicated, branch off, at times become intertwined, and at times also be broken either amicably or brutally through felony, a very serious case of breach of loyalty. The French kings were able to manipulate these feudal ties in a remarkable way: first, by setting themselves at the summit of the feudal pyramid; then by attempting to control their vassals by continually claiming homage; and finally, up to the time of Constable Bourbon under Francis I and even the great Prince Condé under Louis XIV, by using the very serious accusation of felony.

The bonds of feudalism tied together knights who always owned several increasingly powerful war-horses, bred for strength and fed more oats. Like centaurs, men and horses waged war together, getting heavier and heavier as the shield, lance, broadsword, caparison, and the original wooden and leather armor were increasingly adorned with iron. Indeed, in the depths of the forest there were growing numbers of open-pit mines and furnaces next to fiery and frightening workshops where blacksmiths and farriers labored to make helmets and armor for men and beasts, as well as to forge plowshares for deeper and deeper plowing.

In contrast to England and the Empire, the lords, vassals, subvassals, knights, and nobles of Capetian France married only among themselves, thus constituting a nobility in the strict sense of the term—that is, a group in which status in society is normally hereditary. However, a boy could become a knight only after an initiation, a sort of rite of passage: the often described ceremony of dubbing. An adolescent of fourteen or thereabouts, at the age of puberty recognized by the Church, received from an elder the sword and crossbelt, then got a slap on the face called the *paumée* (from the palm—*paume*—of the hand) as a trial and probably also as a reminder of some very ancient custom. Then, showing off his physical strength and equestrian mastery in the presence of his family, the new knight underwent some harsh test, the most innocuous of which consisted of knocking over a manikin. From then on, he could hunt, wage war, and take part in the virile and often dangerous sport of the tournament.

Around the year 1000, the intrusion of the Church into this

barbarous military ceremony seems to have been discreet. The period of reflection and pious vigil, the blessing of the sword, chivalrous morality, respect for holy places, protection of widows and orphans—all this would come later. Yet even at this early date, the church was already trying to impose or recover its ascendancy over this still rough feudal society of which it necessarily, but all too easily, became a part.

THE CHURCH

For over seven centuries, missionaries and evangelists of all types had solidly implanted Christianity in the Frankish lands. The only exceptions to the general religious uniformity were a few backward pagans found in the Basque and Gascon lands, the Norman colonists brought by Rollo and his companions, and the small groups of Jews still tolerated in some southern towns.

The prestige of the pope was tremendous but remote. The true chiefs of what is still called the Church of the Gauls were the bishops, all of whom were established in ancient Roman cities. Bishops usually came from powerful noble families and thus were intimately involved in feudal bonds. In a material sense they led a relatively comfortable life on domains bequeathed by pious lay lords. They enjoyed immunities enabling them to escape comitial and even royal justice. They were often counts and dukes as well as prelates, and almost always masters of their episcopal towns. They conferred minor and major holy orders on those whom they chose from the laity, after a brief education, to be country priests. They had sovereign judgment in many cases and could use the terrible weapon of excommunication. At times, they even performed miracles, albeit mostly after their deaths. Alongside the bishop, the effective masters of the cathedrals were the chapters of canons, remarkable teams of men of birth and talent who reconstructed the great edifices. The chapters were endowed with a patrimony of land, which was often huge, especially in the north and east, and which, until 1789, was always distinct from that of the bishop.

The bishop and cathedral clergy led a life of varying quality in which fasting and chastity did not always play an excessive role. And yet the best of them, often graduates of the schools at Reims or Chartres, maintained a culture based entirely on Latin, Greek having fallen into oblivion. The study of the so-called pagan authors from Virgil to Cicero, from Quintilian to Livy, and even some insipid leftovers from Plato and Aristotle, went hand in hand with translations of the Bible made by Saint Jerome in the fourth century, and rare mathematical reports gathered by exceptional men like Gerbert, the future Pope Sylvester II, who worked around A.D. 970 in Catalonia, learning from neighboring Moslem civilization. But these were brilliant exceptions.

Most of the time, in the peasant backwoods, in makeshift chapels erected as early as Frankish times, priests celebrated mass, distributed the sacraments, and attempted to preach in parishes whose boundaries had often been established and even formalized. These cells remained the basic units of French life for centuries and are at the origin of the present communal units. As early as the reign of Charlemagne, the rural priests, at times appointed by a cleric and at other times by a lay lord, lived off the tithe levied on the "fruits of the earth," or at least the portion left to them by those who were more powerful.

It is difficult to have a clear idea of the practices and pastoral ministries of these priests. Some historians think that they were oriented toward the Old Testament and Revelations, that they stressed preparation for the Last Judgment, and that they had started to cover the old agrarian and magical devotions with a Christian mantle, somewhat like the prehistoric monoliths topped by crosses. What is certain is that these excessively numerous and often wretchedly poor priests lived close to the peasantry, more or less married, attended to each parish, and urged the construction of the first dark little stone churches in Romanesque style.

These priests, later known as secular clergy because they lived in the world, were often tainted by the life-styles of the times, by wealth and by misery, by conflicts and by subjugation. They clearly had less influence on the minds and spirits of the people than either the holy hermits, whose sanctity was established by centuries of tradition, or the then all-male monastic communities which flourished and multiplied. Originally all of them were supposed to spend their earthly lives in prayer, mortification, and chastity; later the laity, in order to expiate their sins more surely, overwhelmed the monasteries and abbeys with gifts.

Such riches inevitably spoiled these pious institutions, where the purity of the primitive rules declined as more and more gifts were presented by repentant laymen. Then there sprang up new creations of faith in the valleys, near the forests, and along the rivers. After 910, the independence and prestige of Cluny and its first abbots influenced the Christian west. When Cluny faltered, Grandmont in Limousin, the Premonstratensians near Laon, and finally the male and female order of Fontevrault in Anjou attempted to return to a contemplative and pure life. All would be eclipsed by Cîteaux (1098), especially after the indomitable Saint Bernard became abbot in 1115.

Perhaps unaware of this renewal, the subjects and vassals of the first Capetians found among the monks and enclosed abbeys not only help against the brigands and hope in eternity, but also the contagious enthusiasm of the great popular orators who urged people to undertake pilgrimages to Santiago de Compostela, to Rome, and soon even to Jerusalem, toward which turned a nobility as eager for glory and conquests as for sanctification. These mass mobilizations marked the beginning of new times starting about 1030–1040, as slow changes and growth affected the kingdom ruled by the descendants of Hugues Capet and his son Robert II.

CONDITIONS FOR A
FIRST GROWTH: 1031–1137

The barbarian invasions had ended almost a hundred years earlier. Three centuries had elapsed since the last great plagues, which did not return for yet another three centuries. The chroniclers placed the last truly calamitous famine around 1030–1035. The Church had contained or pushed back the devastating anarchy of the battling feudal lords and had attempted to Christianize the knighthood by decreeing—with variable results—here the Truce of God (four days a week), there the Peace of God (several years), elsewhere a kind of lenten respite, and almost everywhere sheltered zones near religious houses.

Soon, by preaching the Crusades, it would export the taste for raids and looting, and the overabundance of petty landless knights. In a somewhat fragile peace, the more numerous peasants were able to work better and the merchants to return to the highways and to hold fairs with some degree of security. The anemic economy of the kingdom started to take off.

Technical improvements gradually appeared, slowly spreading southward from the better-managed northern domains. Among them were the harness collar attached to the shoulder rather than the neck of the horse, improved yokes for oxen, and more iron, not only for armor but also for reinforcing the peasants' tools, including plowshares, hoes, and picks. The well-documented extension of triennial crop rotation brought both an additional crop and a good harvest of oats, which made for stronger horses that could plow more rapidly than oxen. Extra crops of precious legumes planted on once fallow fields yielded beans that filled bellies without depleting the soil. Millet and gruel gave way to bread and various cereal grains. Water mills that had been relics of the past multiplied suddenly; there were close to 6,000 in England at the time of the Domesday Book (1086), and 245 in Picardy around 1175. Later, one would be built every year. But mills and other improvements were expensive and were usually built by the lord, who rented them or collected fees for their use. The same was also true for communal ovens, which were built almost everywhere. Finally, windmills, though they did not appear until 1180, would multiply rapidly after being introduced in the still independent duchy of Normandy.

Of course we should not overestimate this progress which was often local and slow to spread, or peculiar to those ecclesiastical domains about which we are better informed. Cattle and therefore manure were still scarce and remained so for a long time. Only on its best lands was the Abbey of Cluny, the most advanced agrarian unit, able to achieve a yield of six to one, or about ten quintals per hectare; and this yield would not be surpassed regularly for many centuries, until the 1700s. These technical and agricultural improvements took place on lands that are known to us. They certainly did not occur everywhere.

GREAT LAND RECLAMATIONS AND DEMOGRAPHIC GROWTH

It is certain that the cultivated area increased. The second half of the eleventh century and all the twelfth saw a great series of land reclamations. These often started quite simply from the areas around the village, within its own enclosure, and on the "house field," or "manse tract," as it was called in the duchy of Burgundy. The arable zone abutting the village spread by incorporating temporary pastures, areas of irregular cultivation, after burning off weeds, brush, and scrub at the edge of the forest. Such efforts required many men, sturdy tools, and the agreement of the lord, which was generally given in exchange for additional payments, the *surcens* or rents in kind. As long as the hunting reserve and free forest grazing rounds were left untouched, the feudal lords found these developments to their advantage, while the Church gained new tithes.

Better known and more spectacular were the land reclamations in the heart of the forest, often undertaken at the initiative of a lay lord or an abbey. Along a valley or an old road that had been widened and reinforced, the owners attracted villeins by an exemption from taxation, from forced labor, and from other obligations; and at times they were helped by gifts of tools and cattle. The settlers were able to build houses, often clustered together with gardens in the back and fields in the distance, advancing deep into the scrub or trees. From such land reclamation came herringbone-patterned villages,

25

cleared grounds, new towns, and exempt lands—some of which languished while others flourished—attracting harshly exploited serfs from the old manses and seigneurial farms.

Along certain marshy rivers and especially wetland shores from which the sea had recently retreated—in Flanders, for example—other techniques and other financial and human means were needed to start building polders. During the following centuries, this system would spread to the lower Somme, the Seine, and the marshlands of Brittany and Poitou as well as to other areas.

These intelligent and necessary reclamations encouraged a certain spirit of freedom. Lords, and even an alert monarch such as Louis VI, ceded to the land reclaimers charters called franchises (the connotation of the word is as important as its legal meaning). The first, at Lorris in the Gâtinais region, was initiated in the middle of the eleventh century. Thereafter, others appeared in the east in the jurisdictions of Beaumont and Argonne, and in the west in areas governed by the customary law of Breteuil in Normandy, from which the movement crossed over to England.

In other regions, peasant expansion took another form: colonization by large families who gave their names to hamlets scattered in the heart of the woods. There they cut squarish fields that were always enclosed—the richest being near the house. In the eleventh and twelfth centuries, small groups of men fashioned farmsteads from the scrubland and moors in the wooded regions in the west that separated the cleared lands of Beauce and Touraine, and spilled over the borders of the duchies of Brittany and even Normandy, and the Poitevin north of Aquitaine.

FIRST BURGHERS, FIRST COMMUNES

On the basis of local examples from Picardy and Flanders, historians think that between the years 1000 and 1200 the population of the kingdom may have increased threefold, although it could hardly have exceeded ten million. It was better fed, housed, and warmed, indoor fireplaces being more common, and it was spared great famines, although local and temporary food shortages occurred until the seventeenth century. The France of this period, where the fundamental wealth was still based on rural land, had been given a new impetus that seemed to propel it toward commerce and urban life.

Security having been restored, several highways were patched up, and most of the old bridges rebuilt—thanks to the labors of curious "bridge brotherhoods," with the help of some grandees who coveted substantial tolls. Commerce on a large scale was renewed with vigor. Trade had never really stopped: furs, gold, and precious objects had always aroused the greed of the powerful, who eyed the wonders of Moslem Spain, the Byzantine world, and the fabulous East, the object of speculation and exaggeration. Despite the hazards of travel, some merchants had always moved from castle to castle to display their treasures. Henceforth they were able to meet and be met regularly in convenient places: at crossroads, confluences, and estuaries, at the bases of mountains, and near famous shrines. Fairs and markets revived, although it was necessary for the merchants to obtain protection and privileges, which were only granted for financial consideration.

As early as the twelfth century, the first merchants set up flimsy huts around a large space for displaying wares and haggling over prices. Most often they settled close to the ramparts of an old episcopal city, built a chapel, then a parish, and at times several of them. These settlements formed the *faubourgs* or outlying neighborhoods that, before surrounding themselves with walls of their own, indirectly gave a new life to the ancient city under the authority of its bishop and chapter. Cities that once counted no more than a thousand souls started to grow and burst at the seams of their stone corsets, enlarging or doubling these walls. Some of the cities reached five thousand and even ten thousand inhabitants. During the following century the growth would accelerate, then stabilize little by little.

Trade associations of guilds (the word *corporation* did not appear until the thirteenth century) settled there, formed groups, and became structured. Among the most powerful were the butchers, who were also involved in rising livestock and tanning hides; the smiths, who worked in towns utilizing raw iron prepared in the heart of the forests and later also along the rivers; the grocers or the haberdashers, who sold a bit of everything including indispensable salt fish and prunes in Lent, and the already costly spices. Between Ghent and Beauvais there quite rapidly developed rather large cloth-producing towns destined to provide the dress of part of the kingdom. Already there were protected caravans going to the centers of fairs: Flanders and Champagne, and soon Lendit.

As early as the middle of the eleventh century an apparently new type of men, called burghers, began to grow in number and in wealth, thus in power. Unconcerned with how they might fit into the theoretician's concept of a society of three orders, they found it difficult to accept the pretensions and control of lords or bishops. Uniting under oaths to form communes, they struggled, often violently, as at Laon in 1112, to extract privileges that would free them from traditional jurisdictions.

To thwart their own adversaries, the still weak kings allied themselves with these burghers and helped them obtain franchises to have a greater say in the government of the cities. For his part in this history, Louis VI earned the pejorative title, "father of the free towns." Like the rebellious Laon, the great cities of the north—Beauvais, Noyon, Soissons, Reims—rose and extracted partial or almost total communal autonomy. In 1127–28, the Flemish towns astutely took advantage of a quarrel over the succession to the county to obtain strong "constitutions" to which they clung for a long time. This movement was by no means universal, let alone democratic. Only the rich, who often came to agreements with the urban lord, could participate in the municipal magistratures that were gradually formed. And yet none of this would have been conceivable a century earlier.

The development of Romanesque art, the renewal of religious teaching, and the appearance of secular literature did not necessarily stem from this simultaneous demographic, urban, agricultural, and mercantile growth. But it is clear that they were all roughly contemporaneous developments. The building fever that included towns, castles, churches, and bridges can only be linked to the abundance of more vigorous men, better transportation, technical progress, an atmosphere of relative peace, and the renewal of the great pilgrimages whose routes were punctuated by sanctuaries and hostels.

Beautiful and (often prestigious) books have attempted to explain the art that was belatedly called Romanesque. It had regional forms that were very different, and was exported as far away as Palestine. It combined sometimes simple solutions to the problems of arc and buttress, of light and shadow, of simplicity of line with a progressive abundance of decoration, which was at times very stylized and at others very convoluted. A horror of bare walls led to painted murals which, together with carved capitals, offered the illiterate a pictorial Bible, which the fifteenth-century poet François Villon later described for his mother.

During the same period or slightly later, monastic and episcopal schools were founded in Tournai, Angers, Tours, Orléans, and above all at Chartres and Paris, which was slowly becoming the habitual residence of the king. Thanks to renewed relationships with Sicily, which had recently been conquered by the Normans, and with Moorish Spain, sizable fragments of the great Greek literary works were rediscovered and translated abroad. Among the most influential were the medical treatises of Hippocrates and Galen, whose ideas dominated the healing arts for centuries, and the works of Aristotle, which fascinated the growing number of literati of the early twelfth century and would soon stir theologians and the first university professors.

At almost the same time, in the circles of knighthood that were less given to feasting and brawling, there arose a new spirit foreshadowing courtly literature. This spirit was found at the court of the counts of Poitiers and in the refined areas of Aquitaine where poetic contests flourished. At times these were even dedicated to ladies, who began to be regarded as more than just serving wenches, bawds, or breeders. Elsewhere the old epic poems about chivalric deeds helped people while away the evenings in knightly castles. The violent *Chanson de Roland,* with its less famous sequel, the *Chanson de Guillaume,* or the blander epics describing the deeds of Girard de Boussillon or Ogier the Dane were the traditional fare for an audience probably composed of old troopers whose elementary culture at best might have been polished by epics based on ancient themes or regional traditions. The Trojan Wars and the adventures of Aeneas were adapted to the taste of the times, and later Chrétien de Troyes, a cleric from Champagne, would revive the cycle of legends from Brittany that included the story of Tristan and Isolde.

Even these literary genres reached far fewer than one Frenchman in a hundred. Five hundred years later, the alert printers of Troyes and the entrepreneurs of the "blue collection" of pamphlets would revive them quite profitably, spreading these chivalrous, mythological, and courtly tales even to the villages: an audience as wide as it was unexpected.

THE KINGS

Historians know very little about the first four Capetians, yet their combined reigns cover more than a century. They left a few diplomas, those official documents ratified with a seal, and we have indirect testimony from clerics whose critical faculties were not, and could not have been, their dominant virtue.

We know that the first Capetians' Crown lands, composed of scattered holdings disputed by pillaging vassals, included estates between Compiègne and Orléans, some titles in Berry and the benefices of several abbeys or bishoprics as far away as Le Puy. They all fought to round out these lands and to give them some cohesion.

Robert settled in Dreux and Melun, his son Henry in the metropolitan see of Sens, while Philip I favored locations in the Gâtinais, Vexin, and especially Bourges. In one hundred twenty years, the original domain of Hugues must have almost doubled. Here and there, provosts of the king, who were stewards of sorts, levied the taxes, exercised lordly rights, and tried to dispense justice.

Around the monarch, the ancient offices of the imperial household (chamberlain, butler, seneschal, chancellor) were monopolized by direct vassals, but their functions remained and would become important again later. The army was little more than a handful of relatives, companions, and vassals who were fed by the king. By calling up the feudal host, the king could in principle expand the army for forty days to fight against the great, ambitious feudal lords of Flanders, Normandy, and Burgundy, or respond to news of danger coming from the Empire to the east. But nothing more impressive than a kind of control of the loyalty of those who had taken an oath to the king resulted from twenty such lackluster expeditions.

In the last analysis, the great merit of this apparently mediocre line was that it endured. The early Capetians' morality was so doubtful that the pope twice used the weapon of excommunication against them because of their marital repudiations, or rather their uncanonical remarriages. The Capetians benefited from two chance circumstances. Their most dangerous neighbors either became extinct, as did, for instance, the dynasty of the Ottonian Holy Roman emperors in 1002, or were busy elsewhere, such as the Normans fighting against the infidels in Spain and Sicily, then in England after 1066. Above all, by repudiating infertile wives, each Capetian king was able to beget at least one surviving son, whom he was careful to have anointed and associated with the throne while his father was still alive, a practice that lasted until Philip Augustus. Thus hereditary monarchy was reestablished as customary practice. The holders of vast fiefs—whose ancestors had elected the first Hugues yet made him aware of his weakness by asking the famous question, "Who made you king?"—were perhaps reassured by the relative weakness of his royal heirs, whom they recognized without difficulty.

Louis VI (The Fat)

The fifth king of the dynasty, Louis the Fat, was well named. According to Edouard Perroy, he was "gluttonous, obese, sensual and brutal." But he was lucky enough to be advised by Suger, abbot and rebuilder of Saint-Denis, who wrote a laudatory biography of his master which impressed historians for a long time. Indeed, the king had some great designs, such as rekindling the internal quarrels of the powerful Anglo-Norman monarchy. But it defeated him several times, and in 1113 even brought the duchy of Brittany under its control. Then, as luck would have it, England was again troubled by anarchy, giving Louis VI a brief respite.

He was more successful in moving twice to punish his vassal Guillaume VI of Auvergne, who was persecuting the bishop of Clermont. An even better omen for the authority of the Capetians was the king's ability to gather enough warriors from among the most powerful lords, who put a stop to their own quarrels long enough to rejoin the royal host before Reims and discourage the attack of Emperor Henry V.

But the real success of Louis VI was at last to pacify his own lands. He devoted almost twenty years to quelling the hard-headed and well-entrenched brigand lords who defied him. His vassals gave him little help, but several communal militias lent assistance. It took him seven years to subdue the lord of Puiset and close to thirty to control the lord of Coucy. He even had to fight against the family of his favorite, Étienne de Garlande, who had confiscated almost all of the royal household offices and held the royal seal. Despite the confiscation of lands and oaths of submission, there was always work to be done.

Having pacified, united, and even somewhat extended his lands, Louis VI ended his reign with a master stroke whose scope he was surely unable to foresee. He married his son Louis VII to the sole heiress of one of his greatest vassals: no less than Guillaume X of Aquitaine, who died shortly before Louis VI and whose duchy, spreading from the Loire River to the Dordogne, had been extended by the acquisition of the duchy of Gascony, abutting the Pyrenees.

To be sure, husband and wife kept their inherited domains separate, but at last the Capetians would venture forth under new skies where they could foresee a considerable broadening of their power; which took far more than a century to consolidate. Meanwhile the ardent Eleanor would shake the Capetian monarchy to its very foundations.

Louis VII and Eleanor of Aquitaine

Louis VII does not usually have a good reputation among those historians who deem it their duty to pass judgment. However, he had some character traits that were found later in his saintly great-grandson Louis IX—quick intelligence, great desire for justice, and profound piety; nevertheless he was quite young and remained rather immature, imprudent, and lacking any great perseverance. A bit too devoted to the interests of the church, he cut a poor figure as a husband.

The brilliant young damsel of fifteen whom his father had chosen for him had been raised at the court of Poitiers, from which she brought a new language, a culture, and a taste for poetry, songs, flowery decor, and courtesy, as well as a certain freedom of manners and conduct that created a sensation and a hint of scandal in the far rougher Capetian milieu.

Eleanor pushed her husband to intervene openly in the appointment of bishops and in other affairs of the Church, for which she had little love. She also incited him to attack his dangerous neighbor Thibaut of Champagne; the encounter was bloody and ended badly. Louis fell back under the influence of the clerics while his wife became more and more estranged from him. At the same time and far away, the Turks who had been contained for half a century by the Christian kingdoms established in Syria and Palestine attacked vigorously and took back Edessa in 1144. From then on, the pious king thought only about the Crusade that he would lead, after being urged on by the influential preaching of Saint Bernard of Clairvaux and by the decision of Emperor Conrad III to accompany him.

We need not recount here how on the First Crusade, after a difficult trip and horrible battles, a troop of knights conquered Jerusalem in 1099 and took the tomb of Christ from the Turks, who had captured it twenty years earlier; nor how a kingdom composed of three Frankish principalities was established in the Holy Land. Not all was pure in this First Crusade, so tainted with greed and lust for power, but at least it can be credited with ridding the weak Capetians of a number of impecunious and brutal knights from the area between the Scheldt and Loire rivers.

By contrast, Louis VII's Christian zeal cannot be doubted. He departed from Vézelay on the Second Crusade in 1147. His failure to take Damascus the following year and his return to France in 1149 tarnished the history of the Crusades. In his absence he had left the kingdom in the hands of Abbot Suger, who died in 1151. But for the future of the monarchy and the kingdom of France, Louis VII's having dragged the queen along on this adventure had a more important consequence, for rumor had it she had behaved very badly, or rather had been too good to a handsome Saracen who, to make matters worse, was a slave.

Whether or not the affair took place, the frivolous lady from Poitou had produced only two daughters for the king, and he was tired of her. In spite of Suger and the pope, he found several bishops who were accommodating enough to annul the marriage, although it had been consummated. After a second and sterile union, a third wife, from Champagne, at last gave the king a son: the future Philip Augustus.

The flighty Eleanor was well over thirty, in those days a far cry from youth, but still in possession of her duchies of Aquitaine and Gascony; she could choose the youngest and most gifted of her many suitors, Henry Plantagenet. Already count of Anjou and Maine as well as effective master of the duchy of Normandy, conquered by his father, he became king of England in 1154. As vassals of the king of France, the couple held lands stretching from Dieppe to the Pyrenees. Furthermore, they had three sons: Henry, Richard the Lion-Hearted, and John Lackland. A storm was brewing.

In the face of impending disaster, Louis VII adopted the safe policy of sowing dissension and avoiding confrontation. He stirred up quarrels between Henry II and Eleanor (now herself disappointed), and between the father and his sons; he also received with great fuss the chancellor and primate of England Thomas à Becket, who had been exiled by his master.

Moreover, his piety gave Louis VII a certain distinction. In Sens he welcomed Pope Alexander III and his court when they were exposed to the hostility of the Emperor Frederick Barbarossa. Approaching the lands of Aquitaine from the rear, Louis VII helped prelates and monks fight warring and brigand lords. He made his presence felt at Vézelay, Cluny, and Mâcon; in Beaujolais, in Forez, and even in Le Puy against the Polignacs, and in Mende where the count-bishop of Gevaudan swore homage to him. Undoubtedly the royal warriors did not always shine, but the many homages they received were good omens, and above all, these expeditions foreshadowed the future penetration of the lands along the Rhône and the border of Languedoc.

All in all, in spite of the false starts and misfortunes (the most monumental of these was Eleanor, but who could have foreseen that?), this pious and often wise king deserves more credit than he is usually given for introducing the thirteenth century: the greatest century of the Capetians and of the Middle Ages as a whole.

Chapter Two

THE APOGEE OF MEDIEVAL FRANCE: THE THIRTEENTH CENTURY, 1180–1314

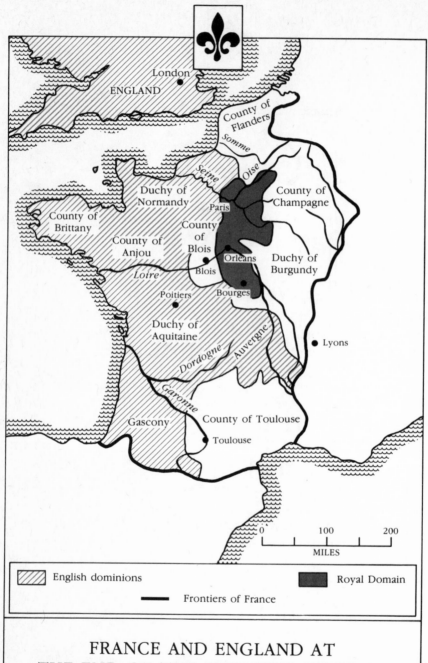

London
ENGLAND

County of
Flanders

Somme

Seine

Oise

Duchy of
Normandy

County of
Champagne

Paris

County of
Brittany

County
of
Blois

County of
Anjou

Orleans

Duchy of
Burgundy

Blois

Loire

Poitiers

Bourges

Duchy of
Aquitaine

Dordogne

Auvergne

Lyons

Garonne

Gascony

County of Toulouse

Toulouse

0   100   200

MILES

English dominions

Royal Domain

Frontiers of France

FRANCE AND ENGLAND AT
THE END OF THE TWELFTH CENTURY

The long period joining the reigns of Philip II and Philip IV is usually described as the age of great cathedrals and Louis IX, the Capetian saint. Indeed these three well-known but quite dissimilar monarchs held the throne, but there were also two others, now nearly forgotten: Louis VIII, who reigned only three years (1223–26); and Philip III (1270–85), whose mediocre reputation may yet improve.

All of them extended their personal domains widely inside the kingdom by successfully waging wars against powerful vassals and dangerous neighbors. These kings were also organizers, because their reinforced power needed at least a rudimentary administration to deal with justice, politics, finance, and military problems. As both enthusiastic and prudent protectors of religion, two of them went on Crusades; but none of them, not even Saint Louis, allowed himself to be dominated by the Church.

ECONOMIC GROWTH

All five thirteenth-century Capetians made contributions to the outpouring of *opus francigenum,* later known as the Gothic style. They encouraged the growth of cities and universities, but they were not alone in this work, for they had the good fortune to rule over a rapidly developing country. Economic growth was apparent, starting in the last quarter of the twelfth century, and represented the first great expansion, or "takeoff phase," of old Frankish Europe.

The conquest of arable land was completed. In Picardy, all usable lands were under cultivation, and triennial rotation and cereal crops were the norm. Villages were growing, too. The better-off peasants were finally using effective plows, powerful horses, and better tools, while iron forges and mills had been built in the countryside.

Two almost unnoticed technical improvements, the spinning wheel and the camshaft for mills, allowed the use of wind and water power for the making of cloth as well as for improved ironworking and hemp manufacture. "Industrial work" in rural areas was now possible, producing additional income and becoming the driving force behind textile manufacturing in the north, led by cities enjoying remarkable growth.

The local economies that had subsisted on barter now entered national and international patterns of trade. Around 1170, the first great European silver mines were opened at Freiberg in Saxony. Later there were others in Bohemia, Spain, and even the Massif Central. Nobles and kings were able to reopen their seigneurial mints and increase the supply of scarce coinage. As early as 1192, for example, Venice struck its first silver gross coins, twelve times as heavy as various local deniers. The new coins were more trustworthy and less scarce, indispensable to a growing trade economy.

At sea there was decisive progress in navigation, with the spread of the compass and a new helm, or sternpost, which was easier to use and more efficient than the ancient rudders employed previously. Large merchant ships came from the north, perhaps from Lübeck. They were heavier and equipped with a deck, carrying cargoes of tar, timber, and furs to hastily prepared harbors between the Loire and Gironde rivers. In exchange, they took back salt and wine, providing new demand for the vast salt marshes of Bourgneuf and Oléron, and for vineyards in the hinterlands.

In 1190, rich Genoese obtained the privilege of crossing the lands of the duke of Burgundy in order to have free access to the famous new fairs that were held almost all year round in four towns of Champagne—Troyes, Lagny, Bar-sur-Aube, and Provins. At these fairs near Paris the great cloth merchants of the north met Italian traders who brought the fine goods of their country as well as the luxuries of the Mediterranean and the Orient. The exchanges of merchandise and silver in the European context could only increase, and helped to support the economy of the kingdom that young Philip II, age fifteen, had just inherited.

PHILIP AUGUSTUS AT
THE SUMMIT OF FEUDALISM

Taking advantage of the king's youth, the rival clans of his Flemish in-laws and his mother from Champagne tried to dominate him. Philip resisted and found himself obliged to struggle against both of them; fortunately they quarreled among themselves and went home.

Three years later, this eighteen-year-old Capetian took advantage of a disputed inheritance in Flanders to impose his arbitration. According to feudal custom, he granted himself Montdidier and the rich town of Amiens, thus extending the frontiers of his personal territories to the Somme River. These actions were typical of a king who was energetic and shrewd and who knew how to exploit both feudal law and armed force in order to expand his domains and guarantee the obedience of his vassals.

Philip II was hardly an attractive character: he was overweight, clumsy, blind in one eye, sneaky, belligerent, and uncultured. Yet he became known as "Augustus" because he was born in August and in time proved himself worthy of this eloquent name. His primary goal was to exalt royal dignity and power by any means, even deceit. His strongest enemy was the powerful Angevin Empire, which stretched from England to the Pyrenees. Philip began his campaign by supporting the rebellious sons of Henry III against their father, who died in 1189. Then he feigned friendship toward Henry's successor, the elegant and cultivated Richard the Lion-Hearted: together they went on a Crusade to recapture the tomb of Christ after it had fallen into the hands of the Infidels. Alas the two monarchs were complete opposites, fell to quarreling, and soon separated.

When the count of Flanders died, Philip left the Middle East quickly to claim his portion of the inheritance, the provinces of Artois and Vermandois. He had even sworn to Richard to do him no harm in Europe. But quite to the contrary, he constantly plotted with Richard's brother and rival, John Lackland. It was arranged for Richard to be held prisoner in a German fortress on his return from the Crusade. When he was liberated in exchange for a hefty ransom in 1194, Richard immediately resumed a generally victorious war against Philip, but during a minor skirmish in 1199, the lion-hearted king was foolishly killed by an arrow before the walls of Châlus in Limousin.

Immediately Philip supported John Lackland's nephew, the young Arthur of Brittany, as Richard's successor. But this move was politically unwise, for John received help from the English barons and the everlasting Eleanor, who brought him her beloved Aquitaine. He humiliated the king of France and received as compensation several villages in Vexin and Berry in the Peace of Goulet (1200). In other areas Philip's judgment also appeared faulty: at almost the same time he brought on himself the wrath of Pope Innocent III. Acting in a canonically irregular way, the king had locked up his second wife, the Danish Ingeborg, on their wedding day, in order to marry a third wife. The fighting pope responded by placing France under an interdict. In principle all religious activities in the kingdom were suspended; this ban, more or less observed, might have meant ultimate disaster for the king.

Recapture of Normandy, Anjou, and Poitou

Starting in 1202, the situation turned around completely. When his third wife conveniently died, Philip became reconciled with both Ingeborg and the pope. He dared to summon to his court his vassal John Lackland, who had unjustly harmed and attacked the Lusignans, other vassals in Poitou. Since John did not deign to appear, he could be legally deprived of his fiefs, made forfeit to his lord. Naturally Philip's sole purpose in this exercise was to get and keep John's best fiefs for himself.

After so many inglorious episodes, it is striking how easily Philip got control of Normandy after the harsh siege of Château-Gaillard and then extended his power in Anjou and Poitou by 1204. Meanwhile John had been poorly supported by his barons and subject to mental crises that made him vacillate between bloody violence and despair; yet he had yielded only temporarily. John thought only of revenge against Philip and imagined that he could get it by forming a coalition with the Holy Roman Emperor and the count of Flanders. But it was not to be. Philip's son, the future Louis VIII, upset John's Angevin army at La Roche-aux-Moines in Anjou, while the French cavalry launched a frontal attack and won a clear victory over the Flemish and Germans at Bouvines on July 27, 1214. These two battles were decisive in consolidating the conquest of the House of Anjou. The joyous homecoming of the victors of Bouvines marked the awakening of national, or patriotic, feeling in the kingdom. Some historians doubt it, yet a French nation without the Midi would be unimaginable.

Not everything was settled in 1214, however. Called on for support by the English nobles, who were in revolt against their half-mad king, the future Louis VIII tried to establish a kingdom for himself across the Channel. But when the death of John Lackland caused the rebels to rally around his young son, Louis returned to France in 1217. When he became king of France in 1223, he quickly put down agitation among the turbulent nobility of Poitou and completed the conquest. Later, his wife Blanche of Castile and their son Louis IX again had to

43

intervene in this region; the English made forays there also. With the recapture of Saintes in 1242, the task was completed, at least for the thirteenth century. By then the Plantagenet domains in France were limited to Guyenne. In the southeast, however, the Capetians were attacking the neighboring territory of Languedoc.

THE CONQUEST OF LANGUEDOC

Count Raimond VI of Toulouse, a distant and powerful Capetian vassal, ruled wealthy and cultured provinces ranging from Quercy and the Agenais in the west to beyond the Rhône River. This area had been profoundly affected by the Albigensian faith, also known to the Church as the Manichean or Catharist heresy. Apparently its beliefs were a purified form of Christianity marked by a somber pessimism and an understandable contempt for the established Catholic clergy. The Albigensians rejected the sacraments as inventions of the Church; instead they held to an ideal of poverty and nonviolence under the domination of an elite of "perfects" who lived in isolated purity.

The papacy could not tolerate such challenges and sent in Cistercian missionaries and energetic legates; they were received with ironic politeness at best. When the annoyed Toulousans went so far as to assassinate one of them in 1208, Innocent III believed he was obliged to preach a Crusade, this time against Christians: he asked Philip Augustus to lead the way. Cautious and otherwise engaged, Philip declined the offer. Thus in 1209, hordes of uncontrolled northern French warriors went south to ravage, pillage, and massacre the population. The invaders were altogether ignorant of the region, the people, their religion, and even their language.

Their mercenary leader Simon of Montfort received clerical support from the legates and from the newly formed Dominicans. He first conquered the estates of Raimond VI of Toulouse; then, at Muret in 1213, he defeated and killed the

44

king of Aragon, who had come to help his cousin the count. In 1215, Montfort had himself proclaimed count by a Lateran Council, which boldly appropriated feudal jurisdiction. The king of France, whose seigneurial rights had been clearly violated, did not budge; he was waiting for the right moment. . . .

Indeed, the former subjects of Raimond VI resisted their conquerors by repeated and successful rebellion. After having massacred Montfort while he was besieging Toulouse in 1218, they acclaimed the young Raimond VII as the new count.

The outraged popes continually pressed the king of France to support the former Crusaders, now defeated. Twice Philip prudently allowed his son Louis to go to their aid with small contingents. As a result, when Louis VIII himself came to the throne in 1223, he had a better understanding of this vast, rich province. First he decided to repurchase his rights from Amaury of Montfort, Simon's defeated young son. Then he procured papal authorization to levy *décimes* (taxes) on the French clergy to finance his own expedition, which traveled down the Imperial side of the Rhône, captured Avignon on the way, and easily obtained the submission of all Languedoc except Toulouse.

After such promising beginnings, Louis VIII died in Auvergne on his way home in 1226. The war for Languedoc began again and lasted three years, until the regent Blanche of Castile made an honorable compromise with Raimond VII. By the Treaty of Paris in 1229, they offered the papacy the Comtat Venaissin, formerly the marquisate of Provence. The Capetians kept lower Languedoc, while the rest passed to Raimond and his young sister, who was hastily married to Louis IX's brother, Alphonse of Poitiers. The absence of heirs on both sides ensured that all these lands would return to the Crown in 1271, establishing the near-definitive union of northern and southern France.

But the subjects of the count of Toulouse had to pay dearly for this peace. Raimond VII had been reconciled with the pope, and thus supported the Dominicans in their work for the extirpation of heresy. Pope Gregory IX officially established this Inquisition in 1233. Its procedures of denunciation, torture, burning at the stake, and confiscation of property were as much in accord with the spirit of the age as with the wretched reputation they have earned from posterity. In response, the dispossessed and exiled population tried numerous revolts; in 1240, the most famous of them brought back to power Trencavel, descendant of the viscounts of Béziers. For a moment in 1242 the count of Toulouse himself together with Poitevins and Gascons joined the rebels fighting against the yoke of the northerners and the Church. Yet the rebellion fell apart at the approach of the royal army. Louis IX, the future Saint Louis, hated Albigensians as much as he did Saracens, and dreamed only of crushing them. While Raimond VII finally surrendered in 1243, the fortress of Montségur, supreme symbol of Catharist resistance, did not capitulate until March 1244, after ten months of siege.

For a long time the Midi was quiet, yet it did not really tolerate royal officials, whom it regarded as foreigners and barbarians. As usual, the elites rallied to the strongest. Yet as late as the seventeenth century Languedoc still held surprises in store for the French monarchy.

LOUIS IX AT THE SUMMIT OF MONARCHY

Louis IX has been completely shrouded in a legend of grace and holiness. In 1297 he was canonized, no doubt to appease his coarse grandson, Philip IV; yet he did possess some claims to this honor.

King at age twelve, Louis was obliged to leave the undisputed regency to his mother, Blanche of Castile. She crushed several feudal revolts, skillfully married her son to Marguerite of Provence, retained all powers for eight years, and kept a good many of them until around 1240. When Louis left on his first Crusade in 1248, Blanche resumed her regency and held it until her death in 1252. Her role as mother and teacher has been praised, and it seems likely that her firm and intelligent

THE LATER CAPETIANS

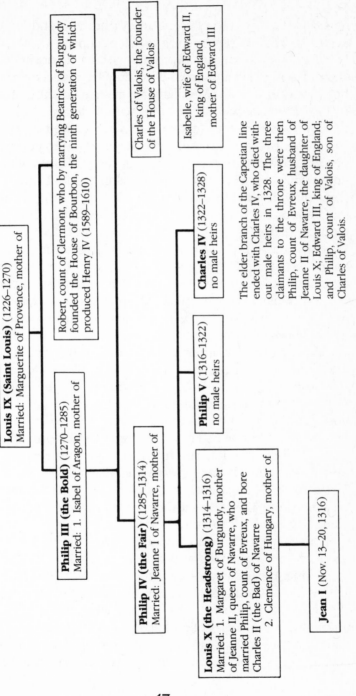

Louis IX (Saint Louis) (1226–1270)
Married: Marguerite of Provence, mother of

Philip III (the Bold) (1270–1285)
Married: 1. Isabel of Aragon, mother of

Robert, count of Clermont, who by marrying Beatrice of Burgundy founded the House of Bourbon, the ninth generation of which produced Henry IV (1589–1610)

Philip IV (the Fair) (1285–1314)
Married: Jeanne I of Navarre, mother of

Charles of Valois, the founder of the House of Valois

Isabelle, wife of Edward II, king of England, mother of Edward III

Louis X (the Headstrong) (1314–1316)
Married: 1. Margaret of Burgundy, mother of Jeanne II, queen of Navarre, who married Philip, count of Evreux, and bore Charles II (the Bad) of Navarre
2. Clemence of Hungary, mother of

Philip V (1316–1322)
no male heirs

Charles IV (1322–1328)
no male heirs

Jean I (Nov. 13–20, 1316)

The elder branch of the Capetian line ended with Charles IV, who died without male heirs in 1328. The three claimants to the throne were then Philip, count of Evreux, husband of Jeanne II of Navarre, the daughter of Louis X; Edward III, king of England; and Philip, count of Valois, son of Charles of Valois.

energy had profound effects on both her son and his reign: after all, she held power for a quarter-century.

The king himself was profoundly pious: it appears that he wanted to become a priest, but his duty lay elsewhere. At least he prayed and fasted regularly, wore a hair shirt, and surrounded himself with clerics. His acts of charity and humility included washing the feet of the poor as well as showing affection for lepers and the blind; they have been popularized by his belated historiographer Jean de Joinville and subsequent imagery. Yet there is no reason to doubt that when stricken with illness in 1244, he made a vow to go on a Crusade. Afterward, his mind was preoccupied with reconquering the holy places.

Having assembled at great expense a fleet at Aigues-Mortes, Louis IX left for Egypt, hoping to strike at the heart of the Infidels. Instead, in 1249 he found defeat, imprisonment, and a heavy ransom to pay. While waiting for a settlement, he installed himself for five years a thousand leagues away from his kingdom, in what remained of the Frankish kingdoms of Palestine. Louis still imagined that he would recapture the tomb of Christ, if necessary with the help of the Mongols.

During his long absence, his mother and counselors managed to keep the kingdom intact and the administration running well. From the moment he returned, he dreamed of leaving again. But he had to wait fifteen years before sailing for Tunisia, where missionaries filled with illusions reported that the Arabic ruler was on the verge of conversion to Christianity. There Louis IX apparently encountered the plague and died on August 25, 1270. His earthly remains worked miracles all along the way back to France.

This fervent Christian, apparently humble in his style of dress and manner of life, was extremely jealous of his authority as king. He did not tolerate any disloyal or rebellious vassals, and punished them severely. He did not allow any other power, be it the Holy Roman Emperor or even the pope, to intervene in the affairs of a kingdom that he was certain God had entrusted to him alone, not merely by the ceremony of coronation but also by an inner conviction that Louis XIV felt as well. Louis IX's tender soul could be harsh or even cruel to Infidels and heretics, but he knew how to be generally just, and thus rapidly acquired popular respect. The fine anecdote about the king dispensing justice under an oak tree at Vincennes survives as testimony to his reputation.

Louis IX could also be generous, and was at times reproached for his actions. Thus to put a stop to continual conflicts with Henry III of England in Aquitaine, he signed a treaty in Paris in 1259. Louis ceded Périgord and Limousin to his adversary and promised him Agenais and Quercy as well, in exchange for definitive acknowledgment of Henry's vassalage and renunciation of Normandy, Anjou, and Poitou. In the same spirit, in 1258, he had abandoned all suzerainty over Catalonia and Roussillon to the king of Aragon when the latter renounced his claims to Toulouse and Provence.

Favorably impressed, other Europeans asked for arbitration by the Just King. In renewed conflict between Henry III of England and his rebellious barons, Louis had contempt for the former, but nonetheless decided in his favor because he was the king. Louis also settled a difficult Flemish succession. In Provence, where he had married off his troubled younger brother Charles of Anjou, the king arbitrated disputes with neighboring Dauphiné and Savoy, thus becoming renowned in Imperial territories.

Within his kingdom, Louis IX wanted virtue as well as justice to rule. Reviving an old Carolingian custom, he sent agents into the provinces to receive his subjects' complaints against wayward *prévôts* and *baillis*. On their return, he proclaimed sound ordinances to establish mutual responsibilities and duties.

Other decisions, of a different nature, were meant to provide complete support to the destructive work of the inquisitors, to expel the Jews (not without confiscating their possessions), to prohibit the carrying of weapons, games, and even blasphemy. These good intentions were continued by his son, who went so far as to regulate the clothing of his subjects by specifying the number and style of clothes they could acquire. These illusory ideas persisted through the centuries:

even Louis XIV in the early part of his reign declared such sumptuary laws. Considerably more saintly than his descendant, Louis IX no doubt believed in them.

Such was the character of Saint Louis, more complex than generally believed. We now turn to his kingdom.

ORGANIZATION OF THE FIRST CAPETIAN KINGDOM: UNTIL 1314

The boundaries given to the kingdom of France by the Treaty of Verdun four centuries earlier had not been achieved, especially not along the Meuse and in the Saône-Rhône Valley. The interior of this apparently unified state contained nothing comparable to the centralized administration of Louis XIV. On the contrary, France was a mosaic composed of three elements: the actual royal domain; the *apanages,* or portions of the domain given as fiefs to the children of the king; and the great fiefs outside the domain, whose holders had sworn homage to the king, but in fact enjoyed considerable autonomy.

The custom of granting *apanages* dates from the Merovingian and Carolingian divisions of property. At that time it was unclear whether these lands necessarily reverted to the royal domain when the holders died, though this became the law in the seventeenth and eighteenth centuries. However, the grants did revert when the princely holders had no heirs, which happened frequently, thanks be to God! For example, *apanages* had been given to Alphonse, count of Poitiers and Auvergne, and to Jeanne, countess of Toulouse, but neither had heirs. On the other hand, Robert of Artois, son of Louis VIII, established a line that lasted for four centuries. Not until 1480 was the grant to his brother Charles of Anjou recovered by the Crown, after the death of "Good King René"; fortunately, by then it had been enriched by the addition of Provence.

Only two great vassals caused serious concern to the French kings: those in Guyenne and Flanders. Since the lords of Guyenne were also kings of England, over a hundred years of

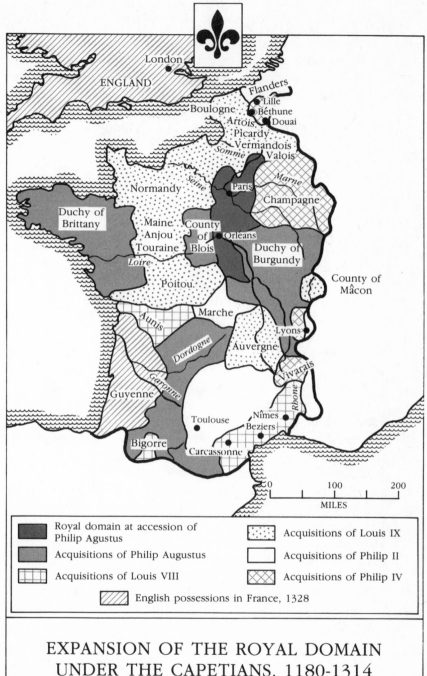

London

ENGLAND

Flanders
Lille
Boulogne
Béthune
Artois
Douai
Picardy
Vermandois
Somme
Valois

Normandy
Seine
Paris
Marne
Champagne

Duchy of
Brittany

Maine
County
Anjou
of
Orléans
Duchy of
Touraine
Blois
Burgundy
Loire

County of
Mâcon
Poitou

Marche

Aunis
Lyons
Dordogne
Auvergne
Garonne
Vivarais
Guyenne
Rhone

Toulouse
Nîmes
Béziers
Bigorre
Carcassonne

0   100   200

MILES

	Royal domain at accession of Philip Agustus		Acquisitions of Louis IX
	Acquisitions of Philip Augustus		Acquisitions of Philip II
	Acquisitions of Louis VIII		Acquisitions of Philip IV

English possessions in France, 1328

EXPANSION OF THE ROYAL DOMAIN
UNDER THE CAPETIANS, 1180-1314

warfare was required to drive them out. The lords of Flanders were extremely rich, and their tempting lands extended into the Holy Roman Empire. Against them the French unsuccessfully tried matrimonial politics, corruption, and inciting revolts among their vassals, as well as numerous military expeditions. Even Philip IV (the Fair) failed to take Flanders, having only momentary success in annexing Lille. The Hundred Years' War stemmed from Flanders as much as from Guyenne, and not until the reign of Louis XIV was a modest portion of the ancient Flemish lands finally joined to the *fleur-de-lis* monarchy.

Against the less powerful vassals, the kings used threats, shrewdness, and seduction with varying effects. Thus the duke of Bar was forced to swear homage for his lands to the west of the Meuse; but Louis IX and Philip IV had to buy territories such as the duchy of Mâcon and the county of Chartres, even though they were quite close to the royal domain. It was also necessary to scheme and toil, using quarrels of the ecclesiastical counts and their neighbors, and finally the intermediacy of the *bailli* of Mâcon to enter Lyon in 1307. Lyon was the ancient capital of the Gauls and their church, but it was also an Imperial city, admirably situated for commercial wealth.

Elsewhere the carefully cultivated support of the powerful bishops of Le Puy, Viviers, and Mende, together with money, smoothed the way for royal entry into these regions on the perimeter of Languedoc. As for encroaching on other Imperial territories such as Lorraine, Franche-Comté, Burgundy, Savoy, Dauphiné, or Provence, the French kings considered such adventures only sporadically and could hardly have foreseen their annexation. The same holds true for distant and wealthy Brittany: though momentarily allied with its Plantagenet neighbors, Brittany constituted neither a danger nor a prey.

The Triple Authority of the King

Two ancient elements furnished the basis and origin of royal authority. The first was the coronation. In principle it took place at Reims, using oil from the holy vial that an angel had reportedly brought for Clovis. Coronation meant anointment, the symbolic equivalent of holy orders; it also conferred on French kings the power to heal the disease scrofula by the royal touch, a power much envied by other monarchs. The second element, astutely used by Philip Augustus, was the king's position at the summit of the pyramid of vassalage. He was the only suzerain not obliged to bend his knee to anyone, certainly not to the Emperor or the pope. Eventually the French kings owed their independence to the long struggle between Philip IV and the papacy. If the popes had formerly been threatening, they were so no more, except in a religious sense. The royal position was ultimately buttressed by bishops who favored a purely French or "Gallican" church—that is, one that recognized only the spiritual authority of the bishop of Rome. This bold interpretation was put forward by counselors of Philip IV, jurists who had studied Roman law and proclaimed openly that the king of France "was emperor in his own kingdom." This was an adroit resurrection of the Roman notion of an *imperium* that had no earthly superiors. An idea unthinkable in the time of Saint Louis, it took some time to establish, but it put the finishing touch on the triple authority of the king of France, already "the Lord's anointed" and the lord of lords.

The Royal Officers

Some time passed before this prestigious and complex kingdom received the organization it needed. The system started with the small Capetian domain where *prévôts* (provosts) collected the lord's revenues on each farm or seigneury. They watched over the work of the peasants and the loyalty of petty vassals, and also rendered justice. The provosts were never abolished and were still active in 1789. On the next level, Philip Augustus had installed *baillis* (bailiffs), who also lasted throughout the ancien régime. They were slowly extended to newly annexed territories or granted with *apanages*; in Aquitaine and the Midi, their counterparts were known as *sénéchaux* (seneschals). They represented the king, transmitted his orders, exercised great judicial powers, and came to hold financial responsibilities as well. When he left on the

Crusade, Saint Louis sent out still other officials, *missi dominici,* to visit and preach to the *baillis* and *sénéchaux;* these travelling representatives were men who held a direct royal commission. They are reminiscent of the envoys of Charlemagne and prefigure the intendants of the early modern period.

Strictly financial agents were occasionally used by Philip IV when he tried to collect such taxes as *fouages* (direct taxes on hearths) and *maltôtes* (taxes on merchandise). But they really emerged later when, with some difficulty, permanent taxation was introduced.

Around 1300, this administrative linkage was neither tight nor systematic, and only became so much later. At the top, around the king, it was at first merely a question of governing the domain. Several men drawn from the good nobility were sufficient to run the household services of chamber, provisions, cellar, and stables. These nobles continued to serve the king and formed the great offices of the *hôtel.* The job of keeping the royal seal was held by the chancellor, who supervised the beginnings of a few small *bureaus.* Philip Augustus lost his archives along with his baggage at the defeat of Fréteval in 1198, but all the same, he organized a genuine chancery managed by a keeper of the seals.

The Curia in Parlamentum

Already the domestic services of the *hôtel* were separated from the king's court (*curia regis*), which consisted of the direct counselors of the king, those who helped him govern and dispense justice as appeals to his authority increased. Some of these counselors met regularly to judge cases. At first they did so in the king's presence and followed him on his travels, but later they stayed more and more in Paris, in the old palace on the Île de la Cité, which was constructed under Louis VII. This group was called the *curia in parlamentum,* or the *Parlement* in good northern French. The Parlement began to record its judgments in large registers, the *olim,* starting in 1268. Its personnel of clerks, scribes, and jurists increased to over one hundred. Beginning around 1240 to 1250, the great customary laws of Anjou and Normandy were compiled. The *curia in parlamentum* divided itself into four chambers, including one for the laws of the Midi; it sent delegations to Rouen and Troyes to receive appeals from Normandy and Champagne. Men from non-noble families were able to sit in Parlement after pursuing studies in the expanding universities, especially the University of Paris. If there had been a duke of Saint-Simon in that age, and it is most improbable, he could already have denounced the intrusion of the "vile bourgeoisie."

Financial specialization came slowly to the curia. From the time of Philip Augustus, the royal treasury consisted of the surplus of domain revenues over local expenditures. It was stored at the Temple fortress in Paris by banker-knights of the order of Templars, originally created to defend the holy places. As in other parts of Europe, the Templars kept the cash and current accounts used by the king to pay expenses.

Periodically, one part of the court went to the Temple to check the accounts: this was the beginning of the *curia in compotis,* later the Chambre des Comptes. When the Templars were placed under suspicion and brutally eliminated by Philip IV in 1307–08, the entire treasury was brought to the great tower of the Louvre. Starting in 1304, a virtually autonomous Chambre des Comptes was installed at the palace on the Île de la Cité. This court received its charter in 1320 and henceforth watched over Crown lands and revenues, and audited accounts and accountants. Nearby, specialists were taking care of the administration of the forests and the mint.

In short, around 1300, the French state had evolved considerably from the little band of warriors, servants, and clerks that followed Louis VI from place to place a century and a half earlier.

The Army and Taxes

Although this powerful monarchy still lacked an army and a tax system, the beginnings of these important institutions can be distinguished.

For centuries, war was a seasonal activity: all fighting was suspended in winter. For brief campaigns the feudal military system relied on the *ost,* service of forty days per year, and the local militias, which regularly furnished several hundred armed horsemen, a few more lightly armed sergeants, and the foot soldiers; there were never more than ten thousand men in all, and most went home when they had done their duty. Since the beginning of the thirteenth century, the kings had recourse to foreign mercenaries, *reiters*—needy knights of the Empire, Genoese bowmen with formidable weapons, and some paid elements of the feudal host.

Starting with Philip III, son of Louis IX, who fought widely without much result, especially in Spain, a good part of the army was composed of bands or routes recruited by generally noble captains. From 1274 onward they received one sou for each *fantassin* (foot soldier) and twenty for each well-armed knight. Marshals and a master of the archers, part of the king's council, set contracts in the countryside and conducted reviews of troops known as *monstres.* There also appeared the treasurers of war, whose offices would last for centuries.

But all this was very expensive, and the kings did not yet have the means to support their military policy. A well-established principle required them to draw income from their domain and customary feudal revenues; this view was echoed down to the seventeenth century. As these funds were insufficient, the kings had to find money elsewhere. Under the pretext of going on a Crusade, Louis VIII persuaded the clergy to pay *décimes,* 10 percent of their considerable revenues. But persistent efforts were required to solicit contributions from the "good cities," good bourgeois, and prelates, as well as to pressure the Jews and Lombards, usurious Italian lenders who nonetheless kept coming back.

Philip IV was more severe than his predecessors. He tried to expropriate the lands of the Templars, which the pope assigned to other religious orders. While Philip also frequently manipulated the coinage, so did almost all of his successors, including Louis XIV; yet Philip received an unjustified reputation as a counterfeiter. In fact he only "devalued" the money, reducing its precious-metal content. This idea with a future was joined by permanent taxes, which flowered around 1303. The first levies included a substitute tax on all men who did not perform military service, taxes on merchandise, and, shortly afterward, taxes on wealth and income—the *centième* and *vingtième*. These also had a lengthy history ahead of them, but they were difficult to collect in the absence of assessments—which appeared in the Midi.

These premature efforts were nonetheless the origin of the *taille, gabelle, aides,* and even the income tax of Louis XIV. The initiatives were regarded as so novel that Philip IV and his counselors thought it prudent to present them to the "estates" for approval. While the composition of these consultative bodies varied, they included some well-to-do bourgeois, especially Parisians, and were the vague forerunners of the Estates General. The king renewed this harmless and intelligent practice from time to time, thus obtaining an easy consensus around political, economic, and religious measures so extraordinary that they are sufficient to place this monarch in an exceptional category. His personality, however, presents problems.

Philip the Fair, or Philip the Great?—1285–1314

Philip IV's contemporaries have told us that he was handsome and deserved the simplistic sobriquet "the Fair," even if none of his supposed portraits give a faithful image of him. Yet he was strikingly different from many of his ancestors, although he thought he was imitating Louis IX. Everything about his reign seemed new: his entourage, his style of government, his haughty discretion, the penetrating boldness and calm with which he attacked the problems of his age. Indeed he faced many problems: a state to administer, an army to build or rebuild, a financial system to master, a military banking order to eliminate, a descendance to savor, an arrogant pope to subjugate, and eternal quarrels to fight with his vassals and neighbors, especially the Flemish and the English.

Even during his lifetime, Philip IV was presented as a weak and confused man, preoccupied with hunting and devotion, dominated and exploited by patently dishonest counselors—suspect because they were southerners and not always nobles. Some who had studied his actions step by step believed that he had a dark side, was ambitious, secretive, unscrupulous, implacable, or even wicked—in short, already a "cursed king."

Yet this king did have a grand idea of his function and his duties. Philip wanted to defend law, justice, and faith as much as his revered grandfather had done; but he wished to do so in his own fashion, showing the mastery and implacability of a great politician. As he was loyal to his chosen advisers, they reciprocated with fanatical loyalty to him. As he was shrewd enough to seek the respectful advice of carefully chosen estates, so he also had the honesty to punish his scandalous daughters-in-law and had their lovers publicly tortured. No doubt he thought that even the progeny of a monarch should be beyond reproach.

Naturally he could not foresee the sudden death of his three sons and the consequences. In 1314, he could die content with the destiny of a dynasty three centuries old and a kingdom whose power he had extended beyond all previous limits.

Philip's harsh quarrel with the papacy produced the most fascinating episodes of his reign, which surprised and often shocked posterity. Previously relations between France and Rome had been good, despite some incidents during Philip II's second marriage. The popes were engaged in long political struggles with the Holy Roman Emperor, endless petty intrigues with the Roman nobility, and more religious wars against Infidels and heretics—Crusades in the largest sense of the word.

The Empire and the Albigensians collapsed around 1250, but all these great pontifical enterprises had been very costly. Indeed, the court of Rome knew how to draw money from Christian kingdoms by diverse means such as the invocation of more or less canonical causes mixed with financial interests, as well as the trade in benefices. Rome also levied tithes and other taxes collected by Italian bankers and the Templars. Sovereigns disliked these activities and reacted even more strongly to the claims of the papal canon lawyers after the death of Emperor Frederick II in 1250. The canonists boldly affirmed that popes held not only spiritual power over Christendom but also the temporal power to judge kings, depose them, and dispose of their kingdoms. Saint Louis would never have accepted such pretensions; neither did Philip IV when he faced the intransigent Boniface VIII.

The conflict began in 1296, abated, then resumed violently. Supported by the estates of 1302, Philip accused the pope of various indignities, some quite plausible. Boniface had pretended to depose the French king and call the French bishops to Rome; in reply Philip ordered him brutally seized at Anagni in 1303—and the pope died of the shock.

After some violent and complicated episodes, two French popes were elected: Clement V from Limousin in 1305, and John XXII from Cahors in 1314. The latter fled from Italian anarchy and settled in Avignon, where he had been bishop. Clearly the papacy had renounced its theocratic pretensions and placed itself under the protection of the most powerful monarch in Europe. Even though it had been acquired by brute force, this sign of prestige was added to others that gave Philip first place in the Capetian dynasty and Christendom of the age. Yet this triumph would be followed by a rude awakening and many long-lasting misfortunes.

THE CENTURY OF SAINT LOUIS

Civilization

As early as the mid–twelfth century, the first elements of Gothic architecture appeared at Morienval north of Chantilly and in several Norman churches. Gothic style was formed by bringing together three known techniques: the pointed arch, cross-ribbing supporting a vault made of stone instead of wood, and flying buttresses to carry the weight of high vaults on stone piers. These developments made it possible to go from small rural buildings to soaring cathedrals. By 1180, the choir and ambulatories with tribunes had been built at Notre Dame de Paris; in 1200, the transepts and the nave were covered. Saint Louis was six years old when the facade was finished.

In the surrounding region, cathedrals were built at Chartres, Sens, and Laon; still higher churches at Soissons, Auxerre, Amiens, and Bourges. At Beauvais the builders attempted the impossible: even after an accident and a risky reconstruction, its cathedral had the highest Gothic arch in the world. In the sixteenth century, it was topped with a spire more than 150 meters high—before it collapsed. This sublime belated folly typified an art of elevation and light, destined to conquer most of Europe.

The Gothic inspiration in architecture, whether simplified or flamboyant, reigned for almost three centuries. Gothic sculpture and stained glass, two other great successes, were at first pure and sublime; then they evolved more rapidly, as can be seen in many great collections of medieval art.

The thirteenth century also saw the rise of universities such as Paris, which acquired its independence between 1200 and 1231. These schools taught the newly rediscovered works of Aristotle as well as theological and philosophical disputation to a meager elite of wealthy young nobles. Simultaneously the study of law flourished: canon law, Roman law from the Midi, local custom, and royal laws all received attention. The universities joined the existing episcopal schools in training future servants of the Church and the monarchy.

When battles and tournaments were out of season, the lordly courts enjoyed songs of troubadours and reveled in the purity of tales of the search for the Holy Grail. Aristocratic audiences delighted in novels of chivalry, which were still found in libraries down to the early seventeenth century. Meanwhile cities may have seen the birth of the bourgeois novel; certainly there were short stories and fables. When they had time, good folk took pleasure in storytellers, exhibitors of curiosities, jugglers, and the interminable mystery plays that were performed in front of the cathedrals.

Yet all this activity happened in towns. Little remains of the culture of simple rural people—a few games and the laughter preserved in timeless stories. The illiteracy of these people was all too evident, yet their spirits were undoubtedly shaped by bursts of faith, fear, and hope.

Economy

None of the signs of thirteenth-century greatness could have existed without a solid economic infrastructure—by medieval standards. Until the beginning of the nineteenth century, French economy was essentially agricultural. By 1200, successful land reclamation had taken place and crop rotation was established. The breeds of horses and cattle had been improved, as had the tools and materials of transformation—ovens, forges, and mills.

Several land accounts from this period show that crop yields continued to improve throughout the thirteenth century, reaching a plateau unsurpassed until Napoleon's time. Agricultural prices also rose gradually as a sign and reward of prosperity. Starting in the following century, people could recall with some reason the happy time of Saint Louis, when there was neither famine nor plague, and almost no ravages of war.

Naturally this prosperity benefited the great landowners and *rentiers*—the entire nobility and clergy, some bourgeois, and indeed the king. Many of them were thus able to grant emancipation to their serfs and villeins in exchange for payments: as a result, the lower orders often became settled tenants who paid annual dues until 1789.

We might think that the time of Philip IV was a golden age in the countryside, but we should not idealize conditions. Medieval lords and peasants knew nothing of valuable crops such as buckwheat and maize, first grown in France in the sixteenth century, or potatoes, which appeared around 1700. The importance of clover and legumes was recognized in Flanders by 1400, but not accepted in the Île-de-France and Midi until two centuries later. Nor did the French have much skill in the domestic cultivation of fruit trees, except for the apples of Normandy. All the same, these relatively happy times did support about 15 million French people. Their population density was close to that of the eighteenth century, a fact that speaks volumes about the miseries of intervening centuries.

Towns, Fairs, and Trades

The newest and most striking manifestations of thirteenth-century prosperity, however, were not found in the flourishing rural areas. They appeared all across the kingdom in the great overland and sea trades and in finance. The dynamic centers of European trade were concentrated farther north, in the Hanseatic League, the North Sea region, Bruges, and other great Flemish towns, as well as in Italy. There the important ship-owners, businessmen, and bankers from Venice, Genoa, Pisa, Florence, and Lucca developed a thriving new trade along with the resurrection of gold coinage. The appearance of the ducat in 1252 and the circulation of instruments of commerce and credit represented techniques at least a century ahead of the rest of Europe.

While awaiting the rise of other centers of trade, medieval businessmen met regularly at the fairs in Champagne, where merchandise and money changed hands actively. The seaports of the kingdom also prospered: in Normandy, Bretagne, around Saintes, and in the Basque country, they participated in active coastal trade and received visits from heavy northern merchant vessels. Meanwhile the English took advantage of Bordeaux and its hinterland. By using frail boats on the navigable rivers and traveling on rough roads, Englishmen carried merchandise, men, and ideas to the interior, especially the rapidly growing towns.

Most towns burst out of their old corsets of defensive walls; they were obliged to rebuild and again went beyond them. As most doubled or tripled their population, they experienced a building boom. Paris had reached 100,000 inhabitants and may have had twice as many. Except for the great cloth-making cities of the north, such as Amiens, medieval French towns were not specialized centers of industry. They combined production, consumption, and exchange, stimulated by ports such as la Grève at Paris and by frequent markets held in the central square. For these markets and seasonal fairs, tables and booths were built. Country people would rise early in the morning, bring their fresh produce, and rub shoulders with traveling salesmen of pottery, cooking pots, and cloth.

Above all, town streets became cluttered with quasi-permanent workshops and boutiques, often specialized so that butchers were in one place, jewelers another, furriers and cloth merchants farther along. Parchment sellers were found near the schools and universities. Everything was organized in guilds of arts and crafts. Étienne Boileau, provost of Paris, listed more than a hundred of them in 1268. These guilds were rigidly structured, with specialization, apprenticeship, and master status defined by statutes, "privileges" at times issued before 1200. Among these different bodies as well as within each one there were frequent and lively disputes, the first sign of urban social struggles that recurred in succeeding centuries.

Around this small world of craftsmen and shopkeepers in the thirteenth century there arose another, the milieu of writers, court clerks, and judges. Later they would wear distinctive long robes. As a growing educated elite, knowledgeable in the law and indispensable to the more complicated society and monarchy, this group quickly acquired both influence and a high standard of living. Especially in Paris and the provincial capitals, they took an active role in public affairs and enjoyed landed income from their investments in town and countryside.

Soon the monarchy would have to reckon with the power of its great servants, and with urban oligarchies and patriciates. Some had even begun to infiltrate the nobility by subtle and indirect means, even before asserting their claims to privileged places. Others were already occupying positions in the Church. Thus we could speak of a "rising bourgeoisie," if this bourgeoisie had not changed in its characteristics and nature by the very act of ascension. Of course we should not exaggerate: although the state of Philip IV no longer resembled the modest monarchy of warriors and serfs established by the first

Capetians, thirteenth-century government and society were still dominated by the powerful royal family, the princes of the blood, and the great vassals of shifting allegiances.

Ebb and Flow

Precisely when the last of the great Capetians and his three sons died, grave threats appeared. Dangers in Flanders and Aquitaine could have been foreseen, but not the terrible problem of succession to the French throne. Even less predictable were the first signs of economic slowdown or stagnation. Shortly after 1300, the Italians decided to avoid the heavily taxed fairs of Champagne in favor of the Saint Gotthard and Rhine routes overland or the Genoese sea passage around Gibraltar. Thus they could reach the centers of northern trade, especially the English wool market in Bruges. Consequently Champagne and Paris suffered a decline in activity, with fewer merchants, less money, and less work.

Much more serious in 1315–17 was the sudden return of harsh famines followed by murderous epidemics. After these shocks, the rural world and in particular the grain-growing economy had difficulty regaining their prosperity. They appeared to lack the monetary means. Shortly the pressure of wars and new taxes would aggravate this difficult situation. A long century of misfortunes was beginning. . . .

To be sure, the Hundred Years' War was not fought because of a worsening economic situation; quite simply put, however, one aggravated the other and vice versa. Neighborhood quarrels and dynastic disputes lay at the heart of the problems of the age. They paved the way for a series of bleak decades; by comparison, the century of Saint Louis and the Philips appears all the more glorious with its exceptional successes in politics, economics, and culture.

Chapter Three

THE MISFORTUNES OF THE FOURTEENTH CENTURY

After the triumphs of the thirteenth century, France passed through more somber years. French art and courtly civilization continued to shine, sometimes with extravagance. But the return of great famines after the death of Philip IV, economic stagnation that soon became deep depression, and the reappearance of plague, that dreaded "evil that spread terror," sent four or five million Frenchmen to their graves. Finally there was the Hundred Years' War, marked by devastating expeditions and companies of wandering soldier-bandits. Meanwhile the Church was racked by division, and it appeared that the papacy might fall. This terrible accumulation of disasters troubled France for more than a century.

THE HUNDRED YEARS' WAR

The traditional dates (1337–1453) for this conflict between France and England show that it lasted for more than a century, but there were more years of truce than years of combat. Even after the war ended, Edward IV of England landed troops at Calais in 1475 to help his Burgundian brother-in-law, Charles the Bold, attack Louis XI. While this episode was a simple epilogue, the long prologue to the conflict had much greater significance.

The origins of the war can be found back in the twelfth century, when the Angevin Henry Plantagenet simultaneously became duke of Normandy, king of England, and master of Aquitaine by his marriage to Eleanor. His power extended from the Scottish border to the Pyrenees, yet technically he remained an overly powerful vassal of the king of France. Philip Augustus and his successors had managed to reduce the continental territory of the English kings to the province of Guyenne. Yet many subjects of dispute remained: feudal obligations, the frontiers of Aquitaine, the north, and the west. Conflict could and did break out at any moment.

For example, in the rich county of Flanders the nobility were largely Francophiles, but the bourgeoisie and artisans in the cloth trade were closely tied to the English, who sold them wool. Terrible battles took place. In 1302 at Courtrai, Flemish foot soldiers humiliated the flower of French knighthood and collected the many golden spurs that gave the battle its name. Later at Cassel in 1328, the French cavalry took their revenge by beheading all their enemies: the cloth workers had rebelled against their lord, who called for aid from Philip VI.

As in Guyenne, Flanders, and the border regions, local conflicts frequently took place in the west. The rich duchy of Brittany was armed with a strong fleet and normally a vassal of the king of France; yet at times the Bretons were allied with the Plantagenets in complex quarrels of succession. One of the candidates would obtain French support, while another naturally went to the English. Struggles continued until the heiress Anne of Brittany finally resolved the question by marrying Charles VIII of France.

In another area King Charles of Navarre, grandson of Louis X as well as count of Evreux, held rich lands in Normandy. He caused no end of annoyance to the king of France by his continuing intrigues and intermittent pretensions to the throne. Charles relied on his Norman châteaux and his Navarrist troops, who nicknamed him "the Bad."

It is clear that private feudal quarrels at first seemed more important than dynastic or national rivalries, which only appeared later. Besides, the fundamental struggle between France and England did not arise before 1337. On one previous occasion, in 1316, the oldest son of Philip the Fair, Louis X, had died leaving only a young girl as his heir; even her legitimacy could be questioned, since the misconduct of her mother was well known. Philip's youngest son, a strong personality, succeeded in winning support from the principal barons. He was crowned king at Reims as Philip V and solemnly recognized by an assembly of notables, lords, prelates, university faculty, and rich bourgeois. At the time no one mentioned the Salic Law, an old bit of Frankish private law rediscovered forty years later by a chronicler, no doubt with the help of a shrewd jurist. Nonetheless, knowing that one princely faction had wanted to place Louis X's daughter on the throne, Philip V found it advisable to call a meeting of the Estates General to declare that women were not eligible to succeed to the throne of France. In reality the decision had been made on practical grounds, justified by the rallying of forces and the personality of Philip V. When Philip died soon afterward in 1322, his brother Charles IV succeeded him without difficulty; but Charles himself died in 1328 without direct heirs.

A new assembly of notables then decided in the first royal election since 987 to choose the oldest and most serious candidate, Philip of Valois, a good knight who was not too authoritarian and who was a nephew of Philip the Fair. King Edward III of England was passed over, even though he was a grandson of the same king. No doubt this decision was taken because of Edward's youth at least as much as because of his mother Isabelle, Philip's daughter: she was notorious for her disgusting character and scandalous life. And of course, as the assembly declared, "It had never been seen or known that the kingdom of France should be subject to the government of the king of England."

Locked in difficult battles with the Scots, Edward III at first agreed to take an oath of homage to Philip VI, who was crowned at Reims in 1329. Yet after Philip's hesitancy and imprudent support for the Scots, as well as local conflicts in Guyenne, the king of England contested the validity of his own declaration of homage, made while he was still a minor. In 1337, he finally sent Philip his challenge—in feudal terms, a declaration of war.

Panorama of the Hundred Years' War

The first period of the war was catastrophic for the kingdom of France. The French fleet was destroyed at Sluis, the port of Bruges, in 1340; the cavalry was decimated at Crécy in 1346; and the fortress of Calais was lost for two centuries in 1347. At the same time, the Black Death first ravaged the land, causing a catastrophe of even greater magnitude.

Ten years later, near Poitiers, the French army was crushed again; King John the Good and one of his sons were captured, taken to Bordeaux and London, and held to ransom for tons of gold. The French estates and the Parisian bourgeoisie found the defeat and its high costs intolerable. They tried to divert to their own ends the power that had fallen to the weak Dauphin Charles, a seventeen year old who had fled at Poitiers. The dream of seizing control inspired Étienne Marcel, provost of merchants at Paris; neither he nor the peasants hesitated to go into revolt.

In 1360, by the Treaty of Brétigny signed at Calais, the captive king and his son handed over one-third of their kingdom to England. Rebellion had been brewing in the countryside and the cities, while famine and plague reappeared. For the first time, the fine kingdom of Philip the Fair and Saint Louis hit rock bottom.

The reign of Charles V (1364–1380) achieved a partial restoration. At the time of his death, the English held only a few ports and surrounding areas. But his successor Charles VI, who went mad in 1392 and was surrounded by bad counselors, delivered his entire heritage to the English King Henry V after yet another bloody defeat at Agincourt in 1415.

The appearance of Joan of Arc along with the slow action of Charles VII's counselors allowed a progressive reestablishment of French power, completed around 1453 when the last English possessions in Gascony were taken. By then the Burgundians had replaced the English as the most serious French political problem.

Louis XI settled everything, taking advantage of internal dissension in England and the foolhardiness of Charles the Bold. At the time of the Burgundian duke's death in 1477, one hundred forty years of troubled history came to a close. The kingdom and its inhabitants had suffered greatly. All this history had to be reduced to its bare outlines for us to undertake an intelligible overview.

THE WAY OF WAR IN THE FOURTEENTH CENTURY

The battles of knights from the age of Philip Augustus and Saint Louis survived in the sublimated form of tournaments. On the battlefield itself, however, several innovations had appeared. To keep troops active over longer periods, it had become necessary to pay them. The word "soldier" comes from the French verb *solder,* itself derived from the *sol,* a modest coin that represented the daily wage for an infantryman. Payment was also required for vassals after the completion of their feudal obligation of forty days' service, as well as for bands of professional soldiers, groups of about twenty often led by noble captains. The obligation to pay troops gradually developed over two centuries and became very expensive. It brought about the introduction of near-permanent taxation and manipulation of the coinage, both of which the French people received badly.

Another novelty was the massive use of more and more effective projectile weapons. The crossbow, a complicated but powerful instrument, was preferred by the French, who used mostly Genoese models. Experienced in guerrilla warfare in Wales and Scotland, the skillfully trained English favored the longbow, which had greater range and could fire three times as rapidly. This weapon was the principal cause of the French disaster at Crécy: by contrast, the English bombardment of the French created more noise than effect, and does not suffice to explain the result of the battle.

Facing these powerful threats, the noble knight was obliged to armor-plate himself more solidly and heavily. By 1400, his articulated shell regularly weighed 60 kilograms (132 lbs). Not only was he unable to dress himself, but he could not even turn around while walking, nor could he get up again once he fell to the ground. Thus he was easy prey for the *coutilier* who struck him on the joints, or held him at his mercy for capture, which was a more common practice than simple murder.

Henceforth, the army was not composed only of splendid armored knights who fought with lance, sword, mace, and battle-ax. The military unit was called the "lance." It was composed of a knight who was a magnificent jouster; two mobile and more lightly armored archers; and a *coutilier*. Minor nobles did not disdain to fullfil either of the latter two functions. Finally came the knight's valet and page, who acted as servants, grooms, and armorers. Thus the "lance" consisted of six men in all.

As in earlier ages, war consisted of alternating long marches and long sieges, which ended with the surrender of the besieged or the departure of the besiegers. In the fourteenth century the role of artillery was not yet decisive, and frontal battles were rare. More common were skirmishes, long periods of rest in winter, and "abstinence from war," which could last three years, seven years, or longer.

Indeed, the real purpose of war, besides honor for the knights, was enrichment. Normally, wealth was acquired by taking spoils: from this point of view, the first English expeditions were nothing more than systematic raids, as long wagon trains carried the booty to waiting ships. After the battle of Poitiers, the French responded with scorched-earth tactics, as if to discourage their opponents. The bands of soldiers that had supposedly been demobilized after the Treaty of Brétigny-Calais also got involved in this destructive activity. These were the "great companies" who enjoyed a well-deserved terrible reputation. Fortunately Charles V was able to use Bertrand Du Guesclin against them.

We should note, however, that the kingdom of France as a whole was not equally or simultaneously affected by these ravages of war. Ruffians habitually followed the same routes; peasants learned to protect themselves by hiding in forests and caves, taking refuge in fortified towns and churches, or buying their tranquility.

Princes and barons did not refuse to stoop to pillage, but they preferred to practice the profitable industry of holding prisoners for ransom. This custom was as old as chivalry itself, and even Saint Louis had suffered it in Egypt. To capture an unhorsed knight, who was thus incapable of moving; to take him prisoner most politely; to treat him with the respect due to his rank; and to extract from him the greatest possible price for his liberty, often raised by the captive himself—this was the supreme goal of a fine and noble war, even if it resulted in ruin for more than half of the kingdom. So it happened to Jean II, called the Good or the Brave, to whom we now turn.

PHILIP VI AND JEAN II

The first two Valois monarchs, Philip VI and Jean II, are not among the kings who have acquired legendary status. It is true that the disasters of Crécy and Poitiers weigh heavily on their reputation. These good and brilliant knights, sumptuously attended and served, vigorously upheld the white standard. Jean and his legendary battle-ax at Poitiers are famous; but Philip pulled in the reins before coming to Crécy—he arrived too late. Neither king had the least notion of strategy or tactics. Like all their nobles, they despised lowly foot soldiers, even their own; they would gladly have ridden their horses over them, without ever understanding that infantry was already

THE EARLY VALOIS

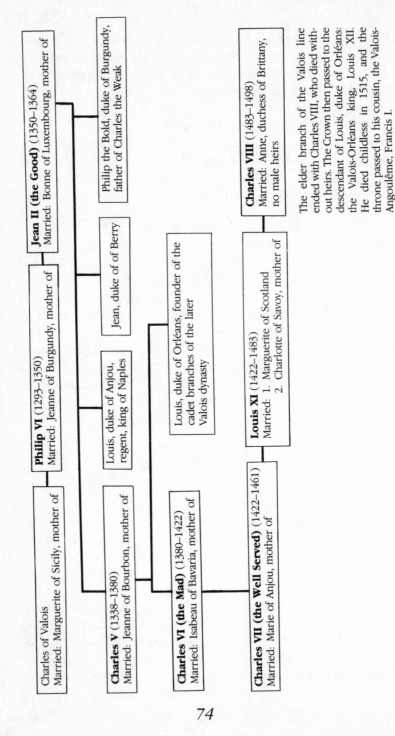

Charles of Valois
Married: Marguerite of Sicily, mother of

Philip VI (1293–1350)
Married: Jeanne of Burgundy, mother of

Jean II (the Good) (1350–1364)
Married: Bonne of Luxembourg, mother of

Philip the Bold, duke of Burgundy, father of Charles the Weak

Jean, duke of of Berry

Louis, duke of Anjou, regent, king of Naples

Charles V (1338–1380)
Married: Jeanne of Bourbon, mother of

Louis, duke of Orléans, founder of the cadet branches of the later Valois dynasty

Charles VI (the Mad) (1380–1422)
Married: Isabeau of Bavaria, mother of

Charles VII (the Well Served) (1422–1461)
Married: Marie of Anjou, mother of

Louis XI (1422–1483)
Married: 1. Marguerite of Scotland
2. Charlotte of Savoy, mother of

Charles VIII (1483–1498)
Married: Anne, duchess of Brittany, no male heirs

The elder branch of the Valois line ended with Charles VIII, who died without heirs. The Crown then passed to the descendant of Louis, duke of Orléans: the Valois-Orléans king, Louis XII. He died childless in 1515, and the throne passed to his cousin, the Valois-Angoulême, Francis I.

74

master of the battlefield. But achieving victory required well trained and respected infantry in the English style. The failure of the French to realize this raised military incompetence to a level rarely seen even among kings.

Both Philip VI and Jean II nonetheless knew how to make ambitious and unruly vassals mend their ways. They bought the city of Montpellier from the king of Majorca in 1349 and obtained the inheritance of the heavily indebted duke or "dauphin" of Viennois, on the condition that his title would henceforth be borne by the oldest son of the French king. Charles V was the first to enjoy this dignity, which had been skillfully arranged by Jean shortly before his own father's death. This acquisition brought the kingdom to the Alpine region neighboring the duchy of Savoy, which was often ruled by related princes; and it also opened the door to the riches of Italy.

The same Jean II knew how to assert his rights forcefully when the last Capetian duke of Burgundy died without heirs in 1361. Jean governed this wealthy duchy himself; Charles V later unfortunately abandoned it to his brother Philip. Yet Jean II, always magnificent and occasionally shrewd, was not always a master of self-control. It is still unclear why he ordered the summary beheading of the former constable Jean de Vienne in the courtyard of the Louvre: the victim had just returned from England after payment of ransom in November 1350. However, this unpredictable monarch did behave like a gallant knight when, after being liberated by the English following partial payment of his own ransom, he returned to their captivity because one of his sons had escaped from the English to be with his young wife; as a consequence Jean died in London in 1364.

Jean and his father had naturally inherited the financial difficulties encountered by the last direct Capetian descendants, mired as they were in long and costly wars. In 1341, Philip VI instituted the *gabelle,* a permanent salt monopoly to produce revenue. As in the past, various taxes presented as temporary measures were confirmed by provincial or regional "estates" whose members were carefully chosen in advance— and yet they tried to control both levies and expenditures.

They attempted to assert even more control in the serious crisis following the battle of Poitiers.

Just as their predecessor Philip IV (the Good) had done, these kings frequently "adjusted" the coinage. The livre-tournois, a weighty monetary unit, was worth 82 grams of silver in 1336, but less than 17 grams six years later. This theoretical decline of 80 percent was the greatest ever seen under the monarchy. As for the modest denier, or penny, 240 to the livre, its value apparently fell by 75 percent between 1350 and 1355. Such devaluations temporarily solved the problems of debtors, especially the kings themselves. They also testify to the astonishing inability of the weak royal administration to deal with the enormous expenses of war; and yet there were always the costs of magnificence, grandeur and vice common to all the Valois. These kings were only establishing an exaggerated model of the manners later practiced all too often by the fleur-de-lis monarchy.

Although complex and not always clear, these financial arrangements were essential. In the middle of the fourteenth century, however, they gave way to a new and formidable force that had nothing to do with politics—the plague.

The Return of the Plague

Six or seven centuries earlier, the plague had disappeared: its last recorded mention dates from 694. God only knows why it stayed quiescent in its Asiatic homelands. Nonetheless its name survived and was given to the most serious epidemics such as dysentery, which may have killed Saint Louis in 1270: experts declare that the authentic plague was not found in Tunisia at that time.

Brought from the Orient in ships, the plague landed in late 1347 in Mediterranean ports. Quite close to the kingdom of France, at Marseille, it killed all the inhabitants of the Rue Rifle-Rafle in November; by December it was in Aix-en-Provence. By 1350 the entire country was infected, with the possible exception of the Massif Central. The last known French cases in this cycle were reported at Tonnerre in 1352. Then the plague took a holiday for several years before its next appearance.

Plague virus, not identified until 1894, was regularly spread by certain fleas. The disease appeared in two forms: pneumonic, which could be transmitted by simple breathing and was uniformly fatal; and bubonic—quickly identified by black spots, or buboes, found on the groin, the neck, and under the arms—from which it was possible to recover. Both forms of the illness lasted only three days and were fearfully contagious.

Startling numbers of victims have been reported, and they were by no means all exaggerations. The most precise document we have is a parish priest's register from Givry in Burgundy. In eleven months of 1349, he buried 649 of his parishioners, whereas in preceding years an average of about 30 had died. The statistics from monasteries and convents are also exact: among the 300 Augustinian brothers of Maguelonne and Montpellier, only 14 survived. Of course, these enclosed houses were ideal for contagion. Numerous studies have shown that epidemics always began during good weather and stopped when the first frost came, although they could return. Mortality varied from 10 percent to 100 percent of the population in each area, but the average was about one-third, suggesting that 5 million French victims died. Although it disappeared in 1352, the plague struck again in force between 1360 and 1362; a third attack occurred in 1374 and a fourth in 1400. From that time until the end of the Hundred Years' War, there were only three years—1403, 1419, and 1447—when plague was not reported somewhere in France. As late as 1669 the disease continued its brutal attacks alternating with periods of remission; after that date it appeared in France only once, at Marseille in 1720. By that time the French had learned to protect themselves with local quarantines, isolation hospitals, and sanitary zones.

In 1349, the horrible Black Death dismayed, deranged, and provoked the population to terrible reactions. Everyone sought the causes and blamed the stars, the devil, human sins, bad air, "plague spreaders," and Jews, who were burnt by the hundreds. To expiate sins there were public flagellations lasting for hours. The saints were invoked and their relics carried in processions, or more simply, people fled, carrying their fleas with them. Christian burial presented a serious problem, as it became impossible to find priests and doctors willing to approach the victims. Blessings were delivered from afar while "carrion crows," highly paid poor devils, pulled out the rotting dead with hooks, tossed them into carts, and dumped them into immense ditches, up to two hundred meters long, outside the cities. Quicklime, if available, was thrown on top of the bodies. Sometimes the dead were left in place and burnt in a purifying fire.

This hideous character of plague dominated the entire century. In the kingdom of France the plague played a much greater role than the Valois, the English, and the roving bandits who carried it among their clothes. Yet the horrors of plague were neither general nor permanent, and in their wake people tried to revive society with an ease that permitted drunken excesses and brutality—all the while awaiting the next attack.

The Other Misfortunes

All four horsemen of the Apocalypse seem to have visited this unlucky century, together or separately. Famine has already been mentioned: it lasted for three years after the death of Philip IV, although sources state that it had always spared the fine century of Saint Louis. The famine was caused by three years of bad weather, which spoiled the grain harvests on which most of the kingdom depended for food. Flour became poor, scarce, and above all very expensive. The common people were thus forced to eat spoiled or infected food, which caused an increase in contagious digestive disorders. Their mortality was aggravated by water pollution and the lack of hygiene.

Apart from a few towns that suffered from long sieges, absolute famine was seldom reported. But the common formula—grain shortage plus price increases plus epidemic equals high mortality—was henceforth repeated an average of once each decade down to the time of Louis XIV. The last great crises occurred when he came to the throne in 1661–62; in 1693; and in the infamous winter of 1709. The series then ended, having been more or less severe depending on the weather. By then people must have been accustomed to it.

Toward the middle of the fourteenth century, the French people had to face other terrors: the excesses of passing soldiers and tax collectors. The soldiers' numbers were suddenly increased when the "great companies" were set free on the roads of the kingdom after the Peace of 1360. The growth and relative regularization of taxes had long been regarded as intolerable and unjust. Besides the old *gabelle* and hearth taxes, now less and less intermittent, there were duties collected on the transport of food and merchandise as well as future "treaties" and "aides" for the so-called absolute monarchy. In the fourteenth century at least these taxes were partially justified by the captivity of King Jean.

It was easy to get lost in the maze of monetary manipulations and to curse the first tax assessors and collectors who were gradually installing themselves across the land. There were *élus* at the cantonal level, *généraux* and receivers of finances at the provincial level. These institutional posts were put in place irregularly and inopportunely: the inhabitants of the kingdom were not in a position to see them disappear.

We should not be surprised that economic historians who have sung the praises of the fine prosperity and growth of the thirteenth century should stress the particularly somber character of the early Valois age in the kingdom of France, a sharp contrast to the situation in Italy.

Economic Stagnation

Not a single technological innovation appeared in the fourteenth century except gunpowder, which was brought from China by the Arabs and the Italians. For the moment it was no more than a curiosity. Agriculture, livestock raising, transportation, and economic centers remained almost exactly the same as they had been earlier. Some had grown, others had not.

Starting in 1303, however, monetary crises began to affect *rentiers* and creditors, as well as debtors and tenants in the other direction. These crises were only the beginning of greater upheavals in the reign of Jean II. The famines after 1315, ravages of soldiers, and the plague worked together to wipe out at least one-quarter of the population. We can understand why so many livestock were slaughtered, so many farmsteads and lands abandoned. Wastelands were expanding. Production and even productivity fell together; landowners and *rentiers* felt the severe effects.

Prosperity in the countryside could not be restored immediately. It grew slowly by the end of the fifteenth century, faster in the sixteenth century, then declined again. Only in the eighteenth century was it truly well established in the grain-growing regions.

As for commerce, it is understandable that great merchants deserted the robber-infested French roads in favor of the Saint Gotthard, Simplon, and Brenner passes. These were the main routes between Italy and Flanders, the two poles of the European economy. The fairs of Champagne, after having drifted toward Châlon, moved to Geneva before passing on to Italy and the German cities. Sailing around Gibraltar was another substitute route: from Italian ports such as Venice and Genoa, vessels could reach the ports of Aquitaine, Brittany, northern France, and Flanders. Meanwhile the Dutch and English monopolized the great trade in salt, wool, salt fish, and products from the north as well as the wine trades of Bordeaux, the Charente, and the Loire. The maritime and land trades of the kingdom were limited to coastal shipping and local markets. Paris was the one exception—the capital of kings, court, parliament, high bourgeois, and great wealth. The Italians had found it easier to settle there permanently even before colonizing Lyon. Yet it should not be surprising that trade had abandoned a kingdom in the throes of insecurity, depopulation, and anarchy.

Moreover, in the important textile industry, styles had changed. Away with the heavy and unfashionable cloth made in northern cities and Paris! Gentle ladies and beautiful girls, infatuated with extravagant costumes, wanted only fabrics that were brilliant, rare, and light—if possible silk embroidered with gold or the supple cloth of Florence. The workers of northern France could not meet this demand.

Cloth-making cities that did not know how to adapt to these changes melted away. Even Arras lost half of its population, most of them workers, but managed to save itself by specializing in the tapestries that made its fortune. Rouen, Beauvais, and their surrounding areas tried to survive by making inexpensive serge for the common people, but it was difficult to sell to an impoverished and decimated clientele.

Fragmentary economic statistics confirm the story of stagnation and decline. The fourteenth century and most of the fifteenth were marked by distressing economic signs. Not until the end of the fifteenth century and the "beautiful" sixteenth century did more favorable trends reappear. Yet aside from the plague, the princes who governed what remained of the French people did much, perhaps involuntarily, to contribute to their misery.

THE POLITICAL CRISIS 1358–1364

Part of the French population had seen King Jean taken as a prisoner from Poitiers to Bordeaux, and the absurd conduct of brilliant chivalry on that day, September 19, 1356, was well known and little appreciated. Paying the ransom was a duty that no one questioned; on the other hand, continuing to maintain a court and government accused of excessive luxury and corruption did provoke some concerns. These were expressed in the meetings of estates held in the *bailliages,* provinces, and linguistic regions (*langue d'oc* and *langue d'oïl*) which were frequently convened to give their consent to new taxation. The weakness of central government encouraged the estates to raise their voices.

The eighteen-year-old Dauphin Charles, weak and sickly in appearance, had reportedly been ordered by his father to flee from Poitiers. First he took the title "lieutenant to the king," then "regent." He kept the untrustworthy and dishonest counselors of his father and grandfather—counselors who were widely hated.

Also momentarily imprisoned was the dangerous Charles of Navarre, a direct descendant of Philip the Fair. Charles was brilliant and unscrupulous, ready to ally himself with anyone in order to assume power if not the throne itself.

Meanwhile at Paris a powerful bourgeoisie had arisen from the cloth trade and passed into finance, particularly into lending money to the monarchy at high profits. Étienne Marcel, the "mayor" of the city, was a son-in-law and brother-in-law of some of the richest members of this group. His enormous fortune in land and personal property did not appear too disreputable. Furthermore, he had talent, prestige, a sense of leadership and of the crowd, as well as ideas that may be called liberal or reformist. Last but not least, he was ambitious. In the seething city there were many malcontents in boutiques and workshops; to the north and east of Paris, honest peasant proprietors and middling farmers who had once been prosperous were now exasperated by the poor sales of their reduced harvests, the price of agricultural implements, and the excesses of tax collectors, *reiters,* and insatiable seigneurs. In May 1358, they launched a revolt, or *jacquerie.* The violence, the extent, and the duration of this uprising were unexpected. As it happened, these forces of opposition did not know how to join together or were unable to do so; in any event the young but already cunning regent was able to overcome them one by one.

Étienne Marcel and the Jacqueries

To the estates who pretended to govern at least royal finances if not the kingdom itself, the regent Charles gave a magnificent gift in the reforming ordinance of March 1357. Just as many other edicts that came later, this one was never put into practice, and the estates got tired of meeting to discuss it.

The king of Navarre had also been busy scheming. Once

he had escaped from captivity, he offered to make an alliance with the unruly Parisians—an act that immediately caused a good portion of the nobility to rally around the dauphin. After some hesitation, Étienne Marcel accepted Navarre's offer and organized riots in Paris. He had two of the future king's counselors assassinated before Charles's eyes. Inaugurating a tactic that would be used again later, the regent fled from his capital to organize a blockade and starve the city into submission. Meanwhile he reaffirmed provincial loyalties.

Marcel negotiated with the *Jacques,* or peasants, whose excesses were well known. He began to have second thoughts about his own involvement, but he nonetheless opened the gates of Paris to Navarre and his soldiers, among them many hated Englishmen. The eternally moderate bourgeoisie, ever *politique,* sensed that the wind was changing and had Marcel assassinated in the street. They expelled Navarre and his troops and shortly afterward allowed the dauphin to make a triumphal entry, as other monarchs did later.

As for the peasants of Beauvais, Valois, Brie, and elsewhere, their anti-aristocratic violence horrified the chroniclers. One recounts that the peasants roasted a knight on a spit and forced his lady, who had been repeatedly raped, to eat a piece of his body. These villains received quick and equally horrible punishment. "Our mortal enemies the English would not have done what our own nobles did then," reads another report.

All these shameful or tragic episodes were but preludes and produced no reform whatsoever of the monarchy, its councils, its financial administration, Parisian "liberties," or the condition of the peasants. Much blood had been spilled in vain.

While Jean II had momentarily returned and dreamt of going on Crusade, the dauphin responded to the seasonal campaigns of the Black Prince and his father Edward III by stealing away his troops. Above all he practiced scorched-earth tactics, causing several thousand English to tire and withdraw, at the sacrifice of a few peasants. Step by step the treaties were signed in 1360, the ransom paid, and the territories of old Aquitaine painfully handed over. English Aquitaine now stretched from the Loire River to the Pyrenees. Renouncing the vain title of king of France, Edward was content to hold complete sovereignty over one-third of its area.

From the French point of view all this was hardly brilliant, but no doubt it was impossible to do any better. Yet the future Charles V would still try.

CHARLES V (1364–1380)
AND THE RECOVERY

The third Valois, Charles V, bore little resemblance to the first two. Charles was awkward, fragile, hardly suited for combat; indeed he was more scholarly, a fanatical collector of manuscripts with more than a thousand to his name, almost as many as the pope. A reader of Aristotle, Charles was subtle and often adroit. He did keep up the family taste for beautifully furnished residences: Beauté-sur-Marne, Vincennes, the Louvre, the immense Hôtel Saint-Paul with its seven gardens, menagerie, aviary, and aquarium.

As a man gifted with good sense, he knew how to choose his counselors: his chancellors, the Dormans brothers; the provost of Paris, Hugues Aubriot; his secretary Bureau de la Rivière; and even an academic, Nicolas Oresme, who translated Aristotle for him and composed a treatise on sound currency. Other writers emphasized the mystical character of royalty in works such as the *Treatise on the Coronation* and *The Vergier's Dream.*

In military matters, this learned king knew how to use the talents of his three brothers, Jean of Berry, Louis of Anjou, and Philip of Burgundy. He also had the courage to appoint as constable Du Guesclin, a minor Breton noble who was both chivalrous and popular. A good trainer of men, he excelled in guerrilla fighting. By his efforts, Du Guesclin was largely responsible for the success of the delayed reconquest, a remarkable and fragile achievement. He restored the best fortresses and understood the coming importance of artillery. He ordered the manufacture of *bouches à feu*, primitive cannons without carriages; at the siege of Saint-Sauveur-le-Vicomte in 1374 he employed thirty of them, each of which could fire balls weighing 100 pounds each. Finally, at the Clos des Galées near Rouen he revived the construction of a powerful fleet. Under the command of Jean de Vienne, this fleet with the help of Castilian vessels regularly dominated the Channel and the Atlantic, and even dared to sail up the Thames!

For all this work, men and money were required. Charles organized his administration solidly, especially in finances. He personally chose the principal treasurers, receivers, and judges of indirect taxes. Most of the old taxes were reformed and acquired some permanence. The *gabelle* and the *maltôte* were levied as usual and joined by a hearth tax devoted to the struggle against highway robbers. This tax was approved by the estates of 1363 and collected anew each year until 1380.

Faithful to the teaching of Oresme, Charles established sound currency—a gold franc of twenty sols that contained nearly 4 grams of gold, thirteen times as much as in the age of Louis XIV. Of course, the bad old money of Charles's predecessors chased away this technical success, as Gresham's law expressed it two centuries later. But on the whole, Charles avoided the cascading devaluations of his predecessors.

This king's patient labor was largely overshadowed by the negotiations with the English, which were complicated by skirmishes, particularly over disputed territories in Aquitaine. The hot war did not begin again until 1369, but in the interval it was necessary to settle new conflicts with Charles the Bad of Navarre, who was finally defeated by Du Guesclin in his Norman possessions at Cocherel in 1364. The French king also had to prevent the English marriage of the only daughter of the count of Flanders, an alliance that would have presented a considerable danger to France. Charles V obtained her hand for his younger brother, Philip of Burgundy, on the condition of handing over Lille, Douai, and surrounding areas. But Charles could not foresee that this momentary success carried the germ of future dangers—the enormous greater duchy of Burgundy and the inheritance of the Holy Roman Emperor Charles V.

As for Brittany, the interminable quarrels about succession were settled provisionally by the Treaty of Guérande in 1365, by the terms of which Duke Jean IV again became a French vassal.

The essence of Charles V's incessant work can be summed up in two main goals: to bring to an end the ravages of the "great companies" that roamed through the kingdom despite the signing of the peace; and to recover from the English the greatest part of the lands abandoned to them earlier.

Against the ravages of the well-organized ruffians, the traditional cavalry made a pitiful showing at Brignais near Lyon in 1362. Du Guesclin intelligently applied the tactics of harassment and concentrated force. After an unsuccessful attempt to send them to Hungary to fight the Turks, he diverted them to Spain, where Aragon and Castile were tearing each other apart, and Castile itself was racked by civil war. Although the bastard Henry of Trastamara won out in 1369 and became an ally of the king of France, while Du Guesclin was momentarily taken prisoner by the English and defeated at Nájera, the constable had succeeded in exterminating a good number of the bandits.

When war with the English resumed, Charles V again employed the shrewd tactic of his regency—making a dramatic withdrawal and leaving a vacuum before the enemy. On their expeditions, the English soldiers exhausted themselves and succumbed along the way.

While these useless cavalcades were in progress, the troops of the king's brothers and his constable slowly recaptured towns and provinces. By 1380, the king of England held Calais, Cherbourg (sold by the king of Navarre before his ruin), Brest (reoccupied during renewed agitation in Brittany), and only a strip of territory between Bordeaux and Bayonne. But no peace treaty except for passing truces ratified this apparently brilliant reconquest.

Another new development was the popularity of King Charles V and particularly Du Guesclin, who was regarded as the scourge of the English: henceforth the traditional hatred of the French for the English seemed deeply rooted. This was the first substantial manifestation of nationalist feeling.

And yet, the grain shortages, plagues, and tax revolts had not really ended. Certain mutinous cities such as Montpellier were harshly punished. The sufferings of his people and a final sentiment of justice led the dying king in September 1380 to abolish at a stroke all the special taxes established during the past twenty years. This was a fine gesture, but it constituted a very bad gift to the next reign.

Charles V left behind other mistakes as well. In 1376 he had not been able to prevent Pope Gregory XI from leaving Avignon for Rome, which had called him back with solid arguments. After the death of this pontiff in 1378, the Italian and French cardinals were so violently opposed that each group elected its own pope. By supporting Clement VII, Charles V sincerely believed he could prevent the schism that he feared. In fact he rendered it inevitable, especially as he was supported only by Scotland, Savoy, and Naples, while Urban VI immediately obtained support from England and the Holy Roman Empire. The schism lasted for forty years and contributed to the poisoning of relations between England and France.

There were more serious errors: Charles V, in contrast to his more prudent predecessors, provided rich and powerful *apanages* for his three beloved brothers. Louis held Anjou, Maine, and later the lieutenancy of Languedoc; Jean took Berry, Auvergne, and Poitou; and Philip received Burgundy, with great expectations of the Flemish inheritance when his father-in-law Louis de Male died. Moreover, Charles allowed his brothers considerable latitude in ruling their *apanages*. This generosity weighed heavily on the first years of the reign of the feeble Charles VI, who became king at age twelve.

Indeed, this apparently restorative reign, idealized in the enthusiastic panegyric written by Christine de Pisan, daughter of the king's astrologer-physician, shows all the signs of a pause for breath among the interconnected woes of the fourteenth century. However, the insolent ostentation of the nobles and the rich could not prevent the Four Horsemen of the Apoca-

lypse (death, plague, famine, and war)—and taxes to boot—
from riding freely through the kingdom. Their ravages were as
harsh as those of the English and the bandits.

THE DEPTHS OF THE ABYSS:
THE BEGINNING OF THE REIGN
OF CHARLES VI, 1380–1392

At first glance it appears that Charles VI ruled for forty-two
years, since he did not die until 1422. In reality his reign
consisted of six years of childhood and thirty of insanity, with
a few years and rare moments of lucidity in between. His
illness sometimes made him furious, at other times deeply
depressed. Around this nearly empty throne swirled all the
ambitions, hatreds, assassinations, extravagance, and depravity
of France. Everything happened in an atmosphere of continuous celebration, delirious luxury, and general profligacy. At
the end of one day in 1420, after having disowned his son, a
wasted and half-dead king gave his kingdom away to an Englishman.

During this time ten or twelve million Frenchmen, the
lowest total population in a thousand years, continued to suffer and die, sometimes in small groups, sometimes en masse.
Plague and famine were never completely absent: they came
surging back in enormous waves every ten or fifteen years.

When the French people rebelled in town and countryside
against the taxes that had supposedly died with the wise king
yet came back as heavier burdens than ever before, the governing princes unleashed their troops to wreak havoc to their
hearts' content. Never before had noblemen found it necessary to cut off so many heads, whether in Paris, Rouen,
Languedoc, Flanders, or elsewhere. Decapitation constituted a
rite, a pleasure, and an amusement.

Before he died, Charles V had projected a sort of regency
council in which his usual wise councillors would make decisions. But within hours the three uncles of the young sover-

eign brushed away all that. They seized power for themselves and kept it for eight years. Philip of Burgundy was especially active while the other two were occupied in Italy or in Languedoc. They set off on several expeditions against the English, went again to Flanders to massacre rebellious "communes" such as Roosebeke in 1382, and above all reestablished and increased the taxes Charles V had suppressed. Thus in the Midi, as in the north, towns and countryside revolted. At Paris the common people seized the lead mallets stored at the Hôtel de Ville and became known as the Maillotins. They opened the prisons, massacred some tax collectors, and pillaged boutiques. At Rouen, Amiens, Soissons, Reims, and Béziers there were also violent disturbances, and in Languedoc peasants called Tuchins roared through the countryside.

The repression, sometimes begun by frightened rich bourgeois, was quickly taken up by the princes. Rebellious cities and regions were punished with heavy fines, and as many heads as possible were cut off. At Paris, after one demonstration, this meant three or four per day, according to the chroniclers of 1383.

Once order was reestablished, the princes continued to exploit the kingdom. There were no more meetings of estates. Instead, the rulers became intoxicated with feasts and cavalcades, and they prepared earnestly for a marvelous expedition to England, which never departed. Meanwhile the duke of Burgundy had received his Flemish inheritance in 1384 and had become interested in Holland as well. He took the young king along to make war against the duke of Gelderland in a hard and senseless campaign.

By the time he returned, Charles VI had reached his twentieth year and suddenly broke free of the tutelage of his uncles in 1388. He recalled the old counselors of his father, good bourgeois and modest nobles who were ridiculed as "marmousets," because they were supposedly as grotesque as certain sculptures on choir stalls. They tried to return to wise and honest government by taking measures to restore justice and financial stability. They even created a commission of "reformers" to investigate abuses and punish those responsible.

This minor palace revolution had little success, perhaps because people had too high hopes for it. In any case, time was short.

In August 1392, while on the road to Brittany to settle a minor conflict, this fragile king was apparently exhausted by the whirl of feasts and pleasures urged on him by his frivolous brother Louis d'Orléans and by his own overly seductive wife Isabeau of Bavaria. Charles VI was seized by a torrid fever in the forest of Le Mans: he suffered a bout of mad fury and attacked his escort with a sword. After this episode, despite increasingly rare periods of calm, the poor king oscillated between fury and dullness. The kingdom fell back into the hands of the princes, uncles, brothers, and cousins.

By happy coincidence England had passed through a series of political, dynastic, social, and religious crises in the last years of the fourteenth century. These were so serious that the English could not envisage a return to war-making on the Continent. After 1389, the truces between France and England were almost continuous. They were broken only in 1415, the year of Agincourt, a lamentable defeat for the French, an even bloodier version of Crécy, and the preface to the supreme abandonment of the kingdom of France to the English.

Chapter Four

THE FIFTEENTH CENTURY: A KINGDOM REBORN FROM THE ASHES

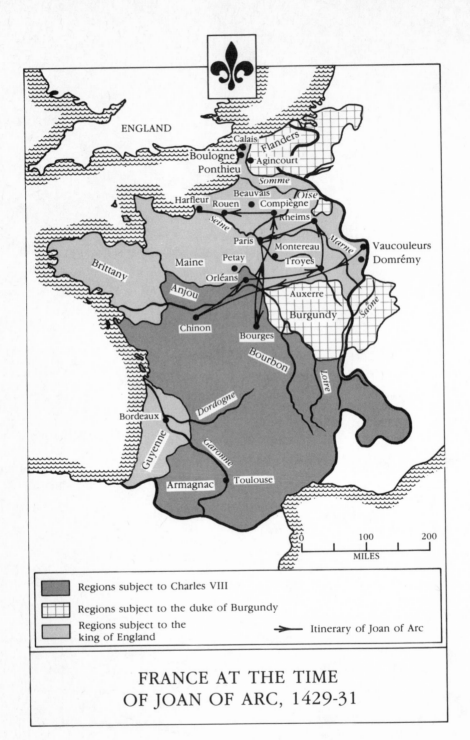

ENGLAND

Calais
Boulogne
Ponthieu
Agincourt
Flanders
Somme

Harfleur   Beauvais   *Oise*
Rouen   Compiègne
Seine   Rheims

Paris   Montereau   *Marne*   Vaucouleurs
Maine   Petay   Troyes   Domrémy
Orléans

Brittany
Anjou   Auxerre   *Saône*

Chinon   Burgundy
Bourges

Bourbon
Loire

Dordogne

Bordeaux

Guyenne   Garonne

Armagnac   Toulouse

0   100   200
MILES

■ Regions subject to Charles VIII

▦ Regions subject to the duke of Burgundy

▨ Regions subject to the
king of England   → Itinerary of Joan of Arc

FRANCE AT THE TIME
OF JOAN OF ARC, 1429-31

While Europe was changing considerably at the end of the Middle Ages, the Church was torn by discord, new worlds were being discovered, and the Gutenberg galaxy was put in place. Meanwhile the kingdom of Charles VI (the Mad) had been divided and pillaged by the princes and the English— and entirely delivered to the enemy after the disaster of Agincourt in 1415. It began to recover under the leadership of Joan of Arc, who made the hesitant king of Bourges into the king of France. And yet Charles VII had to wait a quarter of a century to recapture his kingdom after making such wise reforms as having a standing army and permanent taxation.

The French recovery of Bordeaux in 1453 traditionally marks the end of the Hundred Years' War. It happened at the same moment that the Turks finally captured Constantinople, swallowing the remnants of the Byzantine Empire and completing their conquest of the eastern Mediterranean.

Yet it is hard to say that the Middle Ages disappeared that year and that modern times began at one fell swoop. Even in France, the manifold rhythms of history did not move at the same pace: there were delays in economic development. Royal authority made difficult or deliberate progress. Striking innovations occurred as well—the printed book, the sea route to the Indies, and the mirage that led Charles VIII toward the wealth and danger of Italy in 1494, when the monarchy nearly got stuck in the mire.

Fifteenth-century French civilization is fascinating precisely because of its contrasts: gold and sulfur; mysticism and the stake; the flamboyant Gothic style; the art of Burgundy and Flanders; the first Italian influences; and the literary mediocrity illuminated by the unique genius of François Villon.

ANARCHY: 1400–1428

Heavily endowed with *apanages,* the princes closely related to the mad king had left little territory to the royal government, only distant Languedoc, Champagne, Normandy, and Île-de-France, and even these provinces were administered by their cronies. The holders of Anjou also controlled Maine and Provence; Jean of Berry had Poitou and Auvergne; the Bourbons had acquired Marche, Forez, and Beaujolais. Philip the Bold, besides ruling his duchy and county of Burgundy, also reigned in Nivernais, Artois, and Flanders; in addition he "protected" the principalities of the Netherlands. Louis of Orléans, the king's brother, also held Blésois, Angoumois, and Périgord. The sons of Charles VI, who fortunately died young, also accumulated *apanages.* On the fringes of the kingdom, the counties of Foix and Armagnac were expanding, and Brittany remained hostile.

Each prince, like a little king, had his own palace, council, chancery, and chamber of accounts. Each also levied taxes that rightfully belonged to the king of France. All were occupied with luxury, festivals, and follies; they also practiced intrigue and skillful ways of extracting as much money as they could from the kingdom. Moreover, they were imitated by a multitude of royal officers who dipped freely into the treasury and forged documents at will.

In these circumstances, it is understandable that *gabelle* receipts doubled, taxes on merchandise and the *taille* increased by 50 percent, and the currency was weak. We can also understand why the people could not ignore this pillage and luxury and why anger, revolts, and tenacious hatreds ran through the land.

Armagnacs and Bourguignons

For fifteen years, in the midst of conspiracies, two principal clans were locked in brutal struggle.

Seductive, ostentatious, and depraved—he was overly fond of his sister-in-law, the frivolous Queen Isabeau—Louis of Orléans recommended a prudent understanding with England, but severity toward the "antipope" of Avignon. In his lucid moments, Charles VI supported the opposite policy, as did the Burgundian Duke Philip and his son John the Fearless, who had fought madly but in vain against the Turks.

In November 1407, John resolved to assassinate his enemy. After he left Queen Isabeau, Louis of Orléans was struck down in the streets of Paris by hired killers. Since John the Fearless was easily identified as the man who had ordered the murder, he judged it prudent to flee to his Flemish territories. Civil war with the other princes began almost immediately. Nonetheless, John reappeared at Paris in 1408 and succeeded in having himself absolved of the murder, which was reduced to the status of just punishment for a corrupt tyrant. For all practical purposes John took power and removed the other princes from the royal council. He had the last "marmouset," a hated Montaigu, executed; no doubt the victim was an even greater extortionist than the others. John listened to the rich bourgeois of Paris and the masters of the university who wanted a more reasonable government, a reduced number of royal officials, strict economy measures, and increased surveillance of the financial staff.

In any case, Paris supported the Burgundian. The princes he had removed from power then joined together under the banner of Bernard d'Armagnac, father-in-law of the young Charles d'Orléans, the son of Louis and thus nephew of Charles VI. Bernard and his fearful Gascon forces ravaged several provinces, and were occasionally supported by English adventurers. For more than five years, the kingdom appeared to succumb to anarchy.

In 1413, John the Fearless still held Paris and called for a meeting of the largely forgotten estates of Languedoïl in order to ask them for subsidies. They responded by demanding reforms, and named a commission of inquiry dominated by the theologian Pierre Cauchon, who had several irons in the fire. A partisan of the Burgundians, Cauchon was rewarded with a bishopric and later had the honor of conducting the trial of Joan of Arc.

Outside the assembly, the princes continued their intrigues with the queen and the dauphin. To force their compliance, John organized a terrible Parisian riot led by the head of the powerful butchers' guild, Pierre Caboche. The mob besieged the Hôtel Saint-Paul, residence of the king, and spread through the city to massacre all real or supposed Armagnac infiltrators.

John of Burgundy then published a great reforming edict restating the cherished prudent themes of Charles V. This document was later referred to as the Cabochienne ordinance. But when the riots persisted and became more serious, those bourgeois who always tremble before the people made an alliance with the dauphin and Charles of Orléans. They returned to Paris in force in August 1413, took harsh vengeance, forgot about the wise edict, and resumed their pillage of what remained of the public treasury. John the Fearless had fled again, but he found himself besieged in his good city of Arras. Among these acts of violence and misery, accentuated by the return of the plague and famine from time to time, a great king of England suddenly appeared.

Henry VI, King of England and King of France

As a result of terrible battles, the House of Lancaster had succeeded the Plantagenets on the English throne. Henry IV, the first of the Lancastrians, was preoccupied in his own country and could intervene only indirectly in France. His son Henry V was a just and pious knight as well as an accomplished diplomat and a great warrior; he immediately decided to resume the war. From the moment he came to the throne in 1413, he claimed his "inheritance" in France. After having amused various factions with pretended negotiations, he unexpectedly landed in Normandy in July 1415. In October, at Agincourt on the Artois plain, Henry V found arrayed before him French cavalry composed primarily of Armagnacs. As at Crécy and at Poitiers, the English archers annihilated the French cavalry. There was one significant difference, however: this time the English massacred their noble prisoners, except for the duke of Bourbon and the young Charles of Orléans, who was allowed to exercise his poetic talents in England for a quarter-century.

A lamentable period followed. Besides the bewildered king, Paris contained the constable of Armagnac and the surviving son of Charles VI, the sickly and deceitful Dauphin Charles. The dauphin quarreled with his mother and exiled her to Tours. John the Fearless was already scheming with Henry V of England; he went to deliver Isabeau and tried to create a puppet government at Troyes. In support of a new and violent revolt at Paris, the Burgundian troops entered the capital and massacred all the Armagnacs they could find, from the constable down to his lowliest valets. Dauphin Charles just had time to flee with a few supporters and crossed the Loire to settle at Bourges. At almost the same time a terrible smallpox epidemic struck Paris, killing at least 5,311 persons at Hôtel Dieu and 40,000 in the city as a whole.

Meanwhile Henry V of England conquered Normandy step by step, city by city. Rouen held out for six months, but the English advanced up the Seine and approached the capital. In the face of this threat John the Fearless, who controlled the king and the city, hoped for a reconciliation with the dauphin and the remaining Armagnacs. Negotiations took place. On September 10, 1419, at the second interview, the dauphin's men killed the duke on the bridge of Montereau. Louis of Orléans had been avenged. Dauphin Charles thus gained a reputation as an assassin among the Burgundian partisans: in that group stood practically all of northern and eastern France including Paris.

The new duke of Burgundy was the superb Philip the Good. He hesitated a little, then reached agreement with the English without committing himself too much, even though a joint war against the dauphin had been envisaged. In May 1420, a treaty signed at Troyes by the unfortunate Charles VI gave the kingdom of France to the king of England, who had only to complete his conquest. In this treaty, the French king repudiated and disinherited his son, banished him "for his horrible crimes and misdeeds," and gave his daughter Catherine to Henry V, who was recognized as his "true son and heir." It was agreed that Henry would immediately take over the regency of the kingdom, crush the partisans of the dauphin, and finally join the two crowns to his advantage. From a juridical point of view, even though the traditional French institutions would survive, this was an annexation preceded by an occupation. Two years later, Henry V and Charles VI died, the latter in complete destitution. In accord with the Treaty of Troyes, an infant ten-month-old son of Henry V was proclaimed Henry VI, king of England and of France. For two centuries afterward the English monarchy carried this double title. With the approval of the duke of Burgundy, the regency of France was entrusted to the duke of Bedford, a remarkable man and uncle of the young king.

Of course, the dauphin announced that he would henceforth be called Charles VII, king of France. The people of Paris ridiculed him as the "king of Bourges," where he most often resided.

The "King of Bourges"

In fact, the kingdom was cut in two. The parts north and east of the Loire as well as Lyonnais, a bit of Anjou-Touraine, and Guyenne were under the direct control of the English, their Breton ally, or their Burgundian accomplices of the moment.

At first glance, this collection of lands seemed richer and

better administered, since it included the royal road from Rouen to Paris. But the Burgundian acted in his own interests and was not very reliable. Strong resistance movements against the English occupying forces appeared, particularly in the oppressed and pillaged countryside of Normandy. As for the elites, they acted as usual in accord with their interests and thus collaborated, especially at Paris.

Meanwhile the "king of Bourges" held the calm provinces that had not been ravaged much recently. They granted him important subsidies, two or three times as great as the occupier and his accomplices received; unfortunately his mediocre entourage wasted the money. Great princes supported him: among them were his stubborn mother-in-law Yolanda of Sicily, who held Anjou and Provence; the brave Dunois, half-brother of the captive duke of Orléans; his cousins, the duke of Bourbon and the count of Foix, whom he had appointed his lieutenant in Languedoc. With his former Armagnac counselors, who had escaped from Paris, Charles had reconstituted the Parlements at Poitiers and Toulouse, a chancery and a chamber of accounts at Bourges. Among the company commanders who swarmed around him, Dunois and the Breton Richemont were worthy generals. But Charles's best troops had been massacred at Verneuil in 1424. Afterward, disappointing small skirmishes alternated with truces that were seldom respected.

The most serious problem was that Charles VII appeared to have stopped believing in himself, perhaps in his very legitimacy. The members of his divided and dishonest entourage were even less convinced. Energy and faith were lacking in the dauphin's circle: they had to come from Domrémy.

THE RECOVERY: 1429–1453

Joan of Arc was born into a world of comfortable farm workers on the frontiers of Champagne and Bar, not Lorraine. She was thus a subject of the king of France and not of the Holy Roman

Emperor. Of course Joan was illiterate, as were almost all girls for centuries afterwards. So many mediocre books and pamphlets have been devoted to her that our account must be limited to her historical role, without bowing to legend, hagiography, or even erudition.

Many sincere boys and girls, pure and devout, thought they heard God or his saints and believed themselves destined to save France. Such would-be saviors were found almost everywhere, and no one was surprised. Joan's sole claim to originality lies in her success.

She won her first victory when she persuaded her companions and the lord of Vaucouleurs, an agent of the Dauphin in a theoretically pro-Burgundian area, to give her a sword, a safe-conduct pass, male clothing, and a small escort so that she could travel safely at night on the byroads from Champagne to Touraine.

Joan's second victory was to recognize the king among his courtiers at Chinon and to triumph in little-known tests to which he subjected her before the Parlement of Poitiers—including the verification of her virginity by matrons. She won the confidence and respect of rough soldiers and their brigand chiefs, who knew the legend that a maiden would save the kingdom that had been lost by a woman—Isabeau. To these people, what we regard as extraordinary, the marvelous or divine appeared normal.

On the level of national politics, these victories were surpassed by others. First, acting as "chief warrior" with only a few hundred men, Joan managed to save the besieged city of Orléans on May 8, 1429. Orléans held the key to English penetration of the Dauphin's lands; its relief was a considerable strategic and morale-building success. Then Joan persuaded the wavering Charles VII to take the road to Reims to have himself crowned according to traditional rites. Thus, with oil from the holy ampulla, he became the Lord's Anointed and quasi-priestly ruler who held his kingdom by the grace of God. Certainly by reassuring a monarch whose divine and human legitimacy Joan had always believed, she gave him authority and prestige. Popular loyalty and faith streamed toward him, and especially toward the Maid, for this epic was quickly recognized and interpreted as a sign from heaven.

In four months, from April to July 1429, Joan had accomplished the essential and unexpected tasks. Charles VII was little concerned when she failed and was wounded outside Paris, captured at Compiègne, sold to the English, and judged and condemned by a court specially appointed for that purpose. Since she had achieved her destiny, the king no longer needed her; and the English were delighted to be rid of someone they considered a witch, a tradition still recalled by Shakespeare in *Henry VI*. She was burnt at the stake in Rouen on May 30, 1431.

The extraordinary saga of Joan of Arc and the legends that quickly surrounded her display both the force of medieval Christian faith and the popular patriotism nourished by French hatred of the English, hatred that lasted or reappeared centuries later.

While Joan was sacrificed, the man whom she had made king returned permanently to his beloved Loire Valley, except for a brief excursion to Paris. The monarchy seemed to install itself away from the capital. The best of his captains tried to hold positions in Champagne and Île-de-France, but they had neither the men nor the resources to do more.

The climax of so many years of war finally came in 1435. Philip, duke of Burgundy, who called himself "the grand duke of the West," had in vain tried to impress the English and the loyalists with his ostentation. He had obtained nothing from the former, and thought only of using the latter in order to dominate them. Above all he hoped quietly to expand his territories in the direction of Holland and the Somme River. An arrangement with Charles VII was in order. After three years of negotiations, the Treaty of Arras was signed in September 1435. It sealed the reconciliation of Philip and Charles. The French king personally exempted the duke from obligations of homage and repented for the crime at Montereau; Charles even swore to find the perpetrators, but did not do so. He also recognized all the Burgundian conquests, including Mâcon, Auxerre, the cities of the Somme, and Boulogne.

The English felt threatened, especially as their young king was showing signs of weakness. Bedford had died, the occupation of France was expensive, and a peace party had formed around the Beauforts, relatives of Henry VI. The bourgeois of Paris judged it advisable to rally to the more powerful party; they opened the gates of their city to Charles VII in April 1436.

After some procrastination, Charles VII finally decided upon the indispensable reforms as well as the issue of war and peace. He was receiving better counsel from Pierre de Brézé and others, though probably not from the beautiful Agnès Sorel, his mistress. In 1441, he swept through Champagne and the valley of the Oise north of Paris. In 1442, he led his army as far as Dax and Saint-Sever, to the very gates of the Anglophile province of Guyenne. In 1444, under the impetus of "King René" of Anjou, who had promised his daughter to Henry VI, a truce was agreed: Henry swore to give up at least Maine, but handed over nothing. Charles VII reconstituted his army with powerful artillery built by the brothers Gaspard and Jean Bureau. He was able to take over Le Mans in 1448 and began the decisive campaign to liberate Normandy, with the complicity of the inhabitants. The victory at Formigny in April 1450 achieved this feat. Almost immediately the king headed for Guyenne and Gascony, which had been controlled by the English for three centuries.

For the first time, Bordeaux and Bayonne were conquered in 1451. Yet the English, led by the veteran commander Talbot, landed the following year and were welcomed as liberators, especially at Bordeaux. But the old captain was defeated and killed along with four thousand of his troops at Castilon on July 17, 1453; the French had arrayed three hundred cannons against them. The inhabitants of Bordeaux had to surrender three months later. Because it was impossible for the French to launch an attack to recapture Calais without passing through the territories of the duke of Burgundy, the Hundred Years' War was over. No treaty ratified this fact, which England recognized only much later and with reservations. Although they held only Calais, the English monarchs long carried the title of "king of France."

The Reforms of
Charles VII: 1435–1461

After the signing of the Burgundian peace and the recapture of Paris, the king who had been uncertain and worried for so long was transformed into a determined master, infatuated with reorganization. No doubt he was receiving good advice—he was now called Charles the Well Served—but necessity also required these actions.

Naturally the most immediate concern was the army, which had to be organized from the ground up as an instrument of war and a force for order. With the coming of peace, bands of unemployed soldiers went on worse rampages than ever before. They earned the nickname "fleecers," which barely describes their worst excesses. The king had a certain number hanged and sent others to make war in Lorraine and Switzerland. A better idea was to take the best ones into his own service by paying them, and to try to send the others away, which was done gradually.

The decisive and lasting reorganization dates from 1445, when about twenty "companies under the command of the king" were created. Under the authority of a captain chosen by the king, each company consisted of 100 lances of 6 men on horseback, only one of whom was fully armored; he was the "man of arms," or *gendarme*. These companies were supposed to be billeted in fortresses or with civilians on honest terms. The men were permanent soldiers, regularly paid, and dependent on the king.

These first serious attempts to create a royal army of 10,000 to 12,000 men were complemented in 1448 by the institution of infantry in the English style, the "free archers." In principle, one man was drawn from each fifty hearths, and he was exempted from taxation. These men would train regularly in the use of the bow or crossbow and would respond immediately to the king's call. This institution functioned irregularly because the soldiers were never paid, although it did reappear later, in the time of Louis XIV.

Artillery had improved considerably, from the gross bombard that launched enormous stone balls to the small hand cannons, crude precursors of the gun. Jean Bureau, promoted to grand master of artillery, even used the first bronze pieces that fired cast-metal cannonballs and also employed long culverins that could be drawn by chariots. These weapons were often operated by Italians, Liégeois, or Germans. Although more frightening than harmful to the enemy, they signaled the slow decline of the medieval fortress. Near Rouen the French also resumed the building of a fleet, a project that had been abandoned since the time of Charles V.

This ambitious military program, designed to last, could not be achieved without a reorganization of finances and of government itself. The Burgundian peace and the submission of Paris obliged the king to consolidate institutions that had been duplicated when the kingdom was divided—the councils, Parlements, chambers of accounts, and so forth. Charles took advantage of the situation to hold a wise purge, keeping only the least compromised and most competent of his former adversaries. Picking up again the organization of his grandfather Charles V, he prepared the way for the central institutions of sixteenth- and seventeenth-century France.

Charles VII also laid the foundations of provincial institutions. In the *apanages* as well as the unreliable or distant provinces, rough versions of Parlements, chambers of accounts, and fiscal courts had slowly been established—at Grenoble, Toulouse, Rouen, Bordeaux, and later, Rennes. Of course it was necessary for central government to bear the costs of maintaining them, as well as several universities, all the while trying to limit their freedom of action. Circumstances thus dictated the establishment of a sort of federalism that would not offend provincial sensibilities, even in the essential area of finances.

The tax mechanism of *aides, gabelle,* and *taille* dated back to Jean the Good and Charles V, but it was often subject to the goodwill of the estates of the north (Languedoïl) and south (Languedoc). In northern France, the great innovation, started in 1439, was to dispense with their consent. Thus taxation became regular and permanent. The assessment and collection of taxes were also regionalized, and the distant provinces, which long preserved their estates, enjoyed more independence.

For the greater part of the kingdom, the *taille* was assessed by about seventy-five districts known as *élections,* and the sale of salt was conducted by local warehouses, which naturally did not exist in areas of salt marshes or salt mines. For royal finances as a whole as well as for revenues from the royal domain, the kingdom was divided into four areas administered by *généraux* of finances, the origin of the thirty-odd *généralités* (and *intendancies*) in the time of Louis XIV.

This financial reorganization was directed by Jacques Coeur, master of the mint, finance minister (*grand argentier*), and much more. "To a brave heart, nothing is impossible" was his slogan, reflecting his unbounded ambition. A conspiracy and an accusation of embezzlement put an end to his career in 1451.

Toward the end of the reign of Charles VII, the royal income approached an unprecedented two million livres. Two-thirds of this money came from the *taille*. The little "king of Bourges" now found himself on top of a great and powerful kingdom. He certainly eased the way for his difficult son.

THE STRUGGLES OF
LOUIS XI: 1461–1483

Louis waited for more than twenty years for the death of his father, against whom he had taken up armed revolt. In 1461, he had not even seen Charles for fifteen years, either because Louis ruled in his *apanage* of Dauphiné and plotted intrigue with his neighbors, or because he had taken refuge with his uncle the duke of Burgundy, first at Brussels, then at the château of Genappe, where he plotted still more intrigues.

The prince was thirty-eight years old when he succeeded to the throne, and neither handsome nor likable, but he was obviously possessed of an astonishing intelligence and used it to good advantage in subtleties as well as in excesses. He has unleashed antagonistic passions among novelists and historians, some of whom depict him in darkest hues, while others cannot contain their admiration. No doubt he deserved neither the excesses of honor nor the indignities. To understand him, it is fitting to recall his friend and counselor, Francesco Sforza of Milan or that prince whose portrait was later painted by Niccolo Machiavelli.

Louis XI apparently had none of the Valois characteristics: no taste whatsoever for ostentation, but rather a natural bourgeois simplicity, perhaps slightly cultivated. In contrast to the varied debauchery of his father, Louis displayed a certain chastity. His insistent and devout piety may seem dictated by the fear of death and hell: it led to practices that could be judged mediocre and strongly tinged with superstition. But his political goals were simple—to expand his kingdom and to be obeyed. His methods were more complex; indeed, all means appeared justifiable to him as long as they succeeded. He never allowed scruples to stand in his way, nor did he respect his word, which he always considered revocable. Like Mazarin later, he thought all men were for sale, and he may have been right—he certainly bought many of them.

In the larger European context Louis XI was a diplomat of demoniacal dexterity, but he was eventually entangled in the threads of his own web, either by excessive shrewdness or by haste. Thus we can understand the adventure of Péronne in 1468, when, under the pretext of negotiation, he was arrested and forced to offer aid to the Burgundian duke, whose subjects in Liège he had just incited to revolt. Similarly, his bungling greed led him to seize the entire inheritance of Charles the Bold in 1477, which encouraged the duke's daughter, Marie of Burgundy, to obtain the support and the hand of Maximilian of Austria, the future Holy Roman Emperor. Thus Louis unwittingly helped to install the Hapsburgs on the borders of his kingdom.

Another chapter filled with tales of unsuccessful enterprises could be written about the Spanish policy of Louis XI. He intervened inopportunely in Navarre and the Basque country, provoking the wrath of Castile and Aragon. Taking as payment the province of Roussillon, he helped the king of Aragon fight against the rebellious Catalans, then he changed sides, whereas the Catalans were reconciled with their prince and recovered Perpignan in 1472. It took Louis XI three years of war to recapture the province, which his son Charles VIII gave away in order to enjoy his Italian dreams. During these struggles, Isabella of Castile and Ferdinand of Aragon were married in 1469, preparing the way for the unification of a great state on the southern border of the kingdom, just as Maximilian would later do in the north. It is doubtful whether the diplomatic skill of Louis XI deserves all the praise it has received.

On the other hand, after the initial disasters, Louis did outmaneuver Charles the Bold, duke of Burgundy, in masterly fashion. In this enterprise the overblown personality of Charles simplified Louis's task. Swollen with pride, Charles wanted to unite Burgundy and the Netherlands by grabbing Alsace and Lorraine, then have himself proclaimed king by the Emperor. Louis XI circumvented this move by paying the English so that their army at Calais would not intervene in 1475, and by facilitating an alliance between the free cities of Alsace and the Swiss cantons. Charles the Bold attacked them anyway and suffered two harsh defeats at Granson and Morat in 1476. Mad with rage, he rushed to besiege Nancy, where he was beaten and killed in 1477. Louis XI was then relieved of his richest and most powerful rebel vassal.

Like his predecessors and indeed his successors down to the time of the Fronde in the seventeenth century, King Louis XI had to fight many times against aristocratic conspiracies. They included ambitious and greedy dukes, counts, and barons, and even whole provinces. Three leagues "for the public good" were formed against him. He responded with corruption, promises, and outright violence, including the killing of two Armagnacs in 1473 and 1475.

His constant activity led to numerous additions to the kingdom. Besides Roussillon and his part of the Burgundian inheritance, the duchy of Burgundy itself and Picardy, he collected from his cousins the provinces of Anjou and Maine in

1480, as well as Provence in 1481. He had great expectations for the port of Marseille and for claims to the kingdom of Naples that he was too prudent to pursue.

Such results cannot have been accomplished without considerable funds and a rigorous internal policy. Louis XI was the first of the truly authoritarian kings—that is, he knew how to make people obey him. He made no significant changes in the institutions that his father had put in place, but he did install men who were entirely dependent upon him. Louis preferred men of modest origins because they would owe everything to the king, who reigned by terror.

When *Parlementaires* were occupied with a case dear to his heart, he would force them to relinquish it in order to fulfill extraordinary commissions, and this was the beginning of the Grand Conseil. The cities were asked to elect councillors whom he had chosen. He also held his clergy firmly under control: of course they were Gallican, and left only spiritual authority to the pope. Louis was also the first Valois king to understand the importance of the bourgeoisie. He favored them by creating the fairs of Lyon, giving privileges to the ports and craft guilds, and introducing the silk industry at Tours and Lyon. He continually increased the number of "companies under the command of the king" and had them trained in camps; he always bought more artillery. As for the people, they paid for everything, thus proving that they were not so poor. Within twenty years, the total revenue from *tailles* had nearly quadrupled; to these sums must be added forced loans, confiscations, and benefices from his favorite Italian bankers.

As a result of this harshness and rapacity, as well as the modesty of his dress and his train, Louis XI did not achieve great popularity. The king did not care. He died in August 1483, among the religious medals, saintly hermits, and healers in his well-guarded lair at Plessis-lès-Tours in the Loire Valley, which he had chosen as his capital. Louis was less than sixty years old, yet he had arranged the details of his succession, which on this occasion were carried out. But one swallow does not make a summer, and one observance does not make custom.

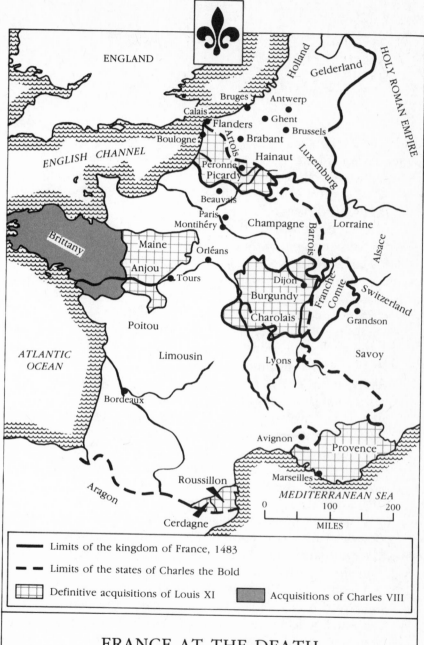

ENGLAND

Holland

Gelderland

HOLY ROMAN EMPIRE

Bruges

Antwerp

Calais

Ghent

Flanders

Brussels

Boulogne

Brabant

Artois

Hainaut

Luxemburg

Péronne

Picardy

ENGLISH CHANNEL

Beauvais

Paris

Montihéry

Champagne

Lorraine

Barrois

Alsace

Brittany

Maine

Orléans

Anjou

Tours

Dijon

Burgundy

Franche-Comté

Switzerland

Charolais

Grandson

Poitou

ATLANTIC
OCEAN

Limousin

Lyons

Savoy

Bordeaux

Avignon

Provence

Roussillon

Marseilles

Aragon

MEDITERRANEAN SEA

Cerdagne

0   100   200

MILES

——— Limits of the kingdom of France, 1483

- - - Limits of the states of Charles the Bold

▦ Definitive acquisitions of Louis XI   ▓ Acquisitions of Charles VIII

FRANCE AT THE DEATH
OF LOUIS XI, 1483

THE GOVERNMENT OF
THE BEAUJEU, OR THE END
OF THE FRENCH MIDDLE AGES:
1483–1493

Charles VIII came to the throne at the tender age of thirteen, and was mediocre in body and spirit. He needed good tutors. For this responsibility Louis XI had chosen his Bourbon son-in-law, Lord Beaujeu, and his daughter Anne, "the least foolish woman in the world," as he said.

This energetic couple encountered the usual hostility from the great nobles, who launched a "mad war" against them, with the help of Maximilian of Austria. But the rebels were crushed at Saint-Aubin-du-Cormier in 1488, where the duke of Orléans was taken prisoner.

Immediately after the death of King Louis XI, it seemed wise to call a meeting of the Estates General at Tours in 1484. This body had not met since 1439. All provinces sent representatives of each of the three orders, representatives who were often genuinely elected. They brought lists of grievances, already collected in *cahiers* (notebooks), some of which still survive. The delegates proposed moderate reforms, reductions in the *tailles,* and the principle of taxation only with the consent of the estates. In response the government made some promises, and everyone returned home apparently satisfied to have been heard.

The most important matter was the succession in Brittany. This rich duchy was theoretically a vassal of the French Crown, but it behaved like an autonomous kingdom. Brittany chose its own allies, nominated its bishops according to a direct agreement with the pope, had installed a Parlement and soon had a university. The Bretons wanted no part of French rule. It so happened that the last duke had died in 1488, leaving as his only heir his daughter, Anne, already a determined young woman of thirteen. She offered her hand to Maximilian of Austria, who was by then a widower, since Marie of Burgundy had died. Happily for France, Maximilian was not able to come to Anne's aid: imagine the consequences of Hapsburg rulers at Nantes and Rennes! The Beaujeu army blockaded the young duchess in her capital of Nantes and forced her to agree to marry Charles VIII in 1491. Admittedly she kept her duchy in her own right, with all of her privileges; but she agreed to marry the next French king if her union with Charles VIII proved barren (which it did). Thus by a simple personal union, Brittany was somehow attached to the kingdom, but not incorporated in it.

This was the last and best achievement of the Beaujeus. By now the king had reached the age of twenty and wanted to govern by himself. He dreamt only of Naples and Italy. It would be tempting to write that the century ended as it had begun, with a mad king, but Charles VIII was merely unintelligent and unaware.

THE BEGINNINGS OF
ECONOMIC REVIVAL

For another half-century, the Four Horsemen of the Apocalypse continued their ride through the kingdom of France. Grain shortages and famines reappeared every eight or ten years here and there, drawing in their wake the usual deadly epidemics. Plague was also still much around, occasionally rising to terrible peaks that affected almost the whole country in 1412, 1438–39, and 1454–57. The worst attack, in 1481–83, saw the plague crisscross France, striking from Abbeville to Toulon and from Laval to Villefranche-de-Rouergue. It is hard to count the number of victims or even to identify the regions that escaped the epidemics. Despite some remission of the disease, the kingdom had difficulty recovering from the ravages of the great Black Death and later paroxysms.

The ravages of war and particularly those of the fleecers were often described in horrifying detail by more numerous and more talkative chroniclers. They tell of countless massacres, burned villages, and deserted towns. Voluminous archival sources allow some estimate of damages, based on contracts for land reclamation and reconstruction. From the middle of the fourteenth century to the middle of the fifteenth, the decline in total population and production exceeded one-third, although some provinces were affected more than others.

Reconstruction had hardly begun before 1460 or 1470, and it required more than two generations to complete. Peace and the elimination of roving bands were the principal factors. New landlords were able to attract workers for land reclamation by offering contracts "for long years"—tenures of twenty-seven, fifty-four, or ninety-nine years, or one or two generations. The general use of such terms in the beginning facilitated the hard work of replanting and rebuilding. By 1500, the results were visible: the entire first half of the sixteenth century rode on a great wave of expansion and prosperity, but always with the possibility of rude shocks.

In the towns, many of which had lost half of their inhabitants, the progress varied. The monarchy provided help as it should have by granting new privileges, franchises, markets, and fairs. Textile production was encouraged, especially of silk and fine fabrics. It is even possible to speak of Louis XI's "economic policy."

We should note that political disorders and the torments of war had isolated Valois France from the greater European trading routes. Italy and Antwerp communicated by other ways, and the rich cities of the Hanseatic League in northern Europe did not extend their activities farther south than Flanders. The fairs of Champagne were forgotten, while the newly founded fairs of Lyon could not yet compete with those of Geneva. Even the Lendit fair at Paris had shriveled up to a mere regional gathering. The great ports of Marseille, Bordeaux, Nantes, and Rouen were controlled by foreigners or depended on them. The kingdom of France held only La Rochelle and Montpellier, from which the adventurer Jacques Coeur briefly launched a few vessels in an attempt to capture the spice trade of the Middle East and Asia. Yet between 1453 and 1491 all these great ports and their specialized trades rejoined the kingdom, and soon afterward the numerous small harbors of Brittany also made their contribution.

In practice the demographic, agricultural, industrial, and commercial revivals occurred simultaneously and naturally supported each other. They benefited from internal peace that was rarely disturbed. Unfortunately, except for a few Normandy sailors, no one in France seemed to think of the future promise of the Atlantic with its sea route to India already opened by the Portuguese and Castilians. Charles VIII was preoccupied with Naples.

The recovery that was already under way in the reign of Louis XI did not affect economic or agrarian structures. The same tools, customs, and techniques were used over and over. But it is possible that the social structure of France was more substantially changed.

A NEW SOCIETY

There is no doubt that apart from the princes the majority of ancient noble families had not survived so many years of wars, massacres, and epidemics. Besides, the surviving members inherited properties encumbered by debts made in order to pay for a horse, a suit of armor, or a ransom. The older feudal military nobility was often replaced by great bourgeois who had become rich from commerce, especially in financial speculation and dealings with the royal and princely entourages.

These new seigneurs bought lands, manors, and châteaux in the Loire Valley. They presided over the reconstruction of the kingdom by recruiting peasants to do the work. At first the peasants had been attracted by very favorable terms, but these were tightened and closely watched by agents experienced in estate administration and greedy for gain. In effect, these agents created such new exactions on the land as the *champart,* a seigneurial tithe. They demanded payment of dues in kind, which was inflationproof. And they insisted upon strict observance of lordly privileges such as justice and compulsory use of mills, presses, and ovens. Nonetheless, the peasants had gained the rights of survivorship, and all but the last traces of serfdom had disappeared.

In the cities, journeymen and artisans had experienced a quarter-century of euphoria. Because of the shortage of workers in the face of greatly increased demand, they were able to sell their labor and technical skills on advantageous terms, receiving higher wages than any of their descendants earned before the eighteenth century.

The most comfortable surviving bourgeois clans had profited from the wars and the court. Their ranks were stuffed with rich shopkeepers and great merchant-farmers. Well established in the towns, they resumed their conquest of nearby countrysides and seigneuries, filling their treasure chests by making loans at interest, a forbidden but common practice, and by discreet usury. The bourgeois continued to ascend to high offices and financial responsibilities. Louis XI had the wit to rely on this class, which controlled the dynamic part of the kingdom's economy.

As for the clergy, while French kings of the fifteenth century had relieved it of its material allegiance and fiscal contributions to Rome, their purpose was to put the Church under their own control. Gallicanism received its founding charter under Charles VII in the Pragmatic Sanction of Bourges in 1438. Louis XI only went through the motions of renouncing it. Of course the pope still held his spiritual authority over the French Church, but that did not bother the kings. In this troubled century, donations, legacies, and offerings continued to flow toward the Church, whose substantially increased material wealth provoked the covetousness of civil powers less than a century later—and not only in France.

Little by little, society became more settled. The estates of 1484 had definitively consecrated the division into three orders. By their very composition, the estates also ratified the relative independence of provinces that had joined the kingdom with their own institutions, privileges, and language intact. This was true for Languedoc, Provence, and Brittany.

And yet, in the heart of the kingdom, in opposition to the rough English enemy demanding tribute or plunder, in accord with the epic of Joan of Arc, French identity was emerging. While this sentiment could be called patriotism, its incarnation was the person of the king.

THE CIVILIZATION OF THE FIFTEENTH CENTURY

The miseries of the age had not prevented the richest princes, the Church, and the financiers from sponsoring the construction and decoration of life to a standard of luxury and refinement that has rarely been surpassed. Their efforts were evident in bizarre costumes, coiffures, and shoes, and above all in sumptuous fabrics; rich tapestries woven at Brussels, Arras, and Paris; marvelously made furniture; and splendid pieces of jewelry.

In church architecture the older French Gothic style became flamboyant and more refined with the use of curves. But churches also contained terrifying images of the Passion of Christ, Death and Hell; they seemed to haunt the epoch, and yet their impression was softened by beautiful figures of the Virgin Mary in a blue cloak and the more familiar intercessory saints. This was the century of feeling and mysticism, in which horror was juxtaposed with tenderness. To some extent these characteristics were found in the works of the only great poet of the age, François Villon, who celebrated his tricks and deceptions, the gallows and beautiful women with the same pen he used to write for his "poor and ancient" mother a sonnet "to pray to Notre Dame."

Aside from this genius who stands somewhat outside his age, the fifteenth century produced interminable courtly novels, interminable mystery plays, and interminable rhetorical and theological discussions in increasingly numerous and less brilliant universities. All the same there were two or three noteworthy minor poets, excellent chroniclers such as Jean Froissart and Philippe de Commines, and the unknown author of the famous farce of Maître Pathelin.

Cultural renewal would come from elsewhere. First stirrings were already seen in Flemish art found in the Burgundian lands, as well as in the first Italian influences in Avignon and Provence. This was a breath of the fresh air that Charles VIII and his successors would bring back from Italy at the dawn of a century that would change the face of the world.

Chapter Five

THE "BEAUTIFUL" SIXTEENTH CENTURY: 1494–1552

THE LATER VALOIS

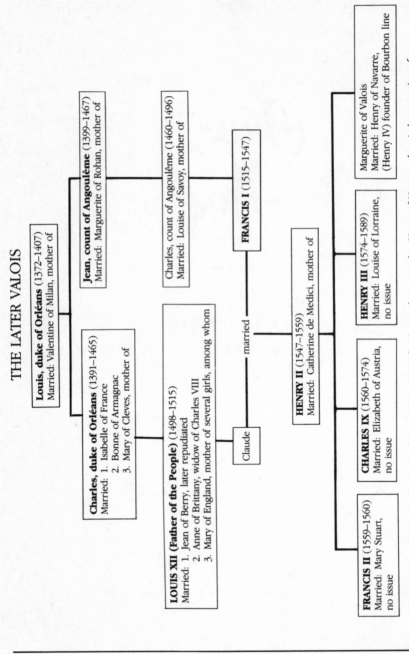

Louis, duke of Orléans (1372–1407)
Married: Valentine of Milan, mother of

Jean, count of Angoulême (1399–1467)
Married: Marguerite of Rohan, mother of

Charles, duke of Orléans (1391–1465)
Married: 1. Isabelle of France
2. Bonne of Armagnac
3. Mary of Cleves, mother of

Charles, count of Angoulême (1460–1496)
Married: Louise of Savoy, mother of

LOUIS XII (Father of the People) (1498–1515)
Married: 1. Jean of Berry, later repudiated
2. Anne of Brittany, widow of Charles VIII
3. Mary of England, mother of several girls, among whom

FRANCIS I (1515–1547)

Claude married

HENRY II (1547–1559)
Married: Catherine de Medici, mother of

FRANCIS II (1559–1560)
Married: Mary Stuart,
no issue

CHARLES IX (1560–1574)
Married: Elizabeth of Austria,
no issue

HENRY III (1574–1589)
Married: Louise of Lorraine,
no issue

Marguerite of Valois
Married: Henry of Navarre,
(Henry IV) founder of Bourbon line

The Valois line ended with the death of Henry III in 1589. The Crown then passed to Henry of Navarre, the ninth generation of a son of Saint Louis, who began the Bourbon line.

The Italian Mirage

Charles VIII embarked on the road to sunny Italy in September, 1494, after having assured himself of the neutrality of his neighbors by proudly giving back to them Artois, Franche-Comté, and Roussillon, the provinces so painfully won by his father. He was accompanied by fifteen to twenty thousand soldiers, one-quarter of them Swiss: an army the likes of which had not been seen for centuries.

King of France, Charles wanted to be king of Naples as well, as his Anjou great-uncles had been. With his young and brilliant companions, he dreamed of a crusade against the Infidels, and even of an imperial crown in the west, perhaps one in the east—or even both. On February 22, 1495, he made quite a scene at Naples by riding in a chariot drawn by four white horses, bearing the crown, the scepter, and the orb of authority. It was a disagreeable sight to his previously divided enemies—suddenly they formed a coalition to evict him.

Indeed, the expedition had begun easily and festively, with a touch of pillage. Since no single Italian state could resist such an army, the kingdom of Naples was occupied at the conclusion of a dazzling promenade. But its loss came as quickly as its conquest. The king had to retrace his steps at the end of three months. Coming out of the Apennines at Fornovo in July 1495, he met the army of the coalition organized by the pope, Emperor Maximilian, and King Ferdinand the Catholic of Spain. Although the French won the day and returned home, their garrison in Naples surrendered a few months later. Charles himself went back to the pleasures of the Loire Valley, where he died in 1498 at the age of twenty-eight, after colliding with a low doorway at his château of Amboise.

His cousin, a great-grandson of Charles V and son of the poet-duke Charles of Orléans, succeeded him as Louis XII. One of Louis's ancestors was a Visconti, and Louis also thought of Italian glory. Soon after he was crowned, he launched his own attack. Louis conquered the duchy of Milan and then Naples, after an agreement with Ferdinand of Aragon. At one point, the gallant French knights fought courteously against the proud Spaniards in a "battle of eleven" that became famous. No doubt tired of these amusements, the Spaniards expelled the French, who retreated in 1504 but kept possession of Milan. The French wars in Italy were by no means over, however, and we shall see that the Italian mirage lasted for at least another twenty years.

Nevertheless the world had changed so much in half a century that we should look beyond these cavalcades and take an overview, momentarily forgoing brilliant Italian reveries: ultimately, they proved not so intelligent anyway.

A NEW EUROPE

Neighboring kingdoms that had long been divided or ravaged by civil war were just recovering their unity and strength, and they presented some dangers to France.

Across the Channel in England, after thirty years of exhausting noble wars between the red rose of Lancaster and the white rose of York, the solid Tudor line came to the throne. Henry VII (1485–1509), the first of their dynasty, found his position strengthened by the extinction of numerous noble families and the confiscation of their property. The English enemy of old would return to France with a burst of glory when Henry VIII, a true colossus of the sixteenth century, succeeded his father in 1509. Just at that moment Louis XII, despite grand victories, was entangled in the Milanese.

Across the Pyrenees in Spain, French monarchs had rarely had serious concerns despite several risky interventions by Louis XI in Catalonia and the Basque country. But the important marriage of Ferdinand and Isabella in 1469 foreshadowed the effective union of the kingdoms of Aragon and Castile, which took place in 1479. The Catholic monarchs then proceeded to conquer Grenada, the last Moorish kingdom in the peninsula, in 1492. That same year Christopher Columbus, a protégé of Isabella, made his famous first voyage. Meanwhile the Spaniards maintained their power in Sicily and Naples, and recaptured part of Navarre in 1506.

The kingdom of Spain was on the threshold of a great destiny, which the last Valois kings hardly suspected. Although Spanish society was vigorously led by institutions of social control such as *la Santa Hermanadad* (the rural constabulary), a royal administration of *corregidores* erased the privileges (*fueros*) of towns and provinces. The nobility was reorganized in prestigious military-religious orders of Alcantara, Calatrava, and Santiago; and religion itself was harshly purified by the action of the Holy Office and the famous inquisitor, Torquemada. On the one hand, the daughter of the Catholic kings had married the son of the Hapsburg Emperor Maximilian, heir to the vast Burgundian domains; his grandson, born in 1500, became Emperor Charles V. On the other hand, following the routes of Columbus and other explorers, Castile acquired the prestigious and fabulously wealthy Indies—the Antilles, the Aztec Empire, and then the Inca Empire, rich in gold and silver. In France, with the exception of a few Norman sailors, almost everyone ignored this New World.

Furthermore, Gonzalo de Córdoba, an eminent Spanish soldier, was inspired by the Roman legions and the new firearms to create rapidly mobile armies of six thousand men, the core of the famous Spanish infantry. At Rocroi in 1643 the young prince of Condé would defeat them for the first time, at the dawn of the reign of Louis XIV. But certainly from 1559 onward Europe and the world saw a century of Spanish preponderance.

The Hapsburgs, The Turks, and Muscovy

While their attention was obstinately fixed on Italy, the French monarchs did occasionally turn toward the north and east. The errors of Louis XI and his son Charles VIII had allowed the bulk of the Burgundian inheritance of Duke Charles the Bold to fall into the hands of Maximilian of Hapsburg. Maximilian became Emperor, and was thus able to join the mineral wealth of his Austrian lands to his lordship of certain German and Italian fiefs, including Milan, the Franche-Comté, and the Netherlands, one of the great models for the world economy with the market, port, and exchange of Antwerp.

In fact the Emperor was camped only steps away from the Somme, on the Meuse and the Saône. When the Holy Roman Empire passed to Charles of Spain in 1519, the kingdom of France found itself caught in a vise. At first there was only one Hapsburg, but after 1556 there were two branches of the family. Their power and lands became an obsession of the French kings for nearly two centuries. The conflicts began badly for the French: Louis XII's successor Francis I was captured at the battle of Pavia, and spent a year rotting in prison in Madrid (1525–26).

However, Francis was able to find at least two worthy replies to Hapsburg policies. The first was getting in touch with the German Lutheran princes, who were naturally in dispute with the very Catholic leader of the Holy Roman Empire. The second, even more astonishing for a Christian prince, was establishing fruitful relations with the nation that had long disrupted the peace of Europe—those Infidels par excellence, the Turks.

From Mohammed II to Suleiman the Magnificent, the vast armies, powerful artillery, and navies of the Grand Turk had come into Europe through the Balkans and the Mediterranean. They advanced to the very gates of the Republic of Venice, which controlled only a narrow strip of the Adriatic. The Turks also challenged Austria after their overwhelming victory at the battle of Mohács in 1526, when the king of Hungary was killed and a good two-thirds of his territory was annexed to the Turkish Empire or placed under its strict "protection." For nearly two centuries the Turks posed a threat to Christianity in general and Vienna in particular. They besieged the Hapsburg capital several times, and even as late as 1683 it had to be saved by a latter-day revival of the crusading spirit—but without the support of France.

Still farther away, in the misty steppes, the great principality of Muscovy was emerging. Under the direction of Ivan III, it expelled the Mongols between 1480 and 1502. The grand duke had married a Paleologus, descended from the former Byzantine emperors. But of course no one at Paris or Amboise took much notice.

The Two Indies

The great changes at the beginning of the sixteenth century were not limited to politics. Three other decisive innovations brought incalculable consequences. The first major change was in the enlargement of the known world by the great discoveries in which the French took almost no part. The essential work was done by the Portuguese, who were encouraged by their learned and curious Prince Henry the Navigator. Portuguese sailors followed the coast of Africa and reached Cape Verde in 1445, the equator in 1471, the Cape of Good Hope in 1488, and the East Indies in 1498 with Vasco da Gama. Then, in less than twenty years, they founded an empire based on Asian trading stations stretching from Aden to Malacca, and from the Sundas to China. The Portuguese discoveries meant that the silk and spice trades, which until then had been dominated by the Genoese and Venetians in the Near East and Mediterranean, henceforth could pass through Lisbon. The Dutch quickly followed the Portuguese, and soon there were thriving African coastal trades in Guinea pepper, gold dust from El Mina, and slaves—sources of previously unimaginable fortunes. Although they embarked later and used different means, the Spaniards also carved out an empire for themselves. Their American lands were crammed with gold and silver, and together with the Portuguese who had casually occupied Brazil they created Latin America.

The discovery and exploitation of the East and West Indies progressively diverted the ships, men, trades, and conquering ambitions from the Mediterranean and central Europe toward the fabled Eldorados of the west. France was momentarily absent from these enterprises, but she would receive considerable monetary and literary fallout from them, including the image of the "noble savage."

The "Gutenberg Galaxy"

The coming of printing with movable type was another great innovation, sometimes called a revolution in the sense of rapid and decisive peaceful evolution, though it touched only a few thousand men at first. Starting around 1450 in the Rhineland and 1470 at Paris, thousands of true printed books appeared. While the goldsmith Johann Gutenberg of Mainz played an important role in this development, he failed to draw much profit from its widespread adoption. By 1480, about a hundred European cities possessed at least one printing house—in France there were only nine but Italy had more than forty. By 1500, the number had nearly tripled. These printed books were twenty to fifty times less expensive than the old copyists' manuscripts. Some twenty million books, mostly religious works in Latin, were printed before 1500. In the sixteenth century the total increased by a factor of ten, with a great proportion in vernacular languages and on secular subjects. Indeed, the essential points of this revolution were price and quantity.

Without the printed book, neither the ideas of the humanists and reformers, nor the great texts of pagan and Christian antiquity would have been known beyond the narrow circles of a few thousand men of the Church, the law, government, and university. These men then constituted the elite of the kingdom, and their libraries could hold hundreds of learned volumes. By 1520, however, the shops of Parisian booksellers such as Janot and Royer contained 50,000 to 100,000 small books of piety or amusement, evidently destined for a different reading public of artisans, shopkeepers, parish priests and landowners.

The presses of Paris, Lyon, Rouen and other cities printed cheap pamphlets and broadsides, which were efficient vehicles for political and religious propaganda. Francis I discovered as much when placards were posted on the very doors of his châteaux in 1534. Then he finally realized the significance of French Protestantism.

The Protestant Reformation

The Reformation constituted another characteristic trait of the sixteenth century that also originated outside France. For the first time since the separation of the Roman Catholic and Eastern Orthodox communions in 1054, division in the Church led to the schism of princes and states. In the course of the century England, the Scandinavian countries, half of Germany, and the Swiss cantons broke away from papism. Part of France nearly took the same road. To these religious ruptures were added political conflicts that were at least as serious, because they engendered incessant wars for more than a century. Learned tomes and cheap pamphlets stirred up quarrels between Catholics and Protestants.

But why did the Reformation happen? The simplest explanation is that the Church was as much a human as a divine institution. Consequently it fell victim to human weakness, particularly when princely families and great feudal lords appropriated its high offices and revenues for selfish reasons. The Renaissance popes, given to excess in erudition and in war, were too Roman and too little interested in evangelical purity. Neither popes, prelates, nor simple priests provided edifying examples to their flock, nor did they always shine by

125

their morals or pastoral care. On the other hand, popular tradition had long made fun of fat canons and lecherous monks. Simple and credulous souls rarely found the comfort they expected from the clergy, which was often mediocre and too rich, or too poor. There was an unsatisfied spiritual need and a call to action.

At a completely different level of learning and culture, the rediscovery and publication of sacred texts of the Bible and of the Church fathers showed clearly the serious divergences that had appeared in Catholic dogma and institutions as well as in the very essence of the faith. An ideal of return to authentic simplicity or Christian poverty was expressed by the elimination of superfluous practices and sacraments, a move supported by elites and simple believers. Even unconsciously, they desired profound reform.

Neither the word *reform* nor the activity was new: there had already been talk of religious reform in the eleventh century. But the novelty consisted of the violent tone of the demands, and their echo in books and pamphlets.

At first there were several cautious groups of reformers such as Bishop Guillaume Briçonnet. The more vigorous initiative had begun in 1517 at Wittenberg, where the Saxon priest Martin Luther made a frontal attack on the massive sale of indulgences by Dominicans allied to the Fugger bankers. Within three years, Luther had broken with Rome, and his writings were spread throughout the German Empire and France. The spur had been given: Calvin and other reformers could come forth.

The sincerity of the original reformers is beyond doubt. However, political implications of the Reformation very quickly appeared in Germany where the Church reportedly owned one-third of the land, and where papal taxes were more oppressive than elsewhere. What a temptation to be rid of them! The reformers who were motivated by spiritual conviction were joined by others with private interests and ambitions. All varieties of reformers, including some who subtly blended their motives, were found in France, to which we now return.

THE "BEAUTIFUL SIXTEENTH CENTURY" IN FRANCE: ca. 1500–1560

The expression "beautiful sixteenth century" comes from economic historians, not from historians of art or culture. The economists have suggested that this cheerful age began about 1475. Some "abstractors of quintessence," as Rabelais called them, extend it as far as 1630 or 1650. Yet it seems more reasonable to reserve the term for the first six decades of the sixteenth century, covering the reigns of three French kings: the sickly Louis XII (1498–1515), his nephew the brilliant athlete Francis I (1515–1547), and his son Henry II, who died accidentally in 1559. Louis XII is popularly known as Father of the People, and Francis I is remembered as a flamboyant cavalier and an intelligent patron of the arts; the more obscure Henry II appears dull, serious, and fearful. All three chose to go to war in Italy rather than seek oceanic glories. Francis I and Henry II were overly cautious in response to Protestantism and vacillated in struggles against the Hapsburgs. Despite their errors, hesitation, and vacillation, the Valois kings often had the good fortune to be surrounded by wise counselors, and they reigned in an atmosphere of cultural and economic expansion, which they encouraged. Furthermore, they took prudent measures that established the monarchy on a firm foundation for their successors.

Economic Expansion

Thanks to better documentation for the sixteenth century, we can speak with more confidence about trends in French society and economy. We can draw demographic statistics from registers of baptisms and marriages and even some censuses taken in the Parisian region, the Loire Valley, Provence, and Brittany. From the end of the fifteenth century until the 1560s, the population of France within constant frontiers doubled, recovering to the levels that had prevailed around 1300. Population density was about thirty-five to forty persons per square kilometer, a figure not surpassed until the end of the eighteenth century. Yet the growth rate was neither uniform nor continuous. In some areas expansion had taken place by 1520, while elsewhere it did not occur until 1570. Population growth was still subject to interruption by epidemic disease, plague, and famine, particularly around 1522–1525.

Overall, the picture of demographic health reflects a return to internal peace, the disappearance of roving bands of vagabonds, and the absence of the army, which was in Italy or on the frontiers of the kingdom. These circumstances favored the peopling of the countryside, the extension and success of agriculture, security along the roads and rivers, and an increase in the number of fairs and markets. Peace and prosperity did much to raise the reputation of Louis XII, who is often presented as a model king.

Henceforth it becomes easier to follow the rapid and sometimes excessive extension of arable land at the expense of forests, which suffered considerable damage in the sixteenth century but were restored in the seventeenth. There was expansion of vineyards and fields of flax, buckwheat, and Indian corn, which came from Mexico by way of the Basque country. At the same time, crop yields rose to their highest levels until the late eighteenth century, and so did the incomes of seigneurial lords, landowners, and clergy, since tithes and other landed revenues roughly doubled.

Toward midcentury this basic agricultural economy reached a sort of ceiling. Poorer peasants had become too numerous for lands that they could not extend or improve, and they were held on a short leash by their masters and lords. The peasants had difficulty paying the increasing tax burden levied by Henry II, and they suffered terribly during the civil wars. But these serious problems arose after 1570 and did not strike everywhere with the same force.

The manufacturing and commercial economy was always secondary to agriculture in this age, despite the thinking of some historians obsessed by great merchants and financial speculators. All their activities can be reduced to buying and selling five commodities that came from the peasants: wheat, wines, liqueurs, salt, and textiles—made of linen, hemp, and wool. Their business improved because their customers, including the court, became more numerous and wealthier.

Statistical studies of the great cloth-making towns such as Amiens support this point: production and sales nearly doubled. Although the luxurious cloth that draped the aristocracy continued to be imported from Italy, the abundant serges and cheaper fabrics were made in France itself—in the north, west, and Languedoc. French manufacturers provided clothing for the common people of Paris and for the kingdom, as well as for the Mediterranean region, Spain, and the Indies.

These growing exports of agricultural and artisanal products helped to bring more gold and silver to France. The country already thrived on a good supply of hard currency, and ritual complaints about the "rarity" of coins were nonsense. In the last analysis, the wars and magnificence of kings were financed by cash advanced by businessmen and bankers, many of them Italians. Naturally, the lenders reserved the right to reimburse themselves generously at the public trough. French national wealth circulated widely even though part of it had been prudently hidden away.

The revived trade of the great French ports still could not compare to Italy, or to Antwerp, the economic heart of Europe. Nevertheless the prosperous French hinterlands and their steady clients supported increased activity. Marseille was establishing its leading position in the western Mediterranean, won in part thanks to agreements with the Turks. Bordeaux continued to ship the wines of its region to its former English compatriots. France as a whole and indeed all Europe needed the salt produced by the areas between the Gironde and the Loire and exported in abundant quantities from La Rochelle and Nantes; these same ports also shipped white wines from the vineyards upstream. The many harbors of Brittany, used for fishing and coastal trade, also handled grain and excellent provincial textiles. Rouen, perhaps the second-largest economic center of the kingdom, was complemented by Le Havre, founded in 1517. Rouen itself was a bustling city of cloth trade and printing, and benefited from the vast wealth of the Seine River Valley and its borders. From Dieppe the brilliant entrepreneur Jean Ango launched his ships for distant seas, captured Spanish galleons, and even reached Sumatra in 1529. These bold moves showed the way to the future, but received only meager encouragement from Francis I and Henry II. By the time of Ango's death in 1551, he was ruined. Despite some striking regional successes, France was definitely not oriented toward the sea.

For a time Lyon was the commercial and banking capital of the country, as well as a center for printing and the silk trade. As a frontier city, Lyon had been colonized by the great Italian bankers from Florence, and by the Swiss and the Germans. Monetary payments were regulated by its four annual "terms" and fairs. Even though the French monarchs long obtained credit there, Lyon really constituted more a focal point of international economic relations for all Europe than a large French city in direct contact with the underlying realities of the kingdom. The international rôle of Lyon declined after 1575, was momentarily taken over by Rouen, and finally fixed on Paris, the true capital. Already the great Italian financiers were settled there, and besides Catherine de Medici had become queen as wife of Henry II. The Italians soon founded dynasties of bishops such as the Gondi, then stood aside in favor of the moneymen of the Parisian region who dominated the finances of the seventeenth century.

From the Economy
to Royal Finances

Increasingly complex wars were fought by armies twice as large as before: while Charles VIII had about twenty thousand men at his command, the French army of 1559 counted nearly fifty thousand. Since these forces could not always live off the land as they had done in Italy, the kings were obliged to establish a solid financial and administrative system. Although this system simply incorporated many older administrative institutions, it did possess at least two new characteristics. The first flowed from an agreement with the pope, the Concordat of Bologna signed in 1516. For nearly three centuries this agreement regulated the status of the Church of France. The king effectively received the right to nominate all bishops and abbots, but the pope reserved the right of spiritual investiture. Thus they jointly suppressed the traditional system of election by cathedral chapters and members of religious houses, who protested against the loss of their independence.

More important, by means of the concordat the king got his hands on a veritable gold mine: the millions of livres of income of the French Church. He could now distribute money and offices lavishly to his family, to the nobles, to his great servants—indeed to anyone whose favors he wished to purchase. The wealth of the Church fell like manna from heaven, joining together political interest and financial interests. Without actually taking anything away from the Church, the monarch was able to make good use of ecclesiastical revenues; consequently he had a powerful incentive to dissuade him from Protestantism, whose precepts included exactly such a secularization of Church properties. These properties constituted about 10 percent of the land of France.

Another precious advantage of the concordat authorized the king to collect *décimes* or taxes from his clergy, which he had already done. In case of need, he could also receive what were modestly and legalistically called "free gifts." They certainly were neither free nor abundant, and around 1560 it was even necessary for the government to go much further, with threats of confiscation.

The second new financial measure dates from 1522: the first "constitution" of *"rentes sur l'Hôtel de Ville"* of Paris and Toulouse. These perpetual loans disguised as annual payments of income represented the first large royal borrowing done through the intermediacy of municipal governments, which were closer to the lenders and more creditworthy than the king himself. Two hundred thousand livres of *rentes* at 8.33 percent (*denier* 12) were offered to the public, which quickly brought in the required 2.4 million livres of capital—in gold and silver. The government promised regular quarterly payments of interest, which was assigned to specific taxes. This pledge of future tax revenues was an assessment on all tax-payers and on the wealth of the growing economy. In 1536 a second issue of *rentes* was made; then, under Henry II, there were no less than thirty-six issues in twelve years. Of course this was too much. By 1561 the monarchy was heavily in debt, to the tune of over 40 million livres, six to eight times its annual income. The king had to threaten the clergy with confiscation of their property in order to obtain a guarantee that the Church would pay the *rentes* from its revenues for a six-year period, later renewed. In reality the city of Paris (that is, the state) paid the *rentes* only when it could afford to do so. And yet this surprising and deceitful system of royal credit lasted for more than two centuries. Financial crises certainly helped to bring about the Fronde of 1648 and the Revolution of 1789, but the system functioned more often than not, despite gimmicks, swindles, and several bankruptcies. The banks of Genoa, Holland, Lyon, and Geneva were able to play a useful and sometimes essential role in intelligently tapping the enormous wealth of the kingdom. Everyone complained and was outraged, but finally paid up.

A TIME OF
POLITICAL REFORMS

The remarkable men of government under Henry II successfully restructured central power and its financial institutions in a lasting way. They skillfully combined an indispensable and elementary centralism in the treasury, fiscal courts, and intendants of finance with the necessary provincial decentralization in an age when it took twelve days to go from Paris to Marseille. France already had its *généralités* and its first delegated commissioners. This system furnished a precedent for Louis XIV, but a full description would have only limited appeal to the reader. Instead, we shall emphasize other, less frequently described but still important aspects of the reforming work of the Valois kings.

One of those long edicts in which the monarchy projected twenty reforms, which often did not come to pass, was proclaimed by Francis I in 1539 at his beloved château of Villers-Cotterêts. It ordered parish priests to keep an exact register of baptisms; marriage registers would be added in 1579. Many priests kept such registers, either in Latin or in French, and some series of the earliest registers have come down to us, especially in Brittany. But this same edict imposed the use of *langue d'oïl,* the dialect of the Loire Valley and Paris, for all official acts. *Langue d'oïl* thus became modern standard French, much as Tuscan became modern Italian. Until this time, in southern France all legal and notarial documents had been drawn up in Latin or in *langue d'oc.* The decision was applied without difficulty, for the elites had known French for decades. But for centuries the rest of the population needed translations into dialect of all royal decisions and official paperwork received at local courts, notaries' bureaus, municipal offices, and parish churches. The monarchy in its wisdom never thought that political unification of the kingdom would require linguistic unity as well.

Another great reform of the sixteenth century was the compilation of customary laws. These traditional laws were sacred, often tacit, and rarely recorded in writing. Custom ruled in large provinces such as Brittany, although there were local variations; it also held sway over large seigneuries or even a handful of villages. Custom regulated marriage and inheritance; rules of agriculture, pasture, and forest; manifold details of everyday life—and it ruled absolutely. Thus there was good reason to establish, compile, and print its texts. This task took more than a century, since information had to be gathered from old judges, notaries, and wise men. As a result, about a hundred local or provincial codes were produced, published, and republished; they were complemented by jurisprudence well into the eighteenth century. The great edicts of Louis XIV were superimposed on these texts without replacing them, and even the Code Napoléon incorporated some of their provisions. Some of them survive today in our local customs.

In the last analysis, slow and reflective initiatives such as these have influenced the life of the French people as much as successive wars carried out by their brilliant sovereigns.

THE KINGS
OF FRANCE AND WAR

War constituted the most noble activity of kings, one that naturally fell to them. They did not fail in their duty but went to war with the help of larger armies often composed mostly of more expensive and better trained mercenaries than in the past. Swiss pikemen were employed after 1516, when Francis I signed the "perpetual peace" with the cantons; they joined German *landknechten,* Basques, and even Greeks and Albanians in his service. Yet it is likely that the majority of soldiers were French.

Firepower increased, both in heavy cannons and in the more mobile culverins. There was even some miniaturization as use of the arquebus spread quickly. The arquebus required five minutes to reload between each shot, but where there had been fewer than a thousand of them in 1520, there were over twelve thousand by 1540. The next innovation, the pistol, appeared in the reign of Henry II.

Apart from the solid *gendarmerie* and several provincial legions supposedly made up of six thousand volunteers each in 1534, the royal army inevitably had recourse to mercenaries, gang-chiefs or *condottieri* in the Italian style. This habit was expensive, but France just managed to pay the bill.

Italian Adventures: Continuation
and Conclusion, 1494–1516

The first two Italian campaigns of Charles VIII and Louis XII (1494–1504) appeared to have left Milan in French hands. But this conclusion did not take into account Julius II, diplomat and warrior pope, who dreamed of uniting all Italy under his holy tutelage. To achieve this purpose he first had to subdue the powerful Republic of Venice, an intermediate goal accomplished by the League of Cambrai (1508), which joined together Florence, Emperor Maximilian, the king of Aragon, and Louis XII. The French were the first to fight. They crushed the Venetians at Agnadello in 1509 and forced them to sue for peace.

The ambitious pontiff then organized a new "Holy" League, in opposition to all-powerful France: its members included Spain, England, the Swiss cantons, and Venice, the former enemy. All of them attacked the French in Milan, where the defense was led by Louis XII's nephew Gaston de Foix, a brilliant young strategist whose military genius and sense of offensive speed made him a forerunner of the great prince of Condé. In midwinter, against all established customs, Gaston led a rapid and victorious campaign against the papal troops at Bologna, then the Venetians near Mantua, and finally the Spaniards before Ravenna. At this last battle, in April 1512, among the fifteen thousand dead left on the field was Gaston himself—wounded eighteen times. His death was the sign of impending disaster. The French were chased out of Italy, and the kingdom of France was simultaneously invaded from the north and the east: Henri VIII, Maximilian, and the Swiss penetrated France itself as far as Dijon. Louis XII bought off the invaders, who signed truces and left.

Louis was succeeded on the throne by his young nephew Francis of Angoulême, whom he had married to his daughter Claude de France, the last heiress of Brittany. This shining knight was also burning with desire to obtain glory in Italy. The two remarkable women who coddled him—his mother, Louise of Savoy, and his sister Marguerite—had described to him the marvels of Italy, as had the young lords who returned from the campaigns.

Several months after his succession, Francis I bought a Venetian alliance and crossed the Alps by a goat path that no one thought worth guarding—the Col de Larche, or Argentera. Three thousand engineers smoothed the way for some forty thousand soldiers and three hundred cannons to appear on the Po River plain in the middle of August. The stupefied Swiss fell back to Milan, which they were supposed to defend. At the battle of Marignano in September, the arrival of the Venetians after two days of slaughter tipped the balance in favor of the French. The echoes of that triumph were heard all over Europe.

The pope gave way to the French king, and signed the Concordat of Bologna, mentioned earlier. At Fribourg the Swiss signed the famous "perpetual peace" by which they promised never to fight against France; on the contrary, in return for subsidies they agreed to furnish contingents of excellent soldiers regularly to the French king. This pattern of service continued until the fall of the monarchy in 1792. By the Treaty of Noyon, also signed in 1516, the young king of Spain, Charles I, agreed that the French could keep Milan in exchange for allowing him the kingdom of Naples.

The French wars for Italy were apparently ended, even though many other conflicts would occur in the peninsula later. The gains to France, however, were greater than simple glory and temporary possession of Milan. The knights who returned from Italy brought some of the Renaissance to France with them. Already there were signs of its influence around Avignon, in Provence, and among the elites. The booty bought or stolen in Italy included antique sculpture, paintings, books, and ideas, as well as art objects made by famous jewelers and craftsmen such as Benvenuto Cellini. Charles VIII recruited twenty-two artists at Florence, and Francis I imported Leonardo da Vinci, who died covered with glory near Amboise.

Shortly afterward, Francis I installed an entire colony of Italians in his favorite château of Fontainebleau. Among them were Francesco Primaticcio, Giovanni Battista Rosso, and even Cellini, but he was unable to draw Titian away from Venice. On the advice of his sister and his counselors, Francis I completed the construction of Amboise and the wing of Blois that bears his name, and began the marvel of Chambord in 1519. He also ordered the demolition of the old palaces of the Louvre and Saint-Germain-en-Laye in order to reconstruct them in grander style. He built "Madrid" in the forest of Rouvroy, the present-day Bois de Boulogne, then Villers-Cotterêts and the new Town Hall of Paris in 1533. He even had Fontainebleau completely remodeled from 1528 onward. This building fever for the new style inspired royal counselors, friends, and financiers. They in turn built Ecouen, Azay, and Chenonceaux. Soon Diane de Poitiers was at work at Anet, and the enthusiasm spread slowly from Île-de-France and the Loire Valley to the country as a whole.

In its beginning at least this artistic Renaissance was marked principally by the opening of space, windows, galleries, antique as well as Italian decoration and furniture. The older French arts survived, and simply came out with new grace. Old châteaux shone more radiantly with a Florentine wing, foliage ornaments, pilasters, pierced staircases. The true Renaissance of classical motifs, antique columns, and more ordered style did not appear in France until the reign of Henry II. For some time the French even continued to build churches in the Gothic style, which more progressive minds now regarded as barbaric.

While all these feverish constructions, reconstructions and decorations were expensive, they provided work for multitudes of stonemasons, carpenters, and woodcarvers. Among them were master craftsmen and sculptors who were purely French, though their inspiration was often Italian. Their names and monuments still survive: Lescot at the Louvre; Delorme at the Tuileries and Anet; Bullant at Ecouen. All of them had made Italian journeys, which became *de rigueur* for serious early modern artists.

Even if the Italian or antique style was later momentarily forgotten, it is clear that during that "beautiful" first half-century the country was practically covered with the scaffolding of new buildings. Everything from the solid new sharecropper's house, the pigeon coop, and the country manor to the grandest royal palaces furnished testimony to the prosperity of the age after the miseries of the preceding century. Unknown to the French at midcentury, the imminent heartbreak of civil war lay in wait.

In the meantime, the two kings had to fight in a terrible war which was not even settled at the end of the century.

Francis I and Henry II versus Charles V

Charles of Hapsburg, king of Spain since 1516, became Holy Roman Emperor Charles V in 1519, after having won an electoral triumph over Francis I thanks to the support of the Fugger bankers. Charles thus added the dignity of the Imperial Crown to the ancient Hapsburg lands, his Spanish territories and the Burgundian inheritance. His domains stretched from the Netherlands to the Indies, and included Spain, Naples, and the Mediterranean islands. With these possessions Charles literally encircled the kingdom of France: his lands came to within one hundred and fifty kilometers of Paris. Furthermore, this young man of nineteen was serious and pious, tireless and multilingual—born in Flanders, he knew French as his mother tongue. Charles V wanted to reconstitute all the domains of his ancestor Duke Charles the Bold—Burgundy itself and Picardy as well. He seemed to have in mind a universal empire. Conflict with the king of France was thus certain to occur: it lasted for forty years. Detailed accounts of these five wars would take up too much space. The first was the most striking, because it was marked by the disastrous battle of Pavia and the capture of Francis I in 1525. From his prison cell in Madrid, the French king promised to renounce his claims to Italy, Flanders and Artois, restore Burgundy, and deliver two of his sons to Charles as hostages for keeping the agreement. Once he was released, however, Francis felt no obligation to observe a treaty extracted from him by force.

The unbounded ambition of Charles V allowed the French king to make alliances with his former enemy, Henry VIII of England, as well as with the German Protestant princes and the Turkish Infidels. The scandal to good Catholic souls was almost too much to bear. By the "capitulations" to the Turks in 1536, the French received enormous commercial advantages in the Levant and the lasting protection of the "holy places." They enjoyed the support of Suleïman the Magnificent's powerful fleet and were able to attack the Hapsburgs from the rear as the Turks threatened Vienna on several occasions after 1528. Despite his triumphs over Francis in Italy, Charles V was thus persuaded to renounce his claims to Burgundy and hand over the two captive French princes in exchange for hefty ransom in 1529.

The third and most glorious war for France led to the total conquest of the duchy of Savoy, from Bourg-en-Bresse to Turin, while Charles V was forced to withdraw his invasion of Provence in 1536–37.

In the fourth war, which saw Henry VIII once again allied with the Holy Roman Emperor, the king of France achieved a brilliant victory in Italy at Cerisole in 1544. At the same time, however, Henry VIII captured Boulogne, and Charles V reached Meaux after having ravaged Champagne. The Emperor was prevented from marching on Paris only because his own sorely tried and unpaid army disbanded. Treaties ensued, but did not change anything.

Henry II, who succeeded his father in 1547, does not have a very high reputation. Yet he understood that establishing secure frontiers in the north and east was more important than going on campaigns in Italy. A strongly Catholic king, he nonetheless had no scruples about making alliances with the German Protestant princes, especially since he had bought their loyalty. They gave him the "right" to occupy the three bishoprics of Metz, Toul, and Verdun, fortified places that guarded the traditional invasion routes of France and Germany. In 1552, Henry II easily managed to take possession of them.

Charles then launched the fifth and final war, whose crucial episode was the siege of Metz, which was defended by Duke François of Guise and ten thousand Frenchmen. The resistance of the French, the winter weather, and epidemics caused the Emperor's powerful army of fifty thousand men to melt away; Charles was forced to retreat. Two years later, suffering from physical and mental exhaustion, he abdicated and retired from the world to a Spanish monastery, where he died at the age of fifty-eight.

To his brother Ferdinand, Charles had left the hereditary Hapsburg domains and the imperial title, which were added to the kingdoms of Bohemia and Hungary, or at least that part of it not controlled by the Turks. To his son Philip, Charles left the rich Netherlands, the Franche-Comté, the Italian peninsula,

Mediterranean islands, Spain, and the colonies in America. Henceforth there were two Hapsburgs instead of one, both threatening to French interests.

The closer and more dangerous ruler was Philip II, the Spaniard. He attacked France in 1557 after Henry II unwisely broke the truce he had signed with the old Emperor. While the duke of Guise left for Naples once again, the spanking new Spanish army crushed the French at Saint-Quentin in August 1557. Once more an attack on Paris appeared imminent; but it failed to materialize because of a lack of money, energy, and intelligence. The duke of Guise had time to return from Italy and recapture Calais from Philip II's English allies in January 1558.

Both sides were tired of war and short of money. The usual bankers and lenders—Italians, Lyonnais, and Germans—declined to act. Consequently, the Treaty of Cateau-Cambrésis was signed in 1559. The English finally agreed to give up Calais; meanwhile Henry II's occupation of the three bishoprics was discreetly passed over in silence, and he agreed to renounce all claims to Italy once and for all. Henry even went so far as to restore to the duke of Savoy all his territories, including Bresse. This incredible gift, for which he has been criticized, was inspired by his strong desire to devote all his strength to fighting Protestantism, then making rapid progress in his kingdom.

Henry II was mortally wounded in a tournament in July 1559. Apparently the official astrologers and sorcerers had predicted an accident. The Most Christian King did not have time to start the Wars of Religion, but he had prepared the way for them.

THE ONSET OF THE WARS OF RELIGION; 1534–1562

The idea of religious reform in France germinated in circles of humanists who had rediscovered pagan antiquity, the correct texts of Scripture, and the Fathers of the Church. The learned teacher Jacques Lefèvre d'Étaples had grouped around him a circle of friends who wanted only a purified Church. Among them was the influential court figure and Bishop Guillaume Briçonnet of Meaux. Francis I, urged on by his sister Marguerite, had a taste for humanism and showed favor to this group. Partly to support their friends, the king created "royal Lecturers," the beginning of the Collège de France. Loud protests against this innovation were raised by the Sorbonne and Parlement, the strongholds of strict and narrow conservatism. And yet this mental ferment barely touched the few intellectuals of the period, people who were more talkative than dangerous.

Matters came to a head around 1520, when Luther's excommunication became known, and his ideas and works were spread in France. Furthermore, in cities on the edges of the kingdom—Strasbourg, Basel, Zurich, Neuchâtel, and Geneva— a more radical Reformation was being preached. The French text of Jean Calvin's *Institutes of the Christian Religion,* originally dedicated to Francis I, dated from 1541. These reformers had rejected the authority of the pope, along with the high clergy and monasticism. They dismissed all sacraments except baptism and communion, and objected to the veneration of saints and images; they asserted that salvation must be by faith alone, not by works. This was going too far for the French monarch, especially when Protestantism won over members of the high nobility—including the three Bourbon princes and the three Châtillon-Montmorency, one of whom was a cardinal.

Francis I had first allowed Protestantism to propagate rather freely, though he had burnt several heretics at the Place Maubert starting in 1523. But he could not tolerate the scandalous anti-Catholic posters that appeared almost everywhere in 1534, even at the Louvre and at Amboise. Royally sponsored persecution followed. After 1540, Francis had such heretics as the printer Étienne Dolet tortured and burnt at Paris. In 1545, he allowed the Parlement of Aix to massacre the peaceful Waldensians of Luberon and ravage their villages. A Dominican Inquisitor was named to the diocese of Paris: he sat in the so-called "Burning Chamber" (*Chambre Ardente*) created by Henry II as a special court alongside the Parlement of Paris. It was already time to extirpate heresy.

More severe and more limited than his father, Henry II was also more threatened by the conversion of a large number of his nobles to Protestantism. He systematized the persecution step by step in a series of edicts ranging from that of Châteaubriant in 1551, establishing the *Chambre Ardente*, to that of Ecouen in 1559, condemning any confirmed heretic to burn at the stake.

At that time, several hundred reformed churches had been established, and nearly two thousand loyal members were enrolled. Almost all the provinces were more or less "infected," and the Protestants were even singing psalms directly opposite the Louvre, on the other side of the Seine. The unexpected death of the king no doubt delayed the outbreak of armed conflict, which had to await the Catholic initiative at Vassy in 1562.

The political situation at the time of Henry II's death was not very promising. The king had left behind three young sons and a widow, Catherine de Medici. The "beautiful sixteenth century" was over. The time of troubles now began.

Chapter Six

DIFFICULT TIMES: 1560–1610

The Misfortunes of the
Age after 1559

The misfortunes were great. Yet they are in no sense comparable to the massive horrors of the Black Death or to the ruin of the kingdom when an Englishman occupied the throne just before the appearance of Joan of Arc.

Misfortune struck first at the top with a succession of weak kings, three brothers—one sickly, another a child, the third a dilettante. Luckily they had a Medici queen mother to guide them. They faced implacable enemies who were both rich and powerful: not the least of these was Philip II, king of Spain, with whom the kingdom was obsessed, directly or indirectly. In France there were great aristocratic families who thought only of their own power and wealth. They regarded conspiracies and revolts as normal behavior. The economy at first prospered, then ran out of breath and began to tire, to stumble, and to fall—but fortunately all crises except the final one did not last long. And above all there was the frenzy of religious fanaticism, which led to furious civil wars in the name of God, who was worshiped in different ways. Simultaneously all over Europe judges sent thousands of witches to the stake. All these disorders, except for the witch persecutions, appeared to end between 1598 and 1603, with the Edict of Nantes, the Peace of Vervins, and the deaths of Philip II of Spain and Elizabeth I of England. And yet, in the completely different climate of the first part of the seventeenth century, the old miseries returned.

A SAD PROLOGUE: THE REIGN OF FRANCIS II, 1559–1560

The oldest son of Henry II was an adolescent of 15, though legally an adult. He was feeble and sickly, completely dominated by his wife, the delectable Mary Stuart, Queen of Scots. She was also the niece of the Guises, a redoubtable family from Lorraine—then part of the Holy Roman Empire; but their lands were primarily situated in France, and they claimed direct descent from Charlemagne. They were and remained the champions of intransigent Catholicism, and they lacked neither ambition nor military and political talent. At this moment there were two Guise brothers: Francis, the glorious general, and Charles, cardinal of Lorraine and archbishop of Reims, the richest prelate in the kingdom. By means of the queen, they continued to exercise power that they had held under Henry II. Their policy was simple: to eliminate the other great families—the Bourbons descended from Saint Louis and the Montmorencys who called themselves "first barons of Christendom." Both of these families were more or less inclined toward Protestantism, which did not give them any advantage.

Henry II had already intensified his campaign against the "heretics" by offering rewards to informers, appointing ardent champions of the faith to judge Protestants, and ordering more arrests and burnings at the stake. The victims included even Anne du Bourg, a moderate member of Parlement who had merely protested against these excesses. The Guises were getting ready to go much further when the occasion arose, the Conspiracy of Amboise in 1560. This was a half-baked plot by the malcontents, one or two Bourbons and neophyte Calvinists, who hoped to kidnap the king and the court. They were betrayed, surprised in the forest, brought back to Amboise, and hanged, drowned, or slaughtered.

These all too visible excesses produced a reaction among the thoughtful moderates around the young king, a group led by Chancellor Michel de l'Hôpital and several reasonable prelates. The Estates General were summoned. Yet violence broke out almost everywhere. The Guises, often hated and threatened, suddenly ordered the arrest at court of the prince of Condé, a Bourbon and chief of the Protestant party. Condemned to death in November 1560, he was saved by the equally sudden death of Francis II. In a trice Catherine de Medici seized power, and tried to resolve the insoluble problems.

The Age of Catherine, "Queen of France, Mother of the King"

So reads the inscription on the great royal seal where Catherine had her image engraved after having sent the Stuart intriguer back to Scotland. Catherine negotiated secretly with all the great families, adroitly circumvented the claims of Antoine de Bourbon, first prince of the blood, and thus acquired the regency for herself.

Although she was the heiress of a great banking family who had become heads of state in Tuscany, Catherine was rather unattractive and had thus been an impatient rival of the "whore" Diane de Poitiers for Henry II's affections. Furthermore, she had been childless for ten years before producing an abundant brood of ten children, seven of whom survived infancy. For a long time she stood in the political shadows, but all the same she was a well-to-do Florentine imbued with the spirit of Renaissance magnificence. She showed her true mettle in December 1560, when her second son Charles IX came to the throne: Charles, age 10, was tubercular and unstable, a neurotic who remained a child all his life.

The genius of this queen in perpetual mourning was to maintain herself in power for nearly thirty years despite often insoluble difficulties of the so-called "wars of religion," which were as much wars of princes and provinces, international conflicts, conspiracies and assassinations, and opportunities for pillage and betrayal. There was nothing simple or exalting about them, and yet they were rather specifically French.

In most European countries, the religious problem had just been solved neatly and brutally. In Spain, Philip II had burned both "moriscos" (Moslems who had openly converted to Christianity but continued to practice their old religion) and Protestants who had not been able to flee or convert in time. On the other hand, grave difficulties awaited him in the Netherlands, where the savagery of his repression in 1581 caused the revolt of the "United Provinces," later known simply as Holland. But this was not a sudden change of fortune.

In the Holy Roman Empire the principle of "cujus regio, ejus religio" was applied: this simply meant that each of the hundreds of states or cities was obligated to adopt the religion of its ruler. In general, northern and central Germany chose Lutheranism, while the rest remained largely Catholic under the dominion of the Hapsburg Emperors and the ecclesiastical electoral princes of the Rhine.

Italy, which was almost entirely Roman Catholic, had never known more than a handful of religious opponents who were quickly silenced or willingly distracted with the most abstract philosophical ideas. As for England, King Henry VIII had decided to become his own pope in order to remarry at his convenience and confiscate the goods of the Church. After Calvinist and Catholic episodes under his immediate successors Edward VI and Mary I (1547–1553–1558), his brilliant illegitimate daughter Elizabeth returned to his original intentions by instituting Anglicanism, a compromise among the sects, but completely and definitively detached from "papism." The Irish, however, remained deeply attached to the Roman Catholic Church, while in 1560 the Scots had just adopted rigorous

Calvinism under the Presbyterian banner of John Knox, at the very moment when poor Mary Stuart, widow of Francis II, returned home.

THE COUNCIL OF TRENT

At the same time the Council of Trent—first called in 1545 and twice interrupted—completed its final sessions. It maintained the totality of Catholic dogma, including the seven sacraments, the faulty and antiquated Latin Vulgate text of the Bible, belief in purgatory, the cult of the saints, and the veneration of images, which had been proclaimed idolatrous by the Protestant reformers. The council also insisted on the exclusive use of Latin for religious services and declared the absolute authority of the pope over the Church: the doctrine of infallibility would come later, in the nineteenth century. Furthermore, the Roman Catholic church was invited to reform its structure and morals. The council recommended that holders of episcopal benefices reside in their dioceses, and it opposed the plurality of livings; but these recommendations were not much heeded. The bishops at Trent also sponsored such wise measures as the creation of diocesan seminaries, which were established in the following decades.

This work in defense of Catholicism was anticipated or completed in 1555 by Paul IV's revival of the Inquisition, known as the Holy Office; it took a prominent role in Italy and Spain. The Counter-Reformation was also strongly supported when the Society of Jesus began in 1537 and was officially recognized in 1540. The Jesuits, a carefully selected and educated army in the service of the popes, grew rapidly. By 1560, they numbered twelve "provinces," fifteen hundred members, forty colleges and six thousand pupils. The Jesuits were intelligent and rigorous, though they could be supple when necessary. They took charge of education and the spiritual direction of prominent figures such as the future Henry III—anyone who was great, powerful, and rich—anyone who might be persuaded to attack heresy on his frontiers, such as in present-day Belgium.

A further step was the creation of the Congregation of the Index in 1571; for centuries afterward it was responsible for the prohibition of "bad" books.

In its ensemble, this Catholic reaction to the Reformation certainly sought "to extirpate heresy," at times with the help of powerful armies. But the Church still had to be reformed from within. This other task, begun at Trent, followed a varying rhythm depending on place and time, as well as political climate. The Catholic Counter-Reformation, however, is not really comparable to the bold and radical efforts of Luther, Calvin, and the other Protestant reformers.

The ebb and flow of the tides of reform all over Europe surely influenced Queen Mother Catherine de Medici. In France nothing had been settled: aristocratic clans fought among themselves, great families and whole provinces taking one side or the other. The exalted Huguenots and the exacerbated papists also had to contend with moderates in both camps as well as ambitious adventurers everywhere.

Although raised at Florence and Rome in the bosom of the Catholic Church, Catherine apparently nourished a lukewarm faith. She allowed her children to pray in French and willingly received polite and well-connected reformers at court. On the other hand she was given to believe in astrology, lucky charms, predictions, divinations, and charlatans of every sort. To accomplish her ends, she would resort to any means, including lying, duplicity, and all possible twists and turns. She gained an abominable reputation as a poisoner and criminal, but she also earned solid friendships and deep devotion from the men of her council and the troop of Italian bankers and military commanders who had followed her to France.

Imperturbable and perhaps the sole virtuous member of her family, Catherine was infatuated with architecture, poetry, music, and ballet. She enjoyed Rabelais and Aretino as much as Ronsard; her fascinating personality dominated the kingdom, though not the age that she had to share with Elizabeth I and Philip II.

EIGHT WARS WITH AS MANY TRUCES AND EVEN MORE MASSACRES: 1562–1593

The Reign of
Charles IX: 1560–1574

For two years, Catherine tried to rule by conciliation, in the absence of true agreement. At the Estates General of Orléans the usual wise speeches and serious proposals for reform of the state were heard, and a famous royal edict accepted them in principle. When the Estates (without the clergy) were transferred from Pontoise to Poissy, they requested and obtained taxation of the Church: part of its lands were sold or mortgaged to pay the enormous debts of the monarchy.

At Poissy there was a discussion between Catholic prelates (including a Bourbon and a Lorraine-Guise) and a dozen reformed ministers, among them Calvin's associate, Theodore Beza. Their dispute was simultaneously precise, eloquent, and intractable. The arrival of Jesuit General Diego Lainez, who described the Calvinists as wolves, serpents, and assassins, quite naturally put an end to any hope of conciliation.

An edict of January 1562 nonetheless granted freedom of worship to the Protestants in private houses and outside walled cities. Several weeks later, the Guises and their escorts discovered a Protestant group in a barn in the town of Vassy. They killed or wounded 178 people, including 30 women. This massacre was the breaking point, but bloody encounters had already occurred in the Midi, at Le Mans, Angers, Beauvais, and even at Paris around Saint-Médard.

Taking advantage of a truce in January 1564, Catherine and Charles IX undertook a tour of France that lasted more than two years. The general purpose was to show the sacred person of the adult king, before whom all disobedience would naturally cease. At the same time Catherine hoped for general pacification after the excesses of the preceding years. The duke of Guise had been assassinated, and his assassin drawn and quartered; Montluc boasted of atrocities in Guyenne and the baron des Adrets of others at Montbrison and Mornas; even the tomb of Louis XI at Cléry had been desecrated. At each step of their "grand tour" the immense royal party encountered feasts, declarations of loyalty, and negotiations for levying taxes: the person of the king proved irresistible.

This spectacular, long, and useful voyage did not, however, prevent the renewal of civil wars, aggravated by foreign involvements. Spain supported the Catholics, while the German Lutherans and Swiss Calvinists supported the Protestants. There was also the revolt of the "sea beggars" in the Netherlands.

With the assassination or disappearance of the first leaders of the two parties, the Guise family still faced the last great Huguenot champion, Admiral Gaspard de Coligny. He was probably, excepting Catherine herself, the only political genius of his time. Aside from some vague inclinations of Francis I, he was the only one who conceived and nearly established two French settlements in the New World, in Brazil and Florida. Coligny won the friendship of the young king Charles IX in one of his lucid moments. Charles admitted the admiral to his council and was even ready to support him when he proposed a war of liberation for the Netherlands, which was already in revolt against Spain. This proved too much for Catherine, who was jealous of her power; it was also too much for the Catholic party and the Guises: they determined to get rid of this intruder. The queen mother had already tried magicians and sorcerers, but in vain. An assassin would be more effective. The Guises found one, yet the blast of his arquebus wounded but failed to kill Coligny on August 22, 1572, several days after the wedding of the Protestant Henry of Navarre and the Catholic Marguerite of Valois, sister of the king. This celebration had brought to Paris a horde of Protestant gentlemen, and it was thus decided to celebrate Saint Bartholomew's Day on August 24.

Legend, fiction, passion, and even history have been carried away by that memorable day's events, which continued for six weeks in the provinces. At first the plan was a simple enterprise of political assassination prepared by the queen mother and the Guises in order to get rid of the entire Huguenot officer corps at one fell swoop, on the pretext of foiling a plot supposedly organized by the intended victims. But the police operation degenerated into terrible popular massacres. Coligny was dragged from his sickbed, decapitated, castrated, and torn to pieces. The bridegroom, Henry of Navarre, escaped execution only by temporarily converting to Catholicism at swordpoint. Others did not have the choice. The total number of victims—ten thousand, twenty thousand, or more—will never be known. All the Catholic monarchs of Europe except the Holy Roman Emperor, who was sickened by the bloodshed, showered Charles IX and his mother with enthusiastic praise. The pope immediately celebrated a Te Deum mass and, like Charles, ordered the striking of a magnificent medal to commemorate this glorious day.

Naturally the massacres settled nothing. The surviving Protestants reorganized themselves in a powerful federation, especially strong in their Languedoc bastion and the fortified places of La Rochelle, Montauban, Nîmes, and Sancerre, which the government had to abandon. A torrent of terrible pamphlets ensued. Serious political theorists such as François Hotman proposed placing the authority of the Estates General over the French kings. Moreover, many sincere but thoughtful Catholics, then known as the "malcontents" and soon to form the "politique" party, practically joined the Huguenot resistance. The agonies of Charles IX continued until May 1574, when he died at the age of twenty-four without a legitimate son. It was doubtful whether his younger brother Henry, recently sent into unenthusiastic exile as king of Poland, would do any better in France.

The Early Reign of Henry III: 1574–1584

Henry III, the favorite son of Catherine, was by far the most gifted and most cultured, though he is not much loved by historians and moralists. He was a true humanist. As a good Valois, he adored pomp, strange festivals, jewels, small animals, and particularly, it is said, young boys—an abominable crime for ordinary mortals in that age. But he did not detest attractive girls either. Except for some unappealing deeds lost

y, however, Henry III left behind thousands of let-
⸺uminating his life, but the voluminous legislative work
of his reign remains little known. Responsibility must no doubt
fall on the terrible handwriting of the time.

The first ten years of Henry's reign were marked by quarrels with his ambitious younger brother, the new duke of
Anjou, and with his unstable sister Marguerite. There was also
a succession of wars, conspiracies, hollow peaces, and reconciliations during the interminable festivals. There was even
another "tour de France" by Catherine in 1578–79. She tried to
pacify the largely Huguenot south and hoped to obtain the
subsidies that had been refused by the Estates General of Blois
in 1576–77. When that failed, however, the French Church was
again obliged to grant more money to the monarchy. Under
threat of confiscation, the clergy agreed to sell part of their
property, though they reserved the right of repurchase.

During this decade, political positions hardened, and parties were set in place. The Protestants, sometimes supported
by the *politiques,* organized a Calvinist Union centered in the
south. This surrogate regime was subdivided into provincial
"governments" with military chieftains and councils adminis-
tering and levying their own taxes. The whole system rested
on the numerous fortified Protestant towns such as Montpellier,
and on the half-Protestant, half-Catholic bipartisan chambers in
regional Parlements.

In 1576, complete freedom of religion was granted, but its
effective exercise was limited to one city per *bailliage,* to the
places where Protestantism was already established, and to
aristocratic houses. Protestant worship was still forbidden at
Paris and at court. These terms were spelled out in the religious peace of 1577, which guaranteed eight years of relative
tranquillity.

Intransigent Catholics, the overwhelming majority, were
also becoming organized. The unwise nomination of the Protestant prince of Condé as governor of ultra-Catholic Picardy
provoked an appeal to the three provincial orders by former
Governor d'Humières, and resulted in the formation of a local
Catholic league similar to those that had already appeared in

several other provinces, even in Languedoc. Their avowed purpose was to restore the state and the religion by a "Holy Union," though at that time without any apparent aggressive intentions. On the other hand, the Guises knew how to take advantage of the Picard League by extending it. With the help of powerful ultra-Catholic bourgeois, they installed the League of Paris, the only real city in the kingdom. In reply, Henry III, who already headed such exalted and expiatory mystical associations as the White Penitents and their flagellant followers, proclaimed himself "chief of the Holy League," and thus cooled tempers for a while.

The French nobility, living anarchically in quasi-autonomous provinces, happily took part in guerrilla warfare, cavalcades, and festivals more pagan than Christian—but tragedies struck as well. In the terrible year 1580, after Huguenot bands had taken up arms at La Fère, in Guyenne, and in Dauphiné, there were earthquakes in a zone from Calais to Rouen and Paris, floods that caused twenty-five deaths in the Faubourg Saint-Marcel, then whooping cough and finally plague epidemics that killed between thirty thousand and sixty thousand Parisians.

Above all, another and even more serious catastrophe struck. The younger brother of Henry III, the unstable duke of Anjou whom his mother had tried vainly to promote first as a husband for Elizabeth I of England and then as king of the Netherlands, died of tuberculosis in June 1584. Henceforth, there was no Valois left to succeed to the throne. The only legitimate heir was Henry of Bourbon, king of Navarre, relapsed heretic. Given the nature of the kingdom and the monarchy, even moderate Catholics found the situation unacceptable, impossible, and insoluble. There had to be a way out.

Henry of Bourbon
in conquest of the
Kingdom of France: 1584–98

Paris was agitated by the Guises as much as by the prospect of a heretic king. Afflicted by high food prices and epidemics, the

Parisians expressed their anger and suffering. The city leadership was grouped around the shadowy "Sixteen," the core of the Catholic League that included parish priests, Capuchins, lawyers, prosecutors, and shopowners; its shock troops were artisans, students, day laborers, fanatics, and riffraff. The three Guise brothers—the scar-faced Duke Henry, Duke Charles of Mayenne, and Cardinal Louis—joined together the fanatics of the moment. They had no scruples about making a firm alliance with the king of Spain. Philip II promised them 50,000 écus a month in exchange for the total "extirpation of heresy," the publication of the decrees of the Council of Trent—which had been rejected by the Gallican Parlements—surrender of the city of Cambrai, and the installation of the old cardinal of Bourbon on the French throne. A priest of Toul had already established that the Guises were descended directly from Charlemagne, thus proving that the ruling monarch was a usurper and preparing the way for their succession.

In the face of these threats, the well-informed Henry III tried by turns to give way, to negotiate, and to make war against the king of Navarre, who defeated and killed Henry's favorite the duke of Joyeuse at Coutras in 1587. Meanwhile the duke of Guise was enjoying greater military successes. At Paris and most other Catholic cities preachers, pamphleteers, and agitators heaped praise on the Guises and excited the badly nourished crowds. Despite the Swiss soldiers employed by Henry III to prevent popular agitation, the duke of Guise entered Paris to wild acclaim, confronted the king at the Louvre, and obtained the dismissal of Henry's other favorite, the duke of Épernon. On the next day, May 12, 1588, as if by coincidence, barricades appeared in the city—and the king fled. The ultra-Catholic League, which was Guisard and pro-Spanish, now held control of the capital and kept it for six years of accumulated excesses.

Henry III at first appeared to yield, and even capitulated by signing an Edict of Union with Guise at Rouen in June. Another Estates General was called to meet at Blois in December. The king took advantage of the opportunity to lay a trap and have the duke killed by his regular assassins, the "Forty-Five." The next day, December 24, 1588, they dispatched his brother the cardinal as well.

The Paris League reviled Henry III as the "tyrant of Sardanopolis," and openly rebelled against him. They purged all neighborhoods, professional bodies and guilds of royal sympathizers, and even imprisoned three *présidents* of Parlement whom they judged "lukewarm." The Parisians joined a federation of most French cities and provinces, declared Henry deposed, and gave a triumphal welcome to the duke of Mayenne. This surviving Guise brother was proclaimed "lieutenant general of the state and Crown of France," while awaiting official recognition of Cardinal Bourbon as king.

In early 1589 Henry III was threatened with the loss of his entire kingdom: he held little more than the cities of the Loire and Normandy (but not Rouen), Bordeaux, and Dauphiné. Catherine de Medici had just died, and Mayenne was already capturing Vendôme and Amboise. There was only one solution for the beleaguered monarch: an alliance with the heretical "natural heir" Henry of Navarre who, since 1582 had been "Protector General of the Reformed Churches of France." In March, Navarre had launched a noble appeal for reconciliation around the legitimate king; he had promised freedom of religion, even in the Midi—for Catholics! After a family reunion of these brothers-in-law and cousins at Plessis-lès-Tours, the two kings and their united armies, more than forty thousand strong, marched up the Loire toward Paris. Along the way they defeated Mayenne at Bonneval. At the beginning of July, they were within sight of the capital, and they jointly prepared to lay siege to it. But on August 1, Jacques Clément, a Jacobin monk inspired by the duchess of Montpensier, a member of the Guise family, stabbed Henry III in the stomach. Before dying, Henry III recognized Navarre as his successor and commanded his subjects to obey him; but Henry III also exhorted the new king to convert to Catholicism.

It took Henry IV four years to make the leap of faith, and nearly ten years against great obstacles to conquer his kingdom. For his entire reign he had to struggle to secure his power before he, too, fell victim to the knife of another fanatic, an emanation of the powerful Holy League.

The Conversion: 1589–1594

In a declaration made at Saint-Cloud in 1589, the new king sought to reassure everyone by promising peace and liberty to all. But half of his army, whether devoutly Catholic or merely worried, abandoned him. The duke of Mayenne, and the people of Paris, the League towns, Spain, and naturally Rome recognized Cardinal Bourbon as "King Charles X," yet he was imprisoned at Loches and died in 1590. To his credit Henry IV still had some excellent commanders in "brave" Biron, Crillon, and d'Aumont, as well as the best regiments of Swiss and gendarmerie. Wisely, he fell back to Normandy, where he defeated Mayenne at Arques near Dieppe in September 1589. When his next attack on Paris failed, he withdrew toward Tours, returned to besiege Dreux, and defeated Mayenne again on the outskirts of Paris at Ivry in March 1590. Then, while his regiments occupied Poitou and Auvergne, Henry once more devoted his attention to Paris, the key to real power.

Despite fatigue and hardships, the Leaguers held the capital. Popular fanaticism was maintained by monstrous burlesque processions of helmeted and armed monks. Negotiations were taking place on a higher level between the chief sponsors of the League, Rome and Spain. In February 1591, Alexander Farnese, Philip II's governor in the Netherlands, sent a garrison of Spanish troops to "save" Paris; they were welcomed.

While campaigns and negotiations dragged on, the Leaguers were divided. The bourgeois "Sixteen" of Paris, composed of merchants, lawyers, and demagogic monks, despised Henry IV and placed their hopes in Spain. Mayenne and his group of nobles were embarrassed, and mistrusted the Sixteen as much as they did the king of Navarre; they hoped for wise guidance from the pope. Finally there was an emerging party of conciliatory Gallican *politiques,* good Frenchmen who hated Spain.

The knotty problem began to unravel when the League summoned its own sort of Estates General in May 1593. At this meeting Philip II's agents proposed his daughter, the Infanta Isabella, as queen of France. She was the granddaughter of Henry II, but had been brought up entirely in Spain. This proposal was a fatal political error. As if he had been waiting for it, Henry IV converted to Catholicism the following month at Saint-Denis. He was dressed in white and cheered by an enthusiastic crowd. Six months later, Henry was crowned at Chartres: the traditional site, Reims, was still in League hands. In any event, he was able to enter Paris on March 22, 1594, and saw the pitiful departure of the Spanish troops who had helped his cause by irritating the Parisians.

The sincerity of Henry IV's conversion has been questioned. After all, it was his second, following his timely switch during the Saint Bartholomew's Day Massacre of 1572. But as a Christian of his time, probably not much troubled by theological disputes, Henry may have passed without difficulty from the religion of his youth to the religion of his subjects, whom he deeply loved. We should emphasize, however, that the beneficial effects of this conversion did not suffice to bring peace to his kingdom. The king had bought the favor of the governor of Paris, and later had to buy most of the cities and provinces, including those controlled by the last holdouts of the Guise-Lorraine family—the duke of Mercoeur in Brittany and the duke of Mayenne in Burgundy. According to his finance minister, Maximilien de Béthune, sieur de Rosny and later duke of Sully, these fine reconciliations cost 32 million livres, double the annual revenue of the kingdom. The Guises collected half of this total. Like Louis XI before him, Henry IV well knew that men were almost always for sale.

Serious obstacles still remained: the pope, the king of Spain, and Henry's former coreligionists who felt they had been betrayed, not to mention peasant revolts by the *croquants* of Poitou and Périgord. The king allowed these uprisings to die out or put them down with a mere flick of his military fingers.

At Rome, where the pope had to pardon the king and even absolve him, the matter dragged on because of the Jesuits. Some members of their order had approved the murder of Henry III, and others were spreading the novel theory of "tyrannicide," a supposedly sacred duty to kill any declared tyrant. The Jesuit Cardinal Bellarmine again upheld the view that the "throne of Saint Peter" should take precedence over any worldly crown, a view that upset the Parlement as well. Furthermore, a student of the Jesuits, Jean Châtel, wounded the king with a knife. Though Henry's injury was slight, this crime provoked the expulsion of the Jesuits from France. For the rest of his reign, Henry IV had to face assassination attempts almost every year. The Holy Father nevertheless granted pardon and absolution to the reconverted monarch in September 1595, and the royal envoys d'Ossat and Perron were rewarded with cardinal's hats.

To deal with the Spaniards—who had captured Calais, massacred four thousand inhabitants of Doullens, and taken Amiens as well—the king desperately needed money for his army. For this purpose an Assembly of Notables was called together at Rouen in late 1596, and Rosny went around the kingdom to collect back taxes. Since both France and Spain were exhausted, the pope sent his legate, a Medici, to mediate and prepare the hollow Peace of Vervins, signed in May 1598. It was nothing more than a restatement of Cateau-Cambrésis: forty years of war had been fought for nothing.

The Edict of Nantes

Concerned by the turn of events, the Huguenots had maintained their political and military organization. They held "permanent assemblies" that alternated among Vendôme, Saumur, and Sainte-Foy-la-Grande; they divided the kingdom into nine religious provinces, and even attempted to bargain with Elizabeth I of England. Using his respected friend Philippe

Duplessis-Mornay to appease their spirits, Henry IV finally had to negotiate with four Protestant plenipotentiaries at Nantes, where he had earlier bought Mercoeur's submission.

The Peace of Religion concluded at Nantes in April-May 1598, included the famous edict granting the Protestants freedom of conscience, equality of rights, and freedom to worship in numerous specified places. It was accompanied by royal letters-patent to help pay the salaries of Protestant ministers, and by two more important sets of secret articles. These allowed the Protestants to keep their politico-military organization—"a state within the state," as Richelieu rightly said—and 151 places of "refuge" or "security," with governors and garrisons theoretically paid only by the king.

The edict and the rumors of its secret appendixes provoked waves of discontent. Even for moderate Catholics, it went too far; for Protestants, it did not go far enough. The pope declared it "accursed," and his successors as well as the entire French Catholic church never ceased to demand its suppression as well as the "total extirpation" of heresy. Indeed, a fully effective Saint Bartholomew's Day Massacre would have raised no more than Te Deum masses from this group.

At a distance, this aggravated fanaticism may astonish us, and yet in the twentieth century we have seen its equal. In that age, it constituted the norm. Tolerance was a word without meaning and virtually nonexistent, except among a few advanced minds. People generally believed that a division into two religions "disfigured" the state, because it existed nowhere outside France. For this reason the French almost unanimously applauded the revocation of the edict in 1685.

To give the edict the force of law, however, it was necessary to have it registered by the Parlements of the kingdom. The judges all resisted for a year or two, and those in Rouen held out until 1609. Henry IV's fiery speeches to these bodies have been preserved: they are a mixture of crude Gascon wit and terrible threats. "Who can win a case at Bordeaux unless he has the heaviest purse? I know you: I'm a Gascon just like you." At another point he declared: "I will cut to the root of all factions and seditious preaching.... Getting along with the pope? I can do that better than you: I will have all of you declared heretics for not obeying me."

In fact, in each province, in every political group, in the middle of plots involving his mistresses and the sons of his friends, in the face of assassination attempts, this king ruled with difficulty. The popular image has depicted the white-plumed "good King Henry" with his fine beard and children on his back, wishing every peasant a chicken in his pot; but these fragments of legend have almost no foundation, having been fabricated much later in the seventeenth century—and not so innocently. Naturally they have been much enlivened since. The realities, as we have seen, were harsh indeed, and it is doubtful whether the king was popular during his lifetime: he levied too many taxes and displeased too many powerful and excessively devout people.

"GOOD KING HENRY" AND HIS TOO-SHORT REIGN

The king of France and Navarre stands in sharp contrast to his fragile Valois predecessors, who were indecisive, ostentatious, bedizened with jewels and plumes, and always sickly. His robust male good health, kept up by escapades and cavalcades of all kinds during his long youth, seems to foreshadow the vigor of his grandson Louis XIV, who had the good fortune not to encounter the assassin François Ravaillac.

Nothing in Henry IV's character bespeaks refinement, courtly etiquette, or the perfumes of Italy and Arabia. He gladly held council meetings while in full stride, tiring his audience— at times intentionally. His inimitable style of short letters, fast notes, and rough speeches adroitly combined finesse and vigor, and his outbursts of Gascon temper were rarely gratuitous. Not much of a theoretician or pompous moralist, he understood his craft of kingship as absolutely as Louis XIV did. "A king is responsible only to God and his conscience," he wrote to James I of England.

This firmness did not preclude an acute sensitivity to nuance, intuition, penetrating understanding, prudence, and cunning seduction. Like all great politicians, Henry could dissemble, deceive when necessary, and quickly seize opportunities. The quality of his entourage and the extent of his work in the midst of serious difficulties must earn our respect. The first of the Bourbons was undoubtedly the greatest—simultaneously the most lucid, the most courageous, and the most perceptive.

If Henry IV had one serious weakness, it was not his immoderate love of women (Louis XIV and Louis XV would have time to exceed him in this quality), but rather the influence that the most seductive females were able to exercise over him. Henry was first married for political reasons to Marguerite of Valois in 1572, but their profligate spirits quarreled and they saw little of each other. They finally agreed to have their marriage annulled by the courts of Rome, again out of political necessity: for dynastic and financial reasons, Henry had to marry the "big banker" Marie de Medici, who was presumed fertile. He very nearly married his mistress Gabrielle d'Estrées, who had given him two bastard Vendôme sons, but she died prematurely. Another mistress, Henriette d'Entraigues, was able to extract a written promise of marriage from him, in case she gave him a baby boy. This was a senseless gesture, even though a boy was born to her one month after the birth of the authentic Dauphin Louis.

The incorrigible "Green Gallant" had much difficulty in extricating himself from his adventures, and it has even been argued that his final military campaign was rushed in the hope of recapturing in the Netherlands a young girl who had been married precipitously to the prince of Condé. This may be nonsense, but Henry certainly wrote too much to women. His weaknesses on this score constitute the only serious defect of an overly generous temperament and spirit that surpassed many others.

In twelve years of peaceful reign marred only by a brief conflict with the duke of Savoy, who was obliged to cede Bresse and Bugey, Henry IV was able to reimpose considerable order on his kingdom. He oversaw everything, but entrusted details to a handful of ministers of state such as Pomponne; Jeannin; Brûlart; Villeroy (the founder of an administrative dynasty); and of course Rosny, who was created duke of Sully in 1606. Sully restored financial soundness to the monarchy, thanks to astute bankruptcies; he trimmed the state budget and encouraged agriculture.

Under the watchful eyes of Henry IV and his ministers, the foundations of the seventeenth-century monarchy were laid. Before discussing them, we should consider what happened, during forty years of wars and massacres, to the kingdom of France itself.

THE DIVERSE MISERIES OF THE
LATER SIXTEENTH CENTURY: 1560–1600

The exhaustion of the kingdom at the end of the wars of religion was so great that people spoke of the "cadaver of France." The soaring prosperity that had marked the first half of the century was interrupted between 1550 and 1570, when all wastelands had been developed, and farms had been subdivided as far as possible. In agriculture, neither techniques nor tools made further progress. Of course, no one thought they could be improved, in an age when any innovation was regarded with suspicion. Consequently the population had reached the ceiling set by the resources available. Economic historians have believed that this ceiling remained about the same from 1250 to 1750, but after a period of growth they thought some decline was inevitable: these two alternating phases established a rhythm over five centuries.

The most readily apparent phenomena were disasters, whether caused by nature or mankind. The old chroniclers recalled horrible events such as eclipses, comets, clouds of blood, catastrophic floods, extreme winters, and summers that were too dry or too wet. Learned studies of climatic change have shown that a "little ice age" began after 1550 and was well established by 1580. This slight cooling was enough to damage harvests of grain and grapes, and sometimes froze trees and livestock. "Spoiled" summers, carefully recorded, caused grain shortages and price increases in 1562, 1566, 1573, and especially 1586 and 1597, when the prices of grain and bread doubled or tripled in most French marketplaces.

Each adult thus expected to encounter such phenomena two or three times during his life and to lose some relative or friend to harsh conditions, which became more frequent toward the end of the century. The plague, which had abated somewhat, suddenly reappeared in 1580 to 1583, and in 1587 started its upswing, the "great Atlantic cycle," reaching a peak around 1600. These terrible outbreaks must have killed many more people than the eight wars of religion, interrupted as they were by truces. Also, the witch persecutions probably killed more unfortunate men and women, perhaps thirty thousand in Europe as a whole, than the Inquisition in search of heresy: but there is really no exact count of persons burnt at the stake.

The destruction caused by passing soldiers, which could occur during truces as well as in wartime, should not be minimized. Villages were burnt, trees cut down, and animals slaughtered—they all took time and expense to restore. Indeed, few provinces escaped these horrors, apart from Brittany, Béarn, and some mountainous areas. Others, such as the Parisian region, were terribly devastated as armies marched back and forth or set up camp. Everywhere in France, even in relatively unspoiled Burgundy, the depths of distress were reached in the last decade, when the Four Horsemen of the Apocalypse enjoyed free rein.

In this period the historians' charts of economy and population become reliable. They show a long upward curve for several decades, brief declines in 1565 and 1574, and a sharp fall in the last years of the century. Population declined as much as 10 to 15 percent. These were terrible years, but they were a far cry from the extended horrors of the Hundred Years' War. Nevertheless, France "needed to catch its breath," as Henry IV said. Perhaps this would be possible in the seventeenth century.

An Old Problem:
The Price Revolution

Formerly it was generally taught that a remarkable rise in prices, on the order of 400 percent or more, occurred over the sixteenth century. The phenomenon was well known to contemporaries: it was discussed by writers such as Jean Bodin, the famous political theorist and harsh persecutor of witches, and the remarkable Jehan Cherruyt de Malestroit, a pioneering economist. In reality, the rise in prices was relatively modest in the first part of the century and benefited all producers, even simple peasants and artisans. Later the movement accelerated, with sharp peaks that meant a quadrupling of prices between Louis XII and Henry IV. Since French currency had been devalued only about 40 percent during the same period, the true rate of the "price revolution" was slightly over 2 percent per year. Whether the increase was caused by the importation of American silver and gold—whose significance has been exaggerated—by the reckless spending of the Valois kings, or by other factors, only one thing finally matters: the effects of this increase on various social groups.

Obviously those who collected their incomes in kind had advantages: they included seigneurial lords with feudal dues and also landowners in general and holders of ecclesiastical tithes. The disadvantages fell on those people, primarily peasants, who had to pay such dues. Conversely, those who owed obligations denominated in livres-tournois profited from the inflation. The state, as the biggest debtor of all, was the greatest beneficiary. Urban wage earners whose salaries were not indexed saw their standard of living decline from the relatively decent levels around 1500 as the prices of bread and wood, rent and household expenses all rose briskly. In the difficult world of money, prices, debts, and revenues, the last years of

166

the century were painful and confusing. When peace returned in 1598, and the currency and interest rates were reformed in 1601–1602, the terrible storms died down. The first years of the new century presented a more stable business climate.

The problems of state revenues and expenditures are harder to understand. Historians have repeatedly described the state as magnificent and yet deep in debt, misrepresenting the subsidies given to the provincial estates, the cities, the well-to-do, and the Church of France. The wealth of the Church had been seriously taxed on the pretext of requiring aid in the struggle against heresy, but it was able to regain its privileged position. Taxation was generally levied on consumption and circulation of goods, and yet the state borrowed repeatedly from Italian and German bankers, from the pope, from merchants at the fairs in Lyon, Paris, and Rouen, and from groups of French financiers.

This constant borrowing furnishes the key to understanding the monarchy, its indebtedness, its lamentations, and its successes. The lenders would not advance their hoards of gold and silver without secure guarantees, which were nonetheless debased by devaluations and bankruptcies. They demanded the security of future taxes and duties, thus placing a claim on the wealth of the kingdom as a whole. Since the king of France controlled twice as much gold and silver as the king of Spain with his Indies, the kingdom of France remained the most powerful and the richest of all Christendom, even during the troubled times of the Catholic League. The point was proved when royal finances were quickly restored to good order after the war and various manipulations: within ten years, Sully was able to accumulate a treasury of more than 13 million livres in the Bastille. Without wavering, France was able to finance a second Renaissance.

The Second Renaissance

During this time France passed from the highly refined Italian style of decor, furnishings, and poetry to a more solid style inspired by classical antiquity. Classicism meant the use of columns, pilasters, superimposed orders, pediments, Roman military attributes, and flowing Greek draperies. The facades of existing churches were rebuilt with so-called Jesuit or baroque porticos, though these terms are not entirely appropriate.

Both during and after the wars, royal, seigneurial, and bourgeois patronage continued. Thus Henry IV enlarged and rebuilt the Louvre, reviving the projects of Catherine de Medici; he also ordered work at Fontainebleau and Saint-Germain-en-Laye, finished the Pont Neuf, began the Place Royale (now the Place des Vosges), completed the Place Dauphine and the Hôpital Saint-Louis. Furthermore, his provincial residences were rebuilt or redecorated in the current style. Almost everywhere the work of Bontemps, Goujon, and Pilon showed the influence of travels to Italy: statuary and bas-relief echoed Roman splendor or Greek grace.

All these artists worked for rich and powerful patrons. Without their protection, hardly any writers of the age could have achieved immediate fame. Except for Ronsard, who survived until 1585, the brilliant generation of poets of the Pléiade had disappeared. Even Rabelais was gone, having died before Henry II. Though generally less famous, the literature of the late sixteenth century was oriented toward "serious" genres of tragedy, political and legal essays, memoirs, and theology. The greatest work of the period defied classification: the *Essays* of Michel Eyquem, sieur de Montaigne. For his contemporaries, Montaigne's *Essays* had as great an influence on thought as Henry IV had on politics.

Chapter Seven

FROM GOOD KING HENRY TO THE SUN KING: 1598–1661

THE BOURBONS

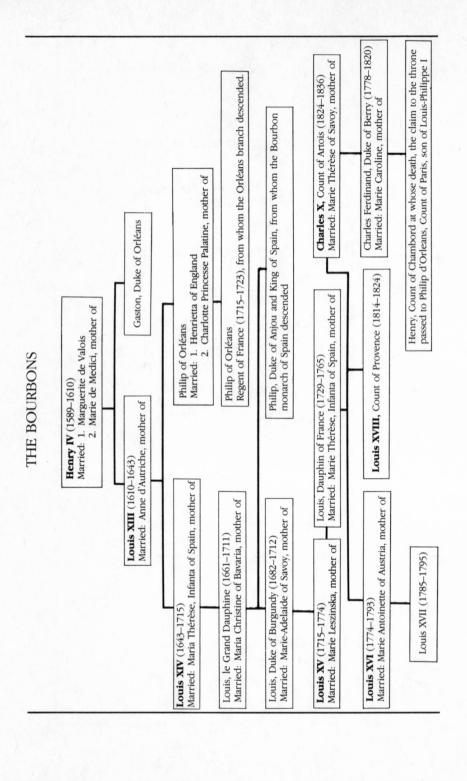

Henry IV (1589–1610)
Married: 1. Marguerite de Valois
         2. Marie de Medici, mother of

Gaston, Duke of Orléans

Louis XIII (1610–1643)
Married: Anne d'Autriche, mother of

Philip of Orléans
Married: 1. Henrietta of England
         2. Charlotte Princesse Palatine, mother of

Philip of Orléans
Regent of France (1715–1723), from whom the Orléans branch descended.

Louis XIV (1643–1715)
Married: Maria Thérèse, Infanta of Spain, mother of

Louis, le Grand Dauphine (1661–1711)
Married: Maria Christine of Bavaria, mother of

Philip, Duke of Anjou and King of Spain, from whom the Bourbon monarch of Spain descended

Louis, Duke of Burgundy (1682–1712)
Married: Marie-Adelaide of Savoy, mother of

Louis, Dauphin of France (1729–1765)
Married: Marie Thérèse, Infanta of Spain, mother of

Charles X, Count of Artois (1824–1836)
Married: Marie Thérèse of Savoy, mother of

Charles Ferdinand, Duke of Berry (1778–1820)
Married: Marie Caroline, mother of

Louis XVIII, Count of Provence (1814–1824)

Louis XV (1715–1774)
Married: Marie Leszinska, mother of

Louis XVI (1774–1793)
Married: Marie Antoinette of Austria, mother of

Louis XVII (1785–1795)

Henry, Count of Chambord at whose death, the claim to the throne passed to Philip d'Orleans, Count of Paris, son of Louis-Philippe I

Strictly speaking, the seventeenth century lasted from 1601 to 1700, and the personal reign of Louis XIV, the "Great King," occupied only the last forty years. The earlier period has been simplistically termed the Age of the Baroque, or the First Seventeenth Century. But labels are less important than understanding the first six decades, to realize how little they resembled the following period, and how they nonetheless made its grandeur possible.

With Henry IV dead and Sully out of favor, Richelieu and Mazarin, two great cardinal-ministers of equal stature, one from Poitou and the other from Rome, dominated the history of the kingdom of France. Two fundamental conflicts radically affected this history: a long international war (1635–1659) and a complex series of internal revolts, exaggerated during the Frondes (1648–1653), when the usual treason and felonious behavior of the great nobility came to the surface on one last occasion.

During this time, the cultural elite could partake of four remarkable intellectual developments: classicism, Jansenism, Cartesianism, and scientific revolution. As for the common people, they apparently enjoyed three decades of particularly comfortable and fruitful life despite routine epidemics, grain shortages, and violence. By 1626–27, however, there were outbreaks of plague in the provinces. Miseries increased when France went to war in 1635. Taxes tripled and inspired revolts; the situation worsened and became unbearable at the time of the Frondes.

In fact 1635 was the turning point of this exciting period, and as often happens, war was the essential explanatory factor. However, it is important to go back further to understand the historical evolution of this powerful kingdom, which was still threatened by so many dangers.

A BRIEF RENAISSANCE: THE WORK ATTRIBUTED TO SULLY, 1558–1610

After long struggles, Henry IV had taken possession of all of his royal powers. For a dozen years, he surrounded himself with a small group of fewer than ten counselors. Sully, the king's old comrade in arms, eventually emerged to lead the restoration of order and prosperity to the kingdom.

The simple fact of peace sufficed to inspire a renewal of activity in the fields, forests, cities, and ports. The work was strongly supported by a demographic revival, plainly evident in the well preserved parish registers of baptisms. By nature a landowner and "grand inspector of roads of France," Sully knew how to encourage this return to prosperity. He achieved a remarkable success with *Théâtre d'Agriculture et mesnage des champs* (1600), the admirable agricultural handbook by Olivier de Serres, a Protestant from the Cévennes. Sully had the book read aloud to the king and the proprietors of great estates. He was also able to lower the rate of general taxation, remit some of the arrears, and start polder works in the marshes of the lower Seine, Poitou, Aunis, and the Gironde. Sully also made astonishing progress in road building, as shown by the elm-lined routes cut or restored from Poitou to Berry. Bridges such as the Pont Neuf and Châtellerault were built as works of art. To improve the less expensive secondary roads, he renewed the work on dikes and levees to contain the capricious but navigable Loire within its banks; he also started the vital work on the Briare Canal linking the Loire and the Seine. The construction was three-quarters completed by 1610.

In the industrial area, Sully's fellow Huguenot and rival Barthélemy Laffemas pushed for the establishment of a guild system of masters and apprentices to ensure the high quality of craftsmanship. He also protected the great entrepreneurs in metalworking and cloth manufacturing at Nevers, Gien, and Bourges as well as the Parisian luxury manufactures of glass, satin, silk, and tapestries. In the great gallery of the Louvre, highly skilled artisans were set to work.

Sully also prepared the way for future triumphs at the Arsenal, where workshops and storehouses kept a permanent stock of fifty cannons ready for use. In the provinces he sent out inspectors of the forests and foundries. He was concerned with the construction of galleys on the Mediterranean coast and with the whole array of fortifications from Amiens to Metz and Saint-Tropez. On the Gironde he had the lighthouse of Cordouan completed, and he encouraged Champlain on his first voyages to Canada in 1603 and 1608, when he reached Quebec. Thus Sully was a forerunner of Richelieu, Colbert, and Vauban.

Naturally all these enterprises cost money. To deal with a debt of sixty million livres and the considerable disorder in finances, Sully was ready to use any means, from brutality to partial bankruptcy. The details are quite complicated, but interest rates were reduced from 8–10 percent to 6.25 percent in 1601, and the currency was finally stabilized in 1602. By 1610, Sully had accumulated a hoard of gold and silver worth nearly 14 million livres.

In the interval, a difficult solution was found for a very serious problem. Royal officials had bought the right to dispense justice or collect taxes in the king's name, but they could only bequeath their offices to their heirs under certain conditions—notably in the forty days preceding their deaths. In exchange for the privilege of transferring their offices as they wished, Sully made them pay an annual premium, something like insurance, equal to one-sixtieth of the value of their posts. The new fee was known as the *paulette,* named after Paulet, the financier who thought of the idea. As a result, a new hereditary caste was born: powerful, proud, and easily promoted to the nobility, whose older members regarded the newcomers with both envy and contempt. This group caused considerable headaches for later French kings.

To reduce the power of these companies of officers, now reinforced by the *paulette,* the government made larger and more systematic use of royal commissioners and intendants. These men were representatives of royal will, imposed permanently in Picardy, Guyenne, and Lyon; in years to come they became part of the essential administrative machinery of the kingdom.

The renaissance of Paris also dates from this brief and prosperous period, only twelve years long. The brilliant capital of the first Capetians with their palace on the Île de la Cité and the Louvre of Charles V had fallen on hard times. French kings of the fifteenth and sixteenth centuries clearly preferred to live in the Loire Valley, and the disorders of the Catholic League had left the capital impoverished and partly depopulated. Yet Henry IV and his family, court, and council settled in the enlarged Louvre in winter, and at the reconstructed palaces of Saint-Germain-en-Laye or Fontainebleau in summer. The population of Paris, which may have fallen below 200,000, doubled in half a century while countless shops, workshops, and houses were built or rebuilt. Furthermore, intelligent urban developers projected, improved, and completed new bridges, squares, and hospitals. Even the old aqueduct of Rungis was restored to working order.

While Ravaillac's knife may have prevented a war and removed a badly aging monarch from the scene, it also cut short this brilliant political renaissance and caused the kingdom to fall into "strange hands," as Sully said.

A LONG INTERMISSION:
LOUIS XIII BEFORE
RICHELIEU'S MINISTRY, 1610–1624

During this decade and a half, Europe and the world faced vast problems. Conflicts arose as a result of burgeoning colonial commerce, the rise of Holland, and religious disputes in the Holy Roman Empire. There was a rebirth of Christian mysticism with the foundation of new religious orders, as well as the beginning of rationalism and scientific thought. The preponderance of the great Catholic monarchies was challenged by the Protestant maritime powers, England and Holland. In the face of these developments, the kingdom of France, which had just forced Sully into retirement, became entangled in petty squabbles.

Crowned on the eve of Henry's assassination, Queen Marie de Medici had been vested with full powers of regency by the Parlement of Paris, which profited handsomely from this ceremony. She governed for nine years in place of the young Louis XIII, her difficult eldest son for whom she had little love and less understanding. To the inherent difficulties of any regency, which was not a "full reign" according to French jurists, the queen added her own evident incompetence. Marie was dominated by a clever Florentine servant, Leonora Galigai and her husband Concini, a greedy and pretentious fop. Together they became all-powerful and used their position to enrich themselves, but they made serious political mistakes in the process. At age sixteen, the outraged and humiliated Louis XIII set assassins on Concini—and the people of Paris gleefully mutilated his corpse. Galigai was executed as a witch, and Marie herself was momentarily exiled from court. Louis then proceeded to delegate practically all authority to his favorite falconer, Charles d'Albert de Luynes, who remained in power until his death in 1621. Then this barely twenty-year-old king hesitated for nearly three years before calling on Armand du Plessis, Cardinal Richelieu. Richelieu's unscrupulous ambition and wavering had long held him back, but his obvious talent happily decided the king in his favor.

Although a new period began with Richelieu's coming to power, we can briefly sketch the history of the first fifteen years of Louis XIII's reign. Immediately after Henry IV's death in 1610, the regent, her supporters, and the high-ranking nobility had dissipated the immense treasury accumulated by Sully. Once this unedifying performance was completed, aristocratic revolts broke out: they had been suspended while money flowed. But when the treasury was empty in 1614, it was decided to call a meeting of the Estates General, as it turned out for the next-to-last time. The three orders worked at cross purposes, though their orators made fine speeches. The most remarkable was that of Richelieu, then the young bishop of Luçon, who fidgeted in the entourage of the queen mother. Then this glittering society was sent home. After Concini had been eliminated in 1617, Marie and Louis engaged in intermittent warfare, each side supported by a fluctuating group of great lords. As for foreign policy, in 1615 the king of France had married an infanta of Spain. The rapprochement between these two Catholic kingdoms caused concern among the Protestants, who proceeded to organize and arm themselves. Soon afterward, Louis XIII and Luynes went to the Province of Béarn to reestablish the Catholic faith; to that end they were obliged to wage war against the rebellious Huguenots of the southwest. Though promoted to constable of France, Luynes did not shine in battle; he became ill and died in 1621. This was not such a great tragedy, for Louis XIII was quickly reconciled with his mother, who brought along her protégé Richelieu. Yet for more than ten years aristocratic factions and religious groups had quarreled and fought. In the face of great European problems, French policy had been wavering, though generally favorable to ultra-Catholic Spain. Nearly fifteen years had been lost in muddle, waste, and mediocrity. Fortunately for his kingdom, Louis XIII successfully found his personal style of government, although it took him six important years to establish it on solid foundations.

THE DECISIVE CHOICES:
1624–1630

This short period determined the European destiny of seventeenth-century France. During these years Louis XIII finally chose Richelieu as his prime minister, who later selected his successor Mazarin, who in turn bequeathed to Louis XIV his greatest collaborators and their progeny: their influence extended the length of the Sun King's reign.

That odd couple, Louis XIII and Richelieu, king and cardinal, already appear quite renowned. The private character traits of the king are certainly fascinating. A victim of harsh upbringing, Louis was unloved by his mother, his brother, and his wife. So often did he suffer illness that it is astonishing he lived to be forty-two; yet he was also athletic, chaste, sentimental, and demanding. Above all, Louis deserves to be remembered for his unyielding authority, the harshness of his justice, and his strong love of military camps and battles. By contrast, Richelieu has been glorified by hundreds of literary works. His political genius was indeed dazzling. He had a supreme talent for going straight to the heart of a matter and holding firmly to it; yet the most remarkable quality of his acute and authoritarian mind was the art of knowing the hearts of men. Richelieu possessed a singular understanding of the psychopathology of his king, without whose agreement he could do nothing, contrary to the legend propagated by romantic writers such as Alexandre Dumas and Victor Hugo. The two great kindred spirits, king and cardinal, found a suitable policy that Richelieu later summed up in three points: 1) to ruin the Huguenot party as a military and political power; 2) "to break the pride of the *grands*," the aristocrats who pretended to govern most of the provinces and played a greater role in the state than they deserved; and 3) "to uphold the name of the king among foreign nations," principally by opposing the designs of the most powerful competitor, Spain.

The liquidation of the Protestants as a political party and

military power was achieved relatively quickly. There were two major campaigns: the difficult siege of La Rochelle in 1628, which the English tried in vain to break; and the struggles in Languedoc against the duke of Rohan, son-in-law of Sully. An "edict of grace" for the exhausted Protestants was signed at Alès in 1629. While freedom of conscience and worship were formally confirmed, the Huguenot politico-military organization of assemblies and fortified places was suppressed. This wise settlement provided forty years of peace for the Protestants and the state.

The struggle against the *grands,* many of whom had never stopped engaging in disobedience, conspiracy, and rebellion, was permanent, brutal, and without decisive results. Indeed several prominent figures were beheaded: the count de Chalais (1626), Marshal Marillac (1632), the duke of Montmorency, and the imprudent and overly seductive Cinq-Mars (1642). Yet these vivid demonstrations were in vain, because plots broke out again after the deaths of cardinal and king. During their rule the repression was also ineffective because all these intrigues were hatched from within the royal family. The king's brother, Gaston d'Orléans, remained heir to the throne until the unexpected birth of the Dauphin Louis in 1638. The king and queen had been childless for two decades. Anne of Austria was not very attached to her husband either: for a long time she remained more Spanish than French. Finally, there was the unhappy queen mother, Marie de Medici. All of them at times knew about intrigues and conspiracies and supported them, often with Spanish intervention.

In November 1630, crisis broke out with the vain and authoritarian Marie de Medici. She was jealous of the cardinal and rather stupid. After having subjected her son to a terrible scene, she thought she had obtained the cardinal's dismissal: at once, the whole court abandoned him and flocked to her side at the Luxembourg Palace. But Louis XIII quickly recovered his composure and placed his confidence entirely in Richelieu. This turn of events is known as "the Day of the Dupes" because the queen mother was sent into permanent exile, and those who had too hastily supported her paid for their rashness.

The issue was not simply a family quarrel or court intrigue, but rather the long-term orientation of French policy. One party, led by the brothers Louis and Michel de Marillac, marshal and chancellor of France, agitated in favor of profound internal reforms in the kingdom and apparently for lower taxes as well. This domestic policy presupposed external peace—that France would not intervene in the Thirty Years War. This war had begun in 1618 between the largely Protestant German princes and the Hapsburg Emperor, supported by his cousin the king of Spain. The key to French foreign policy would thus be an unconditional alliance with the Catholic powers. The matrimonial aspects of this alliance were particularly appealing to Marie de Medici and Anne of Austria—Philip IV and Louis XIII were double brothers-in-law, since they had married each other's sisters. Louis's mother and wife worked together to pressure him during his illness over the summer of 1630, and collected their "devout" supporters. Against this devout party Richelieu and the "good Frenchmen" declared that the most urgent goal was "arresting the progress of Spain." The Spanish had practically surrounded France with their possessions on the Mediterranean, in Italy, the Franche-Comté, and the southern Netherlands; in addition they enjoyed rights of passage through various Alpine, Swiss, and Lorraine territories. To break this chain, the French would have to take action against its links; that meant inevitable alliances with the enemies of Spain. But many of these enemies were fatally Protestant—in Germany, Holland, and Scandinavia. The idea of such alliances was anathema to old and new "devouts," who believed that Catholicism should take precedence over reasons of state. Louis XIII and Richelieu (nonetheless a cardinal!) thought exactly the contrary and clearly demonstrated their view. First they gave subsidies to Protestant enemies of the Catholic Emperor—Germans, Danes, and Swedes. Then they entered the European conflict themselves. This great decision, implicitly contained in the Day of the

Dupes in 1630, took five years to ripen. During that time it was still necessary to struggle constantly against intrigues and plots. The year 1635 was decisive for the entire seventeenth century in France.

THE TURNING POINT OF 1635: THE CHOICE OF WAR

After careful diplomatic and military preparations, France declared war on Spain, the principal ally of the would-be authoritarian Catholic Emperor. The French alliances with Protestant German princes as well as Sweden and Holland showed, however, that conflict with both Hapsburgs was planned. From the Pyrenees to Flanders by way of Italy, Franche-Comté, Lorraine, and neighboring territories, the theaters of war were many. The difficult early years of this conflict were marked by a double invasion of France, in Burgundy and Picardy. While the town of Saint-Jean-de-Losne in Burgundy resisted siege, the fall of Corbie in 1636 and the advance of Spanish cavalry as far as Pontoise touched off panic at Paris. Order was quickly restored as king and cardinal set the example of courage, and numerous volunteers enlisted in the army. The first three years of French involvement did not really produce victories on any front, but the military situation turned more favorable around 1639–1640. The king's regiments occupied Lorraine and Alsace, thus cutting the supply and communications lines of enemy armies. Then the French recaptured Arras in Artois, and finally they marched as far south as Barcelona, taking advantage of internal problems of the Spanish monarchy. In 1640, Spain had to struggle simultaneously against revolts in Portugal and Catalonia, both naturally supported by France. When Richelieu went to his grave at the end of 1642 and Louis XIII followed him five months later, they could believe that a victorious peace treaty would soon be signed, especially since negotiations among all the belligerents had already been opened at two cities in Westphalia. This view was even more believable after the young duke of Enghien (the future prince of Condé) won a brilliant victory over the famous Spanish infantry at Rocroi on the fifth day of the reign of the boy king Louis XIV. Yet France had to suffer sixteen more years of grave difficulties before celebrating a general peace. This long and harsh war had profound effects on the quarter-century from 1635 to 1659.

The Burden of War

The Spanish army was then considered the best in Europe. To sustain campaigns against such numerous and powerful enemies on all fronts, the French required substantial manpower: for the first time their army exceeded 100,000 men. Arms and equipment were needed also, as well as trained crews for new sailing ships and galleys for the navy. As matériel was used up quickly, it was necessary to replenish supplies. Along with munitions, soldiers and mercenaries of all nationalities could be found rather easily, but difficulty arose in paying them. Soldiers of fortune, company commanders, and military suppliers were not satisfied with warm words or even written promises. In short, once again making war boiled down to a matter of money.

Of course it was possible to borrow, and the state missed no opportunity. But the Italian and French lenders demanded a high price for their services. As usual, this burden could only fall on the wealth of the kingdom, its productive capacity, and its riches. Sooner or later, the loan payments would have to be reflected in higher taxes.

The taxpayers had plenty of time to get accustomed to the increases. Between 1635 and 1638, the grand total of all taxes, *tailles,* duties, privileges, *gabelle,* and all the rest was multiplied by a factor of 2.5 to 3.0. Such demands were received badly. Since around 1630, local populations had got into the habit of protesting and even of rebelling against taxes they found exorbitant or whose manner of collection struck them as rough or unusual. Starting in 1635, the situation changed

181

dramatically: entire provinces were in revolt for months at a time, especially in the Midi, the southwest, and the west. To suppress the rebels of Périgord in 1636–37 and the *Nus-Pieds* ("Barefeet") of Normandy in 1639–40, the government had to send troops, organize extraordinary tribunals, and dispatch loyal and harsh plenipotentiary commissioners such as Pierre Séguier in Normandy. The mutinous common people were also afflicted with bad harvests and epidemics, and would not tolerate "novelties" in taxation or tax collectors any more than they would accept increases in their bills. But their rebellions never lasted long because they could not get themselves organized (despite occasional leadership from nobles) or joined in federations. The king was seldom much inconvenienced by the revolts: indeed, he could take advantage of these outbursts to establish permanently the "intendants de police, justice, et finances." These intendants had existed before, though not on a systematic basis. After 1640, they held all financial powers in the provinces, much to the displeasure of officeholders who found their property rights diminished. Disorder thus allowed the central government to reinforce its authority.

Nonetheless, three important points should be kept in mind. First, the king's subjects did truly suffer a great deal from the combination of food shortages, plagues and other epidemics, and devastating revolts. Even more serious were the rampages of marauding soldiers. The sufferings illustrated by the artist Jacques Callot were especially severe in the north and east. Second, and perhaps more surprising, the French people did effectively pay most of what the overbearing tax system demanded. This is further testimony to the great wealth of the kingdom, which had emerged from thirty years of peace. Third, after the death of the exhausted Louis XIII, just thirty-three years after his father, the war continued and revolts broke out on a wider scale, possibly because of an old popular belief that taxation died with the king. The misfortunes of the people continued also, and sometimes got worse; meanwhile the high nobility was engaged in new and often ridiculous intrigues that were at times dangerous or criminal.

The kingdom had fallen into a new regency.

A NEW TWO-HEADED GOVERNMENT: ANNE OF AUSTRIA AND MAZARIN 1643–1661

This unusual couple, Cardinal Mazarin and Anne of Austria, have attracted the attention of historians and romantic novelists. The nature of their relationship has been much discussed: at the very least it was based on the profound affection of a couple in their forties who shared absolute confidence, all that really mattered.

Anne, the scatter-brained and awkward former infanta of Spain, was surrounded by bad advisers. She had been more devoted to her brother than to her disagreeable husband, but as mother of the boy-king she had been transformed and ripened, suddenly becoming conscious of her duties and authority. Cardinal Jules Mazarin, raised in the atmosphere of Rome and the Papal Curia, had been chosen as one out of a hundred by Richelieu—and that spoke volumes. Mazarin pursued the same policies as Richelieu and showed the same energy for achieving them, with at least as much finesse and considerably more dissimulation and patience, which circumstances imposed on him. But it is true that his extreme flexibility, his bad French and his incredible greed could put people off. In any event his role was a thankless one, as it fell to him to play the scapegoat, which he did admirably in order to win the war and leave a powerful throne to his king and godson, Louis XIV.

Fortunately, the manifold forces opposing this couple were in complete disarray. They included *Parlementaires* who wanted greater influence so as to drive out their rivals the intendants. They also wanted to avoid paying even the slightest taxes. Jansenists and crafty "devouts" were secretly conspiring for the true Catholic king, Philip IV of Spain. Court ladies and great lords who were fond of adventures, influence, and pensions did not hesitate to raise armed rebellions or descend to crime to favor their intrigues. And then there were the common people, often hard-pressed, plundered by soldiers, and hurt by the very bad harvests of 1649 and 1652. While fighting half the nations of Europe, the rulers of France had no respite and no quarter.

The greatest revolt, the Fronde, began after dozens of royal disputes with nobles and Parlement. Paris was suddenly covered with barricades in August 1648, for the first time since the days of the Holy League. In order to raze them, Anne of Austria had to consent with tears of rage to the release of Pierre Broussel, an old *Parlementaire* and popular troublemaker who had just been arrested. On January 5, 1649, Anne and Louis even had to flee by night to Saint-Germain-en-Laye. Several months later, with the support of the prince of Condé, then basking in the glory of his latest victory at Lens, the queen mother took her revenge by imposing a military siege on the capital filled with conspirators. In the atmosphere of disorder *Parlementaires,* bourgeois, "devouts," and great lords—Frondeurs all—competed with each other to continue their plots.

Suddenly, in January 1650, Mazarin ordered the arrest of the ambitious Condé; his brother, the prince of Conti; and his brother-in-law, the duke of Longueville. Immediately, the Condéan provinces took up the firebrand of revolt. For two anarchic years, Mazarin schemed and maneuvered, sending the young king and the regent to collect homages and subsidies from loyal provinces: their number increased as the royal mother and son approached. For a time the cardinal himself was obliged to go into exile after having released the three princes. He tried to get the various Frondeurs fighting among themselves, and finally provoked the departure and treason of Condé, the only really dangerous leader. Mazarin accomplished this with finesse by shrewdly exploiting Condé's inexcusable absence during the proclamation of the legal majority of the king in September 1651. The last year of the Fronde proved the hardest of all. Foreign invasion came to the very gates of the capital and was joined with civil war between Turenne and Condé, leading to a second siege of Paris. The concomitant natural calamities were no less terrifying as famine and plague raged at their peak. The divided and beaten Parisians eventually acclaimed the return of the adolescent king and his mother.

Mazarin himself, who had been vilified shortly before, was welcomed back from his second, voluntary exile. He then pardoned almost all the former Frondeurs, while following the old tradition of distributing money to them.

This burlesque episode, often odious and sometimes tragic, marked the end of a certain style of life: never again under the ancien régime did the nobility, the Parlements, or Paris participate in serious rebellion.

In the middle of all these difficulties, Mazarin had pursued war and diplomacy as well. In October 1648, without anyone in France taking the least notice, he had signed the peace treaties of Westphalia. By their terms the king received the greater part of Alsace, though not Strasbourg. At the same time the extreme decentralization of the Holy Roman Empire and impotence of the Emperor were confirmed. Spain finally recognized the independence of Holland and could then concentrate its forces against France, fighting alone and divided within. Ten years of hard struggle followed. While Turenne had to fight the "Spanish" General Condé, Mazarin had to appeal for help to Oliver Cromwell, leader of a Protestant Commonwealth, promising him Dunkirk as a reward. And the young King Louis XIV bravely participated in combat. The victory of the Dunes in 1658 persuaded Philip IV to seek a peace treaty, which was duly signed the following year on a small island in the Bidassoa River, located on the Franco-Spanish frontier. By this Peace of the Pyrenees, France annexed Roussillon, Cerdagne, Artois, and several towns in the Netherlands. With some difficulty Condé was granted a pardon he did not deserve. The marriage of Louis XIV to the oldest Infanta Marie-Thérèse was arranged, and in a crowning diplomatic triumph a dowry of 500,000 écus guaranteed that the young couple would renounce their claims to the throne of Spain. But the dowry was never paid, and we shall mention it again later.

Historians are in the habit of saying that the French preponderance in Europe dates from these two treaties—and indeed they were written in French instead of Latin. But seldom is the genius of Mazarin given credit for these successes. No doubt he was the successor of the "Great Cardinal," but little would have come of Richelieu's policies without the untiring activity of his favorite disciple. In truth, there were *two* "Great Cardinals."

Louis XIV, who was pawing the ground impatiently in his twenty-second year, could now take power: his reign had been well prepared.

Chapter Eight

THE PLEASANT
SEASONS OF
A GREAT
REIGN:
1661–1688

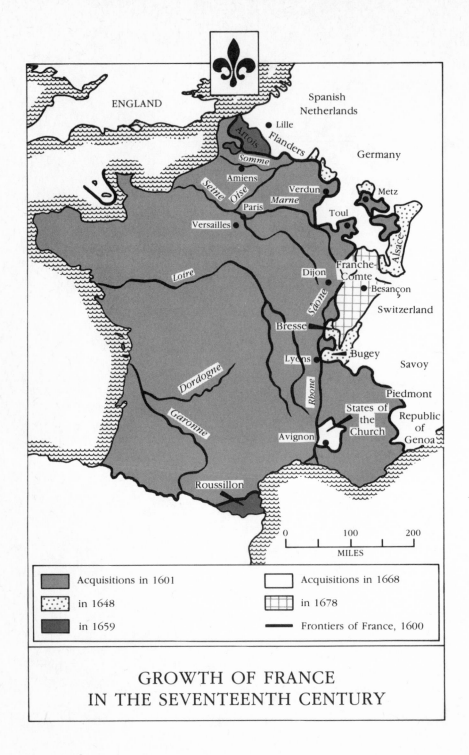

ENGLAND

Spanish
Netherlands

Germany

• Lille

Artois

Flanders

Somme

Amiens

Seine Oise

Verdun

Marne

Metz

Paris

Toul

Alsace

Versailles

Loire

Dijon

Franche-
Comté

Saône

Besançon

Switzerland

Bresse

Dordogne

Lyons

Bugey

Savoy

Rhone

Garonne

Piedmont

States of
the
Church

Republic
of
Genoa

Avignon

Roussillon

| 0 | 100 | 200 |

MILES

	Acquisitions in 1601			Acquisitions in 1668
	in 1648			in 1678
	in 1659		—	Frontiers of France, 1600

GROWTH OF FRANCE
IN THE SEVENTEENTH CENTURY

Legally king since the death of his father in May 1643, the young Louis the God-given had passed his youth and adolescence under the watchful eyes of a mother and godfather whom he respected and no doubt deeply loved. He had turned twenty-two when Cardinal Mazarin died. Inevitably, Louis had great plans: to reign by himself and remain everywhere the master over all others. As a child and young man, he appeared sleepyheaded and not very capable of profiting from his lessons. Even the great Condé, who later changed his mind, looked on him with a certain disdain. Indeed, not until his fifteenth year did he try the first of his master strokes—the sudden arrest of the old conspirator Cardinal Retz, a tough speech to the *Parlementaires* of Paris, and a battle with Spain in the north, conducted with bold ardor. In reality, a couple and a crisis had profoundly affected him.

From his mother he had learned the bearing, exact devotion, courtesy, and requirements of a court in the Spanish style. She had also given him an almost innate sense of majesty and grandeur. From the great cardinal he had learned, first silently during the council and then in private discussions, all about the structure of Europe, courts and intrigues, the sense of the state, the sense of passing time, and a profound knowledge of men, almost all of whom were for sale.

Louis certainly suffered enormously from the humiliations of the Fronde: the sudden departures, uncomfortable or shameful travels and residences. Thereafter he always remembered it and was suspicious of the Paris he abandoned, the higher nobility he domesticated, the *Parlementaires* he treated with contempt, the provinces whose claims he checked, the vague reforming tendencies he rejected, and even the devout party, whether Jansenist or not, whom he harshly silenced for a decade.

This decisive young king also had the good fortune to possess robust health, which four generations of ignorant doctors could not destroy. He ruled as magnificently on the hunt, in the ballroom, at table, and in bed as in the court and council. Mazarin had considerably simplified his task by leaving him peace all over Europe and a group of devoted and capable servants—the brilliant Hugues de Lionne as secretary of state for foreign affairs; the solid Michel Le Tellier and later his son the marquis de Louvois for the war department; and finally the too clever financier Nicolas Fouquet, who was quickly eliminated by the ambitious jealousy of Jean-Baptiste Colbert. Each of these men was succeeded by his sons and an entourage of relatives, a veritable family lobby that surrounded them. Yet the king remained the master who held a tight rein on this team of recently ennobled servants and kept them hardworking, efficient, and reasonably honest.

The real difficulties stemmed from endemic disorder, which "reigned everywhere," as the king declared at the beginning of his brief *Memoirs*. In truth, shortly earlier several noble plots had been discovered—notably in Normandy; the provinces and the large cities of Marseille and Bordeaux were troubled with agitation; peasant revolts, generally directed against taxes, had just disturbed Sologne, and others would break out in Boulonnais, Béarn, and Vivarais. The root of these disorders lay in the general administration of the kingdom, especially in the administration of state finances, which had suffered from quarrels between officers and intendants as well as between ministers—in short, from mismanagement, embezzlement, and chaos due to improvised and corrupt systems of finance.

SPRINGTIME: 1661–1672

The brilliance of the first years of the "great reign" continues to capture the imagination. Yet Louis's personal reign began with a terrible famine in the northern half of the kingdom. Peasant revolts and provincial uprisings broke out here and there until 1675, and the king did not install himself in the unfinished palace of Versailles until 1682, when almost all the great classical cultural figures were dead, aged, silent, or subdued.

Even taking into account these historical realities, there is no doubt that the beginning of the reign was brilliant. The court, which rode back and forth between Fontainebleau and Saint-Germain-en-Laye and sometimes camped at the Louvre, had never been so young, so gay, so gallant, and so light on its feet. Sober virtues were not the order of the day, as the members of the devout party, whom the young king had learned to suspect, were temporarily banished.

Yet every morning, even as early as dawn, the king would meet his cabinet (*Conseil Étroit*), which was composed of three or four men, but did not include his mother, his brother, or any bishop or general. After having heard them, Louis made his personal decisions. At other times he worked face to face with a *commis* (a clerk—this title of grandeur was even applied to Colbert). Nothing of importance was signed by a secretary of state unless the king had seen it. The government really amounted to one man, albeit a very hard worker who listened carefully to his informants.

These twelve years of peace were hardly disturbed by the so-called War of Devolution (1667–1668), which was limited to two brief campaigns that brought Lille and eleven Flemish cities into the kingdom. Peace finally allowed the state to put its financial house in order, which had not been possible since the time of Sully. Under the tight fist of Colbert, the state was relieved of its debts, which were reduced and sometimes simply suppressed. The king's revenues were better collected, and taxation was better regulated: direct taxes were reduced, but indirect taxes increased. The royal domain was reclaimed and made productive, the king was asked to control his expenditures, which he did for some time. Financial equilibrium was finally reached, though it did not last. Colbert, aided by a coterie of administrators and jurists who were often related to each other, gave the kingdom a series of legal codes—civil, criminal, forest, commercial, maritime, colonial—that were often solid syntheses of older arrangements. Indeed, some of these articles still regulate our forests and seas. Colbert's methodical and rather heavy-handed application was aimed at increasing the grandeur of the state, and thus of the king, as well as exacting the most absolute obedience possible from his subjects. Innate provincialism was to be replaced by the hardheaded and meddling centralism that for three centuries has differentiated France from its bemused neighbors. As Ernest Lavisse wrote around 1900, however, it was absolutism "tempered by disobedience," for social control was limited by wily passivity or simple ignorance.

Nevertheless, the influence of Colbert or old Le Tellier over the young king was marked both by a will to restructure the state and a determination to discipline provincial and municipal administrations. Royal orders were prepared at Paris by several dozen councillors of state and masters of requests (the latter were assistants and relatives of the former, whom they later replaced). The orders were slowly sent to the provinces by the henceforth obligatory intermediacy of intendants, trusted men who held practically all powers in the king's name, if they were able to apply them. With varying titles, their successors (representatives on mission, prefects) have grandly spanned the centuries. But in the springtime of the reign there were fewer than thirty intendants, and the offices of each one contained fewer than ten persons; the subordinates—"subdelegates," as they were called—were hardly more numerous, and for a long time were honorary appointees. Yet the intendants could always count on the king and occasionally on the army. Besides, an administration should not be judged solely by the number of persons employed in writing reports and using red tape.

This serious beginning in provincial government was accompanied by a brutal discipline for local administration. Almost all the mayors of the important cities were appointed by the king; municipal finances were strongly purged and on occasion confiscated.

Beyond this necessary housecleaning, Colbert and several others nourished magnificent projects that sought to make France the richest, most brilliant, and most powerful country in the world, a sort of new Rome and new Athens combined. It was a great deal to expect. Colbert was a man of systems and files, and thus was shocked by the irregular production of agriculture. He wanted to make industry better and more competitive by official fiat, while at the same time closing the borders to foreign products in the protectionist tariff of 1667. This was not the best way to promote the export of French goods. For several years, the manufacturing regions, especially the textile areas of the north, northwest, and Languedoc, received artificial stimulation: they were favored by the general peace, the low price of food after 1663, and ministerial subsidies. These subsidies brought to life the large and privileged royal manufactures of tapestry, lace, glass, metals, and ships. To support these industries, the government went so far as to bribe or kidnap the best foreign artists and technicians.

We should emphasize the valiant efforts to remedy the considerable backwardness of shipping and the colonial movement. Henry IV and Richelieu, occupied as they were elsewhere, had thought about them but had been unable to get past the stage of impulses and attempts.

Colbert was moved to rage by his obsession with small, Calvinist, bourgeois, and extremely rich Holland. The Dutch possessed the first bank in Europe, founded at Amsterdam in 1609. They also had a fleet of nearly ten thousand ships, well over half of the world total. Their cloth and linen industries at

Leyden and Haarlem surpassed all others; and their East India Company, with bases almost everywhere and particularly in the Spice Islands and Japan, paid its shareholders an average annual dividend of 25 percent. The Dutch model haunted Colbert, and he resolved to imitate or surpass it. Thus he undertook the construction of a navy. The first vessels were disappointing, but a second series enjoyed more success, and the shipbuilding industry was running well after 1675.

Beginning in 1664, four great French trading companies were founded. The king and the great nobles subscribed to the best known, the East and West India companies; officers and merchants were asked to do the same, but they tarried over it. Small colonies due partly to private initiative were helped and enlarged. Older trading areas enjoying a renaissance—Sénégal, the Indian Ocean, India—could be used by the handful of vessels sent out by these companies. Often these enterprises turned out rather badly, no doubt because French capitalists mistrusted official initiatives, but also because the formerly powerful Dutch did all they could to eliminate dangerous and presumptuous rivals. Colbert was doomed to disappointment in his commercial plan when his exacerbated protectionism naturally engendered retaliation. He thought, said, and wrote that only war could really put an end to the insolence of these terrible "Batavians," who were after all only a tenth as numerous as the French.

For other reasons, the king had come to the same conclusions: the glorious crossing of the Rhine was in sight. . . .

External Magnificence

For the king, for the brilliant and festive court, and for an astonished Europe as well, the reign had begun in magnificence. On the one hand, there was the carnival of feasts, ballets, hunts, mistresses, and the splendor of the first monumental building at Paris (the ceremonial arches at the *portes* of Saint-Denis and Saint-Martin, the palace of the Louvre), Fontainebleau, Chambord and Saint-Germain. Then there was the palace of Versailles, the favorite place for festivals. But the monarch also proudly affirmed in person the total preeminence of "his House, in the entire world, without exception," on the grounds that the Emperor was only elective and possessed in his own right only one residence, "the sole city of Bamberg"; and besides only Louis was "descended from Charlemagne," as he put it in his *Memoirs*. These sincere affirmations resulted in grandiose ceremonies, the "audiences of excuses." The first was for Genoa, which had tried to introduce its representative as a royal ambassador at the Louvre; then came the turn of Spain, whose ambassador at London had the boldness to desire to "march" in front of Louis's own. There was even a ceremony for the papal legate, along with the erection of an expiatory pyramid at Rome, after a papal guard killed a French page in a drunken brawl. More seriously, the king of France sent six thousand men to help the Germans stop the assault of the Turks at the frontiers of the duchy of Austria (1664). The victory at Villaviciosa at 1665 aided the Portuguese in finally liberating themselves from almost a century of Spanish domination.

Spain was already occupying Louis XIV's attention. Since his father-in-law Philip IV had just died without delivering the dowry for Queen Marie-Thérèse, as promised in the Treaty of the Pyrenees, Louis believed he was entitled to claim part of the inheritance. When his lawyers discovered a certain right of "devolution" in Brabant, this name was given to the short but not always easy war launched by several carefully equipped and trained armies in Flanders in the spring of 1667. Then, with more ease, Condé attacked the Franche-Comté. Worried by these feats of arms, some European states led by Holland established a sort of triple alliance, joined by still powerful Sweden, while the duke of Lorraine and even England began to rearm. Louis XIV wisely decided to negotiate and collected a dozen Flemish cities, including Lille; he knew that the Franche-Comté would also soon fall into his hands. The entire kingdom joyfully celebrated this glory and these acquisitions. But this did not prevent the king from backing down before a half-formed coalition, or from bearing a grudge against the Dutch, the instigators of this blocking move. For once Colbert and Louvois were in complete agreement. Henceforth everything would be directed toward the punishment of these "cheese merchants," these "sea beggars," as the Calvinist republicans were called. They had, like Joshua, effectively made the sun stand still, and they even dared to strike a medal for this exploit.

After four years of solid diplomatic, military, and financial preparation, Louis XIV sent 120,000 men and the English fleet "to punish the perfidy" of this people on whom he disdained even to declare war, because it was only a matter of punishment.

THE FIREWORKS
OF SUMMER: 1672–1679

Begun in the spring of 1672, the Dutch war marked the first great turning point of the reign, the full summer of his glory. This war can be summarized in a few lines—first, glorious and easy beginnings; then, rapid and rude surprises with a coalition of almost all Europe; finally, a difficult and brilliant recovery, achieved during the pause provided by a series of treaties, in particular those signed at Nijmegen (1678–1679). For these exciting years, explaining is as important as storytelling.

Several weeks of easy campaign passed with "beautiful sieges" rolling by like a classical spectacle: thirty thousand badly armed Dutch soldiers, curiously abandoned by the republic obsessed by the sea, could not do much against a French army four times as large. A fine flanking movement was a prelude to the risk-free crossing of the Rhine on June 6. Holland appeared lost, and the trumpets of royal renown sounded glorious indeed. For once, on July 8, Colbert allowed himself to daydream: "If the king subdues all the United Provinces of the Netherlands, their commerce will become the commerce of the subjects of His Majesty, and there will be nothing more desirable."

This dream was already obsolete. After crossing the Rhine,

Condé had proposed to finish the business by sending several regiments of cavalry galloping toward Amsterdam, heart and treasure chest of the country; but the king found it more grand to preside over the reestablishment of Catholicism in the ancient cathedral of Utrecht. On the same day, however, the floodgates at Muiden were opened, and Holland reduced itself to a small archipelago, accessible only by sea. Moreover, Admiral Ruyter had just beaten the badly combined fleets of France and England. Everything changed very quickly. In July Prince William of Orange, aged twenty-two, whose military leanings had once appeared suspect to the Dutch bourgeois, was given command of the army, then several provinces, then in August the country as a whole. William had already made sure of help from Spain, from Brandenburg, and from Emperor Leopold, whom Louis had treated so condescendingly. Meanwhile the king of France had returned to his châteaux, declaring that the end of such a war "did not deserve his presence"; he would rather inhale all the incense burning around his person. On December 15, however, William laid siege to Charleroi, which was then under French control. On the Rhine, Turenne was having difficulty resisting the Hapsburg and Hohenzollern forces. Despite Boileau's hymns of praise, the Great King had "ceased to conquer."

The formation of a truly European coalition put Louis on the defensive. Supported by Dutch guilders and the somber obstinacy of William of Orange, the coalition united Europe against him. In February 1674, even his well-pensioned former ally Charles II of England had the cheek to join. The whole year 1674 was difficult for the French. Once more it required the combined genius of Condé, who won a bloody victory at Seneffe, and Turenne, who led an astonishing midwinter campaign in Alsace, to drive away the danger of invasion. At the same time Guyenne and Brittany were in revolt against taxes. Yet misunderstandings among the coalition partners, the power of a better organized and more numerous royal army, several exploits of the new fleet around Spanish Sicily, the inflexible will of Louis XIV, and the astuteness of his diplomats in negotiating as well as buying off the enemy finally ensured success.

As the French were again approaching Antwerp and Holland, which they had evacuated four years before, each of the enemies in turn agreed to a treaty. Spain, the weakest, paid for all the others, in ceding to France several bits of Flanders, Artois, and Cambrésis—as well as the Franche-Comté, which the Spanish had hardly defended. Even Sweden, crushed by Brandenburg at Fehrbellin in 1675 and by Denmark at sea, was able to keep its possessions in the Empire and on the Baltic, only thanks to the protection of its illustrious French ally. More famous than ever, Louis XIV had good reasons to proclaim himself the arbiter of Europe and the greatest monarch in the world.

Nevertheless, not a single one of his anti-Dutch objectives had been attained. Without losing an inch of their own territory, nor for that matter any of their colonies and not much of their navy—except Ruyter, who was killed in action—the Dutch obtained the French evacuation of several advanced positions conquered in 1668 and the abrogation of the rigorous customs tariff of 1667, which had been intended to hinder their trade. Furthermore, their leader William of Orange, the implacable enemy of Louis XIV, would wed Mary, niece of the king of England and future heiress to the Crown.

Praised to the skies by all the writers, artists, and the priests of France, the diplomatic and military results of the war easily veiled these significant shadows. Other problems would appear as a result of the choice made in 1672 by the Great King—the same choice his father had made in 1630: to prefer external relations to domestic affairs, the "exterior" as opposed to the "interior."

In fact the war with Holland and all Europe meant first of all the end of the financial equilibrium reestablished by Colbert and the return to what were called the "extraordinary affairs." In 1672, the deficit reached 8 million livres; it doubled in 1673, and tripled in 1676. Never again under the ancien régime, except for one year under Louis XV, would the budget be balanced. Thus each tax was increased by 4 to 6 million, and the clergy was earnestly asked to increase its contribution, the "free gift." Official pewter marks were invented and widely used, as well as monopolies on tobacco and stamped paper, causing several provinces to revolt. When these measures were not enough, Colbert sold exemptions from taxes and a surprising list of petty offices—regulators of wine and grain, supervisors of the sale of pigs and fish. He also alienated the part of the royal domain so painfully bought back since 1661. To his regret, Colbert was launched as of 1672 on a policy of borrowing, often at 10 percent interest, even though the legal maximum rate was 5 percent. The Genoese and particularly French financiers were involved, graciously (but not for free) advancing the state revenues of future years. All the same, the period of peace had been so long, the preceding policy so effective, and France so rich that financial catastrophe was averted. But from that time on, and for more than a century, with rare exceptions the state lived on loans, advances, and credit, which was not really a novelty. As long as the "peoples" worked, produced, and reproduced, things would go along in the usual way.

In this glorious, long, and certainly costly war, part of Colbert's work foundered—perhaps the part closest to his heart. Except as they supplied the war, most of the royal manufactures were endangered or melted away for want of orders, subsidies, and internal and external markets. The first distant colonists in Canada received help only rarely. The West India Company was dissolved, ruined on its tenth anniversary in 1674. The Northern Company, designed to play a trick on the Dutch in the waters they dominated, the Baltic and North Sea, was unable to send out its ships and had to liquidate its two offices at Bordeaux (1673) and at La Rochelle (1677). The most famous company of all, the East India Company, had to abandon its branches in India and Ceylon—again to the Dutch. It made no profits and renounced its monopoly in 1682, although it was taken up again later by astute traders from Saint-Malo, an event that Colbert did not live to see.

In reality, deeper reasons must explain this partial setback. On the one hand, merchants, wholesale traders, and shipowners, certainly not mediocre men, possessed the ingrained habit of pursuing their activities in their own way and according to their own interests. Their profoundly imbued spirit of economic liberty led them to mistrust any intervention of a state whose capacities they did not find brilliant and whose intentions were not clear. They believed any official initiative might be a hidden tax.

On the other hand, considerable French wealth was invested with great security in buildings and—even more securely in land. The owners lived comfortably off landed and seigneurial revenues; or perhaps, with more risk and greater profit, engaged in all kinds of moneylending from the simple loan (with mortgage) between individuals to bonds of the clergy of France and above all obligations of the king secured by future taxes, thus by the wealth of the kingdom itself. When land and finance were available, why risk gold écus on fragile maritime and colonial dreams?

The Great King was not much preoccupied with all this, however. Louis enjoyed his glory, carried on the construction of Versailles, and dreamed of new laurels, while thanking Colbert halfheartedly for having given the material help to permit the grand ambitions of his maturity and once again astonish Europe at the apogee of his reign. He failed to see that the world was changing, that the seasons were turning, that the great summer was approaching its end.

THE END OF SUMMER: STORMS AND TEMPESTS: 1679–1688

The decade that followed saw a profound inward turn in the personality of the king, in the trends of his reign, and in the destiny of the kingdom.

Intoxicated by praise, Louis XIV dared to do almost anything in religion, diplomacy, and war. Yet though he may not have appreciated their significance, he had the misfortune to suffer the loss of his best servants such as Colbert in 1683, likewise his best generals, and the greatest of the classical cultural figures. He also lost the queen, but replaced her quickly with one of his mistresses, the widow Scarron whom he made the marquise of Maintenon, a woman whose likely private talents were combined with a true genius for education. She helped to educate the royal bastards and later became infatuated with the education of noble girls at Saint-Cyr. Madame de Maintenon also showed a tardy devotion and a certain resourcefulness. She assured the king of pious and proper maturity and old age. While she rendered the recently occupied palace of Versailles rather severe, she contributed greatly to the worldly and intellectual victory of the city of Paris over the court. She may not have concurred with the monarch's despotic inclinations in religion; but while this has often been asserted, in fact no one really knows, and her omnipresence gave rise to speculation.

Religious Despotism

The term "despotism," not used pejoratively, simply defines the will of the king to govern religious affairs like all others. Rather lukewarm in the beginning, he first left the Protestants in peace, much as he gladly made alliances with those outside France. If he followed Mazarin's example in pestering the Jansenists, it was because he well knew that almost all of them had participated in the Fronde. The affair of the exile of the nuns of Port-Royal was noisier than it was significant, and it ended with the Peace of the Church of 1668, a compromise. The peace came apart in 1679, when the archbishop of Paris forced about forty postulants to leave Port-Royal, stopping all recruitment, and when several famous and troublesome sympathizers—"Messieurs" Antoine Arnauld, de Sacy, and Le Nain de Tillemont—were also forced to leave. Louis XIV was not much of a theologian and did not get entangled in quarrels about grace, but he disliked sects, especially rich and powerful ones, and he disliked even more intellectuals who had ceased to adore him systematically. Only the pensioned Racine was an exception.

For the moment, greater matters occupied his attention: the insolence of the pontiff of Rome and of the Huguenots. The second was easier to punish than the first.

The old Concordat of 1516 had settled most of the problems between king and pope: the former nominated and the latter consecrated. Some lacunae remained: for "foreign" clergy (those not part of the kingdom in 1516), for abbeys of women, for the administration of the always substantial revenues from vacant bishoprics. From 1673 onward, Louis XIV decided to resolve all these questions in his favor. Rome protested, but the popes of this era lacked nerve. Suddenly there appeared the only great fighting pope of the century, Innocent XI (1676–1689). Authoritarian, intransigent, and virtuous, he was not afraid of the proud and doubly adulterous Bourbon king. From 1678 he issued curt papal briefs ruling against the king in the complicated affair of the Régale, the pretended royal right over the nominations and goods of the Church. In 1680, the pope refused two royal nominations to the convent of Charonne and the bishopric of Pamiers. When neither side gave way, Louis XIV suddenly called together in 1681 an extraordinary assembly of about fifty bishops, all those who were enjoying court life at Versailles, some distance away from their dioceses. From this little council was painfully extracted a Gallican "declaration of the four articles" affirming the independence of kings in the temporal sphere, the superiority of councils over popes, the undefined "liberties" of the Church of France, and the reversibility of papal judgments. This rather prudent text was simply "torn apart" and "broken" in April 1682 by Innocent XI, who henceforth did not provide canonical investiture for any of the bishops named by the king. In 1683, thirty-five episcopal sees—one-third of the total—were without titular occupants, and the two adversaries nearly came to blows because of the affair of the Roman franchises, which we shall discuss later. The Sun King was living at the edge of schism when Innocent XI opportunely died in 1689.

And yet, in the interval, the king certainly astonished the pope by "extirpating heresy" with the revocation of the Edict of Nantes in 1685.

We should understand that the existence of two religions in one state was then considered an almost monstrous anomaly. The Catholic church had never accepted the opportune and intelligent decision of Henry IV in 1598; it never failed to thunder against the "unhappy liberty of conscience," labeling the Protestant churches as "synagogues of Satan," and the Huguenots as "slaves in revolt." At first Louis XIV was prudent like Mazarin, and attached to a foreign policy hostile to the Catholic king of Spain; for a long time the king opted for wisdom. Toward 1669, however, Louis took more restrictive measures while still adhering to the letter of the Edict of Nantes; then came the buying of souls by the Conversion Fund, offering Huguenots financial incentives to join the Catholic church. At one time it was thought that tardy return to "papism" by the Huguenot Marshal Turenne or the atheist prince of Condé would serve as an example. From 1679, conversion by *dragonnades,* soldiers quartered in heretic houses, had begun; the excesses of this policy were evident, but the intendants sent bulletins of victory to Versailles. Colbert, who knew the economic power of the Protestants, counseled prudence until his death in 1683; but Le Tellier, his son Louvois, and the entire Catholic church were pushing in the other direction. We may consider the deeper reasons for the king's decision: to show himself the master again, to impress the pope, above all to astonish Europe by an exploit that would compensate for his absence from the great victory of the Christians over the Turks at Kahlenberg near Vienna in 1683. The Edict of Revocation, signed at Fontainebleau in October 1685, led in practice to prohibition of all exercise of the "pretended reformed religion," by chasing away all Protestant ministers and obliging all children of ex-heretics to receive instruction in the "true faith," that of the king.

The revocation was welcomed in France by a veritable explosion of joy. From the great nobles and Bishop Bossuet down to the lowest vicars and porters there was praise for the "New Constantine." Rare were those persons such as Bishop Le Camus and the admirable Marshal Vauban who expressed doubts about the quality of forced conversions.

Outside France, the pope and the Catholic princes applauded, but without enthusiasm. A century earlier the Saint Bartholomew's Day Massacre had provoked greater effusions. As for the Protestants, they were reinforced in their hostility, even those of Brandenburg, despite heavy French subsidies. From a diplomatic point of view, the revocation clearly constituted a blunder.

It was certainly a mistake; there can be no doubt about it. Of nearly a million Protestants, at least one hundred thousand chose exile. Few of them were peasants attached to their land, but many were artisans, manufacturers, and merchants who would enrich neighboring countries with their talents, wealth, and moral energy. They populated Berlin, brought the techniques of Angoulême papermaking and Saint-Quentin cloth–making to Great Britain, and installed redoubtable teams of writers and pamphleteers in Holland, whence they inundated their former homeland with skillful seditious writings and formed a likely and active network for espionage in future conflicts. The revocation itself was not much use, since the better part of the Protestants never became Catholic but soon resumed their religious life in the "desert," where they lived in semiclandestinity. Yet the revocation did disturb and impoverish the kingdom by strengthening its principal adversaries. It even helped to prepare the peaceful revolution in England against a "papist" king, whose excesses were also feared. That Glorious Revolution of 1688–89 brought to the throne of the Stuarts the rudest and richest enemy of Louis XIV, William of Orange.

The Great King did not need to make this supplementary blunder: already, by his rash initiatives and peacetime annexations, he had united the majority of Europe against him.

WAR DURING PEACETIME: 1679–1688

After the Treaty of Nijmegen was signed, Louis XIV kept more than one hundred thousand men on wartime footing. The harsh Louvois kept himself busy arming and disciplining them, and Vauban used them to build or repair his famous fortresses. Lodged close to the frontiers, they also supported the proceedings instituted by royal jurists against certain foreign territories that once upon a time depended on fiefs or seigneuries recently acquired by the king. These brilliant initiatives were called the politics of *réunions*. They began in 1679 with Montbéliard, then an independent principality, and were extended to Lorraine, Saar, Luxembourg, and Alsace, which was incompletely annexed in 1648. The most famous episode stupefied Europe, which was nonetheless expecting it: the easy assault on Strasbourg in September 1681 by thirty thousand men "secretly" assembled under its walls. Then, while the Turks were swarming around Vienna, the Great King ravaged the most Catholic Spanish Netherlands, where he had ferreted out several fiefs to "reunite" near Brussels, Ghent, and Bruges.

Outraged, and hoping for Dutch or Imperial help, Spain brusquely declared war in October 1683. Louis continued his ravages, taking Courtrai, Diksmuide, and Luxembourg; he also sent troops into Catalonia. The Emperor and all the rest of Europe were occupied with the victorious pursuit of the Turks; they brought France and Spain to negotiate. Truces valid for twenty years were signed at Regensburg in August 1684: the king of France contented himself with keeping Strasbourg, Kehl, and Luxembourg, as well as several cities of the unfortunate Spanish Netherlands.

Hardly had the truce been signed when Louis XIV chose to make another demonstration of his power. Accused of constructing galleys for Spain, Genoa was bombarded for six days by a French squadron under Duquesne, and the Genoese doge was persuaded to offer his excuses to France. Shortly afterward, the French fleet threatened Cadiz, key to all the rich commerce of the Americas, because the king of Spain had just removed some privileges enjoyed by prosperous French merchants in the city. The privileges were reestablished. Louis also pestered his cousin the duke of Savoy: he even sent Catinat to massacre the duke's Waldensian subjects, who were accused of helping the Huguenots of Dauphiné. This was a wonderful massacre, as Catinat described it in early 1686: "everything is perfectly desolate, there are no more people or animals."

Soon politically more serious matters—the succession to the Palatinate, the nomination to the electoral bishopric of Cologne, and quarrels in Rome—would rouse the nations of Europe. From 1686 onward they concluded a series of agreements that received the inappropriate name of the League of Augsburg. This was not yet the second great coalition, but it was a harbinger of it.

New provocations and even outright aggression in peacetime quickly brought about this generalized conflict, much more formidable than preceding ones. This marked the end of relatively easy French boldness. In the lightning and storms that had announced it, the summer of the Great Century was overwhelmed. In Michelet's seasonal imagery, autumn came. Before we enter it, we should pause to see what had become of the monarchy, the kingdom, and the known world.

Chapter Nine

AUTUMN OF THE GREAT CENTURY: 1689–1715

FRANCE AROUND 1689

Having been installed in the unfinished palace of Versailles since May 1682, Louis XIV was made somewhat wiser in his heavy maturity by the continuous presence of his second wife Madame de Maintenon. He led the grand life so often described, but it was not all elegance and style. Spanish etiquette did not prevent shambles: marvelous decor and filth coexisted in the palace, where knavish lackeys and dubious matrons rubbed shoulders with the highest nobility. Nonetheless, at Versailles the Sun appeared to shine on fascinated France and Europe.

Around Louis, the old and talented team assembled by Mazarin had almost disappeared. Jean-Baptiste Colbert had died in 1683, and Louvois declined in favor as Madame de Maintenon esteemed him little. Louvois finally died in 1691, swollen by ill-gotten gains, food, and vices. Afterwards the king governed with the help of his children, his other relatives, and the clients of his old servants—members of the Louvois family such as Barbézieux, of whom little use was made; numerous relatives of the great Colbert such as his brother Croissy, his son-in-law Beauvilliers, and his seemingly genial son Seignelay, who was quickly destroyed by excesses; still later a nephew, Desmarets, also lived in grand style. The Phélypeaux, a secular ministerial family, finally came to the fore with Pontchartrain, a remarkable man who eclipsed all the others. Of all his clientele of descendants, five of them entered the Royal Council, where the dauphin appeared from time to time. All the rest, even the chancellor, a certain Boucherat, brought themselves back to the level of bureau chiefs directing an administration that finally began to preserve and classify its archives. All essential business was transacted "in private" with the king (and with Madame de Maintenon guiding the direction), by interviews with the controller general of finances, a secretary of state, or a trusted confidant such as the soldier Chamlay or the Jesuit confessor. The decisions taken were frequently noted in *arrêts pris en commandement,* signed by the king and a single secretary of state, usually a member of the Phélypeaux family. Details were handled by correspondence with the intendants. These officials were installed all over France by 1689, even in two difficult provinces, Brittany and Béarn.

Far away from this Versailles where hardly any of the great ministers, great generals, or even great classical figures lived, there was France, the distant domain. The terrible crises of the first years of the personal reign lay forgotten in the past. In the countryside famines as terrible as those in 1662 were rare. Although harsh epidemics still devastated several districts, the plague had declined, and the government had imposed an effective quarantine the only time it had come back in force, at Amiens in 1667–1668. Numerous violent but isolated provincial tax revolts had been controlled either by terror, as in Brittany in 1675, or more often by resignation. Despite several local accidents between 1677 and 1684, the weather had been favorable to harvests. Grain and bread prices had remained habitually low, which satisfied the common people, but not the powerful group of large landowners and farmers.

The farmers had to sell their abundant surpluses at very low prices, and this contributed to a depression in one part of the French economy. The price of agricultural leases declined markedly from the 1660s to the 1680s and beyond. The price of land also fell, by one-quarter or one-third. There were other patent signs of difficulties as the prices of meat and livestock gradually collapsed; even wood, the basic material for heating, building, and energy, which had at least tripled in price from 1600 to 1660, declined afterward.

In manufacturing, which was once encouraged and artificially stimulated by Colbert, there were also difficulties. Credit was lacking and customers were melting away, notably in England, the major buyer of Breton cloth. The English had responded to the unfortunate protectionism of Colbert with retaliatory measures. We also know that the textile production of the northern cities from Rouen to Lille, and particularly the largest, Amiens, began to fall off during the Dutch war. In any case, textile production never again attained the records of the 1630s, rather curiously the best decade of the century.

Not all these signs of depression were tragic, but they seem to have been neither understood nor even perceived at Versailles. They help, however, to explain the difficulties encountered when the people of the kingdom had to pay for the wars.

On the other hand, the industry that was thriving, perhaps too vigorously, was shipping. No doubt the navy did well, since after Colbert it was in the capable hands of his son Seignelay and later Pontchartrain. At times, but not always, it shone in combat, and before the disasters of the later reign of Louis XIV it could even protect the dynamic and essential merchant shipping. In wartime these merchant vessels turned into corsairs armed with cannons, thanks to letters of marque given by the king. The merchantmen of Marseille traded actively in the Mediterranean and dominated the Near East. The great Atlantic ports were always interested in Spain and, by way of Cadiz, in Spanish America, though more and more they turned to the "sugar islands," the Antilles. Le Havre and Saint-Malo had more than a hundred vessels each and dominated the trade; soon the adventurous sailors of Saint-Malo plied the Indian and Pacific oceans to bring home considerable profits. Dutch and English merchants, so influential with Stadholder William of Orange, now King William III of England, thought that French ships and merchants were too numerous and too powerful in the Mediterranean, along the slave coast of Africa and in the West Indies. This competition had to be stopped. Even indirectly, such considerations weighed in the war that was breaking out again. English historians have called this conflict "the war against French commerce," while the French persist in calling it "the war of the League of Augsburg," taking only a partial view of the whole.

This conflict and the following war would henceforth overshadow the rest of the reign, giving it the darker hues that Michelet described as the "autumn of the Great Century."

THE SECOND COALITION: 1688–1697

After his policy of *réunions,* his conflict with the pope, and the revocation of the Edict of Nantes, Louis XIV was engaged in new quarrels. After the death of the German Elector Palatine, brother of the second wife of Louis's brother Monsieur, the king claimed part of the inheritance. Louis made good his threat to use force and aroused the greater part of the Empire against himself. In Rome, he refused to suppress the franchises, or diplomatic privileges of asylum for marauders on the grounds of the French embassy. The French ambassador had been excommunicated by the pope! Louis made increasingly loud threats, in particular to seize the papal town of Avignon. Finally, there were two candidates vying for the archbishopric of Cologne. In September 1688, when the pope chose the imperial candidate in preference to his own, Louis XIV was touched to the quick. He again unleashed his ravaging troops on the Rhineland, burning Heidelberg, sacking Mannheim, Speyer, Worms, and Bingen, and thereby uniting the German princes against him. Then he took Avignon and tried in early 1689 to restore James II to the throne of England. James had just been chased away by his subjects, who had installed William and Mary in the Glorious Revolution. Tourville's fleet fought the English at Beachy Head and carried

James II to Catholic Ireland, where his fervent but poorly armed partisans could not prevent him from being crushed by William at Drogheda. The Stuart king fled back to France, established himself at Saint-Germain-en-Laye, and did not budge. About the same time, the Quebec regiments attacked New York, and wars were systematically extended to the colonies. Far away, Catinat charged into Savoy-Piedmont and carried off without difficulty the victory of Staffarda.

These surprising aggressions resulted from calculations that were not entirely absurd. Louis XIV and Louvois wanted to act quickly. They thought that the partners in the coalition would quarrel among themselves, that the Emperor would be occupied with the war against the Turks (whom he crushed, reconquering Buda and Belgrade), and that William of Orange would get himself entangled in Holland or in England. It so happened, however, that each of these calculations was mistaken. With the exception of insignificant neutrals such as Portugal, Denmark, and Switzerland, all of Europe was arrayed against Louis, and these enemies were led by the tenacious William of Orange. A long and hard war began. It was characterized by the enormity of the forces engaged, at least 200,000 men on each side, the very bloody battles due to progress in weaponry, the high cost of operations, their intermittent and sometimes contradictory character, and the striking emergence of the British navy, which defeated the French at La Hogue in May 1692 and rendered any new invasion of the British Isles impossible.

These nine years of war seemed to repeat the same story endlessly: advance, retreat, victory, defeat; then, finally, a sort of weariness. Thus, after its victory, the British fleet, which could have bombed Dieppe and damaged Saint-Malo, failed in 1694 to carry the day in a landing at Camaret, which was furiously defended by coast guards and Breton peasants. And yet numerous French corsairs—Jean Bart, Duguay-Trouin, Pointis, Forbin—harassed British ships. The same standoff occurred between Piedmont and French Dauphiné. In 1692, Victor Amadeus II of Savoy occupied the French towns of Embrun and Gap; a little later, Catinat entered Savoy and the county of

Nice. In the Empire, the French army managed to occupy Bavaria in 1692, then left again, sacking Heidelberg and the Rhineland once more on the way. The French found it essential to safeguard Alsace. Even in America, the comings and goings between Quebec and New York became ritual. Toward the end of the war, the Canadians seized the region around Hudson Bay, the fur country, as well as Newfoundland and its fisheries. In Spain, a French army took nine years to go from Perpignan to Barcelona, whose capture in 1697, thanks to the Toulon fleet, came at a good diplomatic moment. The greatest battles still took place in the Spanish Netherlands (present-day Belgium). Marshal Luxembourg, the last of the great French generals, stopped the allies first at Fleurus in 1690, then with more difficulty at Steenkerke in 1692, a third time at Neerwinden in 1693—a famous victory, one of the greatest butcheries of the century. After Luxembourg died in 1695, the mediocre Villeroy retreated, taking vengeance by cruelly bombarding Brussels. As a result, the admirable Grand Place had to be reconstructed. Villeroy did no more than wait for peace.

During these hard, often indecisive and dispersed battles, so costly in men and money, the diplomats were holding talks. Negotiations had begun at an early date, perhaps even before 1693. Long discussions were held, with ruses, higher bidding, jockeying for positions. These negotiations were concluded in 1697, in a house belonging to William near Rijswijk, where the treaty was signed.

The Allies, who had intended to bring France back to its frontiers of 1659 or 1648, had to recognize borders that were closer to those of 1679. In addition they ceded Strasbourg, which the Emperor very grudgingly released. But each party obtained some advantages, and for once, the king of Spain lost nothing. It is true that everyone was waiting for his death, since he was very ill and childless, and all hoped to carve up his inheritance.

Despite many difficulties, Louis XIV, could pride himself on a good defense, on several outstanding actions, on much courage, and on having kept Strasbourg. For the rest, he had to pay a high price to obtain the peace so necessary to his fatigued kingdom and his future designs.

He had taken up arms to restore the Catholic Stuart on the English throne, to install his candidate as electoral archbishop of Cologne, to make the pope give way in Avignon and Rome, and to keep all the territories he had "reunited" in the Spanish Netherlands, Luxembourg, Lorraine, and the Franche-Comté. In all these aims he failed. He even had to sign an agreement with the new pope that obliged the French bishops to go before the nuncio and disavow in writing the Gallican Declaration of 1682. He gave back Avignon to the pope; to Spain he gave back Catalonia and all places in the Netherlands annexed since 1679, including Courtrai, Mons, and Charleroi. He had to give back Lorraine to the young duke, and content himself with a right of passage to reach Alsace. To the German princes he gave back the region around Trier, the bit of the Rhineland he still occupied, and the bridge cities on the right bank of the Rhine—Kehl, Freiburg, Breisach, and Phillippsburg, but he kept Saarlouis, which had been laid out by Vauban. The Dutch Republic gave back Pondichéry to the French, but the Dutch obtained great commercial and customs advantages, as well as the precautionary right to install troops at fortresses in the Spanish Netherlands near the French border. This area soon became known as "the barrier." As for England, now the great adversary, Louis XIV had to promise to stop giving aid to James Stuart against William, and to give the English the same commercial advantages as the Dutch. He gave back the conquered territories of Newfoundland and Hudson Bay, in exchange for half an island in the Antilles and two slave-trading posts near Sénégal. Even to the duke of Savoy, soon to be called king, Louis was obliged to give back Nice, Susa, and Montmélian, and to promise a future matrimonial alliance. For a king who had not even been defeated, nor suffered invasion of his kingdom, the peace required much sacrifice. Louis, now approaching his sixtieth birthday, might have learned moderation.

In reality, he understood that his kingdom was tired; but above all he dreamed of the Spanish succession, which promised to become available soon. As it turned out, the long-condemned Spanish King Carlos II took three years to die, giving France some respite and allowing the diplomats to exercise their imagination. This question of the Spanish succession would open the last great war of the reign, the most terrible of all wars of the Sun King.

But the war just ended had plunged the kingdom in very grave difficulties.

The Burden of the War

To feed, equip, and arm for nine years two hundred thousand men and two great fleets on four principal fronts and in as many distant theaters, against the opposition of almost all of Europe, including the banks of Amsterdam and London, was a gigantic task with enormous costs.

To watch over finances after the death of Colbert and the interim term of Le Pelletier (1683–89) who governed honestly but refused to resort to expedients, the king made the excellent choice of Phélypeaux de Pontchartrain. This simple, cheerful, and solid man was sharp and intelligent. He readily used humor and cynicism. Pontchartrain knew how to handle perfectly the strict task that had been imposed upon him: to pay for the war by any means possible.

From the ordinary revenues of classical taxation, hardly anything more could be expected. Revenues increased a little until about 1693, then fell again because of events in 1694, which we shall discuss later. The provinces with estates and the Church agreed to slightly higher "subsidies" and "free gifts." The cities were charged surtaxes twice, but resisted the third time. All of this taxation brought in 20 to 30 million livres per year, but three or four times as much was needed.

Pontchartrain committed himself to "extraordinary means" of fund-raising with a virtuosity reminiscent of Mazarin, although lacking the excessive roguery. He sold, resold, invented and reinvented twenty kinds of offices including official announcers of funerals and oyster sellers. He sold all the mayor's offices at auction to the highest bidder, excepting those of

Paris and Lyon; the same fate befell half of the town council seats. He sold coats-of-arms to commoners. He sold patents of nobility, perhaps with the sneering agreement of the king—who would dare to publish the lists of those ennobled in exchange for payment of 6,000 livres? He sold captaincies and colonelcies in the bourgeois militias that paraded on holidays; and once again, he sold exemptions from taxes.

Like so many others, Pontchartrain returned to the inexhaustible creation of *rentes,* perpetual loans—a hundred million livres at first, with much more to follow, even at 8.33 percent interest. The payment of interest would have to come later, but the capital sums immediately fed the armies. From our perspective, the wealth of the lenders is astonishing, as is the confidence that they still showed in the state. When all this did not suffice, Pontchartrain debased the currency for the first time since two unfortunate attempts by Colbert. As only hard cash in silver and gold counted, all that was required was to change legal value of coins, or to collect them for melting down and minting others. The state could then give them a more advantageous value and begin anew. The minister used these methods beginning in 1689. When they proved very fruitful, he used them with all his might. His successors continued these operations until the end of the reign and even beyond. The poorly paid lenders and creditors, often reimbursed in devalued state paper, complained a great deal but tolerated these repeated devaluations in fits and starts, interrupted as they were by occasional "upward" revaluations, which were always profitable to the state.

In 1694, however, tax collection was difficult; offices, loans, and privileges sold badly. A general exhaustion, aggravated by a sudden economic crisis, had taken hold of the kingdom. While some people were unable to pay, others did not want to lend any more. Pontchartrain was willy-nilly obliged to listen to serious reformers, especially Vauban, who was proposing a shocking innovation—an income tax payable by all, even the privileged. Each subject would declare his income, and officials would verify the declarations. Later the marshal would develop this project in his book, *Dîme Royale* (1708), but a variation of it was enacted in 1695, under the name of *capitation*. This tax touched everyone, even the dauphin and the princes of the blood, though not the clergy, who paid in prayers. All subjects were divided into twenty-two classes according to their profession, their titles, or their "estate"; the lowest class paid only a few sous. This surprising novelty, which went against all earlier legislation and the most sacred traditions, brought in more than 20 million livres annually. But it was suppressed after the peace treaty, as the king had promised. The *capitation* helped to finance the end of the war, whose costs declined in its last years. Resources and armies had been exhausted, not only in France but also among the other belligerents.

Besides, a tragic event had befallen almost the entire kingdom between the summers of 1693 and 1694. After mediocre years marked by epidemics, the harvest of 1693 was spoiled by a humid summer and fell to about half the normal amount. The prices of grain and bread began to rise. Eventually they more than tripled, and the difficulties of communications were mixed with the usual speculation. The result was panic. Except in the south and in Brittany, the population lacked resources and employment. High mortality struck almost everywhere, aggravated by infected food and harsh "contagions." For the first time in more than thirty years, the French people had to eat bread made from ferns and acorns, grains cut before they were ripe, and boiled grass. In at least half of the kingdom, mortality rates were twice or even four times as high as normal, which meant that at least 10 percent of the population died. The increased taxes, the English naval blockade which prevented exports of rural or urban products, and the difficulties of preceding years had prepared the way for this catastrophe. The common people lacked the resources and the reserves to resist. Misery on this scale had not been seen since the Fronde, and even the famous "great winter" of 1709 may not have been so tragic by comparison.

The government readily understood that it was impossible to make a reduced and partially exhausted population pay more. The king showed his pity. Others began to express themselves in a different manner. In 1694, Vauban raised his voice, as he had done after the revocation of the Edict of Nantes; Boisguilbert published his *Détail de la France* in 1695, a critique of the economy and fiscal system. Fénelon wrote that "Letter to the King" so often cited: "All France is only a great desolate hospital lacking provisions." The formula was a bit forced, but it was a sign that firm and respectful opposition was increasing. The *Characters* of La Bruyère, which went through nine editions from 1688 to 1696, already contained sharp critiques. From Holland skillful and inflammatory pamphlets were being spread. The "Sighs of an Enslaved France"— a significant title—was best known. In different but neighboring spheres, Cartesian philosophy was making progress despite prohibitions against it; sacred and biblical exegesis were enjoying a renaissance; and the first critical and free-thinking attacks against superstitions were coming from the pens of Fontenelle and the exiled Pierre Bayle. Bayle's *Thoughts on the Comet* and his *Historical and Critical Dictionary,* two blazing philosophical and political texts, appeared in 1683 and 1696. Although these works were forbidden and prosecuted, they were sought out and read by a still tiny elite, no doubt ahead of its time. But they showed that the age of florid adoration was fading away, and that the Enlightenment was slowly coming on the scene. The aging Bossuet sensed the danger clearly, but the king hardly stopped to notice, as the past and future war almost entirely occupied his attention.

THE RESPITE: 1697–1701

Louis XIV had negotiated with obstinacy and signed the Treaty of Rijswijk with moderation. He might have silenced his internal voices of glory and magnificence in order to listen to that instinct of prudence, which finally emerged from deep in his nature. Perhaps he could give his finances and his subjects the rest they needed. Certainly he decided to do so, because with his diplomats he launched complex negotiations to settle amicably the always imminent Spanish succession. As the question did not come to a head until 1700, the kingdom enjoyed a respite.

The *capitation* and several other wartime taxes disappeared, and the *taille* was reduced by 10 percent, which had not happened in ages. On the other hand, the collectors of indirect taxes levied them with greater facility, showing that the national economy was functioning again. Indeed, the harvests were good from 1695 onward, and the English blockade of French ports was lifted, allowing increased production and exports. The monetary manipulations calmed down, and the state was able to reimburse on good terms some of the loans taken out during the war. The people of the countryside were liberated from the militia, a recently established institution that mobilized one soldier per parish. These recruits were taken first from the bachelors and then the young married men, and supported by the parish. This apparent novelty was in fact a revival of an old custom, but it provoked an outcry from the peasantry more attached to its fields than attracted to military life. Deserters were numerous and given shelter by the general population. Thus the end of the militia was celebrated, but it would return. . . .

On another front, the king began to think that his anti-Protestant policies had not succeeded. In 1698–99 he ordered that persuasion rather than force be used, though naturally he could not give way on the principle of religious unity.

The peace caused an extraordinary burst of energy in maritime commerce, for which privateering had constituted only a last recourse. In 1698, the number of ships leaving Nantes and Saint-Malo for the Antilles tripled. The other ports soon imitated them, and the sailors of Marseille finally ventured beyond Gibraltar. At the same time, serious private companies were founded for trade in the Indian Ocean, in China, and in the Pacific along the coast of Peru. The first merchant ships were making round-the-world voyages taking three years, and trading along the way. This risky commerce brought in great profits or nothing at all. It consisted of taking to these fabled lands the fine cloth and luxury products of France, and bringing back loads of silver bars or coins, especially from Mexico, as well as sugar, silk, lacquer, and spices—the products of China and India. These fabulous trades also included black slaves and enriched generations of famous merchants like the millionaires of Saint-Malo, the Danycans, the Magons, and others. They also brought a breath of sea air to the old agricultural kingdom, as well as indispensable aid to the old king, soon involved in another war. Naturally, this sudden French awakening could not be pleasing to the great maritime powers already established in the islands and the Indies, and accustomed to direct trade between the East and the Far East. These opponents were found principally in Holland, increasingly even in England, and Spain. This trading impulse, supported by intelligent ministers like Pontchartrain, would give new coloration to future conflicts, affecting all those of the eighteenth century.

In the kingdom itself, a survey organized in 1697 "for the instruction of the dauphin" showed that France on the whole was in good condition. Intendants who were working to establish respect for order and regular payment of taxes reported they were reaching these goals. After Colbert's creation of the offices of waters and forests, the stamp tax, and the tobacco monopoly, still more new administrations were established: the Mortgage Agency, the Registry Office for certain notarial documents, and the Department of Bridges and Highways. Lieutenants of police were installed in all the large and medium-sized cities within thirty years of Nicolas de La Reynie's appointment at Paris in 1667. These men regulated the food supply, trades, prices, printing, and public morals. A decision of 1700 established the principle of public education. In each parish two teachers, one male and one female, were to be maintained at the expense of the inhabitants. The intention was simply to generalize what was already being done in the northern third of the kingdom.

The revival of the Council of Commerce, established earlier by Colbert, was more significant and longer lasting. In a move to broaden its representation beyond ministers and great clerks such as d'Aguesseau and Amelot, it was decided in 1700 that twelve great merchants would represent the principal trading cities of the kingdom, which had gradually established Chambers of Commerce. This council advocated the idea of economic liberty and asked for trade agreements with the two great maritime powers, Holland and England. Some of its members, such as Mesnager of Rouen and Descazeaux of Nantes, even played a diplomatic role in negotiations for the treaties of 1713–1714.

During this time, the court, the city of Paris, and also some of the provincial elites were passionately interested in current affairs that escaped ordinary mortals: the excessive and vaguely hysterical quietism centered around Madame Guyon and Fénelon for a time, and the rebirth of a strongly Gallican Jansenism. In these theological quarrels, the near-priestly king laid down his opinion, which was now much closer to that of Rome and its ultramontane supporters. But leaving aside the high society of salon discussions and various forms of libertinage, the Great King was especially concerned with the most important affair of all: the Spanish Succession.

The problem could be posed thus: among the possible heirs to the childless and dying king of Spain, only two really counted: Louis XIV, son and husband of elder Spanish princesses; and the Emperor Leopold, son and husband of younger Spanish princesses. Each had put forward the claims of a son or grandson. Europe could hardly allow the union of the crowns of France and Spain, with its American possessions, under one king. Neither could it tolerate the reconstitution of the empire of Charles V, an idea even less acceptable to Louis XIV. Therefore during these years of peace a series of complex negotiations took place, necessarily involving England and Holland. As a last resort, Louis XIV would have shown much moderation and been content with Milan, a magnificent bargain, allowing the rest of the inheritance, or almost all of it, to go to Archduke Charles, son of the Emperor.

In Spain itself King Carlos II died, leaving behind a will that became known on November 1, 1700. Carlos had insisted on the integral unity of Spain and its possessions, and designated as his heir Philip of Anjou, grandson of Louis XIV. If

Philip refused the crown it would go to his brother; and failing him, to Archduke Charles. Louis XIV and his ministers deliberated for two days, then accepted the terms of the will. This decision meant an inevitable war with the Emperor, who was holding to terms negotiated earlier; but it had the advantage of drawing on the entire and considerable power of Spain, especially its American treasure. This was an important point, because refusing to accept the will would also have led to war, but without Spanish help. Louis XIV could not have accepted the revival of Charles V's empire.

Even though posterity would hold long and useless discussions of this fateful decision, it did not immediately lead to war, except for several months of activity around Milan. The third coalition against Louis XIV was slow to form. First of all, the Emperor could not decide the matter by himself. The young king Philip V had a very successful entry into Spain and made himself popular, especially in Castile. Finally, William III of England and Grand Pensionary Heinsius of Holland seemed determined to wait and see, even though merchants and sailors of their two countries had disliked the accession of a Bourbon prince to the Crown of Spain and its American treasures. Louis XIV spoiled this momentary respite by a return to his old policy of grandeur.

From February 1701, contrary to all earlier agreements, he maintained all the rights of Philip V of Spain to succeed to the throne of France as well. This decision was premature, to say the least, since the Grand Dauphin and his eldest son were still alive and stood ahead of Philip in the French succession. Then, while waiting for the arrival of Spanish garrisons in the southern Netherlands, Louis sent French soldiers to occupy "provisionally" the "barrier places." Thus he took prisoner the Dutch contingents that had been stationed there since the Peace of Rijswijk. Meanwhile at Madrid too many French counselors were helping Philip V govern, while the great French merchants immediately invested in Spanish and American markets. Furthermore, in September 1701, the new king of Spain accorded the *asiento,* the monopoly to furnish slaves to the immense Spanish Empire, shortly before held by the Dutch, to a French company. Philip himself and his grandfather were stockholders in this company, along with the richest financiers and bankers of France—the Crozats, Le Gendres, and Samuel Bernard. This economic triumph was an intolerable affront to the maritime powers. Several days later England, Holland, and the Empire signed the Great Alliance of The Hague. Louis XIV was given two months to negotiate, but he responded in his usual prideful manner. As James II, the dethroned Catholic king of England, had just died, Louis recognized his son James III as king of England *de jure,* while William III reigned *de facto.* This, too, was contrary to Louis's promises to recognize William at Rijswijk, and declared him a usurper. Of course neither William nor the English Parliament could allow this outrage, and William's unexpected death in March, 1702 delayed the conflict for only two months. On May 15, 1702, the three allies of The Hague mobilized the third coalition.

THE LAST COALITION AND THE WAR OF SPANISH SUCCESSION: 1702–1713

Once again, Louis XIV had to fight on all European fronts—in the Netherlands, the Empire, Italy, and Spain—as well as on the seas and in the colonies. And Louis had only four allies: Cologne and Bavaria in Germany, and Portugal and Savoy, both of which abandoned him in 1703. The Portuguese, fearful of losing Brazil, accepted an English protectorate, while the duke of Savoy wanted to be recognized as a king and live peacefully on his lands.

The French army had been carefully prepared, reformed, and trained. The rifle had come into general use in 1701, the attached bayonet in 1703; the artillery was reinforced by an expert, Surirey de Saint-Rémy. An enormous recruiting effort had been completed, and the militia was again called out despite peasant hostility: it would render real services, especially in auxiliary roles. From 1702 the king had 220,000 men at his disposal, and perhaps as many as 300,000 the following year.

Yet he lacked ships: those he had were of high quality, but too few. The same could be said of his generals. It is true he had Villars, the duke of Berwick (an illegitimate son of James II), and above all Vendôme, who was talented but difficult to control. These effective generals were sent from one front to the other, but the king also used incompetent courtiers such as Villeroy, La Feuillade, and Tallard. As it happened, the greater military genius lay with the enemy, in the persons of Prince Eugene and the duke of Marlborough. The English fleet quickly dominated the seas and once again blocked French ports, despite the noble exploits of the French royal navy and privateers.

From the French point of view, the war was composed of two distinct periods: first, grave reversals until 1709; then a certain recovery after that date.

The first disaster took place in the Empire, at Blenheim near Hochstadt in 1704. Prince Eugene and Marlborough crushed the Franco-Bavarian army of Marcin and Tallard: banners were buried, thirty thousand men captured by the enemy, and the rest straggled back as far as Alsace. No one dared to report the rout to the old king. When he found out, Louis recalled Villars from the Cévennes, where he was fighting the Protestant Camisard rebels, so that he could stop the enemy at the Moselle at least. The adversaries then fought on the Rhine without noteworthy results.

The same year, the English took Gibraltar, and the Toulon fleet could not recapture it. The same fate befell Barcelona a while later. To this city the English peacefully brought the Archduke Charles, whom Catalonia recognized as king of Spain. Valencia and Murcia followed suit. The new Carlos III even entered Madrid in 1706, helped by Austrian and English armies, some of whom came from their new ally Portugal. Vendôme, had long held Milan despite the desertion of Victor Amadeus of Savoy at his rear, but he was replaced by La Feuillade, who was immediately crushed by Prince Eugene at Turin. Louis XIV and his grandson had to abandon the defense of all of Spanish Italy in order to obtain an honorable retreat in 1707.

In the north one disappointment followed another. Defeated at Ramillies in 1706, Villeroy lost the Spanish Netherlands, which then recognized the Austrian archduke as their king. Two years later, Vendôme and the duke of Burgundy, who did not get along with each other, were defeated at Oudenaarde by the Allies. The French army fled in disorder, leaving Lille unguarded; despite the efforts of Boufflers, the city fell in October 1708. The invasion of the kingdom had begun. The same year, the king attempted an invasion of Scotland, which was supposedly loyal to the Stuarts, but his fleet was not even able to land and had to return to Dunkirk.

Difficulties had also arisen inside the kingdom. Driven by Catholic intolerance and misery, and encouraged by young visionary prophets, the Protestants of the Cévennes launched an open revolt beginning in 1702. The affair was so serious that it was necessary to send the army under the command of Villars himself. The rebels' principal bands were dispersed in 1705, but despite fierce repression, guerrilla warfare continued until about 1710. The southwest was troubled by other revolts, such as that of the "Tard-Avisés" of Quercy in 1707. On another level, a peace party was forming around the heir to the throne, the duke of Burgundy. Fénelon played a not-always-discreet part in it, visibly preparing for the next reign. At the summit of the kingdom, political will was wavering.

There is no doubt that financing the war presented grave problems. As before, taxes were increased, but it was difficult to collect them; hundreds of offices were sold and every conceivable loan floated. Currency manipulations were also carried to the limits. The expedient of paper money was even tried: it had previously been successful, but the government printed too much and was unable to reimburse the bills at full value. As a result they soon lost half and then three-quarters of their value. In 1708, Controller General Chamillart, an honest sort, wrote a rather desperate letter to the king to tell him of his own and the kingdom's exhaustion. Louis XIV then had the courage to call Desmarets, whom he disliked because of his questionable past; but the intelligence and cynical skill of this nephew of Colbert exceeded all bounds. He succeeded in the impossible task of finding liquid cash to end the war. For this purpose he went to French and foreign businessmen: Crozat, Fizeaux, Le Gendre, Samuel Bernard, and the Genevans Hogger, Huguetan, and Mallet. From them he borrowed at high interest rates, with everything guaranteed by the fundamental wealth of the kingdom. The nation's revenues would have been pledged for several years, if he had not decided to declare a partial bankruptcy once the war was over.

To all these difficulties was added one of those brutal famines that had struck the kingdom at irregular intervals for centuries. It was to be the last, but no one knew that. The "great winter" of 1709 froze most of the cereal grains and trees of France. Olive and walnut trees suffered notable damage. As a consequence there were catastrophically high prices, as much as quintuple those of normal years. These were coupled with epidemics and sudden increases in mortality. Fortunately these plagues were short. Spring cereal crops saved several provinces, and the following harvests were fortunately good. Yet misery was aggravated by the burden of the war and taxes, which were collected only with difficulty. In those years from 1708 to 1710, it looked as if France had reached the bottom of the barrel.

Even though he took great joy in seeing his grandson reconquer almost all of his Spanish kingdom beginning in early 1708, the king decided to negotiate at The Hague. He offered to abandon Dunkirk, Newfoundland, and even Strasbourg; he offered to expel the Stuart pretender, and above all to abandon his grandson Philip to his fate in Spain. But the Allies had the audacity to insist that Louis make war on Philip. The king's sense of honor forced him to refuse; much saddened, he broke off negotiations altogether.

Then hopeful signs appeared. At the end of 1709 in the battle of Malplaquet, a bloodbath and partial victory, the improvised and deprived French armies held in check Marlborough and Prince Eugene. Despite the French military weakness, they were still able to protect the frontiers of the kingdom. At Villaviciosa, Philip V, whom Vendôme was still helping, managed to secure Spain at the end of 1710. In September 1711, what remained of the French royal navy bombarded Rio de Janeiro, and brought back considerable and very useful booty. Finally, the unexpected late victory of Denain in July 1712 prevented Prince Eugene from attacking Paris, and accelerated the negotiations that England had begun in earnest.

Indeed, there had been changes in England. The Whig war party in Parliament and around Queen Anne gave way to a peace party led by Tory landlords, who thought that the conflict had cost too much and become useless. The Emperor was dead and had been succeeded by his son Charles, the self-proclaimed King Carlos III of Spain. Like other powers, the English did not want to see the same monarch ruling over Austria, the Empire, the Netherlands, part of Italy, Spain, and America. From this moment onward, the English and French had common interests. Preliminary discussions held in London at the end of 1711 prefigured the terms of the peace treaties, which were signed in 1713 at Utrecht and in 1714 at Rastatt–Baden.

Louis XIV had to grant formal recognition to the queen of England and her forthcoming Protestant Hanoverian successors, while accepting that Philip V would definitively renounce his rights to the throne of France. In turn his grandson was recognized as king of Spain and the "Castilian Indies" (America) by all Europe, but he had to cede his Italian territories and the southern Netherlands to the Emperor—the Austrian Hapsburg. Louis XIV lost several square miles of territory on the northern frontier of France. He had to agree to demolish the fortifications at Dunkirk, and to allow the Dutch to reoccupy the "barrier places" to keep himself under surveillance. But Louis recovered the valley of Barcelonnette and several Alpine towns from Piedmont. The treaty also marked the beginning of the sacrifices of distant lands that hardy pioneers had conquered for him: St. Kitts in the Antilles, the Hudson Bay region, Newfoundland, and above all Acadia, already settled by French colonists. In comparison with the terms that would have awaited him in a treaty in 1709–1710, this peace was almost a diplomatic success.

Yet the peace is much less imposing in view of the economic and shipping advantages obtained by the maritime powers. France abandoned all vestiges of Colbert's protectionism, renouncing the *asiento* and all privileges in Spanish America. The French allowed the English to obtain considerable benefits: besides the *asiento,* the slave trade, and that "licensed vessel" sent each year to trade along the American coasts. The greatest period of English power started exactly in 1713, and would be an obsession of the successors of Louis XIV.

THE WINTER OF THE
GREAT REIGN: 1713–1715

The king in his seventies maintained his majestic bearing and health despite thousands of purgations, bleedings, and emetics. The surgeons who had broken his jaw to remove several rotten teeth had not encroached upon his frightful bulimia, which pushed him to prefer spiced venison and enormous sherbets. Digestive problems and gout weakened him at times, but not until his last weeks of life did he fall victim to gangrene in his lower members, doubtless undermined by arteriosclerosis.

All around him, the enormous machinery of court continued its motions, its intrigues, and its apparent devotion, but its members distracted themselves at Paris or at the "follies," country houses dedicated to liberty and libertinage. The Regency began in hushed voices. The king often retired with Madame de Maintenon to live with his memories and a few old men like Grammont and Villeroy. For entertainment, he had comedies of Molière played, or listened to the chamber music he had always liked.

This sad gravity, which he rarely showed, came from the reverses suffered in the war and the devastation of his family by smallpox. His sons and grandsons died before him. At the end only one great-grandson remained alive, protected from doctors by the women who raised him. Amid these periods of sorrow and defeat, Louis XIV always forced himself to work hard. Three concerns obsessed him—the establishment of a final, lasting peace; uniformity of religion; and the succession of France.

His recent moderation had already produced the last treaties. Henceforth he thought of reaching a serious agreement with the Emperor, which would complement his uneasy understanding with his grandson in Spain. But he did not have the time to accomplish it.

On the religious question, his tardy devotion, nourished above all by the fear of hell for his past sins had provoked ultra-Catholic attitudes, according to Madame de Maintenon. Twenty years earlier, precise decrees had put parish priests in the hands of bishops, who could even imprison them. After the moderation of 1698, Louis suddenly decided to resume the anti-Protestant persecution by various measures, such as forbidding doctors to visit patients who would not present certificates of Catholic faith. This order was poorly observed in the provinces. While the king lay in agony, the first reformed synod of the century was meeting near Nîmes. Louis also responded rather badly to the renewed theological discussions inside the Catholic Church. Against the new Jansenism, which had become Gallican and Richerist (favoring the ordinary priests), he first ordered the destruction of the Abbey of Port-Royal-des-Champs, having it demolished stone by stone, including the church and the cemetery (1709–1712). Then Louis asked the papacy for help against these insurgents. It was ironic that Louis had to seek help from the same Roman curia he had treated with contempt twenty years earlier. The pope made the king wait, then proclaimed in 1713 the bull *Unigenitus,* drawing opposition from the archbishop of Paris, the Sorbonne, Parlement, more than a dozen bishops, and hundreds of priests and regular clergy. Furious, Louis XIV spoke about "walking on the belly" of such adversaries, and dreamed of calling a petty council, to whom he would declare his own religious law. These too were reveries he did not have time to realize.

Louis feared the inevitable Regency of his nephew the

duke of Orléans, whom he detested for his intelligence and freethinking. He opposed it with a terrible testament giving all power to his favorite bastard, the duke of Maine, a man of valor, whom he had the Parlement declare worthy of succeeding him. But two days after his death, Parlement annulled the will, as though it had a right to do so.

The monarch who completed his reign with these surprising actions died on September 1, 1715, after a brief and pious agony. Almost until the end, he imposed his mood on his entourage as well as on foreign ambassadors.

GREAT KING, GREAT REIGN

Historians have wept a great deal about France in 1715. The country was in rather sad financial condition, having spent in advance its income for the next two years. Nevertheless the Regency was able to put all in order within a decade. The situation was no more terrible than at the time of Richelieu, and less serious than at the time of Louis XVI. In all three cases, war was the principal cause of disorder.

Economic exhaustion was not evident. Granted, the years 1709–1710 were terrible, and a severe epidemic decimated livestock in 1714. But before as well as after the wars, many harvests were good and sold well. After some hard times, farmers and sharecroppers were able to recover in preparation for the bountiful decades of the eighteenth century. With the return of peace, manufacturing and port activity could also resume. In the maritime euphoria of the new century, the ports profited considerably from the slave trade and from sugar and cloth. The sugar islands of Martinique and Saint-Domingue quickly prospered, and serious colonial prospects appeared in India and Louisiana, if not in Canada.

The people of the provinces, for the moment quite calm, did not seem to appreciate the triumphant centralism, the intendants, the militia, and the new authoritarianism of priests who had studied in rigorous seminaries.

As for the elites, they had escaped the suffocating atmosphere of Versailles and the devout life, and were disporting themselves with Cartesianism, Anglomania, critical spirit, and criticism, as well as libertinage in all forms, even noble ones. Obviously, the French Enlightenment was breaking through the Great Century.

Was Louis XIV a great king? Did he have a great reign? It is not the historian's job to make such pronouncements. He must only state that neither the monarch nor the kingdom was the same in 1661, 1688, and 1715. Opinions about Louis XIV have varied a great deal from one century to another, from one group of minds to another, from one country to another. It is well known that Louis was detested in Germany and Holland, and that the English historical school, normally elegant and measured in its judgments, has not been kind to him. It is also significant that the royalists of the nineteenth century evoked his glorious image much less often than the popular image of "Good King Henry IV" or the sad memory of the "Martyr of January 21," poor Louis XVI.

Such as he was or as he is seen, Louis XIV belongs to the French national heritage, as much as Saint Louis, Louis XI, Henry III, Robespierre, or Napoleon.

Chapter Ten

THE AGE OF LOUIS XV: 1715–1774

The long reign of Louis XV, which lasted almost sixty years, has raised often contradictory and sometimes surprising interpretations. Little is known about the personality of the monarch, and consequently he has been seen through glasses of widely varying colors.

A political overview of the "century of Louis XV," as Voltaire and Pierre Gaxotte called it, could be divided into five acts. The first act, or Regency, was imposed by the age of the king, who was only five when he inherited the throne from his great-grandfather. From 1715 to 1723, the Regency was dominated by the duke of Orléans, whose bad reputation should be corrected; it was then followed by the interlude of the mediocre duke of Bourbon, from 1723 to 1726. The second act featured the old tutor of the king, Cardinal Fleury, a supple, authoritarian, and pacifically minded individual who was able to hold power from his seventy-third to his ninetieth year, 1726 to 1743. Next came the time of Madame de Pompadour, nicknamed "Her Petticoat Majesty" by Frederick the Great of Prussia. During her years of influence, 1743 to 1757, the royal mistress made ministers dance to her caprices, but she also shaped court life with her elegant refinement. Act four brought to the stage the likable and inconstant Choiseul, the first to sell the idea of an empire in the period from 1758 to 1770. The fifth and final act of this tragicomedy was the recovery of power by a monarch who finally decided to confound his proud opponents by relying upon two energetic and talented men, Maupeou and Terray. They began the reforms that could have saved the regime, if Louis XV had not been brutally struck down by smallpox.

This political bird's-eye view does not even mention the feeble longevity of most of the ministers: one named Silhouette passed into the language as a common noun. Such a survey also conceals essential developments: economic progress that was both uneven and pronounced, and the rise of powerful opposition elements—religious, philosophical, parlementary, and even aristocratic. These last elements were particularly dangerous because they involved powerful elites. Louis XV's regime had a visceral incapacity to reform itself financially, despite a dozen courageous initiatives. Finally, France enjoyed dazzling bursts of military glory, and even maritime successes; but these were ultimately spoiled by defeats, inconsistencies, and surrenders, which certainly provoked shameful feelings and strong reactions.

THE REGENCY

This Regency in no way resembled its predecessors, those of Anne of Austria and the two Medici queens. It remained "the Regency" par excellence, surrounded with a somewhat exaggerated reputation for licentiousness and financial speculation, but also for elegance and spirit. In fact the Regency was simply a reaction to the hard, sad, and warlike end of the preceding reign. As a first sign, the young king and court left Versailles for Paris, the great city that was once again full of life. The second sign was that Parlement immediately broke the will of Louis XIV, who had wanted to entrust all power to his bastard son the duke of Maine, the devout party, and the Jesuits. In return for this act of Parlement, the duke of Orléans, who had clearly become the master, gave back to the

Parlementaires their lost right of remonstrance. Henceforth they would use and abuse it until their extinction.

Nephew of the Great King, son of the vigorous and delightful Princess Palatine, the Regent had received almost every possible gift: beauty and a commanding appearance; military talents; extraordinary literary, artistic, and scientific culture; a knowledge of character, that great political art which consists of placing realities before doctrines. The Regent even had a taste for work, except in the evening. If he devoted a good third of his time to the pursuit of pleasure, this was neither novel nor rare: his father and his uncle had certainly not been models of virtue. Without modesty or delicacy, the Regent's roué friends and mistresses were content to bring into the light of day what had always been hidden in quiet discretion. And there were constellations of talent in this dissolute milieu: from the pastel artist Rosalba to the painter Antoine Watteau, who died too early in 1721 at the age of thirty-seven; from the sculptor Caffieri to the cabinetmaker Cresence; from the always spiritual Fontenelle to the young impertinent Voltaire, who wrote his first serious work, *La Henriade,* in 1723. The first masterpiece of Montesquieu, his *Persian Letters,* appeared as an unequaled model of the stylish pamphlet. The Regency was also the time of the philosophical salon of Madame de Lambert and of the first cafés.

Accompanying this emerging brilliant civilization were two unsuccessful innovations, one rather mediocre, the other premature but wonderfully clever.

The first initiative, inspired in part by Saint-Simon and the memory of Fénelon, may be summed up as the aristocratic recovery of power from the "vile bourgeoisie," the descendants of Colbert and Louvois. The princes of the blood and the high nobility were persuaded that the conduct of public affairs rightfully belonged to themselves, and that their high birth would take the place of competence. Thus the Regent dismissed men of the "old system," except for a few whom he knew to be useful. Eight councils of the highest aristocrats were created, but experienced and competent bureaucratic servants had to be included anyway. It is usual to mock this "polysynodie," which was dissolved in 1718; indeed, it did not always shine and the "Council of Conscience" unhappily relaunched the Jansenist quarrel. Another council, however, created the Corps of Bridges and Roads, which employed talented inspectors and engineers. The Council of Finances bravely tackled the terrible financial problem. It began without originality by announcing a partial bankruptcy, followed by a classic witch-hunt for corrupt financiers. The ritual Chamber of Justice in 1716–17 threatened several thousand of them and made several dozen regurgitate their wealth. But with some exceptions—Crozat and Bourvalais among them—the announced purge dwindled to the level of a public-relations exercise. The government could not condemn men it could not live without, men who often played an important part in its work. More promising was the project for a *taille proportionnelle,* a tax proportional to declared and verified incomes: it was conceived in 1717 and effectively tried out in several *bailliages.* But to apply and extend it widely would have taken years and much perseverance, just the quality that this government repeatedly showed it lacked.

The Regent then listened to John Law, whose ideas had previously seduced Desmarets, a genius who had been discarded too quickly. More than a hundred books have tried to describe the Scotsman, his financial system, and its collapse—but only the collapse is important.

At first it appeared normal that Paris should henceforth enjoy a strong bank for deposits, discounts, and foreign exchange. Amsterdam and London had such institutions, established in 1609 and 1694, respectively. More daring was the idea of multiplying the quantity and the velocity of money in circulation, in order to support rapid expansion of the internal economy, maritime trade, and colonies. At the same time there was an attempt to reduce if not suppress the quasi-monopoly of monetary gold and silver by substituting banknotes or shares. These paper instruments were guaranteed both by the revenues of the state and by the anticipated resources of the slave trade of India, the Antilles, and above all America. The promising territory of Louisiana had just been acquired from Crozat,

238

and the city of New Orleans founded. The example of Holland and England, both great trading nations with merchant shipping and rich colonies, suggested that the time was ripe for this idea. Both the Regent and Desmarets well understood that Law's proposal lacked neither foundation nor subtlety. It was not well adapted to a large nation with an enormous landed fortune—locked in place, with traditional values, firmly attached to the heavy security of precious metals. Thus the idea came from abroad, and above all it came prematurely. Moreover, this "system" was even less suited to a powerful and related group of high aristocrats, financiers, great officers of finances, and even ministers who had become rich and specialized in speculation by means of tax collecting, supplying the armies, and lending to the king. Striking at hard money was a threat to their fortunes and their power. From the beginning they were hostile to Law, and ultimately they overthrew him.

In fact, the first notes of the private General Bank and the first shares of the Western Company for America were well received. Then the issue of shares in both institutions accelerated, while dividends were slight. Law had to keep money moving constantly, absorbing companies for the slave and Oriental trade. Finally he took over the entire tax-farming system and the title of controller general (1719—early 1720). This was too much for financiers such as the Pâris brothers and their allies, the princes of the blood Conti and Bourbon. In the middle of frantic speculation, these last two aristocrats moved in for the kill. They gave the signal for a general attack on Law when they withdrew carriageloads of gold from the now royal bank in exchange for paper that became *ipso facto* worthless. Everything collapsed quickly. Large and small fortunes suffered and sometimes disappeared; others were simply stolen away.

Much has been written about the consequences of Law's system, too often drawing on pamphlets and passionate testimonies. Several facts, however, are clear.

The obligatory rate of exchange for banknotes, even when devalued, allowed many debtors to purge themselves easily of old debts. They could refinance at lower rates loans made at 5 or 6 percent, or reduce the interest on them. This was not a good time for creditors, but many debtors were thus able to extricate themselves from financial straits. Besides, even though 90 percent of the people of France did not suffer in the slightest from the collapse, they had long been disgusted with paper money, with money made from paper, and even with the nonconvertible banknote. The lesson of this adventure was confirmed by the revolutionary *assignat,* and the popular attitude persisted until 1914. Consequently, as can be verified millions of times, hereafter no transaction whatsoever, not even a small lease, could be concluded except "by good coins of gold and silver, no matter what the prince decrees"; this last surprising formula died hard.

Another observation of the best informed contemporaries has been largely confirmed: the "system" with its great agitation of money and ideas cracked the whip over the French economy. It gave particular stimulus to the great commerce in slaves and sugar with the Antilles. Not only did Nantes and Bordeaux, the slave-trading cities, become rich, but also Marseille and Lorient, which had been renovated by the Indies Company. Law's system also encouraged the refining industry, shipbuilding and fitting (sails, ropes, masts, keels, rivets, anchors, and cannons), and the overseas sale of luxury goods from city and countryside—everything from Aquitaine wheat to Laval cloth and "articles of Paris."

A more far-reaching consequence of Law's system was the stabilization of the *livre tournois* in May 1726. After a series of skillful manipulations, this stability lasted for almost two centuries. Even during the Revolution, following the disorder of the *assignats,* the *franc de germinal* gloriously reclaimed the same definition: 4.45 grams of silver of 90 percent purity. This stability cut across all regimes and was continued in the *franc-or,* which disappeared only during the First World War. This accomplishment, however, was the work of those who governed after Law's flight in 1720 and the death of the Regent at barely fifty years old in 1723. The destroyers of the system were the duke of Bourbon, his mistress the marquise de Prie (daughter of the financier Berthelot), and the military supplier Pâris-Duverney and his brothers. While awaiting the appearance of Fleury and the marquise de Pompadour, both of whom were children of financiers, we should note that the "century of enlightenment" was just as much the "century of finance," and that these two were by no means incompatible.

After the tempests of Law's system, whether power was held by Bourbon, Fleury, or their successors, the so-called absolute monarchy faced the same acutely painful problems. Rather than recount their evolution in detail, it would be better to take an overview and present these problems one by one, just as they overlapped in reality before bursting out all at once in the time of the unfortunate Louis XVI.

The Royal Problem

It is well known that the sacred character of royalty was not discussed, except by a few harebrained crackpots. Popular confidence and affection spontaneously flowed upward toward the king: he was the supreme judge and the last resort. It could happen that bad counselors would mislead him, and that financiers, bloodsuckers of the people, would steal from him; but he knew how to unmask and punish them. He was simultaneously the representative of God, the state, and the nation. Since the *patrie* then constituted only territory, his subjects often limited their loyalties to the areas they knew personally. For the reigning king, the crucial point was not to waste this capital. Louis XV did not seem to grasp this point.

Less well known than his ancestors, Louis XV has been distorted by the adverse passions of contemporaries and historians. In his youth he presented the image of beauty and elegance. His pronounced penchant for women, easily explained by heredity and environment, was only later found shocking because of his less than honorable choices and the savage popular songs composed about him. With the exception of Henry IV, he was probably the most intelligent of the Bourbons and surely the most cultured. Spoiled by soft and flattering education and by the overbearing affection of Fleury,

241

he did not feel obligated to perform the assiduous daily work to which his predecessor had been devoted. Louis XV applied himself only by fits and starts. No doubt he also nourished a likable skepticism, as well as a certain taste for secret diplomacy, in which his personal agents sometimes opposed his own ambassadors. He also experienced long periods of what we would now call depression, during which his spirits flagged. In contrast to his resignation and fits of silence, however, he did have occasional awakenings of pride, majesty, and energy. Nevertheless, he could not disguise a deeper nature, often darkened by mysterious forces. Note his reaction when his father-in-law, the king of Poland, was dastardly attacked in 1733; or his run to Metz ten years later to face the threat of Austrian invasion, only to fall ill and thereby stir up the prayers of his people. They named him Louis the Well Beloved. We can also hear him crush the pride of the Parisian Parlementaires in 1766 in the purest Louis XIV style: "It is in my person alone that sovereign power resides. . . .To me alone belongs the legislative power, independent and undivided. . . .The entire public order emanates from me. . . . The rights and interests of the nation whom you dare to make a separate body from the monarch rest only in my hands."

Five years later, he fully supported the energetic and unpopular ministers, Maupeou and Terray, who took in hand the reform of the regime and might have saved it if the king had not died and if his successor had not dismissed them.

And yet, this royal mastery and lucidity flowered but rarely. The reasons may lie in resignation, fatigue, and a habit Louis XV acquired early of allowing himself to be governed by mentors—Orléans, Bourbon, Fleury—or mistresses, from the four daughters of the marquis de Nesles to the great Pompadour drawn from the world of finance and the Dubarry of low gallantry, who encouraged the satyriasis of his old age. All this may explain the rage of the pamphleteers and his final extreme unpopularity, even though the good people of France had only wanted to adore this very handsome and generous monarch.

Louis XV was indeed very slow to take account of the rise of opposition, occupied as he was by the games and gambles of diplomacy and war, not to mention those of the court. Meanwhile his country was moved by an economic expansion that it had not known for a long time, and certainly not in the emerging new forms.

BRILLIANT BUT UNEVEN GROWTH

Demographic Growth

In 1708, Vauban estimated the population of the kingdom at slightly more than 19 million. Though not uniformly accepted, this figure has served as a basis for discussion for more than two centuries and has inspired the digressions of dozens of historians and demographers. Three points are clear: first, no one knows the exact figure; second, Vauban's total seems too low, perhaps by about two million; and third, whatever other statements are made, France certainly was the most populous country in Europe. Spain and England had only a third as many people, and ultra-rich Holland only a tenth of the French total. Countries like Germany and Italy, which were not yet unified, were only simple geographic expressions; others like Russia were just beginning to emerge from the shadows.

Around 1772, Abbé Terray began serious continuing work on demographic statistics. As a result, we can now see that the kingdom of France, increased by a sizable portion of Lorraine (the three bishoprics added in the sixteenth century) and Corsica, could then count 26 million inhabitants, slightly more in 1789. That would indicate a growth of about one-third in the course of a century. This increase was less than that of the sixteenth century, and also less than those of other European countries. From this time onward, the Austrian and Russian empires, though less unified, probably surpassed France.

This healthy growth can be explained in simple ways. The plague had disappeared, except for a brutal attack at Marseille and its environs in 1720, when perhaps fifty thousand people died. Eighteenth-century wars always took place outside the kingdom, except for a few border areas; and the better disciplined regiments no longer lived off the land. Also, the most serious harvest failures and famines had disappeared after 1710, leaving only very local or minor shortages around 1740 and again around 1770, as well as painful and long-lasting memories of hardships. Finally, the practice of systematic birth control made timid and sluggish appearances in only a few areas, around Paris and perhaps in the southwest.

The whole of the kingdom benefited unevenly from this expansion, which primarily affected the north, the east, the south, the big cities, and the large ports. Meanwhile Brittany, the center, and mountainous regions stagnated or even drifted further backwards.

With some exceptions, this surplus of people to feed and employ did not then constitute a serious problem, because economic growth accompanied, explained, or provoked demographic growth.

Overall Economic Growth

Toward the end of the seventeenth century the first statisticians appeared. They did not have the technical skill of our contemporaries, but sometimes their common sense made up for it. The statisticians of the eighteenth century went even further and with more confidence: they were even found in ministerial offices. At last, carefully kept archives could supply rather trustworthy figures, especially on commerce. We will give only a few examples of elementary but reliable rates of growth.

The value of French foreign trade, which was amply profitable almost every year, tripled from 1726 to 1774, the year of the king's death, this in a period of stable currency. Of course the so-called colonial goods, in part reexported, played a large role in this triumphant increase, but they were more inspirational than decisive.

The trade in well-defined products such as Languedoc cloth, exported from Marseille to the Middle East, rose from about 30,000 pieces per year at the beginning of the reign to nearly 100,000 at the end. Trade at the great regional and international fairs of Guibray in Normandy and Beaucaire in

Provence also tripled. Despite its bad reputation for smoke and dirt, coal was finally put to use in France a century later than in England. Shipments from the region around Saint-Étienne to Paris increased from 3,000 to 4,000 metric tons annually around 1715, to 15,000 in 1774, and to 20,000 a bit later. In the north, great lords such as the duke of Croy founded the Anzin Company. Meanwhile production also increased at the furnaces and forges of Champagne, Lorraine, Nivernais, Berry, Isère, and elsewhere; the names of the great producers—Wendel, Dietrich, and Schneider—were beginning to emerge.

In the textile industry older cloth manufacturing centers experienced slow growth, but the linen manufacturers from Cambrai, Rouen, Lavel, and Voiron tripled their output in half a century. They were soon joined by the "Indian" fabrics— dyed cottons, whose manufacture was finally authorized in 1759. By that date the English "mechanics" John Kay and Holker had arrived and speeded up the production.

Let us take a rest from statistics and examples: this impressive industrial and commercial progress, which followed close on the heels of the English, was unprecedented. It did not attain the dimensions of a true industrial revolution, but it may have been the take-off stage, or at least the preparation for it.

It goes without saying that all these changes meant more work for many more laborers, especially in rural areas. They were the principal ones who made the cloth and worked seasonally at the ovens, forges, mines, and cutting rooms. They also transported the goods. In the cities, there were at times hundreds who worked together in great factories, notably in textile-manufacturing.

In other sectors of the economy, the atmosphere of prosperity was not always so clearly apparent.

Progress and Contrast in the Rural Areas

Rural life as a whole, except for trifling late examples, in no way resembled what the physiocrats and most amateur salon-farmers have reported. In general these writers were content, after 1750, to translate the works of English agronomists. But the English themselves observed the Dutch and Flemings who had accomplished their agricultural revolution almost two centuries before. The elements of this revolution included cultivation of fallow land, abundant use of selected fertilizers, legume crops, artificial forage, and carefully selected varieties. In the greater part of France, however, the rural world passed through a slow evolution. This explains why serious food shortages rarely occurred and also why the standard of living rose markedly. The development of household furniture and especially feminine wardrobes testifies to this point.

In the fortunate areas of the north, the east, the Parisian basin, suburban zones, and all wine-producing regions, we can note a slow but sure increase in the prices of commodities, farm leases, and the value of land itself. Vineyards and meadows in particular rose in value, woods even more so. These increases can be interpreted as further signs of prosperity, interrupted only by rare accidents. It is equally certain that essential grains, the principal source of food, were better planted, better preserved, better milled, and better baked. Good wheat took its place at the top of the list, causing a decline in the popularity of brown and black breads. Some virgin lands were slowly cleared, and fallow lands were planted with legumes—beans, peas, clover, alfalfa. Alert peasants knew their virtues. Vineyards were expanded and produced more—soon too much. A certain specialization was instituted. The higher nobility, judiciary, and clergy were exploiting the best lands by using two new techniques: late harvests and carefully selected grapes. The wines they produced—distinguished old Hermitage and solid burgundies, especially from Beaune—were particularly appreciated in Paris, along with newly fashionable champagne. Farther west, Bordeaux and Cahors wines were still shipped to England and the Netherlands. The same Dutch ships, omnipresent in French rivers, carried Loire wines and liqueurs from Charente and Armagnac. The newly cultivated vineyards of Beaujolais, following the example of those of Lyon, were producing wine for Parisian cabarets. Nevertheless, the largest wine region of them all remained "France"—the area along the banks of the Seine from Champagne to Normandy. This area annually produced 3 to 5 million hectolitres of *gros rouge*. During the eighteenth century this wine became darker and more abundant, flowing freely not only in the north but also in all the small suburban taverns from Belleville to La Courtille to Passy. Thousands of vine growers were thus able to live decently in their tile-roofed two-story houses. Their wives and daughters often amassed sprightly wardrobes.

This slow increase in the comforts of life in part of the rural world can also be measured by changes in household decor, with the appearance of the cupboard, china, silverware, a copper sink, even a mirror. We can also observe prosperity in the increasing yield of indirect taxes, despite occasional strong resistance. Salt sales by the *gabelle* administration increased by more than 60 percent, double the growth of population. Tax collection in general was slow and acrimonious, but much less difficult than in the preceding century.

All the same we should not carry this impression of growing prosperity too far. Some historians deny it entirely, though they have no decisive proof. On the one hand, there were still bad years of spoiled grain and wine harvests, combined with animal and human illnesses. Serious epidemics of influenza, typhoid, and diphtheria continued. On the other hand, whole sections of the kingdom seemed to crawl along or even regress. This was true of the Massif Central, where both population and economy stagnated. In these areas, skilled workmen such as masons, stonecutters, and sawyers left and did not always come back. Other mountainous areas where metallurgy (Allevard) or paper-making did not flourish often exported their younger sons to distant places such as Holland. Population only rose when the "Mexicans" from Barcelonnetta came after 1820. Eighteenth-century Brittany lost population for several reasons: the ruin of the great cloth-making industry after 1680, the decay of numerous minor ports caused by the rise of great ports, and above all the terrible epidemics against which the population was helpless. The Loire Valley seemed sleepy, too, because no new activity of any type kept going for long. The comfortable lives of seigneurs and *rentiers,* gardeners and vine-growers did not push them to make changes they thought useless.

Finally we should emphasize that the rural world as a whole benefited unevenly from the prosperity of Louis XV. Large farmers and wealthier tenants became richer. This became clear when the properties of the Church were sold during the Revolution. *Rentier* owners of the land, nobles, clerics, and bourgeois did even better. Vine-growers and gardeners did well, too, though their prosperity did not last. On the other hand, the poor devils who had barely assured themselves of daily bread received the crumbs of the expansion, and often only because they worked harder. They began to feel the distance between their condition and that of the favored ones. More than fifty years ago the economic historian Ernest Labrousse summed up the situation in three striking figures. Prices in general rose 56 percent in three-quarters of a century; landed income rose nearly 100 percent; but wages rose only 25 percent to 33 percent. Of course, wages were not very significant in an age when many people were self-sufficient and lived outside the market economy. Be that as it may, this century was never so lamentable and tragic as the seventeenth century and its predecessors.

French economic growth during the eighteenth century was encouraged or permitted by a changing but talented administration.

AN ADMINISTRATION
OF HIGH QUALITY

Launched by Colbert, Louvois, and the Pontchartrains, the administration of Louis XIV was both elementary and heavy-handed. After the episode of the *polysynodie,* it reached cruising speed. The historian who uses archives can experience the triple pleasure of reading clear and elegant language that joins precision and extreme courtesy to stern injunctions, all written on everlasting papers scratched by skillful and often artistic pens. Each province was provided with an intendant, who often came from the fishpond of Parisian masters of requests and councillors. These men were the high nobility of the robe, descendants of old royal servants who had regularly been ennobled for ages. Each intendant was supported by a military governor, a great noble of the sword who frequently enjoyed military and political powers beyond the normal apparatus of administration. He was aided by the casual functioning of provincial offices and by the once numerous subdelegates who were often well chosen from the local notables. At the same time the intendant supervised the remaining provincial estates, the Parlements, the bishops (discreetly), the cities, the officials, the food supply, and public order. If the intendant also thought of making a career by a brilliant return to Paris, he often became a man of his province, identified with local interests. The intendants were well known, and most were quite admirable in their qualities of spirit and character. Above all they were renowned for their culture, which their latter-day successors seldom attained.

As for the central government, now based in Paris as much as in Versailles, new traits shone through old structures. Since the king was not always disposed to attend council, the ministers met in committees. These ministers were frequently nobles of ancient lineage, or those who had been ennobled long ago, like the bishops. The essential part of their task no longer concerned justice, but henceforth finances, as shown by the thousands of *arrêts du Conseil* issued each year. After Fleury's death there was no prime minister, even though Choiseul might be considered such. The ministers were responsible for the work of their own departments. Even more striking is the extension of ministers' activity in the national economy.

One example: the Administration of Bridges and Roads, created during the Regency, reached its full development only after 1730. It reached a high level of distinction under the Trudaines, father and son (1743–1777), and Perront. These three founded the first *grande école* of bridge-building in 1747. They used the institution of the royal *corvée* on the great roads in 1738 to force poor peasants (others were exempt) to build that remarkable network of roads so admired even by the English. Their passion for straight lines and infrequent payment for expropriated land raised many protests. Rural people objected to being taken away from their usual occupations, especially during the summer. This gigantic and worthy program was incomplete in 1789. Succeeding regimes would have to finish the work.

Bertin, friend of the physiocrats, was inspired by the fashion for "new" agriculture to enact legislation full of good intentions. Societies of agriculture were sponsored almost everywhere, and some of them were not content to remain debating clubs. The useful veterinary schools of Lyon and Alfort were founded. Attempts were made to "liberate" the grain trade, which involved charging higher prices and thus elicited applause as well as protests. Once again serious attempts were made to regulate the persistent problems of enclosure, the division of communal rights, and the uses of woodlands. In several provinces changes were tried, but they were often favorable to the lords and the richer peasants. The mass of the rural population disliked them, and made its views known.

This benevolent administration legislated in other areas as well, often with happy results. It passed the law nationalizing mineral rights in 1744; it created military schools, at Paris in 1751 and later in the provinces, then schools for military engineers and artillery experts, and many others. The regime's repeatedly stated good intentions failed, however, when it came to essential reforms in the tax system, the hydra of the century.

The Impossibility of Fiscal Reform

The habitual indebtedness of the French monarchy undoubtedly came from its heavy spending. Above all military spending regularly absorbed half of the available sums in peacetime and even more in war. But indebtedness was also due to a surprising fiscal and financial system, which was beginning to be understood. Of course the monarchy lived on taxes, but also on daily cash borrowing and cash advances against future receipts. These loans were granted to the state by the richest members of society. The lenders included the aristocracy in general, above all nobles of the sword, but also the Church, nobles of the robe, and ennobled financiers. The famous *fermiers généraux* served as well-paid intermediaries and occasionally as scapegoats. These agreeable lenders never took less than 10 percent interest, plus costs and "thefts" on rare occasions. Naturally they were able to escape the taxes paid by common mortals. When we reflect upon their situation, we can find a certain logic to it—why pay taxes to yourself?—but this opportunity was not within everyone's grasp.

The various ministers who had succeeded each other since the end of the seventeenth century nevertheless tried, in the face of absolute necessity, to make various privileged people pay up. These favored ones included royal officials, many bourgeois, cities, and even entire provinces such as Brittany, which paid no salt tax. The ministers cherished the hope of establishing some kind of tax on wealth or income, based on declarations and subject to official verification, a tax that everyone would pay. On several occasions under Colbert's administration, they planned and even began making a tax register for the whole kingdom. Indeed, they were only following the established precedent of neighboring states such as Savoy, where even today copies of the "old map" can be found.

We have seen that the process began with the capitation of 1695, levied for the duration of the war. It was renewed with the first *dixième* in 1710, a tax that was closer to the ideas of Vauban. The decree that ordered it specified that "all nobles and commoners, privileged and not privileged" had two weeks to declare all their revenues from "lands, woods, meadows, vineyards ... tithes, dues, seigneurial rights ... and interest income of all kinds." They would have to pay one-tenth of their annual income to the king. But His Majesty soon declared that the clergy were exempt from this new tax. Of course, this declaration was followed by delays, failures to act, protests, reductions, and subscriptions. Yet the *dixième* still brought in many millions, though it provided less than 10 percent of the estimated revenues. Suppressed by the regent, the *dixième* was reestablished in 1733 during another war, and again in 1741 for the same reason, on almost the same terms, and with the same results. In the interval the government tried in 1725 a *cinquantième* tax of one-fiftieth (2%) of income. It produced meager results, however, and was abolished in 1727. After several years of excellent administration under Controller General Orry, who even produced in 1738 the only balanced budget of the century, Machault tried in 1749 to institute a *vingtième* tax of one-twentieth (5%) of income from all properties, notably including those of the Church, and that with the firm support of the king. Naturally, the Assembly of the Clergy in 1750 thundered against this sacrilege, and Parlements and provincial estates reacted vehemently. The king, who had confidence in Machault and was going through one of his good periods, resisted for a moment. Then, as usual, he gave dispensations, reductions, or generous subscriptions to the Church, nobles, and other privileged groups. This tax produced a good yield because it was better established and better collected than others, particularly from commoners who did not enjoy privileges. Later it was reenacted, then increased by a second *vingtième* and momentarily by a third: they both resembled the first, even using the same declarations.

We understand what was at stake. To attack privileged groups was to call into question the foundations, even the nature, of society. No doubt egoism and self-interest played roles in the ferocious and almost always victorious resistance of the complex ensemble of privileged groups. More particularly, clergy and nobility felt dishonor at the very idea that they should be obliged to pay the same tax as any common layman. Indeed it is true that nobles in the Midi were not dishonored by paying the *taille* on their non-noble lands, and the clergy agreed to pay the king a "free gift." The proper role of the nobles, however, was to serve the king with arms and counsel—that is, office. The clergy served him by their prayers.

Facing this same problem, aggravated by a gigantic war debt, the government of Louis XVI ran into the same obstacles. By then they had become even greater, and its policy of trying almost the same remedies was condemned to failure. Changing the basis of taxation would have effectively started a revolution. At times the monarchy felt that such a move was necessary, but it never really decided to accept responsibility. Thus, even though the regime pretended to be absolute, it struck hard resistance.

THE RISE OF OPPOSITION

The philosophy of the Enlightenment has generally been given a prominent place in the history of opposition to the regime. Its smiling or scathing criticism supported demands for more or less radical reforms. Above all the *philosophes* attacked intolerance, obscurantism, and unenlightened absolutism. In the time of Louis XV, however, this opposition was limited to literary discussions and salon life, and was rarely dangerous. Many of its supporters were close to the government or belonged to it, such as the official censor Malesherbes, protector of the *Encyclopédie,* and the physiocrat Bertin. In any event, we shall rediscover the philosophical critics during the reign of Louis XVI, when they were bolder and better organized.

Much noisier and apparently more dangerous were "our lords of the Parlement" of Paris. Louis XIV had reduced them to silence, and to a servility in which many of their members acquiesced. Besides their judicial role, the Parlementaires recorded royal ordinances on their registers in order to publish them, but they claimed the right to make "remonstrances." In principle these were judicial remarks; in practice they were quickly extended to political responses. The regent, who needed the help of Parlement to break the will of Louis XIV, granted the Parisian Parlement and its twelve provincial counterparts this right of remonstrances. Henceforth they used and abused it. An adult King Louis XIV would have promptly silenced them, but except for brief episodes, none of his successors dared to do so.

The first conflict between king and Parlement arose in 1718. The traditional form lasted until the end of the old regime. When they received the text of a law that displeased them, "the court" presented their remonstrances and refused to register it. In order to force them to give way legally, the king came in person to a session of *lit de justice,* surrounded by all of the peers, princes of the blood, and the chancellor. On the following day, Parlement presented "iterative remonstrances"; the king replied with *letters de jussion* to compel their obedience. If the conflict persisted, there could be a judicial strike and a royally ordered exile of the Parlement. In 1720 they were sent to Pontoise, where the judges became very bored. The affair ended with negotiations and compromises.

This power of the "great robes" can no doubt be explained by the weakness of several kings. Also, every law had to be registered in each particular parlementary jurisdiction in the provinces as well as in Paris in order to be published, disseminated, and applied. The decorum, wealth, clientage, and popularity of the Parlementaires themselves played a role, too. In the last analysis, the Parlementaires knew how to participate in passionate ideological movements that echoed the public opinion of the time. Interested parties included the educated elite, even parish priests, and a significant number of the craftsmen and shopkeepers of the big cities. Some controversies took on a religious character, as when the Parlements and the public regularly supported the cause of the rigorous Jansenists and Gallicans. In part, the judges were jealous of the Jesuits and strongly hostile toward them. In 1762–1764, "all the assembled chambers" of the Parlement of Paris practically provoked the expulsion of the Jesuits from France. The second weapon of the Parlements lay in their quasi-systematic rejection of any new taxation. In this cause they put forward the "public good" and the need to spare the miserable people, whose protectors and champions they claimed to be. Indeed, the people often believed them. In reality, the "great robes" thought above all of preserving their own exemptions and privileges. Then the Parlements began to assert that they collectively constituted only the regional representatives of one illustrious body, the true royal council established in the time of Clovis. Moved by collective pride, all of them conducted a concerted revolt against royal authority in the 1760s, in Paris, Rouen, Rennes, Pau, and elsewhere. All proclaimed that the king could not govern without them. They even dared to present the first demands for meetings of now-forgotten former provincial estates such as those of Rouen in 1760, or even Estates General, as at Paris in 1763.

Then, after long forbearance, the king decided in 1771 on a master stroke, known as the "coup d'état of Maupeou." First the vast jurisdiction of the Parlement of Paris was divided into six areas, each containing "Conseils supérieurs" with new magistrates who were paid by the state, thus civil servants instead of officeholders. Furthermore, they would render justice without charge. This reform was extended to the provinces, suppressing venality and hereditary office as well as gratuities to the judges. Voltaire had already struck against *Parlementaire* intolerance in the Calas affair, when a Protestant was unjustly convicted of killing his son, supposedly for converting to Catholicism. Thus Voltaire applauded the king's actions. Beaumarchais took the opposite position, as did public opinion, or what passed for it. It so happened, however, that after a difficult beginning the system functioned well. At the same time the Abbé Terray boldly reorganized royal finances, revived Machault's project for a tax on wealth, started the comprehensive tax register, and created the first official statistical bureau. This courageous and unpopular return to strong government collapsed with the death of the king. For fear of hostile demonstrations, Louis XV was buried quietly in May 1774. Despite his final misunderstood and unfinished efforts, he left a dissatisfied kingdom, notably because of the foreign policy he had pursued or allowed his government to pursue.

FOREIGN POLICY:
FROM GLORY TO RETREAT

After the hard-won treaties of 1713–1714, France found a new situation in Europe and the world.

On the continent, the Austrian Hapsburgs, the traditional enemies of France, had succeeded over thirty years in reconquering all of Hungary, Serbia, and Wallachia from the Turks. Since the Hapsburgs also held Bohemia and the Imperial Crown, they constituted the great power of central Europe. After the fall of the brilliant and ephemeral Charles XII of Sweden, who died in 1718, two new stars appeared on the horizon. Following discreet and systematic ascension, the Hohenzollerns of Brandenburg had become kings of Prussia in 1701. They carved out for themselves a discontinuous kingdom from the Russian frontier to the Rhine, and created a powerful and well-trained army, supported strongly by an efficient tax system. The young Frederick the Great became king of Prussia in 1740 and immediately used these advantages. Frederick was curiously popular in France thanks to his reputation as an enlightened ruler and his military victories. Frederick also benefited from the French ritual hatred of Austria.

Farther east, in Muscovy, Tsar Peter the Great had feverishly begun the work of modernization. He opened Russia to the sea by constructing St. Petersburg and seizing Azov, and he helped to crush the Swedes under Charles XII. After some difficult reigns two of his successors, Elisabeth (1741–1762) and above all Catherine the Great (1762–1796), made a powerful country out of their immense empire. Russia soon rose to claim a secondary place in Europe.

At sea and in the distant colonies, where the kings of France had shown only occasional interest, it quickly became apparent that the prime adversary was England. In its wake sailed Holland, still rich from its overseas trade and commerce with the Indies, and Portugal, still in control of Brazil. After several minor disputes, a tacit agreement known as the "family pact," was instituted between the Bourbons of Paris and the Bourbons of Madrid, who were still drawing on their American riches and being eyed covetously. In addition to their different religions and political systems, France and Britain were opposed in other things as well: their navy, their foreign commerce, their trading posts nearly everywhere, the Antilles, and their penetration into India and North America. More significantly, the English government and elite consisted of nobles and bourgeoisie intelligently blended together. They clearly understood the problem of world power and were ready to do anything to solve it. In France, where continental Europe dominated official thinking, the problem was seldom understood.

In the Western Hemisphere England occupied all the vacant Antilles and sent its religious dissidents to colonize the North American continent from north of Boston to the borders of Spanish Florida. These colonists quickly numbered more than a million. During the same period Colbert and other French administrators forbade the departure of the Protestants from France. Lacking the attraction of El Dorado, the French gave only meager support to New France and occupied themselves more with the Caribbean trade in slaves, sugar, and coffee than with Canadian furs. They were still interested in the trading stations of the Ottoman Middle East or the silk works and Indian cloth-making of Asia, centered in Pondichéry and the islands of Réunion and Mauritius. But this was more the fruit of happy improvisation than of great ideas. Nevertheless, sixty to eighty thousand French pioneers settled in or traveled to the Saint Lawrence River and New Orleans, passing through the Great Lakes, the Ohio and Mississippi rivers, virtually encircling the thirteen British colonies. In India, bold traders such as Dupleix set out from the trading posts of the French Company and approached those of the English. They advanced into the subcontinent by skill and diplomacy, and for a time controlled a Deccan territory twice the size of France. But French administrators found all this very expensive, and French diplomats had eyes only for the Netherlands, the Rhine, or Italy.

Until 1740, the agreements with Walpole's England and

Bourbon Spain prevented serious conflicts, especially as Prussia and Russia did not yet count for very much on the European scene. France played the role of arbitrator, first among the northern countries that had defeated Sweden in 1721, then among the Austrians, Savoyards, and Spaniards who were fighting over bits of Italy. The result was that the Austrians momentarily occupied Parma and Tuscany, Savoy expanded in size by taking over Sardinia, and cadet members of the Spanish Bourbon family became kings of the two Sicilies. There was still more French arbitration in 1739, when Turkey responded to new attacks by recapturing and keeping Belgrade and Serbia. At the same time the economic privileges so favorable to the trade of Marseille were renewed.

In the meantime Louis XV had sent troops to Danzig to save his father-in-law Stanislas Leszczynski, who had been dethroned by an Austro-Russian coalition. He then made war in Italy against the Austrians, carefully avoiding the Netherlands so as not to displease the English. In this conflict the aged Villars achieved his last victories. Long negotiations then resulted in the Treaty of Vienna giving King Stanislas the duchy of Lorraine and the county of Bar, which would revert to France on his death in 1766, usefully completing the northeastern frontier.

After 1740 everything changed. War continued practically without interruption for twenty-two years. Furthermore, by the will of the English, the war was expanded from Europe across the oceans to America and Asia. In 1739, England attacked Spain, the weakest nation, which nonetheless was roused to action against illegal English trade in the Americas. Cardinal Fleury resigned himself to sending two French squadrons to support the Spaniards. Three years later war was openly declared, but the English fleet, three or four times as great as the French, frequently carried the day, capturing the port of Louisbourg in Canada in 1745. On the other hand, Dupleix and La Bourdonnais took Madras, the principal British trading post in India. These distant exploits were overshadowed by the great continental affair of the Austrian Succession (1740–1748). This war began when almost everyone fiercely attacked Maria

Theresa, the designated heiress of her father, Emperor Charles VI. Frederick the Great of Prussia pounced on Silesia and held it. The French marched on upper Austria and, disdaining Vienna, occupied Prague and Bohemia in 1741. The following year, the young queen was able to negotiate with Frederick and obtain the support of the Hungarians, the Saxons, the English, the Savoyards, and the Dutch. The French army was forced to beat a hasty retreat, and the Austrians threatened Alsace. The king and Maurice of Saxony straightened out the situation. After the illustrious victory of Fontenoy in 1745 and several others, the entire Austrian Netherlands and a portion of Holland were solidly under French control. In Italy the French released Milan, but Savoy was firmly occupied. These were considerable spoils, and there was astonishment in Europe and even France itself when Louis XV and his ministers, tired of the war, gave up all their conquests in the Treaty of Aix-la-Chapelle in 1748. This was the pleasant time of the marquise de Pompadour, when court life had an ephemeral, floating quality.

The Seven Years' War, in which France was allied with Austria against Prussia and England, was filled with disasters. In 1755, during peacetime, Boscawen's squadron captured three ships that were carrying supplies to Canada. Several days later, some three hundred French vessels were captured on the open seas and in English ports—a harsh beginning. After successes in Hanover (a possession of the English King George II) and the capture of Minorca, the French army commanded by the incompetent Soubise was crushed at Rossbach in 1757. The national shame was curiously corrected by admiration for the victors, Frederick the Great and his model army.

During this time, the French in America fought as well as they could without support. They held out against enemies three or four times as numerous who were regularly reinforced and resupplied by the British fleet sent out by William Pitt. The war was settled by the sad death of Montcalm, defeated by Wolfe, who also died before the walls of Quebec in 1759; later Montreal and several other forts were lost to the British. In any event, it was unreasonable to expect fewer than

80,000 French colonists to hold out against a million and a half "Americans."

In India, the French Company thought only of short-term profits and recalled Dupleix in 1754. They forced his successor to negotiate with the English East India Company and renounced their protectorate over the Deccan states. After several successes, the last French troops—700 men—were trapped in Pondichéry and besieged by 20,000 English and their ships. The French surrendered in 1761. Curiously, their commander Lally-Tollendal was decapitated on his return to France.

The Treaty of Paris signed in February 1763 signaled the loss of all French possessions in North America. Even the bit of Louisiana left by the English was given to the Spanish allies, who had lost Florida. There were other French losses as well: several Antilles, including Dominica; all of Sénégal except for the small island of Gorée; all of India except for the five dismantled trading posts. In Europe also the war had been fought hard with little result, though Frederick the Great did keep his cherished Silesia.

From a distance of two centuries, it is easy to condemn the government of Louis XV, and the people of Quebec still do so. But it would be more worthwhile to try to understand the ministers and their choices. The men of that age had simply followed the policies of Louis XIV, oriented toward dominating the continent of Europe against the traditional Hapsburg enemy. They used the same type of army reinforced by militia and somewhat improved equipment. Only their commanders were mediocre or worse, with the exception of Maurice of Saxony. As for the East Indian coast and the "Islands" of the West Indies, the French had above all sought profit: cheap goods that could be sold easily at high prices. From a mercantilist point of view, the withdrawal from India may appear surprising, though it was so far away. But this was not the case with the "snow-covered acres" of Canada and Ohio, almost empty territories, not very productive except for a few furs. Their prosperous future was unknown. At the time, keeping Martinique and Saint-Domingue with their enormous production of easily marketable sugar and coffee was surely the better choice, as the best-informed Englishmen well knew.

Be that as it may, the war had consequences in France itself. Choiseul sought partial compensation for the loss of this first empire by purchasing Corsica in 1768. After Rossbach, the need for army reform along Prussian lines was widely felt, as was the importance of building a powerful navy and preparing for some revenge. *Parlementaire* revolts and philosophical propaganda were increasing and becoming bolder. Economic crises and disturbances resulting from high bread prices re-appeared from 1770 to 1772. Meanwhile the first partition of Poland took place without any protest from Versailles, and the courageous royal stance at the time of Maupeou encountered undeserved unpopularity.

A desire for revenge, an unruly opposition, and the eternal financial problem—this was the inheritance that Louis XV, struck down by smallpox at age sixty-four, left to his grandson, aged twenty. Everyone knows that he could not or would not take it on. We must find out why, and how this unhappy situation arose.

Chapter Eleven

LOUIS XVI: 1774–1792

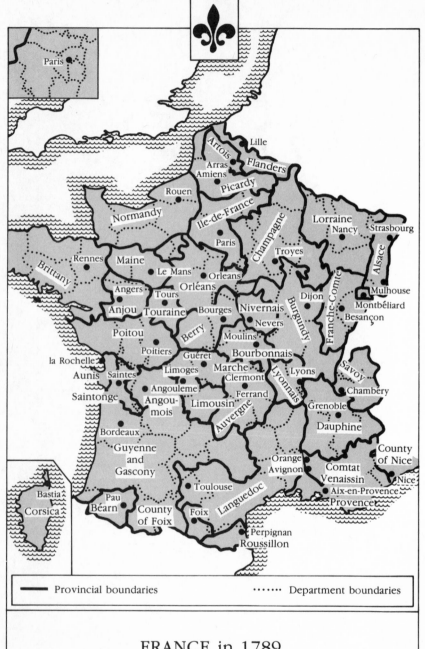

Paris

Artois
Lille
Arras
Amiens
Picardy
Flanders

Rouen

Normandy

Ile-de-France

Lorraine
Nancy
Strasbourg

Paris

Champagne

Troyes

Rennes

Maine

Le Mans

Orleans

Alsace

Brittany

Angers

Tours

Orléans

Dijon

Mulhouse

Franche-Comté

Montbéliard

Anjou

Touraine

Bourges

Nivernais

Burgundy

Besançon

Poitou

Berry

Nevers

Poitiers

Moulins

la Rochelle

Guéret

Bourbonnais

Lyons

Savoy

Aunis

Saintes

Limoges

Marche

Clermont

Lyonnais

Chambery

Saintonge

Angouleme

Ferrand

Grenoble

Angou-
mois

Limousin

Auvergne

Dauphine

Bordeaux

Guyenne
and
Gascony

Orange

Avignon

County
of Nice

Bastia

Comtat
Venaissin

Nice

Corsica

Pau

Toulouse

Aix-en-Provence

Béarn

County
of Foix

Foix

Languedoc

Provence

Perpignan

Roussillon

——— Provincial boundaries   ······· Department boundaries

FRANCE in 1789

For nearly two centuries the pitiable and courageous deaths of Louis XVI and Marie-Antoinette on the guillotine have touched French hearts. More recently they have provoked controversial and sometimes ridiculous interpretations by psychoanalysts and their followers—such ideas as the murder of the father-figure. In this area the historian should not choose sides but rather try to retrace events and understand situations. No one could have foretold what would happen, let alone predicted any difficulties, when in May 1774, two sympathetic and popular young sovereigns aged twenty came to the throne. They themselves were not expecting to receive power so soon, or to hold it for such a short time.

Despite their apparent complexity, these fifteen years of power presented only two striking novelties. First came the War of American Independence, whose importance cannot be exaggerated, because it helped to unleash the French Revolution of 1789. The second noteworthy feature was the complex economic crisis, which curiously culminated in July 1789. We shall return to both these points later.

As for the rest, France experienced the same things it had known for sixty years. Good projects for reform were aborted by the weakness of the king or by the ferocity of blind aristocratic opposition. Also, there was a crescendo of even bolder and more widespread philosophical ideas, thanks in particular to various *sociétés de pensée*. The Freemasons were only one such group. Many others had been born well before the reign of Louis XVI, and their ideas were henceforth brought down to a more popular level by itinerant peddlers of increasingly rude and critical illegal pamphlets.

THE KING AND
HIS ENTOURAGE

Well informed on some topics, the young monarch nourished many good intentions, but he did not really know which way to turn. To guide him, his pious aunts, the daughters of Louis XV, found an unlikely mentor: the comte de Maurepas, then seventy-three years old. Maurepas was a skeptical, spirited, scheming man. Some of his epigrams against the marquise de Pompadour had caused him to fall out of favor many years before, in 1749. Now the comte was to help his young master reign for seven years.

Louis XVI might have been the best possible father of a family, despite initial physical difficulties, or one of the finest artisans or geographers—if chance had not placed him on the throne. He did not know very much about the art of governing. He was given to fits of enthusiasm, toward Turgot, for example; these could be followed by timidity, weakness, and even energy, but they often came at the wrong moment. From the queen, whose extreme charm and unhappy end have attracted so many admirers, he could expect nothing. Marie-Antoinette was obsessed with her appearance and busied herself with feasts, balls, and indiscretions. She liked to play shepherdess, and for her own pleasure and her beautiful friends she spent money without a thought in the world. Her infrequent interventions in government affairs resembled whims and were often made at inopportune moments. She caused distress first to her mother Maria-Theresa and then to her brother Emperor

Joseph II, who came incognito to France in an attempt to bring her to reason. Adored by the French people at the beginning of the reign, she quickly became unpopular because of her pride, prodigality, and entourage. Although she was completely innocent in the unfortunate "affair of the queen's necklace," which should have brought ridicule only on the richest and most noble bishop in France, her reputation was stained. The peevish pamphleteers had a field day. Later events would show that the harsh-sounding epithet of "the Austrian woman" (l'Autrichienne, or Ostrichian) with which many Parisians stung her was not entirely inaccurate.

As for the rest of the royal family, there was nothing better to be expected. The comte de Provence, the future Louis XVIII, was a refined epicurean who helped to make the queen unpopular. His brother the comte d'Artois, quite the opposite in character, tried to exceed him in futility and waste. The princes of the blood Conti and Orléans played roles in the opposition. Conti cooperated with the Parlements, while Orléans, the richest man in France, had some ambition and sponsored reformism in the English style, which would carry him far. At court, in between feasts, there was petty clan warfare. The last members of the devout party, the lingering Choiseulistes, the Anglophiles, and the decorated physiocrats formed cliques supporting one faction or another.

Nevertheless, excellent ministers worked on the reforms they felt were necessary. One by one they failed, just as all their predecessors had done since the time of Vauban. They were liquidated by incomprehension and egoism.

THE FIRST OPPORTUNITY LOST:
TURGOT, 1774–1776

After his initial monumental error of recalling the Parlements and dismissing Maupeou and Terray, the last great ministers of Louis XV, Maurepas made Louis XVI choose ministers of the first rank: Sartine, Saint-Germain, Vergennes, Miromesnil, and Lamoignon de Malesherbes. The first two devoted themselves to the work of rebuilding the army and navy, which would one day make people forget the humiliations of the Seven Years War and the surrender of the Treaty of Paris. Vergennes long directed diplomacy superbly. The others took on the rest of the administration, with the exception of finances, which were left to Turgot.

Turgot, experienced as intendant of Limousin, was the son of a *prévôt des marchands,* an appointed mayor of Paris. He had a solid reputation for economic and philosophical understanding. He had succeeded in provincial administration, and he had character and ideas. His rough frankness and his concern for the public good pleased the king, at least for a while.

In the administration of finances, Turgot proclaimed his opposition to bankruptcy of any kind, all tax increases, and all borrowing. He undertook a sound campaign of budget reduction, even affecting the *Maison du Roi,* thus the expenses of the court itself, which did not appreciate his efforts. To make the fiscal system more just and more productive, he decided to extend the *taille tarifée* applied in the *généralité* of Paris, yet another tax on declared and verified income. The archives show that assessments were done in an admirable manner. Turgot dreamed of a state agency for collecting all taxes, and thereby aroused the hostility of private tax-farmers and collectors, financiers large and small who preferred to collect the taxes themselves.

As a champion of economic liberty, Turgot reestablished a free internal trade in grain. But the misfortune of a bad harvest, aggravated by the usual maneuvers of speculators to jack up the prices, was followed by a parade of false rumors. As a result, a series of bread riots and attacks on storehouses broke out in the provinces as well as at Paris. This "flour war" of 1775 was harshly repressed by troops. During its troubled course new phenomena appeared: voluntary taxation—maximum prices imposed by the mob—and denunciations of "bandits, brigands, and monopolists." These manifestations and upheavals would reappear during the Revolution, but the Revolution certainly did not invent them.

To complete his philosophy of liberty, Turgot proclaimed in 1776 the "liberty of labor," which meant the abolition of state controls on trade and craft guilds, though there were exceptions such as surgeons, armorers, and printers. At the same time almost all of the privileges and wardenships of the guilds were suppressed. The Parlement thundered against this "undefined liberty" and shocking equality of rights. It also had an opportunity to denounce tax projects that risked "confounding" all the orders and "degrading the nobility"—that is, itself. Turgot had already begun to replace the royal corvée on the new great roads with a tax on all landed proprietors, including privileged groups that owned almost half the land of France. Turgot took other provocative measures as well. He finally extended the official population register to include Protestants, removed education from clerical control, prepared the "general tax register," and even forced the clergy to pay taxes. At the same time Malesherbes thought of abolishing press censorship, which was only moderately effective anyway, and considered restoring the Edict of Nantes. All this was too much for the high nobility, the court, the Church, the military, and judicial nobles. Even worse, Turgot, the minister they abhorred, was also preaching the repurchase of certain feudal rights and the creation of local and provincial assemblies. These new bodies would have infringed on privileges of the all-powerful intendants and governors. With the help of the queen, Louis XVI curtly dismissed Turgot in May 1776.

In the weeks that followed, all of Turgot's decisions were countermanded. Only the Discount Bank he had authorized survived. Apart from bills of exchange, it accepted deposits and soon issued reasonable quantities of convenient banknotes, which were warmly welcomed for several years before suffering from speculation.

After some hesitancy, during which the royal lottery was reinvented and a convenient bankruptcy prepared, Maurepas decided it was a good idea to give Jacques Necker complete authority over finances. Finances, with foreign affairs, constituted the essence of government.

THE SECOND LOST OPPORTUNITY: THE FIRST NECKER PERIOD, 1776–1781

While Jacques Necker was indeed a rich banker, he was also a foreigner, commoner, and heretic to boot. The French bureaucracy had never seen anyone like him, even if he had to be content with the modest title of Director of the Treasury. The popularity of this stout, moderate man may be surprising. He was an opportunist, rather vain, but also skillful. Necker's wife, daughter of a Swiss Protestant minister, and his daughter Germaine, the future Madame de Staël, held a brilliant salon where philosophes, writers, and high society met—and no doubt that counted in his favor. At least as important were his close connections with powerful Swiss bankers. Besides, he had achieved a good reputation as a philanthropist. He founded the hospital that still bears his name, created the first French "Mount of Piety" (two centuries after the Italian foundations), liberated the last serfs on the royal domains, abolished the use of torture in judicial interrogations, and prepared a sound proposal for public welfare aid.

Necker's great popular success was to pay for the American war without raising taxes. "He is a god!" said Mirabeau ironically. As a good banker, he was happy to borrow 550 million livres, twice as much as the ordinary budget of the state, at 8.5 percent and then 10 percent. All that remained was to pay it back. Unfortunately, this considerable debt was added to others and grew like a rolling snowball as interest and partial reimbursements increased from one year to the next. And thus the eternal question became even more urgent: Would the rich finally agree to pay taxes? In their answer lay the revolutionary crux of the problem.

The immediate concern, of course, was how to make ends

meet. Thus we find Necker trying to cut each budget, even those of the army and navy, which did not endear him to his eminent colleagues Vergennes and Sartine. When his subordinates on the council and in the treasury were uncooperative, Necker dared to get rid of them and surround himself with simple salaried clerks whom he had known in the banking world. Outraged by the bad will of the intendants, he returned to one of Turgot's proposals, to create provincial assemblies that could levy taxes in their stead. He even installed some at Bourges and at Montauban. These assemblies, partly appointed and partly co-opted, contained as many men of the Third Estate as of the other two orders combined—another scandalous innovation.

These initiatives inspired a whole cabal against the Genevan financier. He replied with a great blast: the publication in 1781 of his *Account Book for the King,* an almost sacrilegious revelation of the secrets of official finances. The work was a shameless apology for himself which made it appear that there was a budgetary surplus. In fact the trick was to exclude "extraordinary" expenditures, and the deficit exceeded 80 million livres. At last the one hundred thousand purchasers could find out the amount of pensions, gratuities, and festive expenses of the royal family and the entire court. The sum was considered astronomical, even though it represented only 6 to 8 percent of all expenditures. As an example of extravagance, critics cited the dowry given by the queen to her dear friend Polignac: 800,000 livres, equivalent to the annual wages of two thousand Parisian journeymen. All of this contributed to the disgrace of Necker, who was dismissed in May 1781.

Two conscientious clerks, Joly de Fleury and d'Ormesson, took their turn at the helm of royal finances. Naturally they were obliged to order some economy measures and new taxes. Suddenly, at the end of 1783, the queen had Charles-Alexandre de Calonne named controller general of finances. This supple and optimistic man of the world arrived on the scene at the same time as peace, and presided over a few months of euphoria. He also quickly understood that it was necessary to reform the old machinery, and he set about the task.

There is something vain in this parade of often talented men who just missed achieving success, or were forced to renounce it. For several years the essential political developments had already been taking place not at Paris or Versailles, but elsewhere. While the heart of the kingdom was burdened with dark forces that would all break out at once, America had come to the fore.

THE WIND FROM AMERICA

None of the thirteen English colonies established in America between 1607 (Virginia) and 1732 (Georgia) closely resembled its neighbors. They differed in religion, economy, ethnic composition, and even political systems. Nevertheless, a governor represented the king of England in each colony, and one or two legislative assemblies held a great deal of local power. These assemblies constantly invoked divine protection and were elected by almost universal suffrage, except in Massachusetts. Almost everywhere there reigned a climate of liberty that the French *philosophes* could have envied: popular consent to taxation, election of judges, quasi-compulsory school attendance, and freedom of the press—as long as it did not shock morality or established religion, which could be Puritan or Quaker.

Hard pressed financially by the Seven Years War, England wanted to make the Americans pay a portion of her debts and reinforce her commercial primacy—or rather, monopoly. During the protests and violent movements that broke out across the Atlantic, resounding documents were written, voted on, and published, starting with the Declaration and Resolves of the First Continental Congress at Philadelphia in 1774. Others, more renowned, included the Virginia Bill of Rights in June 1776, and finally, on July 4, 1776, the Declaration of Independence of the United States of America, proclaimed by the Second Continental Congress in Philadelphia.

These documents, warmly received in the United States,

272

quickly became known to enlightened parts of France and other countries. They unleashed both enthusiasm and concern. Their texts, which contain both English and French philosophical ideas, represented a challenge to the very bases of absolute monarchy.

> All men are by nature equally free and independent. . . . All power is vested in and consequently derived from the people; . . . the magistrates are only their trustees and servants, and at all times amenable to them. . . . The legislative and executive powers of the state should be separated and distinct from the judiciary . . . (Virginia Bill of Rights)

Or, as the Declaration of Independence stated,

> We hold these truths to be self-evident, that all men are created equal and that they are endowed by their Creator with certain inalienable rights, that among these are life, liberty, and the pursuit of happiness. That to secure these rights governments are instituted among men, and deriving their just powers only by the consent of the governed . . .

It is striking that these American documents greatly influenced the proclamations of 1789, including the Declaration of the Rights of Man and Citizen, and the French Constitution of 1791. Some historians have even seen a direct connection between the American Revolution, an anticolonial insurrection, and the French Revolution, whose immediate and perhaps far-reaching consequences had quite different meaning and importance.

Nevertheless it is clear that the "rebels," those armed colonists in revolt, also inspired sympathy because they gave the French people and their government an opportunity to take their revenge on the victors of the Seven Years War and redeem the shame of the Treaty of Paris. Patriotism and preromantic generosity caused young French officers to cross the Atlantic and place themselves at the disposal of General George Washington's troops, at first ill-favored indeed. Among them were the marquis de Lafayette, who was barely twenty years old; the dukes of Lauzun and Noailles; the count of Ségur, and many others. The flower of the French nobility went to fight shoulder to shoulder with the republican rebels! Most of them would later form the core of the liberal nobility in the first months of the Revolution of 1789. Almost at the same time, the good-natured Benjamin Franklin arrived at Paris, reinforcing with his sly, wise simplicity the "American air" that blew through the capital and the principal cities of the kingdom. Franklin had come to negotiate for French intervention.

Vergennes and Louis XVI had already helped the American insurgents with money and munitions. After some hesitation, they decided to take military action as well. They had secured the neutrality of continental Europe, then made alliances with Spain and even Holland. The surrender of a British army at Saratoga in October 1777 encouraged their decision to send military aid. Since Choiseul's efforts, the French army and navy had been greatly reformed and invigorated; they had also acquired modern weaponry, which would benefit succeeding regimes. In the end, the French navy played a considerable role in the American Revolution. It made a powerful contribution to the decisive victory at Yorktown in 1781 and distinguished itself in the Mediterranean, in the Antilles along the Indian coasts. By the terms of the Treaty of Versailles in September 1783, Britain recognized the independence of the United States, and victorious France was content with reclaiming one of the Antilles (Tobago, lost again in 1815), Sénégal, and the fishing posts of Saint-Pierre and Miquelon.

This obvious glory was accompanied by considerable debt, from which the regime could not escape. We have mentioned that Necker had to borrow more than 500 million livres, but other spending, particularly on naval operations, must be added to the total. The historian Michel Morineau has recently evaluated the cost of the American war at more than 1.3 billion livres in gold, which had to be added to the unpaid debts from the previous war twenty years before. The English, whose expenses had been comparable, were able to surmount a crisis thanks to William Pitt the younger, who laid on a crushing fiscal burden. But in France no one was able to do it. After careful reconstruction, the last budget of the monarchy shows that more than half of the expenditures went to debt service, a proportion that had more than doubled since the beginning of the reign.

The wind from America had simultaneously brought glory, ideas, and a deficit that could lead straight to bankruptcy—in short, some of the important elements that led to the Revolution. When Calonne was called to head the ministry of finances, yet another miracle worker had appeared; but he, too, suffered the fate of the others.

THE LAST EXPERIMENTS:
1783–1788

With the celebration of peace came six years of whirling festivals and quarrels, books and pamphlets, Swiss banking and speculation, scandals, and riots—a period both brilliant and worrying. The outclassed Louis XVI sent away three prime ministers—two new ones, Calonne and Brienne, and one old hand, Necker. They tried three new experiments, which resulted in three new failures, each time for the same reasons: the enormity of the deficit and the refusal of the aristocracy to contribute to solving it.

The likable Calonne bought Saint-Cloud and Rambouillet for the king. He embellished Bordeaux and Marseille, finished Cherbourg, opened canals in the Center and Burgundy, and revived the French East India Company. He also surrounded himself with economists and physiocrats, and signed the first free-trade treaty with England in 1786—for which he was roundly blamed. That same year Calonne could no longer find enough money to borrow, not even in Switzerland. Predicting an increased deficit of 150 million livres, he returned to a sort of Turgotism. He presented a six-point recovery plan, including the establishment of a State Bank and a general and proportional income tax, which would be applied by elected provincial assemblies. To ratify these bold measures, the government revived the antique institution of an Assembly of Notables, last called under Louis XIII. The king designated the 144 members of this body, overwhelmingly nobles of the sword and robe, together with several recently ennobled persons. They accepted the entire package, except for the essential point, the universal "territorial" tax. Just as Necker had done six years before, Calonne appealed over the heads of the notables to enlightened public opinion. Naturally this did not endear him to the court and the assembly, and they had him dismissed in April 1787.

Once again under pressure from the queen, Louis XVI then called on the chief of the aristocratic opposition, Archbishop Loménie de Brienne, a prelate who was distinguished more by culture, suppleness, and spirit than by devotion and good morals. Brienne also embarked upon useful reforms, such as the army reorganization accomplished with the help of the harsh Guibert, supporter of the Prussian system. Protestantism was given legal recognition, and a number of serious budget cuts were made in administration, in court expenses, and even in the officer corps. Brienne successfully raised a loan of 400 million livres. But, after having sent away the troublesome notables, he encountered the systematic and sometimes violent opposition of the Parlement of Paris, soon imitated by other Parlements. The *Parlementaires* hoped thus to achieve popularity. Besides the ritual demand for taxation subject to their consent, this opposition was fixed on two points.

The first consisted of the proposal, this time serious, to create a cascade of provincial elected assemblies, going from the level of the *Généralité* down to the parish, passing by way of the new subdivisions of *département* and *arrondissement,* later taken up by the Revolution. In each assembly the representation of the Third Estate was systematically doubled, and the method of election approached that of popular suffrage. The majority of the population, those who paid more than ten livres in taxes, could vote; but fewer than 10 percent, only those who paid 50 livres or more, could be elected. The financial powers of these assemblies would in fact have abolished the powers of the intendants and the ancient officers of the fisc. Indeed, this measure prefigured the terms of the Constitution of 1791. And Brienne thought to crown the whole reform by the Estates General.

The Parlements, whose members were unevenly divided between semireformers and antireformers, were first and foremost defenders of tradition as they understood it. They held sacred their power to control all legislation, especially financial legislation; they claimed to work for the public good and to protect the good people of the kingdom. These causes habitually dissimulated their egoism and vanity. At Paris there were new remonstrances and royal sessions, *lits de justice.* When the *Parlementaires* still refused to co-operate, they were sent into exile at Troyes. Negotiations were followed by their triumphal return to gaping crowds, then by further recidivism. The Keeper of the Seals Lamoignon then announced the Edict of May 8, 1788, a version of the "Maupeou Parlements" of 1771, suppressed in 1774. Henceforth, forty-seven *Grands Bailliages* would accomplish the judicial tasks of the old Parlements, whose jurisdiction would be reduced to considering cases of their own privileged members. An appointed *Cour Plénière* would take over the registration of royal edicts and ordinances. This energetic but tardy reform unleashed fiery protests, violent pamphlets, and even authentic provincial revolts, notably at Rennes and Grenoble. Just at this moment the Assembly of Clergy decided to refuse any subsidy to the king. Brienne was forced to suspend all state payments on August 16, 1788, which was a serious matter. Eight days earlier, he had called the Estates General for May 1789; nine days later, he left office.

To try to ward off bankruptcy, the king recalled Necker, from whom impossible miracles were expected. With great risk, he recalled the Assembly of Notables: they were now resigned to fiscal equality and divided on the doubling of representatives of the Third Estate at the forthcoming Estates General. In the general agitation, this question became crucial. In pronouncing against the doubling of the Third Estate, the Parlement of Paris definitively brought itself into disrepute in September 1788.

At the end of 1788 and the beginning of 1789, the king granted the doubling of the Third, and authorized infinitely generous, almost democratic electoral rules for the Estates General. After a flood of scandal sheets, pamphlets, meetings, and petitions, he brought to Versailles a large number of lawyers among the Third Estate, a majority of parish priests among the Clergy, and a minority of reformers among the nobility. Would they join together? The king tried to prevent them from doing so. On June 23, 1789, he was still declaring, "I alone can bring about the happiness of my people." Four days later, he yielded. The three estates joined together henceforth represented, against the monarch, the "Nation Assembled," and this National Assembly soon declared itself "constituent" of a new regime.

In this beautiful summer of 1789, the first retreat of Louis XVI foreshadowed others, which constituted so many steps in the decline of the monarchy and in his own fall.

STEPS TOWARD A FALL: 1789–1792

At the beginning of July, the king reacted to the political crisis by dismissing Necker and concentrating reliable regiments around the city of Paris. The popular reply to this action was the capture of the Bastille on July 14. Once again the king gave way and recalled Necker; Louis XVI even went so far as to don the tricolor cockade hat of the people. Municipal and rural revolts followed, with the "destruction of the feudal regime" when the National Assembly abolished many privileges on the night of August 4, 1789. Louis refused to ratify most of their decrees, but on October 6 he was forcibly brought to Paris by a mob. After intermittent resistance, attempts at corruption, complex intrigues, and obscure plots, the king left Paris only once more, in June 1791, on a clumsy flight toward Germany; but he was rather wretchedly arrested at Varennes. By his failed escape and his almost funereal return, Louis XVI had shattered the confidence that "his peoples" (as he said) still held in him. He was the king of only part of the French people.

And yet the National Assembly still treated him with respect, pretending to believe that there had been an attempt to kidnap him. He was for all practical purposes a prisoner of Paris. His last attempts at resistance and his ultimate appeals to the absolute monarchs of Europe only worked against his cause. The threatened invasion, the "revolution of August 10, 1792," which led to his suspension and the proclamation of the first French Republic, his painful trial, and his execution, decided only with great difficulty—all these events were present in embryonic form in the sad escapade that ended at Varennes.

Profoundly wounded in his sense of the monarchy and in his sincere faith, Louis XVI was surrounded by bad counselors and was himself too hesitant. He was unable, did not know, and did not want to understand how to give way frankly or command firmly when he could still have done so. Indeed he was unfortunate as a monarch and a man. The role of history, which is in no sense a tribunal, is not to judge him but rather to understand him in his age.

And this age certainly accounts for much more than his person.

*Chapter
Twelve*

THE
REVOLUTION
DURING
PEACETIME:
1789–1792

There is no hope of ever reconciling Frenchmen of diverse opinions around their first Revolution. Antagonism and passion have carried them away, and the coming bicentennial will stir them up again. The quarrels have already been renewed. Since the role of a professional historian does not consist of delivering praise or blame, we propose here to take on the difficult task of rising above the debate in order to see clearly and emphasize what appears essential.

Defining the Revolution

True revolutions, and there have been few of them, upset the very bases of government and legislation. They rearrange social groups, bring to power new and often young men, redistribute property (at least partially), and generate a significant renewal of ideas, mentalities, and passions. The Estates General of May 1789, which became the Constituent Assembly of June and July and then the Legislative Assembly of 1791–1792, accomplished all these upheavals in less than three years, in the first genuine and unpredictable revolution. These assemblies benefited both from the mediocrity of their adversaries and from general European peace, as the monarchs were otherwise engaged.

Everything changed with the war, declared in April 1792. The invasion of France brought panic, violent and divergent movements, enormous expenditures, the concentration and radicalization of power, and the fall of the monarchy. Starting in the summer of 1792, almost everything can be explained by the defense of French national territory, a hard task accepted by the Revolution. Once victories had been won at the end of 1793 and in 1794, the provisional suppression of constitutional guarantees was no longer necessary. The emergency measures of the revolutionary government and the Reign of Terror could be abandoned. The most extreme revolutionaries did not understand the changed situation and were locked in their own quarrels. They fell from power between May and July 1794. At that time the reaction set in—a climate of intrigue, speculation, and mediocre coups d'état; but the great institutional and legislative work of the Revolution continued. When the war broke out again very soon after the treaties of 1795, a strong man appeared to take power in November 1799: a "saber," just as Robespierre had predicted eight years earlier. If Hoche had not died too soon, he could have played the part; or it could also have been Moreau or Pichegru. But instead it was Napoleon Bonaparte, a man whom others thought they could manipulate. He became the Emperor Napoleon in 1804. War then lasted for more than ten years. The main point is that the Revolution began in peacetime; from 1792 to 1815 war was the principal explanatory factor.

Let us see why this Revolution took place.

ON THE TRAIL OF THE ORIGINS OF THE REVOLUTION

It is always necessary to go back to elementary facts: the Revolution did not occur simply because the Estates General were called. Rather, the Estates were summoned because total bankruptcy appeared inevitable. This bankruptcy had been brought on both by the enormous expenses of the American war, and by the refusal of the aristocracy as a whole and the bankers to make a serious financial contribution to the state. This is so well established that we can say that the aristocracy—at court, in the Church, robe and sword—started the Revolution by its blindness. This would not have been enough to guarantee revolution, however, if other factors had not played a role.

If two hundred parish priests, deputies of the clergy, had not joined the reformers of the Third Estate, the three orders that the king wanted to keep separate could not have met together as one body, the National Assembly. This fact, often overlooked, underlines the secession of the educated and worthy lower clergy from the ranks of the privileged orders, whose arrogance, luxury, and carelessness shocked them. The aristocratic agitators should have foreseen this possibility and treated the priests with great care. As it was, the Constituent Assembly was moved by a spirit of systematizing and lacked political experience. It very quickly lost this precious clerical support in less than a year. And yet, clerical support was decisive in June 1789.

Without the intervention of the poor people and the modest bourgeois of Paris who captured the Bastille on July 14, 1789, the king and court would have had their loyal regiments disperse the insubordinate subjects who pretended to represent the nation, "which is not incorporated in France, but resides entirely in the person of the king," as previous monarchs had affirmed. Without the powerful intervention of Paris, whose weight would continue to be felt throughout this period, the work of reform and revolution would not even have begun.

In the following month, the Assembly went much further, "destroying entirely the feudal regime" in the psychodrama of the night of August 4, when speaker after speaker offered his sacrifice for "the Nation." "Feudalism" could be abolished precisely because the majority of French peasants had already rejected it by not paying their dues. Occasionally peasants had even dared to take up arms. They destroyed the record books and attacked the landlords and lawyers who were the champions and beneficiaries of feudal claims. This process had gone so far that the decrees of August 1789 were more a sign of slowing down than of acceleration. But why did the peasants, who had been so calm for a century, suddenly come to life and completely change the direction of the Revolution that had just begun?

It was not clear what the 800 or 900 deputies to the Estates General wanted. More than 500 of them were from the Third Estate, and nearly 200 were from the clergy, whereas only a handful were nobles. As a group they called themselves patriots, nationals, reformers, and constituents. They soon showed their seriousness of purpose by enacting abundant legislation, some of which still regulates life in France today. But in 1789 it was by no means certain that they would adopt a "philosophical" program such as that discussed by the *sociétés de pensée*.

Four great problems, fundamental for an understanding of the events of 1789 and the years that followed, must be considered from both long-term and short-term points of view.

The Distant Origins: Society, Church, and State

For more than two centuries sharp criticisms had been leveled against the intransigence, wealth, and relative corruption of the French clergy. Their collective income was almost equal to that of the king. Satirical attacks were first directed against monks and monasteries. Victims of ridicule since the time of Villon and Rabelais, they were hit strongly by the cruel irony of Voltaire and his followers. In a serious attempt to reform monastic life, Louis XV finally created a Commission of Regulars in 1766. Not all forms of monasticism were found to be in decay: higher traditions were still upheld by teaching orders such as the Oratorians, certain learned scholars among the Benedictines, and the admirable hospital keepers and servants of the poor. On the eve of the Revolution, these groups still showed signs of vitality.

During the Wars of Religion in the sixteenth century, the

French kings forced the Church to sell a considerable part of its property (though with the right of repurchase) to pay for the struggle against the Protestants. Naturally the Protestants did not treat their heartless adversaries kindly either: they made a point of refusing to pay tithes and complained of clerical oppression. Even Louis XIV in his *Memoirs* had fumed against the "great number of clerics . . . useless to the church . . . [and] burdensome to the State." He was justifying in advance the nationalization of Church property enacted by the Constituent Assembly beginning in November 1789. Even moderate writers had to admit that the Roman Catholic church of France enjoyed enormous privileges, particularly financial advantages.

In addition, the eighteenth century saw the rise of a secessionist movement within the Catholic church among the lower clergy. Worthy and knowledgeable priests could not tolerate the arrogance, lukewarm faith, and overwhelming opulence of the bishops. Naturally the bishops were almost all drawn from the highest noble families. This noble monopoly reinforced the opinion of those who saw an "aristocratic reaction" in the second half of the century. This reaction provoked the rancor of some of the "excluded ones," many of whom were very competent and rich bourgeois.

Indeed we should keep in mind that except for Necker all the ministers of Louis XVI, all the bishops, virtually all the high administrators, the *Parlementaires,* and the officers of the army and the navy belonged to the oldest, most titled, and richest nobility. Granted, after a hard struggle a few useful commoners, notably technicians, slipped into the ranks of the civilian and army hierarchy. But they never advanced in the officer corps of the navy, unless one counts the despised clerical types. The bourgeoisie of talent—experts, men of letters, lawyers, *rentiers,* wealthy merchants, shippers, planters from the Antilles, bankers, and businessmen—warmly desired to acquire offices for which they had the qualifications. Their ambition was one of the driving forces of a Revolution that eventually did employ them and brought them to the fore. The bourgeois were particularly prominent in its first period before August 10, 1792, and after Thermidor (July 1794), as well as under the empire that followed.

This essentially bourgeois ensemble, along with the "enlightened" members of the nobility and clergy, had received the uneven influence of the *philosophes,* those would-be moralists, political scientists, and sociologists. They had also pondered the English example of parliamentary monarchy, and more recently the American model of a federal republic with widespread suffrage. They had debated a great deal in the salons, cafés, clubs, provincial academies, agricultural societies, and Masonic lodges, which were not then anti-religious. Among the wealth of ideas expressed there, we can note only a few that were truly influential.

Most significant was the rejection of pure despotism and absolute monarchy. These men showed a marked preference for intermediate bodies at the provincial level as well as legislative chambers elected by limited suffrage. The vote, as they envisioned it, was never universal, but always reserved for respectable property owners. Following Montesquieu, they habitually accepted the separation of powers and sought a complete reform of the judicial system to make it clearer, more unified, more humane, and non-venal. The dogma of religious tolerance was often linked to a certain deism, for atheists were rare indeed. They also favored serious philanthropic efforts, general plans for public welfare, and a cult of respect for virtue, family, and old age, modeled on classical antiquity. Finally, the *philosophes* warmly supported education, though not for all people. They admired science, technology, and the unceasing progress of the human spirit.

This body of ideology inspired the majority of the deputies elected in March and April 1789, and their work evidently bears its stamp. But they would not have been able to accomplish it without the intervention of the people of Paris, the new municipal governments in the provinces, and above all, the peasants. These interventions, however, must be placed in the context of recent short-term crises.

The Economic Crisis and Popular Movements

Since the monetary stabilization of 1726, the French economy had enjoyed steady and moderate growth, though the effects were spread unevenly. There were several fortunate developments such as the beginning of the oil industry, the soaring cotton manufactures, the growth of the large seaports (though not during the wars, owing to the English blockades), and particularly the explosion of colonial commerce. Saint-Domingue stood in the foreground of this trade. The standard of living in city and country was slowly improving, with the exception of several backward regions and gloomy years. Great famines and plague had practically disappeared.

In this relatively happy climate, the slightest difficulties acquired new significance. Toward 1771–1772, bad harvests brought inevitable increases in grain and bread prices, which touched off disturbances at Paris and elsewhere. These were severely repressed by force. At the same time an epidemic of bankruptcies shook the world of business and manufacturing, causing financial difficulties and unemployment. This was a first warning of what would follow.

The real "crisis of the old regime" began between 1775 and 1778, as the historian Ernest Labrousse explained fifty years ago. Overproduction of wine caused falling prices and low profits, despite adult per capita consumption of a liter a day in the large cities. But there were tens of thousands of specialized wine-grape growers, particularly in Île-de-France, and peasant cultivators were even more numerous. For these people the sale of wine made their lives easier, allowed them to pay their taxes and buy goods in the marketplace. The depression in the wine trade lasted seven or eight years. It was followed in 1785 by a great drought, which made forage scarce and expensive and caused the death of thousands of livestock of epidemic diseases. For about one-third of the French population who lived in mountainous and wooded areas and were dependent on livestock-raising, this was a heavy loss. Their flocks could not be reconstituted quickly or without cost. From

1778, the price of grain languished or fell, affecting countless small sellers, farmers, and sharecroppers. By contrast, the landlords, tithe-collectors, and large proprietors always collected their *rentes.* Suddenly, from 1787 to 1789, an old-fashioned cereal crisis broke out with a vengeance. In the northern half of the country, the old patterns, once thought to be passé, were present in full force. A mediocre harvest was followed by the catastrophic hailstorms of July 1788, then by a very harsh winter—and the prices of grains and bread rose between 50 percent and 100 percent. In Paris, the highest price was reached on July 14, 1789. Of course this record price did not provoke the capture of the Bastille, but it aggravated the rioters' grievances.

The tightening of rural purses had already caused falling sales in the industrial sector, especially in textiles, an area of prime importance. In 1789, the textile industry was working at only half of its productive capacity. Low sales meant unemployment for the workers, who of course did not receive any welfare aid. There was also unemployment in the overpopulated countryside, causing young peasants to migrate to the cities. And these cities were rife with rumors and speculation. Various fears were stirred up by lively pamphlets, cruel songs, and inflammatory harangues from speakers heard in cabarets, at crossroads, in public squares, and at the Palais-Royal of Paris.

July 1789: The Eruption at Paris

In overcrowded Paris, 700,000 inhabitants—many of them young and unemployed—knew how to read or how to listen. They were living in the streets that beautiful summer, in hot and sultry surroundings, reading the pamphlets and posters that had multiplied since the elections for the Estates General. They responded quickly to the most surprising reports, which were transmitted at breakneck speed. At the beginning of July, Parisians learned that the king had concentrated troops around the city. At the Invalides, people sought and found weapons to defend themselves; they hoped to find more at the Bastille. Those who attacked the old fortress-prison were in no sense bandits, beggars, or representatives of Freemasonry, as some ridiculous reactionary historians have pretended. Rather, they were the little people of the Faubourg Saint-Antoine: workers, journeymen, shop assistants, supported by several small shop-keepers and even modest *rentiers.* Their successful attack on the Bastille struck a responsive chord and became a popular symbol. In the following days it led to blind and cruel executions, claiming such victims as the intendant Bertier de Sauvigny, one of the best administrators of the kingdom, who was accused of speculation. Its immediate effects were the establishment of a new municipal government with the astronomer Bailly as mayor, the transformation of the bourgeois guard into a national guard, and the inglorious capitulation of Louis XVI.

Thanks to Paris, the National Assembly was saved from the expected dissolution; the delegates could set about their work. But the Assembly did not work in an atmosphere of tranquility. Disturbing news was arriving, not so much from the cities, where other municipal governments and national guards were establishing themselves, as from the rural areas, where discontent had taken unexpected forms.

The Impact of the Countryside and the End of the Feudal Regime

Although they had been peaceful since the death of Louis XIV, the rural areas were no less troubled than the cities. Rancor, quarrels, and complaints were expressed in a novel fashion. There was much litigation (rarely successful), and above all peasants had recourse to the powerful weapon of passive resistance.

The infrequent disputes between the peasants and the Church were essentially related to the tithe, which was collected unevenly on variable harvests. Against the demands of the royal treasury, the peasants tried fraud and foot-dragging, but the administration became quite effective. Nonetheless encounters with "gabelous" (salt-tax collectors) and "cave rats," agents of the indirect tax farms who checked the sales of wine, at times went beyond the excesses of popular farce and reached the level of tragedy.

Henceforth the novelty, brought on in part by the crisis, was for peasants to attack their lords, whether small or great. It mattered little whether they were living on the land or absentees represented by shrewd bourgeois agents who searched out forgotten feudal rights and closely supervised payments. Peasant anger was directed in the first place against game: hunting rights were among the chief complaints of 1789. The peasants also agitated against rules that prohibited them from grazing their animals, suppressed their traditional privileges of using the forests, divided their common lands, and required them to use the lords' mills and ovens. The first violent rural disturbances occurred during the winter of 1788–1789. In the North, in Picardy, Alsace, around Paris, in Anjou, even in Brittany, Dauphiné, and particularly in Provence, peasants refused to pay tithes and taxes. They destroyed seigneurial insignia, openly hunted on seigneurial land, and even began to burn châteaux and their feudal documents, often after having drained the wine cellars. Some recalcitrant nobles were molested, and one or two were murdered at Aups in Provence in March, 1789. The "feudal regime," as they said, was already in upheaval before the Estates met.

By July and August 1789, the situation was quite different. The distorted echo of Parisian events and harsh conditions caused fears of brigands and invasion. Irrational panic radiated outward from half a dozen places in a "great fear." Only Brittany, Lorraine, and part of the south were immune. There were repeated attacks on châteaux, abbeys, and their archives, and even several assassinations. There was no question any more of paying dues to the lords, tithes to the Church, or even taxes to the king. And where prohibition had once reigned, all people were now free to hunt, fish, graze animals, and cut wood anywhere they liked.

The Constituents and their friends, whether or not they were bourgeois and tied to landed income, feared that the disorders would spread. They pushed for the formation of national guards on the Parisian model, charged both with saving the nascent Revolution and protecting the interests of property owners, which most of them were. The fine generosity of the night of August 4, with its proclamation abolishing "privileges, tithes, and feudal rights," thus takes on its true meaning. What the deputies abandoned had already been lost. They could only hope to calm the peasant fury, which they were momentarily able to do. Afterwards, the Assembly took back its all-embracing generosity in detailed decrees. It wanted to distinguish rights that had been suppressed altogether from rights that could be "repurchased" by the peasants. But the peasants repurchased hardly anything, and the successive assemblies ratified their refusal. Despite several attempts after 1815, the "feudalism" that was abolished in 1789 was never revived: the age of lords and tithes died that year. This was a significant event.

On October 5–6, one more attack of panic and high bread prices at Paris rudely brought the royal family from Versailles to the Tuileries, as the mob carried away "the baker, the baker's wife, and the baker's boy." The Constituent Assembly soon followed them. It had already done a great deal. For two more years it would show what it could do, but it had to act under the watchful eyes of armed and organized Parisians.

THE WORK OF THE CONSTITUENT ASSEMBLY 1789–1791

The Constituent Assembly worked hard and very systematically, perhaps too much so. It wanted to recast the old Kingdom completely as the new Nation. Institutions, legislation, administration, justice, finances, weights and measures (the admirable metric system), even religion—all appeared ready for renewal.

Following the American precedent, the Assembly logically based its constitutional work on a Declaration of the Rights of Man and Citizen. This firm, sober text recognized the authority

293

of a "Supreme Being," a broad expression of divinity that would suit Protestants, Jews, and *philosophes* as well as Catholics. Article X officially recognized freedom of religion: "No one shall be persecuted for his opinions, even in (matters of) religion." The proclamation was wisely addressed to citizens, not to subjects. It spoke of Man in general and not merely of Frenchmen. And it gave more attention to his rights than to his duties. All of these were notable innovations. The key words were equality before the law and liberty. Almost all liberties were explicitly stated: freedom of work, press, speech, and personal security—"every man is presumed innocent." Property was described as inviolable and sacred, and resistance to oppression was also included as a right. The only limits on personal freedom were the liberty of others and the supreme interests of the state. These were fine principles: all that remained was to apply them.

The king of France became king of the French, although he had already held the title *rex Francorum*. His power came not by the grace of God, but after an oath to the Constitution. He held important executive powers and restrained the legislative body through the veto, the right to suspend the application of laws for a time. Louis XVI seldom used the veto and not always wisely. In any case, a single Assembly held the essential powers of government. It was elected by a voting system based on ownership of property, which excluded the poor, almost half of the men and of course all of the women. Only rich property owners could be elected: this was enough to qualify the regime as new, as far away from democracy as it was from absolutism. The system did not last long, but reappeared from time to time until 1848.

The structural reform of the kingdom was more fundamental and long-lasting. Most of the administrative divisions disappeared forever: *prévôts, bailliages, généralités,* and some twenty other divisions were swept away. Everything was reorganized into *départements,* which were almost geometric units, such as the quadrilateral of the Oise. In these eighty-three *départements* and their subdivisions, finally known as *arrondissements* and *cantons,* the boundaries of a rural community often reproduced exactly the limits of the old parish. These units contained all political, financial, judicial, and even religious administration. Officials were systematically elected. Even judges, tax collectors, parish priests, and bishops were chosen by ballot. In practice, local councils held considerable authority, and the result was real decentralization, far removed from the centralism that had gone before and would follow again from the time of Napoleon onward.

The entire ancien régime tax system was abolished. Three out of four traditional taxes—landed property, trading licenses, and personal property—began their long careers. Collecting them was another matter. It was soon necessary to have recourse to so-called "indirect" taxation.

Justice was made more humane and simplified. Cambacérès was already working on the civil code. The useful institution of the cantonal justice of the peace was established, and the English system of trial by popular jury was adopted. An appeals court was also created. Here, too, the Revolution had achieved remarkable results, but it suffered from a serious weakness in the area of religion.

THE STUMBLING BLOCK OF RELIGION

Following precedents in other countries, the Assembly decided in November 1789 "to put Church property at the disposal of the Nation" in order to help resolve financial problems. The Church owned at least 7 to 8 percent of the land of France. These "national properties of the first origin" (the "second origin" would be the properties of exiles, seized later) were sold very quickly in various forms. Bourgeois, rich peasants, and even some nobles acquired good lands and scattered parcels spread over hundreds or even thousands of hectares. To facilitate this massive transfer of property, the state issued *assignats,* paper certificates whose value was assigned to these lands. It allowed sales to be settled in this currency. Until the end of the Constituent Assembly, the *assignat* lost little of its value in terms of hard money, gold. After 1792, however, it fluctuated, then came crashing down. Those who were clever enough to wait could pay for their purchases with paper that became almost worthless after Thermidor. This wide-ranging operation took on an irreversible character and attracted to the revolutionary cause a crowd of comfortable people who professed no other ideology than their own interest. All that they asked of succeeding regimes, including the Restoration, was the confirmation of their purchases in perpetuity. Of course this did not prevent them from later entering the ranks of right-thinking notables and champions of the established order.

Few people were shocked by the prohibition of further perpetual monastic vows, as well as the reorganization of the few remaining religious houses. Their inhabitants returned to civil society and received honorable pensions. In any event, the revolutionaries had shown an intelligent respect for charitable orders.

The Civil Constitution of the Clergy, however, appeared more surprising and dangerous. Faithful to their principles, the Constituent Assembly placed one parish priest in each community, and of course more in the cities. They established one bishop in each *département,* and several metropolitan archbishops above them. These functionaries were appointed, or rather elected by the richest of their flock. This could have surprised honest clergymen. It was perhaps less shocking to good Gallicans that henceforth the procedure of consecration would bypass the pope, even for bishops, and that no more money would be sent to Rome. What troubled clerical consciences the most was the duty to take an oath to the Constitution beginning in November 1790. Those who refused would be replaced but would receive a pension. Most bishops refused. Among the lower clergy jurors and non–jurors were about evenly divided in France as a whole, although the distribution varied widely from one region to another. Even some who had taken the oath expressed reservations. As the law was applied, a new clergy was installed with some difficulties. In reality, the revolutionaries were waiting—and they waited for a long time—for the pope's reaction. They knew that Pius VI was hostile to everything that had happened in France since May 1789. But Pius did not publicly pronounce judgment until March 1791, when he issued two burning briefs. From this time onward there was a schism inside the French Church, and between France and Rome. Many of those clergymen who had already taken the oath were now inclined to retract. The matter did not stop there, because other oaths were demanded later and largely refused. This schism might have been avoided. It aggravated the growing internal disorders of revolutionary France as well as the external threat, which was as yet only theoretical.

For the most part the members of the Constituent Assembly were representatives of the cities. Often they were shocked by the behavior of high and middle clergymen, but few deputies indeed were truly devout and even fewer were atheists. They had completely misunderstood the profound attachment that many people in the provinces, particularly in western France, felt for their priests, their only guides and continuously resident pastors. In the preceding century these parish priests had been well trained at diocesan seminaries. Their lives of service contrasted sharply to the unedifying careers of most of the clergy at court.

The Mounting Threat:
March 1791 to April 1792

The agitation, which had temporarily subsided in 1789, was renewed in the cities and the countryside. The flight of the king, like a bolt from the blue, exaggerated everything, bringing on first the war and then the Republic. These violent upheavals naturally provoked much discussion and activity.

Besides in the cabarets and the streets, political action in cities occurred in neighborhood meetings or sections, as they were known in Paris. These sections took the place of town halls and even clubs such as the Jacobins, Cordeliers, and Feuillants. Powerful orators, often drawn from the lower levels of the law, journalists, and shopkeepers, expressed themselves on every topic. They denounced the hoarders and the plotting aristocrats such as the first group who had gone into exile in July 1789 with the king's brother, the comte d'Artois. They also distrusted the "refractory" priests who refused to take the oaths. Soon enough they saw conspiracies everywhere, and indeed there were plots afoot. They began to talk of "suspects," people who were disloyal to the Revolution. Fortunately, bread was cheap and unemployment was not rising.

In the countryside, the situation was often anarchic. Cloisters were destroyed, woods were despoiled, and livestock wandered about everywhere. People were not paying taxes, not even the tithe to "good priests." Entire provinces—the Comtat, the west, the center—were divided by struggles between revolutionaries and royalists. The affair of the oaths made everything worse. Whole cantons refused to accept the "constitutional" priests who were sent to replace "refractory" ones. On April 11, 1791, the Constituent Assembly followed the example of administrators of the Parisian *département* and authorized the refractory priests at least to say mass, though not to administer the sacraments. This reservation could not be enforced.

During this period, quarrels between ideological factions were tearing the Assembly apart. The last champions of absolute monarchy and the dominant party of ambitious moderates including Lafayette and Barnave were struggling against a handful of daring revolutionaries supported by the Parisian clubs. From this latter group emerged several sorts of democrats, soon to be republicans, such as the journalist Jean-Paul Marat and the lawyer Maximilien Robespierre.

After failing in his rather naive plan to escape in order to intimidate the Constituents from across the border, Louis XVI provoked a reshuffle of the cards, a renewal of popular agitation, and a decisive turn of events toward true tragedies. On June 21, 1791, the day after his recapture at Varennes, some Frenchmen apparently thought that a king should not abandon his people. Others thought that he must surely have had good reasons to seek help from foreign princes and the thousands of exiles who were agitating across the eastern frontier. For a moment the Constituent Assembly suspended the king. Then, accepting the peculiar thesis that he had been kidnapped, the Assembly reestablished him, seeing that he had sanctimoniously ratified the Constitution of 1791. But they also sent a goodly portion of the National Guard—100,000 men—to the frontier areas. The Assembly was unable to prevent violent popular reactions as nobles and refractory priests were molested, and more châteaux set ablaze. At Paris, the Cordelier Club demanded a republic. They laid a petition to that effect at the "Altar of the Fatherland," the same spot where the king and Talleyrand, then bishop of Autun, had presided on July 14, 1790, when the federated provinces had sworn their loyalty to the laws and solemnly constituted the nation. The men in power, ambitious moderates who had little liking for the common people, ordered guards to fire on the "republicans" who had just ratified this petition. From this moment, July 17, 1791, there was a split between the two branches of the former "patriot" party. Henceforth the Parisian sections viewed the Assembly with suspicion, which resulted in many other days of revolutionary action.

Shortly afterwards the new Legislative Assembly was elected by limited suffrage. In accord with Robespierre's proposal, never again enforced, no deputies from the preceding Assembly were allowed to sit in the new body. Nevertheless it contained a near majority of sincere supporters of the Constitution, who were determined to make the system work. Another party, composed largely of members of the Feuillants Club (about 260 strong), tried to help the king, but they were blocked by conflicting ambitions. To the left of the presiding officer in the Assembly sat almost 140 deputies, often enrolled members of the Jacobin Club or the Cordelier Club. From this group, men of talent soon emerged: they were of relatively modest origins and often Girondin in their thinking, as Lamartine described them. Some, like Vergniaud, were eloquent. Both generous and a bit lazy, they were grouped around Brissot, a journalist with a doubtful past who mixed appealing ideas and disorderly activities. These men met at brilliant salons, where they were readily seduced by luxury and by women such as Madame Dodun, Madame de Staël (née Necker), and especially Madame Roland. In the clubs, powerful personalities such as Danton and Robespierre harassed them continuously.

Among countless intrigues, provincial disorders, and the fall in value of the *assignat,* there was only one important question: peace or war. Although the revolutionaries chose to go to war on April 20, 1792, we should not forget that the Revolution benefited from three years of peace. This period of peace facilitated its work, but also requires historical explanation.

The Abstention of Europe: May 1789 to April 1792

The first misfortunes of Louis XVI were vividly felt by the kings of Europe, or at least so they said. Those who were crying out the loudest included some who were farthest away, such as Catherine the Great. Others had no intention whatsoever of coming to Louis's aid, such as the king of Spain and the petty monarchs of Italy. The rulers of the three great continental states—Austria, Prussia, and Russia—were thinking more seriously about seizing bits of territory from Turkey and treating themselves to a second partition of Poland while awaiting the final division of that country. Furthermore, some had their own internal problems. In particular the brothers of Marie-Antoinette, Emperors Joseph II and Leopold II, faced near-revolts in the southern Netherlands and Hungary. Even though reports of the first revolutionary acts had been too warmly received for their taste by their liberal elites, all these great powers and above all England looked on these strange agitations with a certain favor. In their opinion revolutionary upheaval could only weaken a country that had just won a great war. Thus they were content to issue indignant protests and friendly, dilatory answers to their brother and sister in France, who regularly appealed for their help. Besides, the National

Assembly had solemnly declared peace in Europe and the world.

Nevertheless two matters complicated European relations. Since 1789 the people of Avignon, subjects of the pope, had "given" themselves to revolutionary France, which did not know how to refuse and finally accepted them. The Sovereign Pontiff was furious; the Civil Constitution of the Clergy and the controversy over the oaths only increased his anger. The violent condemnation that he issued certainly made an impression on Catholic princes, who were also upset about the fate of the French clergy; but it was not enough to prod them to action. The second matter also dated from 1789, when the abolition of feudal rights affected Alsace, where princes of the Holy Roman Empire had kept their possessions since the French annexation in 1648. Feeling themselves wronged, they appealed to their sovereign, the Holy Roman Emperor. But since the Alsatian municipalities had joined others in the grandiose ceremony of federation on July 14, 1790, the Assembly considered that the will of the Alsatians took precedence over ancient rights of foreign landlords. Thus they stated the redoubtable principle of popular self-determination. Emperor Leopold II, wise and rather liberal, gave several worthy speeches and contented himself with diplomatic protests. Even after the attempted escape and suspension of his brother-in-law Louis XVI, Leopold declared that he could foresee armed intervention, however desirable it might be, only if all Europe would join him, which he then knew was impossible. Even his famous warning that he would act if any harm came to the French royal family, the Declaration of Pillnitz, which he published jointly with the Prussians in August 1791, did not in his eyes constitute a real engagement. Yet the French revolutionaries, even the moderates, perceived it as an insulting threat, which in fact it was not.

Six months were sufficient to turn the situation completely upside down.

Many things had changed in Germany as in France. Outraged by the indignities suffered by the royal family and the refractory priests, who were threatened with imprisonment, Austria and Prussia made an alliance in order to restore the ancient form of monarchy in France. They would each supply fifty thousand troops, but in good time. The unexpected death of Leopold, who was succeeded by his neither prudent nor liberal son Francis II, accelerated the process. But France had taken the initiative on April 20, 1792.

All the important French political figures, with the exception of Robespierre, wanted war. The king and queen were betting on the defeat of the Jacobins. Ambitious officers, such as Lafayette and Dumouriez, thought of using the army to play a prominent role alongside a monarch who would be forced to recognize their talents. Ardent idealists, too, supported war as they dreamed of bringing liberty to the enslaved peoples of Europe. The Girondins held this view, and also hoped to reinforce their domestic political position. In short, in this war military operations often had unfortunate results or were detoured from their objectives simply because they had to serve contradictory political ambitions.

FROM THE WAR TO THE REPUBLIC: APRIL TO SEPTEMBER 1792

The French armies had to fight not only the Austrians but also the famous Prussian army, which they were not expecting.

Indeed the French possessed the best weapons and the finest artillery in Europe, brought up to date by technicians and ministers of Louis XVI. But the army was composed of two diametrically opposed elements. First came the old troops, who were well trained, but in complete disarray. More than half of the officers had emigrated, and the rest were slack and incompetent. Their lukewarm attitude toward the revolutionaries can be seen in thousands of desertions. On the other hand, the 100,000 soldiers drawn into the National Guard in 1791 were often enthusiastic and full of good intentions, but lacking in instruction and experience. At the first skirmishes with the Austrians near the present-day Belgian frontier, part of the army disbanded. Some officers such as Dillon were killed by their own soldiers. Chance had it that the enemy armies were not ready to attack, and the Prussians allowed a good two months to pass before resuming the offensive. Arriving on the boundaries of Lorraine at the end of July, they captured Verdun on September 2, and already threatened Paris. From this date, the fate of the monarchy, which had never stopped supplying information to its German allies, was sealed. The people of Paris had decided its doom.

With the first military setbacks, threats from the exiles at Koblenz, revolts in the west and south, the imminent treason of Lafayette, and the formation by the king of a trusted "constitutional guard," the atmosphere in Paris was a mixture of anger, anguish, and suspicion. Revolutionary Paris and the Legislative Assembly accepted the necessity of harsh measures. In noisy meetings the revolutionary *sansculottes,* wearing their Phrygian caps and carmagnole jackets, carrying their pikes, cried out for vengeance. They demanded the dethronement of the king whose sympathies could only lie with the enemy. In order to foil the omnipresent "aristocratic plots," the Legislative Assembly threatened to banish the refractory priests. They harassed the families of exiles and called up twenty thousand *fédérés,* National Guardsmen from the provinces, to protect Paris.

When Louis XVI vetoed these last measures, thousands of threatening demonstrators invaded the Tuileries and abused him. The king showed his habitual quiet courage and drank to the health of the nation, but refused to give way on June 20; this was a clear warning.

In July the Prussian army began to move. Defying the king, the Assembly declared "the Fatherland" in danger, and openly recruited numerous "volunteers" while the *fédérés* were converging on Paris, some of them singing the celebrated "Marseillaise." In this extraordinary atmosphere the duke of Brunswick's famous manifesto, published at Koblenz on July 15, suddenly became known at Paris on August 1. This insensitive and rude text was composed by an exile, probably on instructions from Marie-Antoinette. It threatened death to all French people who resisted the "imperial and royal" army under Brunswick's command, and promised "military execution" and "total subversion" at Paris if the king and his family were not respected and restored in all their powers. The effect it produced was not that which was intended.

At the instigation of the Faubourg Saint-Antoine section, the neighborhood sections of Paris, composed of workers, artisans, and small employers, expelled the legal administration and replaced it with an insurrectional commune. With the help of the *fédérés,* they brutally assaulted the Tuileries on August 10, and forced the hand of the Legislative Assembly. The resistance was spirited and murderous, but the king tried to stop it and took refuge within the Assembly itself. That body could only suspend and imprison him, and call for a new Constituent Assembly or Convention, because the Constitution of 1791 was obviously obsolete.

Almost two months of anarchy, passion, and violence followed. This disorder was explained in part by the fall of the *assignat,* commodity speculation, high food prices, and the requirements of the war effort. A wave of antireligious feeling swept over France and was accepted by the deputies, who were not very religious anyway. It did lead to the banishment of the refractory priests, who numbered some thirty thousand. Convents and bishop's palaces were closed; religious orders were definitively dissolved; sacred vessels and precious crosses were confiscated, melted down, and sold. Even the wearing of clerical garb was forbidden. Divorce and civil population registers were introduced.

The roll of unsettling events continued to inspire fear. The Prussians were besieging Verdun; Paris was constantly aroused by the incessant alarms. And at the front, there was the treason of Lafayette, whose army refused to follow him. To spur them on, the revolutionaries had the burning harangues of Danton, who was calling for "Boldness, even more boldness." The agitation of the *sansculottes* led to the creation of an extraordinary criminal tribunal, which was supposed to work in the prisons. When Parisian mobs killed prisoners outright in the

September massacres, an expression of unbridled panic and fury, fewer than one hundred aristocrats, more than two hundred clerics, and over a thousand commoners died. Half of the two thousand eight hundred prisoners were spared, including all but thirty-five of the women; but among the victims was the Princess de Lamballe, whose executioners were taking vengeance on her friend "the Austrian," Marie-Antoinette.

Fifteen days later at Valmy, an astute maneuver by Generals Dumouriez and Kellermann cut off the retreat of the Prussians. The young guards and old soldiers of France courageously resisted cannon fire and made the reputedly invincible enemy turn back. Indeed the Prussians were surprised, but they were also mired in the mud, decimated by dysentery, and demoralized at not receiving any help from their Austrian allies. They returned quietly to their quarters in Germany.

On the following day, September 21, the new Convention abolished the monarchy. On September 22, year I of the Republic was inaugurated. This reply to Brunswick, the exiles, the aristocrats, and the internal plotters was harsh and unexpected. The Convention had been elected in a fearful atmosphere, with only revolutionaries voting, about one-tenth of the total electorate. For the moment, the Revolution had been saved. But it still had to survive in an almost entirely hostile Europe. Even in France more than half of the nation was against it.

Chapter Thirteen

REVOLUTION AND WAR: 1792–1799

Most French people have passionate and contradictory feelings about those two hard years of their history, from the summer of 1792 to the summer of 1794. Yet they do not always take into account either the object of the conflicts or the fundamentals of the situation.

The essential point is that war against England and the greater part of Europe lasted from 1792 to 1815. It was continued by the will of successive governments and interrupted only by two brief truces—in 1802–03, after the Peace of Amiens, and in 1814, at the time of the first Restoration. Directly or indirectly, this war often ruled internal politics as well as economic and financial development. The war brought about the dictatorship of the Terror as well as that of Napoleon. Of course, the war does not explain everything, particularly not details of internal quarrels and religious affairs. But for a long time the war weighed heavily on France, and may have left as many new weaknesses as glorious memories.

THE JACOBIN CONVENTION AND
THE TERRIBLE YEARS:
LATE 1792 TO JULY 1794

Many dense volumes have been devoted to the twenty-month period between the end of 1792 and mid-1794, an era that was complex and heavily laden with history. To go to the heart of the matter would constitute an almost impossible task, but the war does provide a continuing theme for understanding.

The young Republican Convention had been saved in September 1792 at Valmy. The revolutionaries took comfort in the brilliant victory by Dumouriez at Jemappes, and they exulted in the rapid conquest of all Belgium, and the Rhineland as far as Mainz. The armies of the republic also captured Savoy and the county of Nice from the king of Sardinia. On November 19, the Convention declared that it would henceforth bring "fraternity and help to all peoples who wanted to recover their liberty." This proclamation could hardly be pleasing to the monarchs of Europe. Even the English, who had been prudent and quite good-natured toward the French Revolution up to this time, were worried. They had to deal with their own democrats and with the Irish. Then, in a new breakthrough, the victorious but poor Republican Convention covered its war expenses by confiscating the properties of princes and churchmen in occupied countries, as well as pillaging their lands. Danton and other revolutionaries formulated or rediscovered the theory of frontiers "marked by nature." They had in mind the Rhine and the Alps. Several months later, while the trial of Louis XVI was taking place, the countries conquered by the republican armies were simply annexed by France.

The reaction was violent, particularly in England, which would not then allow a French squadron to occupy Antwerp, and indeed has never allowed it. Using as pretext the execution of Louis XVI on January 21, 1793, the British expelled the diplomatic representative of the French Republic. Flush with victory and fired with youthful enthusiasm, the Convention replied on February 1 by declaring war on Britain and, for good measure, on Holland as well. To their dismay, the Dutch had become neighbors of France and would now have to pay the price. The exhausting war against Pitt's nation lasted for more than twenty years. At the beginning, Austria and Prussia were still at war with France, too, even though they had taken part in a second partition of Poland. These four partners in the anti-revolutionary coalition were soon joined by many others: Spain, Portugal, Piedmont-Sardinia, the kingdom of Naples, and Russia, although Russian involvement was purely theoretical at first. This poorly organized group of nations was known as the First Coalition.

The dangers for the French army were great. It was still uncertain and divided, improvised and suffering from uneven leadership. Several weeks later, catastrophe struck. Expelled from all their conquests and betrayed by certain officers including Dumouriez, the troops of the Republic could not prevent multiple invasions of France. The Austrians laid seige to Maubeuge and Valenciennes, the Prussians invested Mainz and then Landau, the Piedmontese were on the move in Savoy, and the Spaniards crossed the Pyrenees at both ends. Even the British, though they had eyes mainly for the rich Antilles, invested Dunkirk and Corsica. The British navy soon captured the Mediterranean naval base of Toulon, which was handed over to them by local royalists.

As if this sixfold invasion was not enough, the Convention also had to face internal revolts in the spring of 1793. In a good part of the south and in cities such as Lyon and Marseille, royalists had been hard at work for months. Grave difficulties could be expected. Within the Convention itself, the dominant Montagnard faction was centralist in principle and, out of necessity, in practice. When the more extreme Montagnards eliminated the Girondin party in May and June after long personal quarrels, the most important effect was to accentuate and extend the so-called federalist revolts, which covered a good third of France, including Normandy. The soldiers who were sent to check these "enemies of the interior" acted ruthlessly.

The most serious revolt by far broke out in the Vendée, the wild country of the west—first in Anjou, then in Poitou, later in

Maine and Brittany. This civil war at times reached the summits of horror and aroused violent opposition then and now.

The revolt took place at the exact moment the Convention decreed the conscription of 300,000 men in March 1793. Men from Choletais and surrounding areas refused to register for the draft. Stirred up by popular leaders such as the game-warden Stofflet and the coachman Cathelineau, they refused to leave their villages to fight the distant enemies of a little-known and unsympathetic government. Accustomed to their "good priests," they had rejected the new Constitutional Clergy. But they had accepted with joy the abolition of seigneurial rights, because they hated their contemptuous absentee lords. The peasants had responded badly to the installation of new municipalities and administrative units dominated by bourgeois. Furthermore, they were not pleased when the latter made massive purchases of national properties, which they had silently coveted for themselves. The revolt was supported by former salt-smugglers who had been made redundant by the abolition of the *gabelle*. In the beginning the conflict was savage and chaotic, at least as long as the nobles were not tempted to organize it. A few nobles did eventually allow themselves to be persuaded. The few Republican troops in the area suffered from poor commanders and were often trapped and massacred. They received only mediocre reinforcements and retaliated against the rebels with the same unspeakable cruelty. In three months the Vendéean rebels had captured Cholet and Saumur, threatened Nantes, and veered northward, supposedly to join with forces supported by the English. At that time France was being invaded from all directions, while Normandy, Franche-Comté, Provence, and part of the southwest were ablaze with revolts.

This conjunction of dangers required a strong central government. The Convention, after having written an ultrademocratic constitution that was carefully laid aside in a magnificent box, declared that the government of France would be "revolutionary until the peace." Great, energetic, and often excessive measures led to the dictatorship of the Montagnards, the Committee of Public Safety, and the Terror. In view of the fearful external and internal dangers, the historian must agree that to save "the *patrie* in danger" the men of that age had to make a choice between harsh measures and outright surrender. Twenty years later, even Napoleon did not have to make that choice.

The core of the government of the Terror, several dozen dedicated members of the Convention, was composed of lawyers, journalists, technicians, groups of centralizing and not very Catholic republicans. Their salient characteristic was youth: their oldest member, Carnot, was barely forty. They exhibited habitual competence, strength of will, and, at times, burning ardor. But they were also prone to nervousness and fatigue, and the force of contradictory passions eventually tore them apart. The radicalized Parisian crowds, armed and organized in sections, excited these leaders with their cries, hatreds, and acclaim. Nevertheless, these men were united in their firm decision to defend the *patrie* by all means, even the most horrible. The present-day sense of the word *patrie,* or "fatherland," as they finally called France, dates from this period. Their *patrie* was truly in danger, as much from real internal enemies as from the invaders, whom they had the audacity to provoke by their declarations of war.

The means of the Terror are well known, though they are usually presented with an equally superfluous enthusiasm or hatred.

First of all, there was a progressive concentration of power in the hands of minority parties in the Convention: Girondins, then Montagnards, then various committees, especially the Committees of General Security and Public Safety, then the pure Robespierrists. Through prudence or cowardice, the bulk of the Convention, the Center party known as the *Marais,* supported these minorities in rapid succession—until it decided to take all power once the danger had passed, after the Thermidorian reaction in 1794. This collective magistracy, in which everyone nonetheless had a specialty (Carnot, for example, was in charge of the armies), needed supporters and listening posts, "antennae," in the *départements* and armies. This role fell to the representatives on mission, plenipotentiary members of the Convention similar to the old intendants.

There was also a national agent in each district or large commune, supported by a popular society, the local branch of the Jacobin Club. In order to watch "suspects," aristocrats, priests, federalists, lukewarm people, and "enemies of the interior" in general, a revolutionary committee operated in most communes, similar to the Committee of General Security in Paris. The first Revolutionary Tribunal was created at Paris by the Girondins in March 1973. This special court and its provincial counterparts were charged with judging opponents of the Revolution. At first the courts operated with moderation, acquitting about half of those charged. Then the multiplication of dangers as well as pressures from above and from the fanatical *Enragés* made justice terrible indeed. In 1793, the tribunal at Paris pronounced 243 death sentences, almost as many as at Bordeaux or Marseille, cities that were hostile to the Revolution; but Paris condemned only one-tenth or one-fifteenth as many people as the courts at Lyon, Angers, and above all Nantes, cities in open revolt against the Revolution or at the center of an insurgent region. The most extreme incident, the insane drowning of thousands of people ordered by Carrier at Nantes, was a prelude to the "putting to right" of the Terror by the Montagnard Convention. In fact the Great Terror of 1794 was limited to specific areas: 70 percent of the deaths occurred in the Vendée and Provence, while there were none at all in six *départements,* and an insignificant number in more than thirty *départements* of the Center and the Alpine regions. In Paris the Terror was spectacularly tragic: more than 2,000 persons were guillotined in sixteen months. Of the 14,000 victims of the Terror who have been definitely identified, fewer than 15 percent were nobles and clerics, and nearly 60 percent were workers and peasants. With the killings in the Vendée, the total number of victims was well in excess of 100,000, and perhaps nearly twice as many. Passion, hatred, and madness contributed as much to the Terror as did the quest for national security, which nonetheless cannot be discounted as a cause.

After the internal reconquest of France, which remained uncertain for several years, the other priority was protecting the frontiers. To do this required reinforcing the disparate, unreliable, and badly equipped army. The widespread custom of electing officers and noncommissioned officers was considered democratic. Under the absolute authority of Carnot, the organizer of victory, attention was devoted to the fourfold problems of recruitment, weaponry, discipline, and tactics.

Shortly after drafting 300,000 men, the Convention decreed the *levée en masse*— that is, the mobilization of all men from eighteen to twenty-five. Despite resistance and desertions, this decree ensured numerical superiority for the French armies, which were about 600,000 strong at the end of 1793, and perhaps 800,000 in 1794. The combined forces of the enemies were considerably smaller, and of course they could barely communicate with one another.

Discipline had never been perfect, but it was greatly improved thanks to two measures. First came the consolidation of demibrigades, composed of one-third "whites," or experienced soldiers, and two-thirds "blues," or new recruits. Then there was progressive purification of the officer corps thanks to the elimination of treasonous commanders, who were dismissed and at times executed in case of defeat. This made the work easier for Carnot and the Convention's representatives on mission. Setting aside the inefficient system of election, they singled out or promoted very young generals: among the eldest were Jourdan and Pichegru, aged thirty-two and thirty-three. Often they chose former noncommissioned officers, men who were competent, dynamic, enthusiastic, good republicans, and frequently of modest origins. The names Hoche, Marceau, and Kléber suffice to show that military talent does not come only with noble birth or age. The excellent weaponry left behind by the ancien régime, especially the artillery, was renewed and improved. Factories were sometimes installed in disused monasteries and convents. Thanks to the factories of Saint-Étienne, Le Creusot, and Allevard in particular, France was able to produce up to 700 cannons and 250,000 rifles per year. For several years, until Bonaparte allowed it to be destroyed at the Battle of the Nile, even the French navy was well maintained and could hold its own against the British, who blockaded almost all the great ports. The corsairs also captured a good number of enemy merchant ships.

The tactics so intelligently preached by Carnot and followed by the army were really of the utmost simplicity. The French armies took advantage of numerical superiority, the revolutionary ardor of the soldiers, and the superior quality of weaponry. They attacked the enemy massively at a single place, without wasting time in long sieges or subtle maneuvers. The result was that by the end of 1793 the federalists and Vendéeans had been defeated or contained, and the invading enemy was pushed back almost to the frontiers. Beginning in the spring of 1794, French successes included the victory of Fleurus in June and the reconquest of Belgium, the Rhineland, Savoy, and the Spanish border areas. Most members of the First Coalition wanted peace. Meanwhile the great revolutionary drama reached its climax between March and July when the Montagnards carried their quarrels to the point of fratricide.

Life and Death of the Mountain: 1794

The more moderate Girondins having been eliminated in June 1793, it now fell to the Montagnards at the head of the French Republic to assume the almost impossible task of defeating the internal and external enemies. Instead, they tore themselves apart from March to July 1794.

And yet, despite increasing difficulties, their accomplishments represent something both gigantic and monstrous. First of all, it was necessary to feed, clothe, supply, arm, and pay the masses of troops and maintain the still numerous ships. Prieur, a former officer of the corps of engineers (like Carnot), and Lindet—both members of the Committee of Public Safety—assumed responsibility for munitions and supply. These men wisely surrounded themselves with famous experts—Monge, Berthollet, Chaptal—to improve and expedite the manufacture of gunpowder and weapons. They organized the necessary work force, which included women. As for the rest, the harsh requisitions, forced taxation, and exploitation of conquered territories helped ensure success. But to achieve this success, it was often necessary to use the traditional services of arms merchants and traffickers in order to find the indispensable credits and supplies. Thus, this honest Montagnard republic was unable to keep its hands clean. The following regimes had even more difficulty, because fighting wars demands more than just large numbers of men. In 1794 the Republicans nevertheless executed several shady operators such as Choiseau and d'Espagnac, who had stolen too much.

These trials and successes had harsh effects. Despite its wealth and power, France could not tolerate the multiple exactions of a merciless authoritarian regime. A large part of the citizenry detested the government for its religious attitudes, policies that were politically insensitive in a country that still contained a Catholic majority. They could not accept the persecution of priests and the revolutionary calendar with its suppression of Sunday. The abhorred the revolutionary civic festivals with the goddess of reason or the Supreme Being, let alone the savage attempts at dechristianization. These extreme measures pleased only an exalted "philosophical" minority. It is impossible to argue that the state of war demanded these incredible blunders, which appeared to oscillate between the ridiculous and the hateful.

There were other genuine and quite sufficient obstacles: rising prices, inflation, underemployment, embezzlement, commodity speculation, and riots here and there. The local agents of the Convention were implacable when dealing with profiteers, wealthy peasant and bourgeois monopolists. The "revolutionary armies" of the interior, several thousand men with a guillotine in tow, were employed to ensure the movement of supplies and enforce the fixed maximum prices. These domestic military expeditions naturally provoked the black market and harassed workers as well when the regulations were extended to wages. Fortunately, the harvest of 1793 was rather good, the war provided employment, and the *assignat* did not fall too quickly. The currency fell most rapidly after Robespierre's demise.

But everything changed in the winter of 1793–94. The harsh

weather, the subversive activities of royalist agents supported by English money, the incessant quarrels between the Parisian neighborhood sections and the Convention, the factions within the Convention itself, and of course the sincere authoritarianism of Robespierre provoked a series of purges. In March, less than a year after the fall of the Girondins, the first to go were the Enragés and Hébertists, supporters of intensified terror. In April, it was the turn of the Dantonists, supporters of reduced terror after the internal and external victories. The Robespierrists and their leader had been cut off from the people since March. They aggravated the Terror into a fit of madness and decreed the "Cult of the Supreme Being" with its theatrical festivals. They provoked the weariness, disgust, and above all suspicion of the last members of the Convention, who were worried about losing both their property and their lives. The least acceptable act was probably the law of Prairial, which called for the confiscation of goods of "suspects" and their redistribution to the poor. In the eyes of most French citizens, attacking property was the supreme sacrilege!

On 9 Thermidor (July 27, 1794), the accumulation of rancor and the ultimate blunders of Robespierre led to the elimination of the Mountain and its crest.

The prudent and wise men of the *Marais,* often mediocre at best, had survived the Jacobin torrent and would henceforth occupy center-stage from Thermidor to Brumaire. Almost all of them showed up during the Directory. Yet in these five years of dull or shady transition, the armies of the Republic continued their exploits. Let us rejoin them.

FROM THERMIDOR TO BRUMAIRE: WAR AND CONQUEST

Thermidor was the end of the ascendant Montagnard phase of the Revolution. It was also the beginning of an apparently less harsh period of reaction, certainly less "pure" and in some ways more "bourgeois," but it had little influence on the fate of the French armies. They continued their conquering march to the north, the east, the southeast, and the southwest. What was now called "the Great Nation" stretched as far as the Rhine and beyond the Alps and Pyrenees. The Spaniards were inclined to negotiation, and the Prussians earnestly desired it because they wanted to join in the final partition of Poland, which the Russians had already started. Even Britain wanted peace as long as it could continue to dominate the seas and capture what remained of the French colonies. The British decided to stop subsidies to their Prussian allies. But in January 1795, Pichegru launched his cavalry attack on Holland and captured the Dutch fleet, which was blockaded in frozen harbors. Even though the Convention was now "Thermidorian," it was still revolutionary and proceeded rapidly to transform the United Provinces into a Batavian Republic, a sort of younger sister of France itself. England could not tolerate this affront. While seizing the Cape of Good Hope and Ceylon, two former Dutch colonies, the English decided never to negotiate with this continental neighbor that had become too powerful and too close for comfort. The other belligerents, Austria and Piedmont, still had resources and thus maintained their hope of taking revenge on France. Eventually, Prussia and Spain came to terms with the French Republic at Basel between April and July 1795. The Prussians recognized the French occupation of the left bank of the Rhine, in exchange for a promise of unspecified compensation in the future. The Spaniards ceded to France their half of the rich sugar island of Saint-Domingue, which was at that time occupied by the English. Spain also promised to form an alliance with France. The young Batavian Republic came to an agreement giving the French several Flemish territories, an alliance, and above all the help of its fleet.

It appears that the Thermidorian conspirators were replaced by the men of the Directory government in October 1795. In fact most were the same men, including Carnot, and represented the same interest groups. They found themselves confronted by two powerful adversaries. Against Britain with its privileged island status, they could do almost nothing. The invasion attempts of Hoche at the end of 1795 and Humbert in 1798 failed, despite Irish support. For all practical purposes, the British Royal Navy controlled the seas, despite the exploits and attacks of French privateers.

Against Austria, Carnot employed an old strategy of the late French monarchy: attacking Vienna simultaneously via the Main and Danube River Valleys. Two fine armies of 80,000 men each were entrusted to two brilliant young generals, Jourdan and Moreau; but Archduke Charles, brother of the Emperor, stopped both of them. There remained a third, more modest army of 40,000 men, stationed near Genoa, which was supposed to lead diversionary attacks against the king of Piedmont and the Austrian possessions in northern Italy. Carnot was resigned to giving this command to Napoleon Bonaparte, then aged twenty-seven, an artillery officer with a complex past. Bonaparte was neither well known nor much appreciated for his remarkable role in recapturing Toulon at the end of 1793. He had helped to repress the coup d'état of Vendémiaire with the famous "whiff of grapeshot" (October 1795). Most other officers looked on this Corsican as an intriguer who owed his position to the protection of powerful but shady characters such as Barras. Shortly before becoming his faithful lieutenants, Masséna and Augereau were quite critical of him. Masséna labeled Napoleon an intriguer, which he was; Augereau called him an imbecile, which he may have become later. From the end of March 1796, however, opinions changed as the new general immediately showed a political and military genius that almost no one had suspected he possessed.

The story of the Italian campaign has been told many times in grand epics. Often these accounts were based on documents that were rewritten by the immediate entourage and zealous admirers of the hero. Yet this famous campaign still reveals a military genius who was gifted, like Condé, with a sharp eye, intuition, rapid thinking, and a certain charm. Equally evident was his political genius, which blossomed quickly and had already achieved triumphs in a shrewd public-relations effort. In reality, the campaign consisted of two brief and brilliant episodes framing the eight terrible months of the siege of

Mantua from June 1796 to February 1797. First, in two months, Bonaparte separated the Piedmontese armies from the Austrians, forcing the king of Piedmont-Sardinia to hand over Savoy and Nice immediately. Then, having surprised the Austrians at Lodi, he occupied Lombardy. Once Mantua was taken, he climbed up the road through the Alpine valleys, and in two months found himself only a short march away from Vienna. The Austrian Emperor Francis II was then forced to sign an armistice at Leoben; this was later transformed into the Treaty of Campo-Formio in October 1797. By its terms he abandoned to France his possessions in the southern Netherlands, which had in fact already been annexed by the Republic; he also surrendered Milan and (secretly) the left bank of the Rhine as far as Koblenz.

This brilliant campaign relieved the Republic of the most powerful of its continental enemies, at least for several years. Furthermore, Bonaparte had systematically organized the pillage of northern and central Italy, which he soon occupied. The peninsula fed his armies, paid the suppliers, and enriched him and his entourage. Italian booty also provided powerful support for the finances of the Directory, which received "help" as well as works of art by the wagonload. This same Directory, however, had some reason to be worried by the "proconsular" conduct of the Corsican general.

In a château near Milan, Bonaparte held a sumptuous court for several months. He had negotiated with the Austrians practically on his own account, following or ignoring the instructions of his government as he pleased. Whether or not they approved, he had remodeled Italy. With the support of the Directory, he had invaded the papal states and taken some of their lands along with Bologna and Ferrara. Besides these territories and the definitive surrender of Avignon and the Comtat-Venaissin, he obtained from the defeated pope a substantial indemnity in gold and works of art, which were immediately shipped north to the French treasury and the national museums. On his own, Napoleon then found a vague pretext to attack the venerable Republic of Venice; he kept half of it, and gave the rest to the Austrian Emperor at Campo–Formio.

About the same time, he had transformed Lombardy into the Cisalpine Republic; later, after an ultimatum to Genoa, he invented the Ligurian Republic. In 1798–99, shortly after his departure, the Directory, carried away with enthusiasm, created three other "sister republics"—the Helvetic, the Roman, and the Neapolitan—bringing the total to six. Certainly the French Republic was giving Europe in general and Italy in particular something quite different from liberty.

After the epic campaign enhanced by Bonaparte's own publicity machine, the French government still faced recurring internal problems and two other concerns: the continuing war with Britain, and this overly popular general. The incredible expedition to Egypt could have resolved them both, because it might have struck at British trade with the Orient, and even—in wilder French dreams—helped part of India to revolt against the British. At the same time it would have rid Paris of this troublesome hero. For Bonaparte, whose ambition knew no bounds, this campaign flattered his old dreams and satisfied his desire for increased glory. It also gave him some room to maneuver, for he could plainly sense that the time for political action had not yet arrived.

We shall not recount in detail that romantic and tragic adventure, the game of naval hide-and-seek with British Admiral Nelson, Bonaparte's easy victories over the Mamelukes and the Turks who came overland from Syria and by sea, the plague of Jaffa and elsewhere, the deep hostility felt even by ransomed Moslems against Christians dedicated to cutting their throats (like Kléber in 1800), the attempt at "enlightened" government in this old country (which Mehemet Ali would take up again later), and the very fine work of the hundred scholars who went with the French army.

The significance of the campaign can be summed up with two facts. First, by abandoning his army in Egypt, Bonaparte was somehow able to return to France in secret to accomplish his coup d'état. Second, a year before, on August 1, 1798, Nelson had surprised and sunk the entire French fleet anchored near Aboukir in the "Battle of the Nile." As a prelude to Trafalgar, Aboukir should have shown the French precisely where the danger lay—in Britain. It should also have made clear to them how limited the Revolutionary and Imperial dreams of continental annexation were, and how they would eventually be destroyed.

While this sad escapade was unfolding, Europe had formed a Second Coalition against France in the summer of 1799. This time the distinguishing feature was the arrival of numerous well-commanded Russian armies. They gave powerful support to the Austrians and to several English regiments, and expelled the French from practically all their conquered territories, particularly in Italy. A devastating general defeat loomed on the horizon until October, when the tide turned for Brune in Holland and Masséna around Zurich and Saint Gotthard. These two French generals succeeded in redressing the balance of an almost desperate situation. But it was becoming patently clear that the Republic could have been saved without Bonaparte.

Returning just in time to succeed with difficulty in his coup, Bonaparte had to liquidate the Second Coalition in order to consolidate his power. As Russia had retreated after its defeat and the assassination of the half-crazed Tsar Paul I, and Britain was inaccessible on its island, once again there remained only Austria to fight.

After a difficult crossing of the Great Saint Bernard Pass, a maneuver that has been transfigured by Bonapartist imagery, Napoleon was barely able to defeat the Austrians at Marengo in June 1800. In fact Desaix saved him from disaster, but he had the misfortune to get himself killed shortly afterwards. Moreau inflicted a crushing defeat on the Austrians at Hohenlinden in Bavaria in December 1800, and Bonaparte felt some jealousy toward him. Overall, the French were victorious in continental Europe. The Austrian Emperor Francis had to negotiate the Treaty of Lunéville in 1801 under conditions similar to those of Campo-Formio in 1797.

Far away, the Turks had compelled remnants of the Egyptian expedition to surrender without glory, but allowed them to return to France in 1801. Of course Britain still remained immune to attack. But on that great island, economic and financial difficulties were increasing. The public was more and more irritated by rising taxes and the high cost of living. Some very difficult negotiations resulted in the Peace of Amiens in March 1802. The British agreed to return Malta and, in principle, some of the French, Spanish, and Dutch colonies that they had occupied without much risk. Nothing was said of French conquests or maritime and commercial affairs, which shows that the agreement was really a truce rather than a general peace.

The truce lasted hardly more than a year. Once again, and for twelve long years, war would pervade everything, dominate everything, and explain almost everything. To magnify and thereby excuse the war, the artisans of the Napoleonic legend had been hard at work since 1796. But they could not have foreseen what would happen.

FROM THERMIDOR TO BRUMAIRE: THE GOVERNMENT OF THE MARAIS AND THE COUPS D'ÉTAT

After Robespierre and his followers were executed, the conspirators of Thermidor attempted to govern for five years, from 1794 to 1799. Among them we find repentant Montagnards, revived Girondins, and that majority of the "Plain," or *Marais,* who had until that time tolerated everything. They had acted out of faintheartedness and prudence but also out of necessity. Besides, their convictions had changed. Among them were a good number of regicides, many fervent republicans, and even some devout Catholics. Not many of them had clean hands, but all were champions of the sacrosanct rights of property, which some Robespierrists appeared to threaten. To maintain themselves in power, they were not above using clever devices such as the so-called decree of the two-thirds. This decree effectively decided without elections that two-thirds of them would belong to the assemblies of the next regime, the Directory. In the same category was their simple annulment of elections that went against them in May

1798, and on half a dozen occasions their recourse to use of force and coups d'état that are hardly worth mentioning, except to show the increasing role of the army. Just as Robespierre had predicted in 1792, that army would finally overthrow the regime.

Their immediate concern after Thermidor was alleviating the Terror and bringing about a time of ease, real or feigned. There may have been fewer tumbrils on the road to the guillotine, but that instrument continued to function. It is true that execution was supplanted in part by deportation, generally on old naval hulks, a punishment known as the "dry guillotine." A certain number of priests and exiles who came back too soon died in this manner, as did the excluded deputies and overly talkative journalists who were "fructidorized"—that is, eliminated in the coup d'état of 18 Fructidor in September 1797. This government of the Marais can hardly be described as one that restored the joy of life.

There were some delights for the solid bourgeois and resigned aristocrats. They were reassured by the abolition of the Montagnard laws on property and by the rapid fabrication of the new Constitution of Year III, which effectively gave power to the richest inhabitants. The new France had hardly more than 20,000 electors, who were carefully defined by their fortunes. The bourgeois and aristocrats were also reassured because they could still buy confiscated national properties and pay for them in *assignats,* which had fallen to one-tenth of their value in Robespierre's time; they were then able to resell these properties in smaller lots for gold coin. Despite the furious rhetoric of the Montagnards, it was only now that the greatest monuments of the Church and the deserted châteaux were sold and demolished—stripped stone by stone and bit by bit of furniture. Groups of merchants known as "black bands" took part in this activity. Traces of most of their operations have been preserved in archives, but naturally these have never been analyzed, out of regard for the "interest of families," more particularly the concerns of descendants. Under the regimes of Thermidor and the Directory, these members of the eternal Marais also became rich through grain speculation.

Such free enterprise was especially lucrative after the bad harvest of 1795, which once again plunged the urban poor into semi-destitution. Speculators found opportunities in supplying the armies in cooperation with the great international bankers of Amsterdam, Hamburg, and London—who were, incidentally, the subjects of enemy nations. Fine fortunes built up by intrigue and war were put on display openly, at least in the cities. In rural areas the richer farmers stayed more discreet. This was the happy time of extravagant costumes and customs. In the streets foppish youths thrashed suspected republicans, and the general tone of Parisian social life was set by various scandalous female marvels such as Madame Taillien, Madame Récamier, and Joséphine de Beauharnais. The last of these was everyone's mistress, and was particularly favored by Barras, who may have passed her on to Bonaparte. Napoleon's blindness on this point (and there were others) has frequently been recorded.

This general laxity met with varying reception and was accompanied by a classic crisis of subsistence. Meanwhile, the rulers of the moment had to fight the right as well as the left.

The fate of the left—what remained of the Montagnards and the Parisian *sansculottes*—was decided on the first of Prairial, May 20, 1795. Calling for "Bread and the Constitution of '93"—that is, more democratic government—they had invaded the Assembly and killed a delegate. What remained of the Convention then called out troops, the likes of which had not been seen since July 1789. The *sansculottes* were disarmed, and Paris did not rise up again until 1830. Montagnards who had not yet been guillotined were killed, deported, or imprisoned. The purged ranks of the National Guard were entrusted to the good bourgeois of western Paris. The Jacobin Club was demolished, and the word "revolutionary" was forbidden, in a ridiculous valedictory to this liquidation.

Suddenly, royalists and counterrevolutionaries believed that their day had come. The exiled nobles had never been very numerous. Hardly more than twenty thousand of them had left France, while more than ten times as many remained undisturbed, apparently resigned to the Revolution. Now these exiles began to return. A smaller number of priests also returned, but the rump Convention and Directory did not welcome them very warmly. Almost everywhere—in Paris, the Rhône Valley, the region of Toulouse, and the former war zone of the Vendée—there were groups of "companions of Jéhu and Soleil," overexcited fanatics mixed with bandits who organized a "White Terror." They hunted down supposed Jacobins, robbed and executed them savagely, sometimes in large numbers. This White Terror would be continued later. Encouraged from Verona by the future Louis XVIII, Charette in the Vendée and Cadodal in Brittany renewed their struggles, in violation of the agreements they had signed with Hoche. The British finally decided to help these rebels by furnishing ships and uniforms to several hundred courageous exiles, who landed at Quiberon in July 1795. Hoche was waiting for them: he cut them to pieces and had the survivors legally shot. This did not discourage the Parisian royalists. They were embittered by the decree of the two-thirds, which the frightened Convention had just voted in order to survive. In October, the revolutionary month of Vendémiaire, a great hue and cry led to the mobilization of thirty-two of the forty-eight bourgeois sections and threatened the Convention, which entrusted its defense to a five-member committee dominated by Barras. To quell the disturbances, Barras appointed Napoleon Bonaparte, a minor general who had been imprisoned and long suspected of Terrorist views. Nevertheless, Barras had appreciated his talents at Toulon. On this occasion, Napoleon's role was reduced to sending squadron chief Murat to get some cannons at Sablons near Neuilly. He then deployed them in the avenues leading to the Tuileries, where the worried assembly was sitting. Nothing more, but for this he was wrongly called General Vendémiaire. Barras and his accomplice Fréron had only used Bonaparte. As compensation for his artilleryman's initiative, he received Joséphine and was promoted to brigadier general, then given command of the army charged with maintaining order in Paris.

The regime put in place by the Marais was soon installed.

Its offspring, the so-called Constitution of the Year III, defies understanding. There were two legislative houses, elected by the twenty thousand richest men in France. They were required to achieve unanimity to vote the most petty law. Five directors held the executive power, and that was all; they could be replaced one by one, while one-third of the legislators were replaced each year—the whole every three years. Instability, internal quarrels, and inefficiency could have been predicted, and they soon appeared. The only solution to governmental problems was the coup d'état. Four such coups are regularly cited: two against the right, and two against the left.

In the spring of 1796, the government began by eliminating a small but bold group inspired by the former feudal lawyer Gracchus Babeuf. This group had attracted some support in the aftermath of a difficult winter. They advocated crushing the million aristocrats and bourgeois who held the wealth of France and giving all wealth and power to the other 24 million, the poor. The Babeuvistes would also have organized public assistance and work. Even when simplified in this way, what has been called the "communism" of Babeuf bears little resemblance to the late-twentieth-century species. Nevertheless, having plotted against the regime, the theoretician and his friends were captured and executed. Despite short bursts of alarm, the "million rich" would sleep soundly for decades.

Soon it was necessary to strike a blow against the right also. In September 1797, the legal reselection of one-third of the deputies had removed two hundred former members of the Convention and brought about an enormous majority of royalists. They did not hesitate to encourage the return of noble exiles and refractory priests, and prepared an accusatory decree against three vaguely Jacobin directors. The directors sought the help of any prestigious general, Hoche or Bonaparte. From Italy Napoleon sent Augereau, who rapidly restored republican order on 18 Fructidor by military arrests followed by imprisonment, expulsion, and harsh penalties such as the convict-ships. The majority of both houses found their authority overturned. The returning exiles were threatened with death, and the refractory priests with deportation; freedom of the press was suspended. The Directory had allowed Catholicism and other religions gradually to reestablish themselves, but now went back to vaguely Robespierrist ideas of civic religion. There were parades, songs, and dances in celebration of Republican festivals of *decadi,* the tenth day, chosen as a substitute for Sunday. The officially sponsored faith was *Théophilanthropie,* a melange of deism, Rousseauism, and the national good. A handful of ideologues and idlers found these inventions touching. In the rest of France they encountered at best indifference, amused stupor, or indignation. The essential point was that the army had decided everything, and brave Augereau openly boasted of it.

In the following year, new elections gave the Jacobins a strong advantage. The incumbent regime found it convenient to exclude the elected candidates and replace them with most of the defeated ones. This indelicate centrist maneuver was given the grand name of the coup d'état of Floréal (May 1798).

And suddenly, in the next year, the neo-Jacobins and revisionists who wanted to reinforce the power of the five directors won the elections. This time a series of gross financial scandals and military defeats in Germany and Italy facilitated the takeover of the Jacobins. They forced the resignation of three directors, whom they judged "soft," in the coup d'état of 30 Prairial (June 1799). Then they went back to policies that gave them a new lease on life: persecuting families of noble exiles, refractory priests, and hoarders; voting a forced tax on the rich, who went into hiding; and enacting a hostage law that frightened people more than it punished them. Public opinion was indifferent or resigned to these moves. Everyone wanted above all to live in peace. The people showed their lack of enthusiasm by helping military deserters, young men from twenty to twenty-five, who were expected to serve for five years under the terms of the Jourdan law of September 1798. In the provinces, particularly in the south, the White Terror was resumed with ferocity.

This discord, these fears, these political excesses, the evident inadequacies of the Directorial regime, and the growth of many interests and ambitions—all help us to understand the relative ease of the only coup d'état that really counted, the coup of 18–19 Brumaire.

The experienced men who had governed since Thermidor were often intelligent and competent, if not honest. They certainly knew that this unstable and threatened regime could not last. Some were not lacking in ambition and had no scruples to hold them back. Sieyès, the former priest from Chartres, had enjoyed his moment of glory in 1789 when he published the sensational pamphlet *What is the Third Estate?* Afterward he had sunk into obscurity, but he now returned to the foreground. Sieyès had prepared an admirable constitution, in which he had reserved a leading role for himself. He also had a useful circle of friends, but he needed accomplices and financial guarantees as well as a "saber." The accomplices were soon found: Cambacérès and Merlin, old and remarkable servants of the state for thirty years; Fouché and Talleyrand, superbly capable of anything. Talleyrand even had to buy the cooperation of Barras, perhaps with money furnished by Bonaparte. The "intelligentsia" of the time—Daunou, Cabanis, Volney, and Destutt de Tracy—were sympathetic to the Sieyès plan, and a significant number of worried and well-off men also appeared disposed to rally round him. With the exception of Perrégaux and perhaps Lecouteulx, two future founders of the Banque de France, the bankers were hesitant. But the munitioneers and army suppliers were much more forthcoming. Collot, a supplier to the Italian campaign, and Simons, timber merchant to the navy, advanced the necessary money. As for the saber, the plotters had first thought of Joubert, but he was unfortunately killed in August; then they considerèd Moreau, who hesitated. The unexpected return of Bonaparte provided the solution to their problem. Preceded by the account of his prestigious victories (but not of his defeats) in the distant Orient, the general who had abandoned his army was acclaimed all along the route of his return. Rather naively, Sieyès thought of making Bonaparte his instrument and set in motion his coup d'état, "one of the worst conceived and worst executed that anyone could imagine," as Tocqueville judged it.

On the 18th of Brumaire, almost everything went well. On the pretext that they were threatened by an anarchist plot, both legislative chambers decided to decamp to Saint-Cloud, and entrusted the garrison of Paris to Bonaparte for their protection. On the 19th, almost everything failed. The general spoke very poorly in the upper house, was heckled in the lower house and threatened, as a would-be dictator, with being declared an outlaw. His brother Lucien Bonaparte, presiding officer of the lower house, opportunely went to speak to the indecisive soldiers outside, while Murat simply told his grenadiers: "Get this mob out of here!" And that is what they did, almost too well. The soldiers did, however, find a few deputies to organize a triumvirate of consuls to replace the vanished directors. Sieyès still thought he would dominate Bonaparte.

A handful of politicians and soldiers had just given a master to France, in the face of jubilation or indifference on the part of most of its inhabitants.

The man who would become Emperor Napoleon said, in rapid succession, "I am the Revolution" and "The Revolution is over"—two almost contradictory affirmations. Historians are in the habit of ending the Revolution at this point.

But a revolution, especially a great revolution such as this one, is never really over. Anyone who declares it insignificant is fantasizing. The French Revolution left behind accomplishments, expectations, promises, disappointments, and, naturally, mistakes. In any case, it left a deep and almost indelible mark on France, because it lives on in spirit.

AN OVERVIEW OF
THE FRENCH REVOLUTION

On the day after 19 Brumaire, only a very astute observer could say what the Revolution had really accomplished. First

Consul Bonaparte was concocting the Constitution of the Year VIII. This document apparently instituted universal male suffrage—a right that was never applied; it also established four assemblies that were quickly debased or suppressed, and appointed three consuls. Of these, only the First Consul really counted, though Cambacérès and Lebrun were excellent administrators who had served every regime since that of Louis XV. Much of the work of the Revolution was continued and completed in the following years of Consulate and Empire with the appointment of prefects, the writing of the Civil Code, the signing of the Concordat, and the creation of the Banque de France. Napoleon Bonaparte was simultaneously the expression of the Revolution, its logical conclusion, and its liquidator.

Henceforth it would be difficult for so-called absolute monarchy to return. Even when monarchs reappeared, as they did five times between 1804 and 1870, they could not dispense with a written constitution that gave at least a semblance of a separate legislative branch and an electoral system. The vote itself was reserved for the richest citizens until 1848 and was, of course, only for men. The separation of the executive, legislative, and judicial powers, a dogma that came from Montesquieu, would be respected at least in appearances, except in cases of grave danger.

As was happening little by little to other churches all over Europe and indeed had already happened some time before in Protestant states, the Church of France lost its considerable privileges. These included its official status, special justice, exemption from all taxes, and the right to collect between 6 percent and 8 percent of the harvest. Above all the Church lost its enormous fortune in goods and lands. Without remorse, the more comfortable peasants enthusiastically joined the bourgeoisie and even some nobles in buying church property—goods "put at the disposal of the Nation." Their purchases were frequently made with paper money, which gave rise to shameless speculation that did not even end in 1799. The middle class and some rather modest peasants had also participated in this enormous transfer of property, which affected nearly 10 percent of the landed wealth of the country. But these operations had lesser effect on the properties of second origin—those confiscated from exiles. Many exiles were able to maintain their ownership through their families, friends, and tenants who stayed on the land. All these large and small purchasers of national property became powerful reinforcements for what Quesnay termed "the proprietary class." The upper part constituted the fortunate ones, or notables, who thought that power should come with wealth; they played an important role for decades. Thus these men did not accept that their enrichment at the expense of the Church should be called into question. Napoleon understood this perfectly and found support among them. Despite strong pressures from their entourage, the restored Bourbons were forced to accept the *fait accompli.*

The Church of France later recovered a large part of its prestige and was able to receive landed property in gifts, but it no longer enjoyed the political role it held under the ancien régime. There were three periods when it appeared to reassert its claims under Charles X, under the authoritarian Empire, and under the Moral Order of 1871 to 1877. But these were brief episodes. By accentuating the so-called Voltairean tradition, the revolutionary spirit led astray a growing number of minds. That the head of the Church and its members would condemn the Revolution for more than a century was to be expected.

The ancient nobility suffered less than has sometimes been claimed. Other groups, such as the imperial nobility, soon tried to attach themselves to it. But apart from revolutionary crimes and mistakes, nobles who were executed or died in combat knew what they were risking. Most of the exiles, a small minority, came from frontier and coastal provinces. Often part of the family stayed behind to try to preserve properties that were threatened and sometimes pillaged, sold, and burned. After Thermidor, the exiles gradually returned to a mixed reception: some were tormented, others were warmly welcomed. Emperor Napoleon opened his arms to them, and most rushed to embrace him. The incorrigibles would not return until 1814 or 1815, "in the baggage wagons of foreign-ers," as the cruel but just saying goes. The nobles as a whole had lost part of their property. In 1825, Charles X gave them compensation in the "exiles' billion." They also lost their seigneurial powers and rights. And yet, in 1800 as in 1815 and for at least half a century afterward, the nobility remained by far the richest social group in France. Only a few great bour-geois—bankers, industrialists, even fewer merchants—man-aged to join this well-known group of the richest taxpayers of the empire and the kingdom that followed it: the list of their names was then publicly printed.

All the peasants, without exception, benefited from the disappearance of seigneurial rights and the ecclesiastical tithes. Some of their former masters did try to recover these privi-leges by diverse shrewd maneuvers such as increasing the rents. A good third or more of the peasantry acquired at least a small piece of land. Though they were at times troubled by requisitions, many profited from the high prices and the needs of the army by selling their produce advantageously. They tried to obtain payment in gold. The landless peasants gained hardly anything, except the glory of serving voluntarily or un-der duress in the valiant republican armies. Often they did not come back, more likely having fallen victim to epidemics and the lack of medical care than to the enemy.

Only the little people of the cities gained absolutely noth-ing. They had consistently supported the revolutionaries until 1793 or 1794. They suffered from the high cost of living, in-security, riots, and conscription. In 1791, by terms of the Le Chapelier law, they even lost their previous right to organize themselves into "corporations." In the name of "liberty" any association or coalition of workers became illegal. This pro-hibition remained in force until it was partially lifted by Na-poleon III. Only at the end of the century was it abolished. Henceforth the consortium of great noble and bourgeois land-owners, the wealthy and the notables, found themselves hold-ing the reins of power. They maintained their hold for a long time and hated like the plague the increasingly impatient stirrings of petty working people. They were especially afraid of those swarming and nervous hordes in Paris, the crucible where the history of the country has so often been made.

France had been profoundly transformed by the men of the Revolution and the Consulate. They were, of course, partly the same people, often the former servants of the monarchy.

To the motley collection of unequal provinces with different statutes, venerable privileges, and abundant local customs, Bonaparte soon added prefects whose authority exceeded that of the old intendants. After some hesitation, the countryside was subdivided into *arrondissements* and *cantons.* The commune often prolonged the life of the former parish. Little by little the political, financial, and judicial administration of modern France was established. It was essentially put in place by revolutionary governments from the Constituent Assembly to the Consulate, and much of this administration survived until the middle of the twentieth century.

Naturally there would be no more provincial law: instead there was only a single national law, soon consolidated in the Civil Code. Other laws would be added after years of preparation by solid jurists, especially by the man who became the Second Consul, Cambacérès.

For the profoundly centralizing and unifying spirits of the revolutionary age, national law entailed a national language. We can hear Abbé Grégoire thundering against *patois*—the dialects in which the counterrevolution was expressed: *French* was the language of the Republic. On this point, the abbé gradually obtained success. His discourse was integrated into the national will, a general feeling of living in a single nation at last. The *patrie* no longer existed only in the person of the king, but rather in the unifying federation that was expressed in so many festivals, speeches, songs, and victories: the epic of the Revolution.

The French Revolution is sometimes praised for having achieved the "natural frontiers" of France, and for having raised its flag over the Europe of the kings. The tricolor symbolized not only liberty, but also subjection and pillage. Of the disputed and ephemeral conquests, nothing remained in 1815. Hundreds of thousands of men had been sacrificed to a glory that was as brilliant as it was short-lived, bringing on the resentment of the former "sister republics," the loss of almost all the colonies, and the destruction of the navy, which was practically turned over to Nelson by Bonaparte. French sailors would wear the mourning dress of Aboukir and Trafalgar for more than a century.

This Revolution had not yet resolved its financial or religious problems by 1799, though it would soon do so. It had divided the French people into two irreconcilable camps, those who were "for" and those who were "against"; each side was subdivided into fanatics and moderates. For some, unquestioned legitimacy passed after the death of Louis XVI to his son, the uncrowned boy "Louis XVII." When he disappeared, the royalists looked beyond the frontiers of France itself to the person of the comte de Provence, who called himself Louis XVIII. For others, no doubt the majority, legitimacy was found in the heart of the *patrie*.

After Brumaire there would be a redistribution of prizes, whose significance and duration no one could foresee.

Chapter Fourteen

FRANCE AGAINST EUROPE: THE NAPOLEONIC ERA, 1800–1815

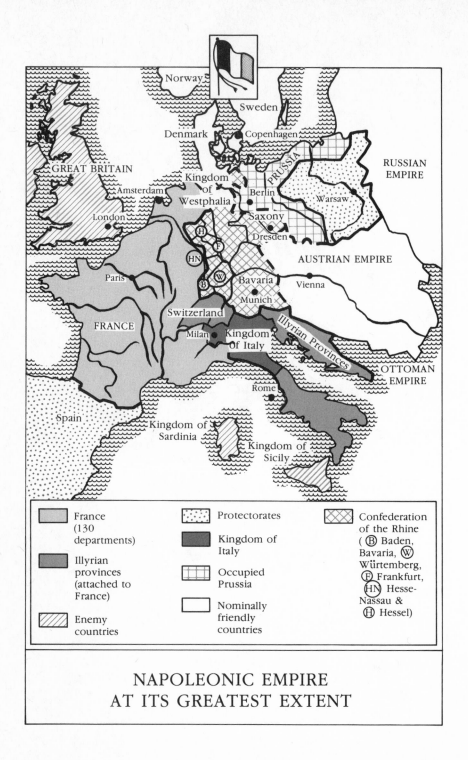

NAPOLEONIC EMPIRE
AT ITS GREATEST EXTENT

For twelve years Napoleon passed like a meteor across France and Europe. His brilliant genius seemed unlimited. From a distance of nearly two centuries the whirlpool of events still fascinates us today. We are captivated by the stunning impression made by the surprising ease of his success and then his defeat, the pounding of cannons, trumpets, proclamations, delirious joy, and violent hatred. Napoleon has inspired imitations and denunciations, and Napoleonic legends have been carried by the press ever since. His image has inspired and influenced speech, poetry, music, and all the arts. Few Frenchmen can truly ignore the Napoleonic era, and most take great pride in it. In other Europeans, however, it produces mixed or hostile sentiments. Exciting as it may appear, the foaming surface of history nonetheless conceals the essential point: the Napoleonic epic rests on solid granite foundations.

GRANITE FOUNDATIONS

In largely completing the considerable work of preceding governments, including the Directory, the Napoleonic regime quickly succeeded in establishing legislative, administrative, financial, judicial, and even religious foundations of France that would last throughout the nineteenth century and even into the twentieth.

The Civil Code, later known as the Code Napoléon (1806), has regularly been praised for its rigid clarity. It spread rapidly throughout Europe and the world in general, though to a lesser extent than the admirable metric system of 1793. The Code was the work of excellent jurists of the ancien régime, who served all the revolutionary assemblies. On many points the Code was more severe than older customary law, notably on the subjection of women and children. But at least it recognized the principles of civil liberty, equality before the law, and the secular character of the state. The sacrosanct basis of the restored Nation was Property, jealously protected. Previously, the right of primogeniture applied mainly to the nobility and only in certain regions of France. The Code established the general rule that inheritances should be divided equally. Above all, the Civil Code ratified the immense transfer of property accomplished by the sale of nationalized lands, which guaranteed the loyalty of bourgeois and peasants. The beneficiaries were not much troubled by sentimental considerations of the old Church and nobility.

Departmental administration, which still rules France in spite of recent modifications, dates from the Constituent Assembly. In 1800, however, there was a near-definitive partition into *arrondissements* and *cantons*. Elected administrators such as judges, tax collectors, and even parish priests were replaced by appointed functionaries—mayors, prefects, and subprefects. In addition, diverse municipal, neighborhood, and departmental councils were established. Their members were chosen from lists of notables; in general these were the richest inhabitants. Revolutionary Paris again had the privilege of being governed by two chief authorities. One ruled at City Hall as prefect of the Seine and thus was the successor to the former mayor, also an appointee; the other was the prefect of police, successor to the former lieutenant of police created by Louis XIV in 1667. Naturally the fundamental governing institution was the prefecture. Prefects were direct agents of central authority chosen from deputies of all former revolutionary assemblies, even including some regicides. These appointments were made by Bonaparte and his closest advisers: his brother Lucien, the two consuls, and Talleyrand, a striking constellation of talents. The all-powerful prefects personified Napoleonic government. They held more powers than the intendants of the ancien régime and were effective instruments of a unifying centralism that owed much more to Bonaparte than to Louis XIV. As uniformly shaped millstones that ground down local differences, they imposed obedience over two centuries. They still produce at least ironic surprise in most Western countries, which have often adopted the federal system without apparently suffering too much. All these servant-prefects were directly dependent on the minister of the interior, that is, on the chief of state. This dependence still exists today.

Starting in 1800, the departmental model and the system of appointed control from above were extended to the bureaucracies of law, finance, and even religion—in principle at least until 1905.

Under the Consulate the hierarchy of civil and criminal courts was also fixed, as were the twenty-nine appellate courts and the supreme court. At the summit of administrative justice stood the *Cour des Comptes* and the *Conseil d'État,* with the largest jurisdiction of all. In essence, these were revived institutions of the ancien régime. All judges were appointed rather than elected. Their permanent tenure was balanced by the exorbitant powers conferred on imperial prosecutors, who could be removed from office. These prosecutors were responsible for watching over not only the judges but also the spirit of other civil servants and of the *départements* as a whole. When they later became royal prosecutors, then general prosecutors, their reign seemed permanently established.

Up to a point, financial and even ecclesiastical administration obeyed the same regulations. But these two areas, where the revolutionary assemblies had encountered such great difficulties, deserve a more detailed examination, especially since the Consulate found lasting solutions to their problems.

The Revolution had come about in part because of a great

financial crisis and a refusal to sacrifice any privileges, above all tax concessions. The first assemblies swept away existing legislation and tried to establish a universal regime of direct and general taxation levied on land, personal property, and commercial activities. Soon afterward "doors and windows" were taxed, and many of them disappeared from houses of thrifty taxpayers. These levies constituted the traditional "four old taxes" of France. Since they did not produce sufficient revenue, the revolutionaries thought to solve the financial problem by confiscating and offering for sale all the properties of the Church and the exiles. Their worth was then assigned to paper money. As we have seen, after a promising beginning, the *assignats* lost their value slowly, then more rapidly after Thermidor. Naturally, the French people preferred gold or commodities to paper *assignats.* Excellent ministers such as Cambon and Ramel then tried to substitute another form of paper money, the "territorial mandate," but this offspring of the *assignat* was no more successful. In 1797 Ramel had to resort to the "consolidated third," a grand bankruptcy in the style of the old kings. At a stroke, two-thirds of the public debt was suppressed, and the remaining third was consolidated into annuities at 3 percent. This operation was recorded in a magnificent *Great Book of the Public Debt,* which can be seen today. At the same time the state was collecting unpopular but effective indirect taxes. This was first done discreetly, but even then included a shameful tax on drink. In reality, the revolutionary regimes had lived off impositions, requisitions, exactions, and outright pillage: in this area, Bonaparte had shone, as had others such as Masséna.

Once Napoleon had taken power at the end of 1799, he chose Gaudin, one of Necker's former clerks, to be a quite competent minister of finance. Not only did Gaudin resuscitate the whole gamut of indirect taxes of the ancien régime, but he also made them produce almost as much as direct taxation. No doubt this was because he entrusted their assessment and collection to well-selected, competent, and powerful civil servants. Helped by the peace of 1801 and a group of intelligent bankers who understood the foundations of French wealth,

Gaudin gained confidence by stabilizing the currency and paying the *rentiers* in gold. These *rentiers,* together with landowners, constituted the inalienable base of every regime that respected their interests—in fact every government right down to 1914.

Like almost all of his colleagues, the banker Perrégaux had managed to survive the revolutionary tempest; he may even have profited from it. In 1796, he created a *Caisse des Comptes Courants* (Current Account, or Giro Bank) to aid commerce. This bank faded away. It was followed in February 1800 by the foundation of the Banque de France, a private institution which offered discount operations, loans, current accounts, and bearer-bills. The principal directors of the new bank were Perrégaux, Mallet, Perier, Lecouteulx, and Récamier—extremely rich, prudent, and powerful men who bridged the gap between the ancien and the nouveau régimes. In April 1803, the bank was given a monopoly of issuing notes, at first for fifteen years and in moderate quantities. The extension of its privileges was progressive. Since 1800, a *Caisse d'Amortissement* (Refinancing Agency) had been directed by Mollien, who had worked for the Fermes Générales of Louis XVI. This agency was supported by the guarantees and advances of powerful *receveurs généraux*—departmental treasurers—whose offices and advances still exist today. With their support it was possible to repurchase burdensome state annuities at a discount, thus reducing the public debt.

But this government's most important financial act, which probably had greater effects on nineteenth-century France than all the various regimes and military campaigns, was the law of March 1803, which finally created the *franc* of germinal requested by the Convention. Its value was fixed at 4.5 grams of silver, or about 0.3 grams of gold. This franc took on almost exactly the definition of the *livre tournois* of 1726. No one could have foreseen its destiny over more than a century, as it proved the perennial nature of that powerful French wealth which had nonetheless passed through so many trials. Only the war of 1914–1918 could destroy this near-monumental stability.

The religious reconciliation, more difficult to achieve and

less successfully accomplished, nonetheless provided a general solution to an apparently insoluble problem. Apart from a few exceptions, the fate of the regular clergy was no longer a concern: the Concordat of 1801 does not even mention it, but the Jesuits were able to rise to the surface again. The revolutionary assemblies had not been very Catholic; indeed, they were vaguely deist or at times atheist, and they had forced the clergy to take a series of oaths. Only the first of these oaths was acceptable; the others met with massive rejection. Consequently two orders of clergy had been created, then torn apart. The priests rapidly became suspect, as they often supported the great insurrections of the Vendée and elsewhere; they were persecuted and sometimes killed. In an attempt to replace the old rituals of Christianity, the government had organized secular festivals of virtue, youth, philanthrophy, and the Supreme Being, all with parades and songs: they were placed on a new revolutionary calendar that featured mathematical and poetic names for weeks and months. But all this activity lacked conviction. Hoche wanted to treat robust Catholic royalism humanely, while Thureau favored savage repression; but to finish it off, the regime had to come to an accommodation with the traditional religion. Church doors were first opened slightly, then thrown wide open, sometimes to different services in succession; at times the refractory priests were allowed to officiate. In short, with the complicity of the Angevin priest Bernier and others, Bonaparte succeeded, not only with the people of western France, but also with the new pope. After months of negotiation and some twenty proposals, the Concordat was signed by Pius VII on August 15, 1801. For more than a century it regulated relations between France and the Holy See; it still applies today in Alsace-Lorraine.

The Roman Catholic religion was recognized only as that of "the great majority of the French people." Afterward Protestants and Jews were recognized and protected also. Atheism was always tolerated, and Freemasonry inundated by the Bonaparte family. The Church was resigned to the loss of its properties and promised never to trouble the purchasers, a very important clause. The map of dioceses was redrawn, and henceforth the chief of state would nominate bishops with the tacit agreement and immediate investiture of the pope, as in 1516. Parish priests were strictly subordinate to bishops, much more so than in the time of Louis XIV. All would take a strong oath of loyalty to the government and receive salaries. Churches and pious organizations could again receive gifts of money or property from devout individuals, and they soon began to solicit them skillfully. There were some complaints to the First Consul, in the assemblies, and in the army, where traces of republican spirit and lukewarm attitudes to religion were still found. And there were some difficulties in filling posts, since some were occupied by the old refractory clergy, others by the constitutionals, and still others by entirely new men. Bonaparte added to the Concordat some "organic articles" with a strong Gallican flavor. These articles instituted uniform French rather than Italian clerical garb and a cathechism that rendered unto Caesar as much as unto God. At a stroke, Minister Chaptal issued organic articles for the Protestants, whose pastors were also now paid by the state. The settlement as a whole was reminiscent of the Concordat of 1516, the legislation of Louis XIV, and the work of the Constituent Assembly. In fact this lukewarm reconciliation of Church and state took the wind out of the sails of the royalist opposition and some of its supporters, too. In regions where peasant revolts against the Revolution had occurred, there were only a few plots and outbursts of rage, and of course there was banditry.

Despite several serious difficulties at the end of the First Empire, the Concordat constituted one of the bases on which modern France was built. Two others should also be noted: the University of France, and the Legion of Honor.

The university was conceived as a hierarchical pyramid, entirely at the service of the emperor. At the top stood the "Grand Master." At the bottom was primary education, which had been almost abandoned, since the empire needed only disciplined bodies. Not until the July monarchy was the government enlightened enough to take a different view. The essential units of secondary education were the *lycées,* quasi-military barracks directed by celibate servants. Everywhere they taught the same subjects at the same time, carefully controlled to prevent any danger to the state. Their goal was the formation of cadres who could follow orders. This was all that remained of the liberal and intelligent central schools instituted by the Convention, schools that were devoted to modern scientific and technical culture for a large public. The "great schools," also created by the Convention, were stripped of their high objectives. The Polytechnique was reduced to manufacturing soldiers, and the Normale to producing *lycée* teachers. But the structure as a whole, including the faculties and institutes at the top, lasted over a century and was liberalized and enlarged only very slowly.

With the Legion of Honor, Bonaparte wanted first to establish regional cohorts of the decorated faithful: they would follow his orders and take a personal loyalty oath to him. In view of the resistance to this new vassalage, he reduced the scheme to a constellation of medals and ribbons, "leashes by which men can be led," as he said. They still function as always.

This network of institutions, a compromise between the old France and the new, guaranteed the preeminence of the bourgeoisie both old and recent. Many aristocrats came to join it. These *notables*—the very word acquired a sort of nobility—survived after Napoleon. As Jean Tulard has stated, "Regimes came and went, but the consular institutions were not changed. ... Empire, Monarchy, and Republic were only epiphenomena. Behind the political instability, we must keep in mind the permanence of administration put in place during the Consulate." We may be forgiven for thinking that it still governs France today.

Once these durable masses of granite are firmly fixed, it is tempting to write that all the rest is literature. Yet the Napoleonic era profoundly affected arts and letters, thought, imagination, and politics in France and all over Europe. These effects, good and bad, should be mentioned by the historian, if not judged.

346

THE DREAM

There are some moments when the historian pauses for contemplation and hesitates before trying to explain. Within five years the cautious young officer who had been loyal in succession to Paoli, Robespierre, and Barras, and who had wavered before the Council of Five Hundred at Saint-Cloud, had crowned himself emperor at Notre Dame de Paris. Before a crowd of eminent persons and upstarts, he faced Pope Pius VII, successor of the pontiff who had crowned Charlemagne a thousand years earlier. With a sense of respect for decent formalities, the new Caesar had submitted to a religious marriage ceremony only the preceding night. Five years later, after extraordinary campaigns of genius and luck, he seemed to dictate his will to all Europe. Only Britain escaped him, after its navy won the Battle of Trafalgar (1805), but only the British noticed. Meanwhile, Napoleon annexed provinces, offered kingdoms of his own making to his numerous family, and imposed his protectorate on the rest of the Continent. Later he even married the daughter of the last descendant of the leaders of the Holy Roman Empire of the German nation since 962. Thus Napoleon became the nephew of the late Marie-Antoinette and Louis XVI. Napoleon founded a completely new dynasty and dreamed of conquering the Ottoman Turkish Empire and even India. These tasks would be shared with Tsar Alexander I, his friend of the moment. Then this Corsican Alexander the Great who knew little geography and less of his own limits threw himself into the Spanish maelstrom, where he met stubborn popular resistance. Even more disastrous was his invasion of the snowy vastness of Holy Mother Russia, which smothered him just as it had Charles XII of Sweden and would later engulf a minor Austrian housepainter. Beaten, exiled, returned, and beaten again despite lightning strikes along the way, he left his country five years later without a fleet and almost without colonies. In 1815 France was smaller than it had been when he was a ten-year-old cadet at Brienne military school. Its territory as far as the Loire was held for six months by ten foreign armies, even including the Swiss—a shame unknown since the time of Charles VI. For three years 150,000 men would occupy the northern and eastern frontiers, and in a further refinement of humiliation French museums and palaces had to give back all the works of art stolen from abroad in the preceding twenty years.

Is it necessary to recount the well-known details of Napoleon's marvelous campaigns? They were distinguished by the victories of Austerlitz against the Austrians (1805), Jena against the Prussians (1806), and Friedland against the Russians (1807). Granted they have not always been scrupulously explained. But to discuss them in detail, we should have to present the Grand Empire with its 130 *départements,* its satellite and allied kingdoms, and the last great triumph at Wagram (1809), which was followed by Napoleon's Austrian marriage and the birth of his son, the "King of Rome" (1811). Finally there came the fall: in Spain, Russia (1812), and Germany (especially the disaster at Leipzig in 1813); the enemy invasion of France and the first abdication (April 1814); all before the dizzying return from exile and the Hundred Days, which ended at Waterloo in June 1815. There Napoleon made his supreme tactical error, a repeat of Marengo, but without Desaix to save him. In any event, his destruction at the hands of the irresistible force of unified and outraged Europe was inevitable.

The more important questions faced by the historian of Napoleon are those of the man, the war, Europe, and the nation.

The Man

According to Jean Tulard, Napoleon has inspired the writing of more books than there have been days since his death. As early as 1837, Ozeki Sane'i wrote a biography of him in Chinese. The fascination he exercises comes from the almost unbelievable character of his adventure, the repeated and insipid comparisons to Alexander the Great and Julius Caesar, the extraordinary publicity he constantly raised, and the little-noticed fact that for almost twenty years he had the entire world as his stage. While this may indeed have happened indirectly, he succeeded in pushing the English, the successors of the dethroned Spanish Bourbons and the occupied Dutch, into the Indian Ocean, to Java, the Antilles, the former Spanish colonies of America, and even Brazil, following in the wake of the king of Portugal.

Napoleon was the second son of a family of minor but rather comfortable Corsican nobility. He may have inspired Freud to speak of a "younger son complex." He was protected by the intendant Marbeuf: there were even rumors that the intendant had been impressed by the beauty of Napoleon's mother, "Madame Mère." Marbeuf helped Napoleon by attesting to his noble status and poverty, which allowed him to win a scholarship to the junior military school at Brienne. Later he entered the École Militaire, but he does not appear to have been a brilliant student, having finished forty-second in a class of fifty-eight. Then followed a long period of hesitation and trials. As a minor garrison officer at Valence and Auxonne he was often absent from duty, spending his time reading bits of everything, especially Rousseau. He tried to write and had some passionate involvements here and there. At one moment he enthusiastically supported and fought for Corsican independence. Later he joined the radical party of Montagnards and enjoyed the patronage of Augustin Robespierre, younger brother of the famous Maximilien. For these connections he was briefly imprisoned after Thermidor. But having attracted attention at the siege of Toulon by his adept deployment of artillery—four cannons and two mortars—he was promoted from captain to brigadier general with the help of Barras. Barras used him in October 1795 to save what remained of the Convention. At last his period of wandering ended: the exceptional man burst out in the Italian campaign of 1796–97 and remained on stage for more than fifteen years. Yet before this time the character of Napoleon was entirely shrouded in that of Bonaparte.

His political and military genius shone from the legendary encounter at the bridge of Arcola to 1809, with very few errors in between. It is almost too easy to appreciate his gifts two centuries later. The military side of his genius owed much to solid study of the terrain, visual acuity, and the frequent use of flanking attacks behind a sham front. He divided enemy armies into manageable pieces, then defeated them one by one, using the extraordinary velocity of light infantry and numerous cavalry. These were directed by magicians such as Murat, and took advantage of temporary superiority in numbers and weaponry. Napoleon also exercised an uncanny seductive power over his closest subordinates, frequently those who had served with him in Toulon and Italy. He knew how to speak to the troops on their own level, as no one had ever done before. But this genius had limits as well, as Clausewitz clearly saw: resistance to technological innovation, belief in the virtues of a perpetual offensive that finally consumed itself, obstinate confidence in the superiority of his forces and matériel that did not last, and a rejection of any suggestion of criticism. Nonetheless, Napoleon still preserved the illusion of brilliant generalship by a series of lightning strokes in 1814 and 1815.

His political genius was based on a profound and cynical knowledge of the vanity and above all the venality of men. For a long time he knew exactly what was possible. There is little need to add that he treated almost all human beings with utter contempt. This was his attitude toward the humble workers who were required to carry their passports and permits, little people who were locked in pious ignorance, and his own massacred infantry at Eylau, where the spectacle of carnage horrified even Percy, surgeon of the Grande Armée. He reserved the same contempt for ideologues, learned men and republicans, his former Montagnard friends, and companions in Egypt. Likewise he had contempt for almost all religions and even the popes, for he mistreated Pius VI under the Directory and exiled Pius VII to Savona. At times he even showed contempt for the members of his own family and his marshals, whom he gorged with extravagant honors and money in order to rebuff them more easily. As is almost always the case with political geniuses, Napoleon had a facility for dispensing as quickly as possible with such biological necessities as sleep, food, and love. In his brain he could classify problems like files in a cabinet. His greatest gift—his charisma—lay in his sense of carriage and manner, which were simple and unique. Napoleon was habitually somber, his voice and pen rapid and precise, his look defying verbal description: he exemplified brilliance, charm, and magnetism.

This extraordinary mental machine with its power to grasp, organize, and command wore itself down with fatigue, mediocre health, excessive pride, and dreaming. He was subject to serious errors such as the invention of imperial nobility, brutality toward Pius VII, and ignorance of the Russian winter. At this distance it is no doubt ridiculous to stress the weaknesses of a man who was "defeated by his conquests." We should keep in mind, however, that while England held the key to victory after the Battle of Trafalgar, the Napoleonic Empire became both heterogeneous and heavy on its own. It could not carry the day against internal resistance and the nationalism it had helped to inspire in other countries.

Europe and the Napoleonic Empire

Once the first wave of pillage ended, the diverse Latin and Germanic peoples who had been annexed, occupied, or "protected" were at first able to appreciate the advantages of exported French legislation. These included the abolition of serfdom, remission of feudal rights, sale of Church lands and suspension of the tithe in Catholic areas, introduction of the Civil Code, and a measured dose of the principle of liberty (the exact meaning varied). Princes who had governed these peoples were in some cases driven out, made vassals, or pushed aside. Naturally they appreciated the system much less. It was the same with churches and churchmen, inasmuch as Napoleon was in dispute with the pope from 1809 onward and kept him prisoner for four years. Furthermore, despite the incessant call for younger and younger French conscripts, the strength of Napoleon's forces was sapped by high rates of draft resistance (at times 20 percent), desertion, and death (at least

800,000 in fifteen years). He was forced to recruit soldiers not only in the forty newly annexed *départements* but also in the allied and satellite kingdoms. Thus the French half of the Grande Armée was rejuvenated while the other half became multinational. Perhaps it did not really contain twenty nations, as the Russians said, but it certainly comprised some 300,000 Dutch, Westphalians, Saxons, Bavarians, Poles, Croatians, Dalmatians, Swiss, Italians, Spaniards, and, in supreme irony, auxiliary corps of Prussians and Austrians in June 1812. From those who had been defeated shortly before, and from the shivering Mediterranean contingents, not much could be expected in Russia. Illnesses and desertions helped the natural wasting away, which culminated in the near-dissolution of the monstrous military conglomerate in disarray at Moscow.

Napoleon's fall appeared evident at the beginning of 1813, when dispossessed and submissive princes courageously asserted themselves. Often their peoples had preceded them in opposing Napoleon's armies. Spaniards and Russians had risen up with courage, constancy, and cruelty. Thus Kutusov's army, the burning of Moscow, and winter do not suffice to explain the Napoleonic debacle. Guerrilla fighters and scorched-earth tactics came from the Russian peasants, the muzhiks, who were driven to fanaticism by orthodox priests. They saw Napoleon, son of the Revolution, as the devil or the Antichrist. Spanish priests told their flocks similar stories about the soldiers of atheism, and their terrible guerrilla activities were effective well before Napoleon's first major defeats.

The elites, especially in Germany and Italy, had been seduced in the beginning by the great principles of the Revolution, but they were quickly disillusioned by the harshness of the occupation, the inconvenience of the blockades, and conscription. Yet one idea persisted, that of the nation, accompanied by the right of peoples to self-determination. Italian officers and intellectuals sometimes found themselves simultaneously in the army and in secret resistance organizations. The first of these, the *carbonari,* was formed in the south; there people dreamed of liberation, unity, and the fatherland.

In the Germanic world, enthusiasm for liberty and reform had not lasted long. A century earlier, the still vivid ravages of the armies of Louis XIV had already provoked an outburst of German national sentiment. The Napoleonic conquest hastened its evolution. Intellectuals, poets, politicians, and academics such as Fichte acted with new force. Going further, the Prussian nobility under Stein, Scharnhorst, and others rebuilt patriotism and an army that could take effective action against the tottering empire. German unification appeared on the horizon, and another Bonaparte would help achieve it.

Thus one part of the people effectively supported the now-reconciled kings of Europe. By the summer of 1813, they exploited Napoleon's errors and condemned him to defeat. Then, in two stages, before and after the Hundred Days, they moved in for the kill. By the terms of two treaties signed at Paris in May 1814 and November 1815, they succeeded in reducing the size of France and taking away its colonies and fortune. France was occupied, put under surveillance, brought low, and reviled. The restored Bourbons had to accept all of this, in a fatigued and apparently resigned country.

But the French people had cooperated to some extent in bringing about this sad state of the empire.

The Country and the Emperor

From the beginning, Bonaparte faced adversaries on several fronts. After some violence and mistakes such as the kidnapping and execution of the duke of Enghien in 1804, he had succeeded in seducing a good part of the royalists, even the exiles. The Concordat had temporarily satisfied the Church and most of the Catholics. His old Jacobin and republican friends had been converted, bought off, or discarded. We have already mentioned his contempt for "ideologues" or intellectuals. The creation of the imperial court with its ostentation and affected manners quite consciously aped the Bourbons, and it disgusted those who were not seduced. In 1809, the dispute with the pope naturally offended the clergy as well as many Catholics and revived royalists. The most astute politicians, who also happened to be the most corrupt, understood quickly that the system could not last. Talleyrand, who served and betrayed so many regimes, was already negotiating with the tsar in 1807. From time to time, plots were foiled by the excellent police work of Fouché and Savary. In 1808, stubborn rebels were shot for sailing between Brittany and Jersey—and among them was a cousin of Chateaubriand. The same year, a general in retreat, Malet, organized a conspiracy: when it was discovered, he was arrested, and when he plotted again in 1812, he was shot.

The discontent among intellectuals and liberals, while not an immediate threat, was limited in 1810 by stricter censorship and by several more-or-less voluntary exiles such as Benjamin Constant and Royer-Collard.

More serious was the changed attitude of the people, who had long appeared to glory in the victories of their emperor; now they appeared almost indifferent to his fall. Several reasons exist for this lax attitude. There were of course taxes. At first war had paid for war, but then the campaigns in Spain and Russia became expensive. The indirect taxes on drinks tripled from 1806 to 1812. Once again there were riots against taxation, as under the old monarchy.

The situation worsened when the economy began to decline. It had long remained tolerable despite the English blockade of continental ports and the corresponding continental system against English ships and goods, since both were unenforceable. True, there was a lack of colonial goods, but people became accustomed to that. Thus sugar became ten times as expensive when beets could not supply as much as the cane of the West Indies. Shipments of raw cotton were interrupted, but despite official encouragement, French manufacturing lacked markets more than raw materials. The usual continental clients found themselves impoverished and unwilling to buy. As a result there were bankruptcies and unemployment. At Lyon more than half of the workers were jobless in 1811, and aid had to be given to twenty thousand unemployed people in Paris. Several banks had to be liquidated, even at Amsterdam. Only the munitions industry prospered.

Even worse was the return of the old grain crises typical of the ancien régime. The first alarm came in 1805; the second and much more serious one occurred in 1811–12, when the price of grain doubled. There were violent scenes in the marketplaces with pillage and riots. At Caen several workers were shot. There was even genuine famine. The government was forced to resort to soup kitchens, public works projects, and even to price controls of the discredited "maximum" variety, but these were poorly organized and little respected.

The good harvest of 1812 resolved the food crisis, but not the others. As the military defeats struck, commerce and manufacturing deteriorated, bankruptcies increased, and, most alarming of all, the government's 3 percent bonds, the financial barometer, suddenly fell below 50 francs (par = 100). In short, the confidence of notables and businessmen collapsed, in keeping with the worsening political climate and popular fatigue.

In the countryside, where the royalists were again beginning to agitate and prepare for vengeance, the people were tired of conscription. Although draft dodgers and deserters were protected by the population, the incessant demands for draftees could at any moment set off a new Vendée. According to Jacques Godechot, 20 percent of those drafted between 1806 and 1815 never returned. Indeed, the reconstructed age pyramid for 1815 appears to lack one million men in the age group twenty to fifty-nine. And these men were almost all peasants, which may suggest that the title "Corsican Ogre" was not such an exaggeration.

All these factors combined may help us to understand the indifference with which news of Napoleon's abdication was received in April 1814. On his way to the island of Elba, especially in the south of France, the defeated emperor was insulted and threatened, and even had to disguise himself as an Austrian officer to complete his journey. And yet, many of his soldiers and the common people remained faithful to him.

They showed their devotion after the restoration of the inept Bourbons, during Napoleon's rapid return to power for the Hundred Days, and in the rise of the great legend.

TRANSFIGURATION

Just as the memory of Napoleon lives on, so his legend is not dead. Launched by his own initiative and the skillful pens of his close companions during the Italian campaign, the legend ran through all the bulletins of the Grande Armée. The image of Épinal soon took charge of it, and the *Mémorial* and songs of Béranger made it even greater. There was the romanticism of the "children of the century" (Musset), transferred from the legitimate king to the absent, proscribed one. Finally, popular literature and lithography, imitated and reproduced countless times by Charlet and Raffet, propagated the figure and myth of the eagle right down to the beginning of the twentieth century, when the sonorous poetry of Rostand's play *L'Aiglon* (1900) aroused fervent praise. Even as late as 1930 many humble French homes contained tarnished images celebrating the grand Napoleonic gestures. These were taken over by film-makers as well, but not always with the same talent as Abel Gance. We must recognize without the least reservation that this heroic tale, though it contained less of the gods and more of the truth, acquired as much grandeur as the epics of Homer. Furthermore, it carried nationalism or patriotism to a frenzy, because never again was France as large in territory, as powerful, or as terrible.

That said, the historian must return to earth and make two simple comments. The first is that the legend has profoundly transformed the reality—which was of course its function—and transfigured Bonaparte the man. The second is that from the time of his exile, his great stature dominated more than half a century of French history, and for almost as long haunted the peoples and kings of Europe.

The great confusion that was fabricated from the bridge at

Arcola to Saint-Helena and beyond became truth to the French imagination and heart, and thus to politics. The Napoleonic image of the conqueror and dictator fused with the revolutionary image of liberation from all anciens régimes. Even the "Marseillaise" and the tricolor flag, with or without eagles, often became symbols of the *patrie,* glory, liberty, and revolution. It is curious that this image frequently became an international rallying banner for citizens of other nations who fought or believed they were fighting against tyrants and for a happy, progressive future.

In large measure this amalgam came from the policies of the victorious enemy kings, who distrusted France and wanted to wipe out all memory of the quarter-century that shook their thrones and gave such bad ideas to their peoples. But the image also came from the Bourbons.

They had not defeated anyone, yet despite the wisdom of the former comte de Provence and some others, they did not know how to conquer a people who were tired of war and taxes. The majority of Frenchmen were not at first hostile to them, at least not in 1814. But the Bourbons tried to restore the white flag and divine-right monarchy at one fell swoop. They brought back the exiled nobles and priests with their antiquated costumes and ideas. Many of them thought of nothing but exacting vengeance for themselves. They wanted to preserve all imperial taxes, including the indirect ones, and find a war-indemnity of 700 million francs. And they had to bear three years of foreign occupation in a country of shrunken frontiers, a country that was suffering slow destruction. The whole situation was not well suited to a joyous return to power, which was legalistically reported as having occurred nineteen years earlier anyway. After the astonishing episode of the Hundred Days, almost nothing changed. The disillusionment of so many Frenchmen could only engender nostalgia mixing the tricolor and the nation, the "Marseillaise" and the eagles, the Republic and the empire. And the magnified memory of Napoleon the Great later engendered the easy triumph of the agile Napoleon the Small, as Victor Hugo called him.

The Europe of the kings, meeting at the Congress of Vienna

in 1814–15, was not content with waltzing and dividing the spoils of the Napoleonic Empire. The powers of the day wanted to exorcise the double danger of the spirit of liberty and nationalistic fervor. Their "Holy Alliance" of aging anciens régimes could not prevent the birth of revolutionary movements. These groups were still in their infancy from 1820 to 1830, but they came of age in 1848 and later. Long afterward they placed themselves in a line of direct descent from the "great Revolution." It was the subject of their songs and dreams, but in fact they knew little about it.

What would have become of this Revolution without the emperor who rubbed out its excesses, saved it, and prolonged the reforms that, at the end of the day, suited those who had brought it about? They were the notables, that bourgeois soup mixed with resigned and liberal aristocrats. Indeed, the French nation often appears to require a savior to consolidate the power of the notables and set aside the popular dangers of "the crowd" and "the street." From 1848 to 1958, there were at least four good-sized saviors and several smaller ones as well. Whether any of them achieved the genius of the little corporal, the historian cannot boldly say.

Chapter Fifteen

FRANCE IN THE NINETEENTH CENTURY: A PANORAMA

As we approach our own era, we must take an overview of the evolution of France in order to understand its history. In 1815, the nation had just endured and lost twenty-three years of war. A century later, it would enter a shorter, crueler conflict, emerging victorious on that occasion but suffering serious consequences.

As always, the clearest evolution took place in politics. The monarchy passed from Charles X, the last Bourbon, to his cousin Louis-Philippe d'Orléans thanks to a three-day insurrection at Paris in July 1830. Then it went from Orléans back to a latter-day Bonaparte after a true revolution, which was quickly hijacked just as the preceding ones had been by fearful propertied groups and a risky coup d'état on December 2, 1851. The next change was from an empire to a republic as a result of a senseless war and an inexcusable defeat on September 4, 1870. The Third Republic, which began with the bloody struggle of the Paris Commune and the quarreling of inept royalists, was born of defeat in 1870 and died in defeat in 1940. And yet it was the longest regime France had known since Louis XIV, and the one that worked best despite tempests, real or imagined. The politics of the entire century was ruled by successive constitutions, but what really mattered was their application. At first, the right to vote was reserved for the very rich, fewer than one hundred thousand men until 1830, when the electorate was doubled; in 1848, suffrage was extended to every adult male. The Second Empire ingeniously manipulated the system to give the desired results; the Third Republic practiced these gymnastics less often, and its electoral campaigns became expressions of public opinion. Until 1875, no true parliamentary regime existed, since the elected or appointed assemblies did not really have control of the government: kings and emperors chose their ministers.

Throughout this century a movement for change grew in strength. At first it was indeed reformist, then republican, and finally "social," or socialist. All three tendencies came more or less directly from the Revolution of 1789, whose influence and memory remained strong among its supporters and opponents. Then the concentration of workers in the new industries and overcrowded suburbs, as well as the growing exploitation to which they were subjected, aroused powerful workers' movements. The first such movement was at Lyon in 1831, outside the political context. The socialist thinkers and the union movement were slow to assimilate these forces, which were only partially taken over between 1885 and 1900. Successive governments violently opposed all centers of resistance and action, and their official efforts achieved results, thanks to the use of the army, the police, and the courts. The grand bourgeoisie that effectively dominated the country after 1830 never wanted to share any of its power with those whom it called "the crowd, the depths, the dividers, the reds, the suburbs, the street, the barbarians." When the plebeian forces did triumph much later, in 1936, it was for only a short time.

Behind the succession of governments—eight of them between 1799 and 1870, then only one for the next seventy years—the French population, economy, and society would undergo transformations at least as important, but much slower. These changes gave nineteenth-century France specific characteristics that were not necessarily beneficial.

THE ORLEANS

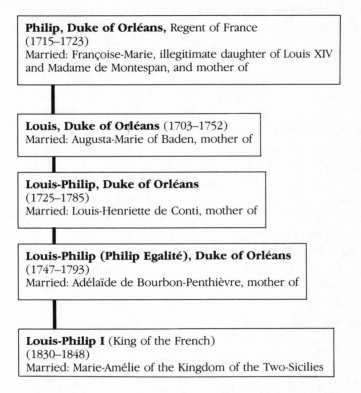

Philip, Duke of Orléans, Regent of France
(1715–1723)
Married: Françoise-Marie, illegitimate daughter of Louis XIV
and Madame de Montespan, and mother of

Louis, Duke of Orléans (1703–1752)
Married: Augusta-Marie of Baden, mother of

Louis-Philip, Duke of Orléans
(1725–1785)
Married: Louis-Henriette de Conti, mother of

Louis-Philip (Philip Egalité), Duke of Orléans
(1747–1793)
Married: Adélaïde de Bourbon-Penthièvre, mother of

Louis-Philip I (King of the French)
(1830–1848)
Married: Marie-Amélie of the Kingdom of the Two-Sicilies

From this marriage are descended the Orléans claimants to the throne of France. The current head of the family is Henry, Count of Paris, born in 1908.

DEMOGRAPHIC TRENDS

The demography of France in this period was quite different from that of other European countries and the world in general. Amid the mass of detail, a few facts clearly stand out. At the beginning of the century, with slightly more than 30 million inhabitants, France was the second most populous country in Europe; only Russia surpassed it. Yet on the eve of the First World War, the population of France had fallen to fifth place in Europe and seventh in the industrialized world. The United States had nearly 100 million people, and Japan had 50 million. French growth rates after 1870 were the lowest in Europe, and French population density was only just above that of Spain. On balance the political annexation of Savoy and Nice in 1860 and the loss of Alsace-Lorraine in 1871 reduced the total population by one million, but these developments did not change French rank in Europe or the growth rate.

This unusual pattern is easy to explain. The mortality rates—especially infant mortality, which still stood at 17 percent in 1895—declined very slowly. Emigration was not very great. But above all there was an unexpected, continuing, and pronounced fall in the birth rate. During the time of Louis XV, the rate had been 40 per 1000 inhabitants; by 1815, it was 31 or 32; by 1850, 27. The decline continued to around 20 in 1900; and below 19 on the eve of World War I. This trend later became general, but it can be seen much earlier in France than elsewhere. Historians and demographers agree that the majority of French couples deliberately practiced birth control by *coitus interruptus,* frequent and illegal abortions, and the use of pessaries and other devices in high society; these practices had already appeared around 1770 in the Parisian region. But why did they do it? We are uncertain whether birth control stemmed from the desire to give better economical and social chances to fewer, better educated children, or from a reluctance to divide family inheritances. There may also have been male indifference to religious precepts. The ultra-chaste Roman Catholic church permitted sexual intercourse only within the bonds of marriage, for the purpose of procreation, and if possible without pleasure. For us it is more difficult to probe hearts and minds than to record statistics, but apart from speculations about causes we must note the results.

The average age of the French population was rising in the nineteenth century, as several figures show. Around 1815, young people under twenty years of age constituted 44 percent of the population, while the elderly (over 59) made up only 7 percent. By the census of 1911, the younger group was just over one-third of the total, while the elderly population had risen to 13 percent. This was regarded as a serious weakness in comparison with unified Germany, where the younger group was almost twice as large.

Nonetheless, thanks to the slow progress of hygiene and medicine, in particular pasteurization and vaccination, infant mortality finally fell below the 17–18 percent level of 1890 to reach 10 percent by 1914. Today, it stands at less than 1 percent. Adult mortality fell more slowly, especially in the poorest neighborhoods and regions; it did not keep up with the relentless fall in the birth rate.

If the growth of the French population was stagnant, its movement to the industrial cities was also slow. The census of 1846 showed that 75 percent of the French population was still rural and that only thirteen cities had more than 50,000 inhabitants; in 1911, the rural proportion was still 56 percent. By this latter date, urban populations had long predominated in the most powerful European states, Germany and Britain. Thus while the industrial revolution did indeed have some effects, France entered the Great War as a nation of peasants.

GREAT CYCLES
IN ECONOMIC TRENDS

Mechanization, the concentration of factories and workers, the spread of the steam engine and metalworking, new roles for banking, the acceleration of transport, and the triumph of the railway—all of these phenomena characterize in summary fashion the first industrial revolution. Others would follow later.

The industrial movement began in England in the second half of the eighteenth century. It had spread slowly in France on the eve of the Revolution, which acted as a brake on its progress. The conservatism of French investors was also a factor, for they were content with purchases of land, gold, and state bonds. The French have always liked peaceful, sleeping wealth, which allows the eyes of the past to contemplate the future.

Two statistical series will prove the point. The first deals with world railway networks, which increased a hundredfold between 1840 and 1900. The United States, which cannot really be compared with other countries, always accounted for half the total mileage. Britain, whose network in 1840 was six times as great as that of France, held first place in Europe until 1870–80, when Germany surpassed it. France was far behind these nations and even trailed behind Russia in 1900, although Russian distances were of course greater. Even under the Second Empire, French railway development lagged, just like the French industrial take-off as a whole.

The second statistical series is taken from a 1945 publication which estimated the value of world industrial production. For many years Britain held first place: in 1870 it was still producing 31–32 percent of the total, while France was in fourth place with only one-third as much. After 1885, the United States came in first, and Germany exceeded Britain in 1905. By 1913, French industry had fallen to only 6.4 percent of the total, and Russia was close behind, Britain and Germany were each producing more than twice the French total, and already the United States had overwhelmed the rest of the world with industrial production as great as that of the three largest European powers combined.

These few figures have been presented as a brief sample, but because they are credible they put the situation in perspective better than a long and depressing discourse. The report card of French industry reveals timidity, delays, and a casual slide from an A to a gentleman's C. To nineteenth-century observers this trend was barely visible, and besides they refused to see it. The country remained proud of itself, of its past glories, of the examples it thought it had given the world. And in fact its solid peasantry, its hoard of gold, the stability of its currency, its diplomatic and supposed military influence, the rebirth of its colonial empire, and the brilliance of its literature, art, and language accepted by elites every-where, like the still glowing attractions of Paris, gave it a solid reputation that was only momentarily tarnished by the hazard-ous adventures of Napoleon III and his final shameful defeat.

But it is now time to study the events of the nineteenth century on a more down-to-earth level.

FROM ONE NAPOLEON
TO ANOTHER:
1815–1852

The Restoration

The very name of this regime—the Restoration—implies a return to the past. But the question is how far did it go. It certainly provoked concern among former participants in the Revolution and to a lesser degree among Bonapartists. Perhaps the most worried were the purchasers of national properties, people who had remained in place during the quarter-century of upheaval or had rallied to the emperor. Those who had always remained fervent royalists and Catholics, and even more so those who came back with the king and his baggage, as-serted their will for absolute vengeance. They demanded with restitution of their property from the "despoilers," reestablish-ment of the seigneurial regime and the tithes, and exemplary punishment for all who had been guilty of rebellion against the monarchy. Most French people probably wanted nothing more than an end to war and a reduction of taxes. They were nearly exhausted after twenty-five years of struggle, but they were to be disappointed. Indeed, those who harbor such hopes almost always are.

Returning after a long exile, the count of Provence, now Louis XVIII, had gained considerable wisdom and lost nothing in refinement. Desirous of not "recommencing his travels," he sought to satisfy all who were reasonable. He received little help from his entourage, who thought of nothing except re-establishing the ancien régime. They did not shine with reason or intuition either. The new king found himself among the most exalted of the former exiles, born-again priests and Je-suits, who were forming secret societies with noble and cler-ical members. Among these were the strongly devotional Congregation and the Chevaliers of Faith, a much more polit-ical group whose history has been written by Bertier de Sauvigny, a descendant of their founder. All these "ultras" be-sieged the king.

Louis XVIII was obliged to let the storm run its course. In the western and southern provinces, a new White Terror raged against the owners of national properties, former revolution-aries and followers of Napoleon. Many were threatened or molested; others were assassinated, among them the Mameluks at Marseille, Generals Ramel and Lagarde at Toulouse and Nîmes, and Protestants who suffered new persecution at the hands of papists. A number of common criminals were in-volved in this reaction. Hoping to calm and control it, the government took charge. Eighteen Bonapartist generals were called up before the Council of War: the executions of La Bédoyère and Ney caused a sensation. After having purged the army, retired the grumblers (veterans of Napoleon's old guard), and put numerous officers on half-pay, the government in-stalled nobles in their places. Many of them had fought against France in the enemy armies. A so-called amnesty law had the effect of banning the Bonaparte family, the regicides, and the new "suspects." Official administration and even the Institut de France were swept clean. Distinguished men such as Carnot, David, Lakanal, and Monge were removed. Thanks to various laws against "seditious cries," the "troublesome ones" were brought before special tribunals from whose judgments there was no appeal. The firing squads were in operation until July 1816: at Lyon, they claimed the life of General Mouton-Duvernet. Of course the press was muzzled by requirements for financial surety, official stamps, censorship, and prior approval. The political police distinguished themselves by their activity.

Once the fury had passed, Louis XVIII tried to govern moderately, assisted by the kind minister Decazes, whom he addressed affectionately in familiar forms of speech. Nonetheless, he used the resources of the Charter of 1814, which he had unfortunately pretended to grant freely. It was a relatively liberal document, although it allowed the two legislative chambers no initiative whatsoever. One of these chambers was elected, the other appointed, thus establishing the second constitutional monarchy under the Bourbons—we should not forget Louis XVI and the Constitution of 1791. Political participation was limited to the *pays légal,* fewer than 100,000 voters, all of them the richest members of society and a majority of them old nobles. Although the first chamber was elected, even the king called it "incomparable" (i.e., unbelievable). It was dominated by the most exalted ultras, who were quickly dissolved and put in their proper places. About 100 of them sat on the right of the presiding officer, while 120 "Constitutionals," faithful supporters of the charter and Decazes, and about 30 "Independents" sat on the left. This last group gained some seats in by-elections. Their numbers included liberals in the English or American mold such as old Lafayette, admitted Bonapartists, and several republicans such as Manuel. The republicans were supported by a weak and persecuted press, as well as by the stinging pamphlets of Paul-Louis Courier and the extremely popular singer Béranger, an inspired satirist of the priests and those former exiles, the marquis de Carabas and the marquise de Prétentailles. Later Béranger even dared to ridicule the old-fashioned coronation of the ineffable Charles X.

Four rather peaceful years passed with only a few small plots at Saumur and Strasbourg, involving units of the Charbonnerie, a vaguely republican secret society. These were quickly nipped in the bud, and the government passed some milder legislation. A military law instituted a small professional army, to be supplemented as needed by a lottery. The lottery was not absolutely random, of course, since the results were affected by the use of substitutes by those who could afford them. Promotion was given to officers according to seniority and merit, which the right-wing judged scandalous. In a sage move, electoral laws indirectly favored bourgeois. The laws regarding the press were also liberalized slightly. At the same time prudent financial management allowed France to pay both the Allies and its debts, and to institute regular budgetary procedures that restored confidence. While the first 5 percent loan had to be negotiated at 52.50 francs, the last in 1830 was sold above par at 102, an unprecedented occurrence. Furthermore, under the supervision of the kings of Europe and their Holy Alliance, international peace was naturally assured.

When in February 1820 a Bonapartist worker assassinated the duc de Berry, the only direct heir of the Bourbons, the semiliberal period ended, and the ultras returned to power. Louis XVIII was ill from the end of 1821 onward, and no longer able to supervise his entourage. Charles X, his brother and successor in 1824, had nothing to recommend him except his amiable elegance. Under the governments of Villèle and Polignac, the delayed rancor of aristocracy and Church were unleashed. They had forgotten nothing and understood hardly anything. They tampered with electoral procedures to exclude the bourgeois; they multiplied the financial and police obstacles to freedom of the press and expression. They appointed a bishop to head the state university in order to drive out lively minds; they sponsored loud campaigns called "missions" of reparation and planted crosses all over the countryside, some still visible today. They dared to promulgate a law against "sacrilege" that fixed harsh penalties for anyone who disrupted religious ceremonies or profaned "sacred vessels," although it proved impossible to enforce. And finally they passed the "billion for the exiles" in 1825, a simple indemnity of modest 3 percent bonds for those who had been "despoiled" by the

Revolution. This act scandalized and terrified the former owners of national properties. There was also discussion of reestablishing the right of primogeniture, which had never applied generally throughout France. At the same time an expedition blessed by the absolute monarchs of Europe went to Spain to restore the despot Ferdinand VII to his throne after he had been threatened by a liberal rebellion at Cadiz. The duc d'Angoulême and several regiments carried the day without risk after the capture of Fort Trocadéro. This easy exploit was praised by some, ridiculed by others.

After several years, the struggle against the regime had been organized among the bourgeoisie and the upper levels of the common people. In large measure the organization rested on secret societies of the Italian *carbonari* type, which played on nostalgic memories of the Great Emperor and the Revolution. These sentiments were openly expressed at the funerals of opposition figures such as Foy and Manuel. Even in the chamber, the left and center groups were momentarily united by circumstances. When a constitution was proposed by the Polignac–Bourmont–La Bourdonnaye ministry, composed of the most extreme ultras and even traitors among the ultra party, a majority of 221 deputies quite legally voted for an "address" to the king. This uncooperative chamber was dissolved, but the malcontents increased from 221 to 274 despite the booming noise of the difficult capture of Algiers. The opposition press defied the censors, and the industrial suburbs were rumbling. To silence them, all that remained was a coup d'état, pushed along by force if necessary. Four absolutely unconstitutional orders were published on July 26, 1830: they sought to clamp down on the press, dissolve the chamber once again, and restrict the vote still further. But by then the government was completely out of touch with the nation.

Exasperated by ten years of provocations from the throne and the altar, bourgeois, journalists, and Parisian artisans and journeymen almost immediately went into action. In its blindness the Restoration, that negation of political intelligence, had unwittingly prepared the way for the next act, which could hardly be called a revolution.

THE THREE GLORIOUS DAYS:
HOW TO AROUSE AND THEN
HIJACK A REVOLUTION

Exasperated indeed by the excesses of Charles X and his ministers, the good French bourgeois desired a true constitutional
monarchy in which they would play the leading role. To achieve
this end, some pretext would be required—and Charles X
could be counted on to provide one. They would also need
manpower to raise the barricades, a group of crafty politicians,
and a recycled king who would be acceptable to the people of
Paris, the only ones who really mattered: they were overwhelmingly republicans. Planned since 1827, the farce was performed
in less than two weeks. The leading players were well chosen:
Talleyrand, an old hand at treason; Lafayette, a tired hero, not
very subtle, once a republican but still popular; Adolphe Thiers,
a writer consumed with ambition, a condensed version of
Rastignac; and finally the prince with carefully cultivated bourgeois appeal, a soldier who had fought at Jemappes and yet
went into exile afterward, son of a regicide, heir of the Orléans
family who had stood so close to the throne for a century and
a half, Louis-Philippe. These men pulled the strings. The indispensable manpower was supplied by students, printers,
journeymen, and artisans of Paris. They were hostile to royalty
in general and had shown their hostility during various funeral
processions; furthermore, they were outraged by the high price
of bread and high unemployment. They first assembled around
the office of a liberal newspaper when the police wanted to
seize the presses; then they built barricades only in the eastern
and southern parts of Paris, the classical revolutionary action.
The king made the supreme error of trying to repress them
with several regiments commanded by Marmont, the traitor of
1814. The battles in the still-medieval streets of Paris were
violent, and as the royal troops could not occupy the terrain,
they broke ranks and disbanded in part. (In his reconstruction
of Paris, Baron Haussmann would remedy the problem of

crowd control by cutting wide avenues suitable for cavalry charges and cannonades.) Marmont fled to the west, of course.

The difficult moment had arrived: the time to trick the victorious people who wanted a republic. A risky strategy nonetheless succeeded. Supported by his friends, the duke of Orléans marched from his home at the Palais-Royal to the Hôtel de Ville, the customary seat of the victors of the day. Orléans began the trip with difficulty but finished in near triumph. He appeared on the balcony with Lafayette and the tricolor flag. The crowd, at first astounded, cried tears of joy and applauded wildly, except for several republican leaders, who understood what was happening. This took place on July 31; a few days later Charles X abdicated and went to Austria, where he died in 1836, four years after the young "king of Rome" who would have been Napoleon II.

The duke of Orléans, momentarily known simply as the "lieutenant general," now found himself "king of the French," with the tricolor flag and the famous charter, slightly liberalized as its unhappy formulas were expurgated.

The mass of the French population, still almost entirely composed of peasants, was occupied with the harvest and did not budge politically. Whether they had one king or another was of no importance to them, as long as they were sure of keeping their national properties and hoping not to see taxes increased. In half a century, they had seen so many regimes come and go.

LOUIS-PHILIPPE AND
THE BOURGEOIS MONARCHY

The year 1830 marked a great turning point for the old aristocracy, as they unanimously rejected the reign of Louis-Philippe, the tricolored intruder. They retreated into touchy legitimism in their châteaux and on their considerable lands, where they often devoted themselves to remarkable projects of agricultural and forest improvement. They preached by example to "their" peasants, and were supported by strict authoritarian priests, who long remained as legitimist as themselves. Their combined influence had marvelous effects on the use of universal male suffrage, which was rashly conceded in 1848. For the moment they sulked, but they also worked.

Around Louis-Philippe and his family, a tender spectacle of both princely and bourgeois virtues, there stood a group of bankers (Lafitte, Perier), historians (Mignet, Guizot, Thiers), and grand bourgeois. Some survivors of the empire (Soult, Mortier) were among them: they did not have to make much of an about-face. Apparently debonair, sincerely conciliatory, quite intelligent but aging rapidly (he had been born in 1773), Louis-Philippe was in the end just as authoritarian as his predecessors, but he knew how to use time wisely, and never rushed anything. He could play on rival ambitions and did not give way to popular disturbances until his fall. By doubling the electoral rolls he had made sure of a chamber that reflected the good, triumphant bourgeoisie, who asked for little more than the opportunity to make money and enjoy a bit of liberty for themselves alone. For the time being the bourgeois rejected a republic and were little concerned with the rising numbers, misery, and anger of the working class, whom they often treated with contempt.

This regime left behind a more-or-less deserved reputation for external peace (if colonial conquests are excluded), prosperity, and economic progress at home. These achievements and the honest and efficient administration were under the ultraconservatism symbolized by the dry silhouette and soul of Guizot. Nonetheless it did run into grave difficulties.

The agitation of the legitimists and Bonapartists, however, was never serious. In 1832 a plot was hatched. Known as "la rue des Prouvaires," it was aimed at kidnapping the king, but it was discovered by the police, and the conspirators were imprisoned or deported. In the same year the duchess of Berry, widow of the prince slain in 1820, landed in Provence and in the Vendée, both old legitimist provinces. She hoped for a massive uprising, but the venture was a pitiful failure that became ridiculous when she was forced by her pregnancy to reveal a secret marriage to an Italian diplomat from the minor nobility. The future for "Henry V" was not promising.

Since Napoleon's son, the Eaglet, had died, the heir to the Bonaparte legacy was Louis Napoleon Bonaparte, a nephew of the emperor who attempted military uprisings at Strasbourg in 1836 and Boulogne in 1840. These also failed miserably and resulted in punishment—first expulsion, then imprisonment at Ham. From there he escaped while wearing the clothes of a mason named Badinguet: this became his nickname. Nonetheless, to appease those who were nostalgic for Napoleon, Louis-Philippe's government had the ashes of the emperor brought back to France with great ceremony—probably a political mistake.

The revolutionaries of 1830, who knew they had been tricked, reacted more strongly to the failure of the "sister revolutions" in Germany, Italy, and Poland. Only in Belgium were the forces of change victorious. The French welcomed numerous refugees from other countries and followed their example by forming secret societies such as the Rights of Man in 1832 and the Seasons in 1839. Ardent young men took part: Carrel, Cavaignac, Garnier-Pagès. Later they were joined by the more dangerous socialist Louis Blanc, the retiring Ledru-Rollin, and the Abbé de Lamennais, talented founder of "liberal" Catholicism, who was quickly disowned by it. There were also literary romantics with a touch of social conscience—George Sand, Lamartine, and Victor Hugo. Apart from the innocuous social reformers and pre-Marxist utopians, there were soon violent demonstrations against the new regime. In 1831, a memorial service for the duke of Berry resulted in the sack of a church and an archbishopric. During the funeral of General Lamarque in 1832, and again in 1834, there were barricades and street fighting between insurgents and the armed forces that left hundreds dead. The massacres of Saint-Merry cloister and rue Transnonain were depicted in a terrible lithograph by Daumier. Three years earlier at Lyon, when their salaries were reduced by 75 percent, the proletariat had come down from their

Croix-Rousse neighborhood in a black-flag procession and occupied the city. On this occasion the government sent Soult with an army but killed no one. The workers, as badly paid as ever, continued "to go completely naked."

The skies had cleared somewhat by 1835, when the July monarchy began a great judicial and legislative purge. Two hundred republicans were arrested, and most were imprisoned or deported. Several members of the "Rights of Man" club were involved in Fieschi's attack in the boulevard du Temple in July 1835. The king escaped but several members of his entourage did not. Suddenly, the September Laws silenced the republicans by placing harsh restrictions on the courts, on trial by jury, and on the press. Even Monnier and Daumier had trouble publishing their caricatures. Despite several minor incidents such as the Seasons riot with Blanqui in 1839 and the anti-English agitation with singing of the "Marseillaise" in the streets around 1840 and 1845, the regime enjoyed twelve years of relative tranquillity. Cholera, which raged through France several times after 1832, was not an object of government intervention, even when it eliminated ministers such as Casimir Perier. Leaving aside these troubles, the government did accomplish a great deal internally and externally.

In foreign policy, there were two main concerns: keeping the peace and reconstituting the colonial empire. In both areas Britain, the traditional French enemy from the time of Joan of Arc to Waterloo, always presented problems. The British barely grumbled when the absolutist rulers of Europe allowed French troops to intervene in Spain in 1823 and in Algiers in 1830. On the other hand, they prohibited the newly independent Belgians from choosing a French king, a fact that Louis-Philippe and the eternal Talleyrand had to accept after difficult European negotiations. In Egypt, after Napoleon's time the French exercised great influence on the reforming Mehemet Ali Pasha, who defeated the Turks twice. Europe became involved, and Britain arranged the situation without French participation in 1840. Public opinion was outraged, the "Marseillaise" was sung everywhere, and the sons of Louis-Philippe taunted the

British. Prime Minister Thiers, thinking himself a little Napoleon, mobilized three contingents of draftees, bought weapons, and began to consider battle plans. Louis-Philippe dismissed him from office and calmed down inflamed spirits. Afterward, despite naval and colonial incidents (in Tahiti, for example), and the agitation produced by Algeria, a sort of *entente cordiale* was reached between the old king and the counselors of young Queen Victoria, who received each other at Eu and at Windsor. Passing clouds, however insignificant, showed that French public opinion was unhappy with this *entente* and judged it humiliating.

This did not prevent the kingdom from enjoying thirty-three years of peace, with good effects on finances and administration as a whole. However, the preceding regime had left behind the difficult Algerian problem. For some years, Louis-Philippe knew only too well what to do with it: he occupied several port cities and their immediate hinterlands. Britain, many members of the French chamber of deputies and businessmen, inhabitants of Bordeaux and revenge-minded patriots would have preferred leaving it at that. Others dreamed of genuine colonization, with the settlement of soldier-peasants. Abd-el-Kader, a young chieftain who claimed descent from Mohammed, simplified the problem by declaring holy war and forming a temporary alliance with the sultan of Morocco. In reaction to massacres organized by the emir, Louis-Philippe sent out Clauzel, an experienced soldier, but with inadequate troops: the French were defeated at Constantine (1835–36), which was nevertheless captured the following year. But Clauzel was recalled, and the government hesitated for three years and even negotiated with Abd-el-Kader. The rebellious chieftain took advantage of the delay to extend his influence, reorganize his forces, and seek diplomatic help from as far away as Britain. Then he resumed the holy war by massacring the colonists of Mitidja. This time Louis-Philippe sent 100,000 men commanded by Bugeaud, who understood the terrain and knew how to organize the army accordingly. All the same it took him seven years and a campaign against Morocco to force Abd-al-Kader to surrender. By 1848, the only parts of Algeria not under French development were the large area of Kabylia and the territories in the south.

Despite British recriminations, by 1842 the youthful but still modest French navy had acquired bases in the Ivory Coast, on the Comores, at Nossi-Bé, and in Polynesia. These were added to the remnants of the old empire—the towns of India, Réunion Island, the Antilles, the forts of Sénégal, impenetrable Guiana, and the cod-fishing islands of Saint Pierre and Miquelon. No one could then predict the future grandeur and fall of the colonies: neither French public opinion nor even French banks were very concerned about it.

The considerable internal achievements aroused more attention. Guizot was the first to pass a law requiring every commune to maintain a primary school. Around one out of every three *départements* also established a teacher-training college. The French people were not entirely uneducated (except in the west, part of the Midi, and several non-Alpine mountainous areas) nor did they wish to remain so. Numerous religious schools had existed since the seventeenth century. Although education was not compulsory, many children went to school in winter. Traditionally parents paid a modest price for instruction, but poor pupils could attend for free. The effort was great, and the first great school crisis caused a serious uproar. Jules Ferry, the educational reformer of the Third Republic, had only to complete, democratize, and republicanize the work of the July Monarchy.

In other areas, various networks were established or created. The great ancien régime policy of building bridges and roads was continued by the Revolution, Empire, and Restoration. Under the July Monarchy it was carried still further, with the construction of 6,000 kilometers of new main roads, 17,000 km of departmental roads, and nearly 300 bridges. The great innovation was the law of 1836, which launched a major program of local road building: 60,000 km were laid out or repaired. At last all French villages benefited from improved traffic flow and were connected to a main road. This was the first step in the transportation revolution, without which no serious economic or social progress would have been possible.

As for the English-style "canal fever," which had already gripped the country, it continued for a while, and navigable waterways increased from 2,000 to about 4,000 km, but it really affected only the north. More significant was the coming of the railway age. The English model and the construction of several segments around Saint-Étienne and Paris, as well as in the south and in Alsace (less than 500 km in total by 1840), did not suffice to convince businessmen, politicians, or even scholars. Around 1840 there were fierce disputes, which seem grotesque to us. The government resolved the problem brusquely by enacting the law of 1842, which designated the axes of the future network and the principles of concessions to be made. Within six years, 4,000 km were allocated to seventeen companies, and the great bankers finally became interested. Laffitte was a participant in nine ventures, and the Rothschilds took part in twelve. The active presence of such persons gave a certain hue to both the business and the regime. Nonetheless, less than 2,000 km of railways were in service in 1848: the railway revolution would take place later.

Indeed, the time of Louis-Philippe still belonged to the ancien régime as far as the economy was concerned. Transportation remained slow and costly, the national unification of markets and prices was far from accomplished, and agriculture still took precedence over industry by important criteria—the number of workers, the amount and value of production. Among the industries that did exist, the older textile manufacturing, now mechanized, was still more important than metallurgy, which had difficulty modernizing. Forges fired by wood continued to produce more than those using coke. Furthermore, in view of the monetary stability and the high premium placed on bonds, regularly traded above par, the numerous banks were too narrow-minded or ridiculously cautious like the Banque de France; they were hesitant to mobilize the enormous national savings and invest in industry or great construction projects.

Agriculture was still king, and still had the sole power to

provoke economic crises. There had been some progress in the mix of crops and techniques, but there was really no general agricultural revolution in France before the mid-twentieth century. In the countryside the great majority of small proprietors, tenant farmers, and sharecroppers lived in near autarchy and isolation.

The foundations of the great economic changes were sketched and partly laid down by the July Monarchy as early as 1842–45, but they would be completed only in later decades. In 1848, France and many other European countries saw the emergence of rumors, crises, revolutionary battles, and defeats.

HOW TO KILL
A REVOLUTION: 1848*

The bourgeois monarchy of Louis-Philippe had been born in July 1830 during three days of republican insurrection in Paris, which it betrayed. In 1848, it melted away almost naturally in three more days; shortly afterward other politicians appeared to hijack this revolution after a premeditated murder. On this occasion, however, a kind of republic had time to exist, first in spirit and then in fact. It had a socialist tinge to its appearance and law, before being silenced by a new autocracy and a new savior. Certainly no one expected much from Louis-Napoleon: Thiers took him for a cretin and thought he could be manipulated.

The insurrection had two origins. The first was in the political world, thus essentially from the bourgeoisie with proper reformist intentions, moderately republican and rarely touched by romantic sensitivity for the people. The other came, as usual, from the common people of Paris themselves, who henceforth included genuine industrial workers with an elite

*From this date onward, it will be clear that the author's sympathy naturally extends more to the victims than to the victors. He hopes his readers will excuse him; he will try, however, to remain honest.

of skilled craftsmen such as furniture makers, gilders, and printers. The crowd no longer consisted only of shop clerks, journeymen, and the unemployed. Although touched by some socialist sentiments and slogans, these people were moved far more by an economic and social crisis that had struck all Europe for more than a year. Just like the grand crises of the ancien régime, this one had begun with a bad harvest in 1846, accompanied by a disease that destroyed the potato crop, the precious successor to cereal grains. In Ireland, the return of famine resulted in massive emigration to America. In France the price of grain, and thus of bread, had doubled. The consequences included riots in the marketplaces, pillage of bakeries and even châteaux, armed banditry, arson, and assassination. The common people were forced to limit their spending to food, and could buy hardly anything else. Manufacturers and retailers saw their sales fall, and as a result there were bankruptcies, falling rates of return, and a budget deficit as tax collections declined. Much more serious was the rise in unemployment, for which there was no assistance except for a few charities. As the republican idea became popular, caricaturists and songwriters ridiculed the king and Guizot. The first socialist ideas were spread, and it is understandable that the proletarians were ready to take action.

Part of the bourgeoisie was outraged by the government's soft diplomacy toward Britain and Austria, and the disreputable though rare scandals that involved peers of France and former ministers, who sold decorations and influence. Tocqueville dared to ask in the chamber whether this regime "by its indifference, its egoism, and its vices" had not become "incapable and unworthy of governing." There soon arose in the country a vast English-style campaign in the form of grand banquets with more and more inflammatory speeches by young "radicals" (a English word) or democrats—socialists such as Ledru-Rollin, Louis Blanc, and the idealistic Lamartine. Guizot and his master remained impassive. When a Parisian banquet and parade were forbidden on February 22, 1848, loud demonstrations took place, but no blood was shed. A frightened Louis-Philippe decided to sacrifice Guizot, yet that concession proved insufficient when a brawl between the crowd and soldiers on the boulevard des Capucines degenerated into a gun battle. The sight of the bodies of sixteen victims drawn in carriages by torchlight unleashed popular fury. On February 24, two days later, the Second Republic was proclaimed at the Hôtel de Ville, and it was the old king's turn to depart, after a failed attempt to bequeath power to his grandson, the count of Paris. Rather curiously, the country and Europe as a whole (also occupied with revolutionaries in Germany, Austria, Italy, and elsewhere) responded favorably, or at least silently. Even the army rallied quickly to the new regime, and parish priests provisionally blessed the new trees of liberty. This era of warm unanimity did not last.

The provisional government consisted of a handful of republicans of various shades, along with Louis Blanc, Marrast, Flocon, and the symbolic "Worker Albert," four socialists chosen on principle. Naturally this government contained all the seeds of quick discord. However, in the first days of enthusiasm it proclaimed pell-mell all sorts of liberties and distributed freedoms generously. There was freedom of the press, and in five months nearly three hundred new newspapers appeared in Paris. There was freedom of assembly, and an explosion of political clubs such as those of Blanqui and Barbès took place. The slaves in the colonies were liberated, corporal punishment and prison for debt were abolished. And there were two magnificent but perhaps unwise novelties: universal male suffrage at age twenty-one, and the national workshops so dear to Louis Blanc, ostensibly created to help and keep busy the swarming unemployed, 100,000 strong in May.

Universal suffrage increased the electorate from a quarter of a million to more than 10 million, of whom three-quarters were peasants and a good third were illiterate. Many had heard about the Republic. Some—owners of national properties, artisans, and lumberjacks—looked on it with favor, while others were negative, particularly in the old provinces with traditions of counterrevolutionary peasant revolts, royalism and fervent Catholicism. No one really knew what "socialism" meant, but parish priests, landlords, and a good number of propagandists took the trouble to explain it. Note, for example, the words of Henri Wallon, who later became the "father" of the Third Republic: "A red is not a man, he is a red. . . . He is not a moral, intelligent, and free being like you or me. . . . He is a fallen and degenerate man. His face is marked by signs of that fall. A beaten appearance, brutalized . . . eyes as colorless as those of a pig . . . the mouth as mute and senseless as that of an ass. . . . The 'dividers' have written on their faces the stupidity of the doctrines and ideas by which they live" (May 1849).

This is a good and vivid example of the "red scare" that was used with the same success for many decades, and not only in France; it may still function today. In 1848, it awakened the fears of the bourgeoisie, who suddenly joined forces with the Church and achieved the desired results in three elections that followed the February revolution. In the voting for the Constituent Assembly in April 1848, the socialists obtained 100 out of 900 seats, while the moderate republicans, many of whom were Orléanists in disguise, held an overwhelming majority. Eight months later, when the new and hastily written constitution had imprudently invented the office of president of the republic, the French people voted en masse for the "nephew of the Great Emperor," strongly supported by local notables and champions of "order." One opponent, Cavaignac, was an unknown, and hardly anyone had read Lamartine. As for the other candidates, Ledru-Rollin and Raspail were known as "reds" and "dividers." The same phenomenon took place six months later, in the campaign to elect a new assembly in May 1849. With the help of the bankers and the Church, a remarkable electoral group, the Party of Order, suddenly appeared to defend "family, property, and religion." This was one of the great moments of exploitation of the red scare, as the reds were denounced by tens of thousands of unforgettable brochures. The champions of order won 450 seats, two-thirds of the total. The 75 surviving moderates threatened no one, but there were 180 democrats and socialists, chosen from Paris, central France, and the southeast. Their presence in government could not be tolerated, and they were soon made to know it, in 1849 as in 1848.

To eliminate them, force was required; to justify it, the forces of order could count on the naive passion of the "reds," and above all on provocations. While awaiting the coup d'état, the mission was accomplished in two phases.

In the name of the "right to work," proclaimed on February 25, Minister Marie had called together at the Palais de Luxembourg an enormous commission with nearly 900 members to discuss proposals. Simultaneously, national workshops were created in Paris and in the provinces. With the complicity of the Administration of Bridges and Roads, it was arranged that the unemployed in these shops would have nothing to do, although they were paid a half-salary of one franc a day. Thus hundreds of thousands of people were kept in misery while putting a drain on the state budget. Socialist and Bonapartist propaganda was spread among the idle workers. The moderate assembly elected in April had to deal with the problem. They thought of putting the unemployed to work in the vast projects of railway construction, but business interests rejected this idea. At the same time it so happened that banks closed and bankruptcies were announced; stock market prices fell by half, as did treasury bills and 5 percent bonds. Tax increases were declared unavoidable, and overall economic confidence declined impressively. On June 15, 1848, Goudchaux, mouthpiece of the bankers, urged the assembly to close down the workshops. On June 22 the assembly agreed, and announced that some laborers would be sent to Sologne to work on useful drainage projects, while youths could choose between dismissal and enlistment in the army. Two days later, the first barricades went up, and the insurgents quickly took over the southeastern half of Paris. The assembly then delegated full powers to General Cavaignac to defeat those it called "the enemy." As they were harshly pushed back, the insurgents took refuge in the "old faubourg" Saint-Antoine, where they were bombarded by cannon fire. About 1,000 soldiers were killed, and perhaps 5,000 to 15,000 insurgents (the exact number is unknown). Some of them were simply assassinated in the cellars of the Tuileries. Even Ernest Renan, who was hardly a revolutionary firebrand, wrote on July 1, "The atrocities committed by the victors make me shiver." Some 15,000 prisoners were brought before the "war courts" (what war?); 5,000 were deported to Algeria, others remained in prison, and still others went into more or less compulsory exile. Lamennais, more eloquent than other disenchanted writers, found a felicitous phrase to describe it all: "the saturnalia of reaction."

These were not the last, either. Following the elections of 1849 in which they had been too successful, the democrats and socialists led by Ledru-Rollin decided to demonstrate against French military intervention in favor of Pope Pius IX, who had been dislodged by Garibaldi and the Roman republicans. From June 13 to June 15, the army crushed demonstrators in Paris and the provinces. At Lyon, for example, two hundred people were killed. Then justice and legislation took over: thirty-four deputies were hauled before the high court, newspapers were suppressed, freedom of assembly was suspended, and a state of siege was declared. What remained of the republican party was effectively silenced.

The prince-president and the assembly, momentarily in agreement with each other, had successfully destroyed freedom of the press and freedom of assembly. Now they handed over almost all education to the clergy in the Falloux Law of 1850. They amputated one-quarter of the voters from universal suffrage by excluding the young and mobile—the local residency requirement was raised to three years. Suddenly, government finances and the economy staged a remarkable recovery. The stock and bond markets climbed again, the loans of the Banque de France to the state shot up by 85 percent, and exports increased by 50 percent. This was a wonderful result.

When all danger of republican and socialist deviations had been destroyed, the happy victors had to decide on the future regime. The death of Louis-Philippe in August 1850 was an opportunity for the elder branch of Bourbon and the younger branch of Orléans to reconcile themselves and restore a monarchy that would have been accepted without difficulty, provided they could live with a good bourgeois constitution. However, the two branches could not come to an agreement, and unfortunately for them they have never been able to do so.

From that moment onward, the door was open for adventure, and particularly for an adventurer. Louis-Napoleon was waiting.

His first priority was to have himself reelected president in 1852, but this was forbidden by the constitution, and the assembly refused to change it. This assembly contained a royalist majority and a republican minority, and it had no particular love for Louis-Napoleon. Furthermore, it was largely composed of provincials and landowners who understood neither Paris nor big business and who lacked the will to industrialize voiced by progressive men often influenced by Saint-Simonism. By contrast, the Saint-Simonists supported Louis-Napoleon, who appreciated them, favored them, and took advantage of their money.

Apparently disdaining intrigues and rumors, the prince-president traveled through the provinces and tried to win popular acclaim with the active support of the prefects. When the results were mixed, he decided on a coup d'état, covertly prepared by a very small group of close friends—his half-brother Morny, Persigny, Rouher, Prefect of Police Maupas, the banker Fould who provided the money, and Saint-Arnauld who was the necessary "saber." Saint-Arnauld was an energetic fighter with limited intelligence and no scruples whatsoever: he had been made minister of war.

On the night of December 1–2, 1851, the army occupied all the strategic points in Paris and arrested possible opponents such as Thiers and Cavaignac, as well as a handful of deputies who tried to organize "legal" resistance. The last remaining republicans exhorted the people to build barricades, but the memory of recent experiences was enough to keep the workers quiet, even in their own neighborhoods. Order was quickly reestablished. On the December 4, crowds shouted and demonstrated a bit on the boulevards. Morny fired on them, and there were two or three hundred victims. Paris now remained quiet for a long time.

The provinces, however, reacted harshly. Republicanism and social spirit had taken hold strongly among the petty bourgeoisie, artisans and skilled craftsmen, the powerful associations of lumberjacks, sawyers, carriers and river-transporters of wood, and among certain day-laborers. Violent riots broke out in the Yonne, Allier, Lot-et-Garonne, Hérault, Var, Basses-Alpes, and Nièvre *départements*. At Clamecy, a printer and his sons led a revolt, which was quickly joined by the woodworkers and peasants of the area; elsewhere, carpenters, masons, and innkeepers played leading roles. The government troops quickly finished off these "bandits and assassins," as the prefect of the Nièvre called them. They were also discouraged by the course of events in Paris. The repression was severe: 84 deputies were expelled, 32 *départements* were placed under martial law; 27,000 "reds" were brought before mixed commissions presided over by a general assisted by a prefect and a prosecutor. More than 10,000 were deported to Algeria and Guiana; 2,500 were interned; 1,500 were exiled. In the Nièvre alone, 800 were deported, even more in the Basses-Alpes, fewer in the Var. Thus the regime created its own future adversaries. At the end of December 1852, some 7.5 million people voted in a plebiscite on the coup d'état; 650,000 had the courage to vote no, and 1.5 million abstained.

A year later, Louis-Napoleon had promulgated yet another constitution, which gave him full powers. He also made a provincial tour that had been carefully organized by Persigny and his prefects. Then he had himself proclaimed emperor in a new plebiscite, which 2 million voters ignored. He decided he would be known as Napoleon III, and that his as yet unborn heirs would succeed him. On December 2, 1852, on the first anniversary of an elevation that he did not dare to celebrate, he could cherish these hopes.

Once again a new revolution, characterized and weakened by idealism, had been methodically and coldly assassinated. In reality, the course of events had been set in those days of June 1848.

Chapter Sixteen

FRANCE UNDER NAPOLEON III: 1851–1870

THE BONAPARTES

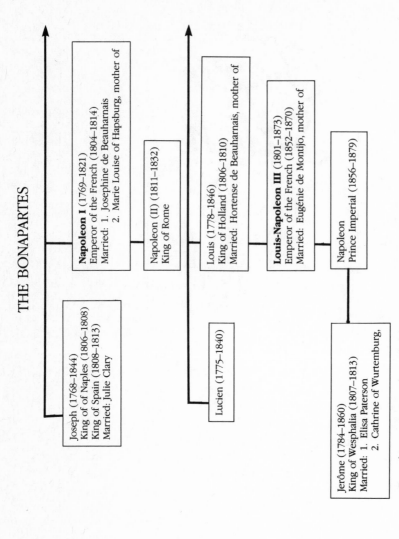

Joseph (1768–1844)
King of Naples (1806–1808)
King of Spain (1808–1813)
Married: Julie Clary

Napoleon I (1769–1821)
Emperor of the French (1804–1814)
Married: 1. Josephine de Beauharnais
2. Marie Louise of Hapsburg, mother of

Napoleon (II) (1811–1832)
King of Rome

Lucien (1775–1840)

Louis (1778–1846)
King of Holland (1806–1810)
Married: Hortense de Beauharnais, mother of

Louis-Napoleon III (1801–1873)
Emperor of the French (1852–1870)
Married: Eugénie de Montijo, mother of

Napoleon
Prince Imperial (1856–1879)

Jerôme (1784–1860)
King of Wesphalia (1807–1813)
Married: 1. Elisa Paterson
2. Cathrine of Wurtemburg,

From this marriage are descended the Bonapartist claimants to the throne of France. The current head of the family is Louis-Napoleon, born in 1914.

A REGIME AND A MAN

For the sixth time in less than forty years, France changed its regime. The Second Empire resulted from a coup d'état that had been better prepared than the 18 Brumaire of the first Napoleon. Like all the preceding regimes, it followed a goodly mix of massacres, imprisonments, and deportations. Indeed, the Third Republic had arisen in the same manner, under the watchful eye of the occupying forces, as had the Restoration in 1815. In 1870, the retrograde Second Empire died the same way as the first, in defeat and occupation; seventy years later, the Republic that succeeded it died the same death. Despite some glorious episodes, we must admit that wars, especially great wars, did not bring success to the French state or nation. This statement may appear cruel, but the historian has a duty to bring to light the evidence, and not to hide it behind the veil of modesty or hypocrisy.

Helped by a tight circle of fiercely loyal, remarkably intelligent, and passably dishonest advisers, the nephew of the Great Emperor had brutally seized power. His personality has been subjected to the most varied analyses and opinions. To tell the truth, it is tempting to write that his end was his judgment. A lack of intelligence marked both the incredible expedition to Mexico (1862–67) and the six catastrophic weeks of the war of 1870, which, for all practical purposes, ended at Sedan on September 2. It is true that Louis-Napoleon in his seventies had lost both Morny and his own health, and that his entourage (whom he had, after all, chosen) showed an undeniable and vain mediocrity.

But the Second Empire cannot be judged only by its dénouement. These twenty years had profound effects on France, primarily because they included the nation's first industrial revolution, some hundred years after the English example. This revolution may be summed up in four words: *credit, banking, railways,* and *metallurgy.* It had begun under the preceding regime, and had far-reaching social consequences.

Napoleon III well understood the importance of change and encouraged it as much as he could. He pushed for the organization of the six large railway companies, offered to display innovations at the two great expositions of 1855 and 1867, and had the audacity to prepare secretly for the shift from the old French protectionism to the first free-trade treaty, which was negotiated by the Englishman Richard Cobden and the French economist Michel Chevalier. The treaty struck like a bolt of lightning in January 1860, startling French industrialists out of their sleepy routine. They had grown fat and complacent because of the disparity between very high prices for their goods and extremely low wages: now they would have to change both traditional policies.

The former prince Louis-Napoleon had written a tract entitled "The Extinction of Poverty." At one time, in 1831, he had been a *carbonaro* and petty revolutionary in central Italy. He was interested in the workers and wanted to solve social problems in his own way. After pursuing a generous policy of assistance and charity, he dared in 1864 to allow strikes, as long as they remained nonviolent and did not interfere with the freedom to work. He also authorized several cooperatives and workers' unions on the condition that they remain moderate.

These examples only serve to underline the character of the man and his regime. He alternated between generosity and authoritarianism. The latter tendency was especially visible in political life, which was reduced to nothingness between 1852 and 1859. Two examples suffice: during elections, which lasted two days, the appointed mayors took home the unsealed ballot boxes. Minister Fortoul even prohibited professors from wearing beards because, he explained seriously, he wanted to eliminate "the last signs of anarchy": a certain Francisque Sarcey was so bold as to ask if he might be allowed to wear a mustache. Starting in 1859 the regime became slightly more liberal: in the legislative body there were even several opponents such as Thiers, who was thus able to restore his much needed illusion of political virginity. The opposition was even successful in increasing its numbers, and the emperor relaxed his rule somewhat. In 1870, people could believe that a "parliamentary empire" was about to begin. However, the same clique always dominated the administration, and the ministers always belonged to it. Fond of secrecy, Napoleon III continued to direct foreign policy by himself; but after Morny had disappeared in 1865, he listened too often to the Empress Eugénie, whose political intelligence never equaled her piety.

The heart of the matter was that this intelligent man who knew how to listen and often understood politics, even when he appeared lost in reveries, still suffered from the weakness of being and wanting to remain a Bonaparte. He wished to assume a heritage that legend had rendered inaccessible.

Thus Napoleon III wanted to recover military glory: after forty years of beneficent peace he plunged France into four wars. The first two, in Crimea and Italy, were difficult but victorious; there were also colonial expeditions such as Faidherbe's brilliant exploits in Sénégal, but they did not excite the mass of his subjects. Napoleon III wanted to correct the contraction of French frontiers imposed by the victors in 1815: he succeeded in acquiring Savoy and Nice, which the Bourbon kings could easily have annexed long before. This was accomplished thanks to services rendered to Piedmont, and after plebiscites organized in the name of the sacred right of popular self-determination. Napoleon III sincerely believed in this idea and tried without success to apply it elsewhere, in Rumania and Poland. He attempted to negotiate as a neutral between Prussia and Austria, while belatedly claiming territory in Luxembourg or north of Alsace as a "tip" for his services, as Bismarck said. Yet the former conspirator was inept: instead of the genius of his uncle, he had inherited his weaknesses. Furthermore, he faced adversaries of rare talent such as Count Cavour, a Piedmontese genius who needed only a temporary military alliance with France to kick the Austrians out of Italy, and would have caused more trouble if he had not died in 1861. Otto von Bismarck frankly surpassed Napoleon III in astuteness, in strength of will, and particularly in the total absence of scruples that makes men great politicians. Napoleon III, on the other hand, was hesitant, secretive, sensible, dreamy even though intelligent, and yet an autocrat. In short, "Napoleon the Small" was a lightweight. Thus he melted away in an instant, and his regime went with him: hardly anyone thought of defending it. Its legacy, however, was the real prosperity that it had allowed and encouraged.

A NEW ECONOMY?

Many historians think that we can speak of a break between old and new economy only if four conditions apply. The first concerns transport—its extension, acceleration, and reduction in cost, which allow the development of a unified national market. Isolated provinces must be brought first into the national and then into the international economy. The second condition is the rise of industry over agriculture, as measured by the value of its production as well as by the number of workers. In France this condition was not established until the twentieth century. The third condition looks at the composition of industry itself: leadership must pass from older textile industries to renovated metallurgical industries, where only the problems of overproduction can cause cyclical crises. This also did not occur in nineteenth-century France. Finally, the last theoretical condition argues for the importance and new complexity of finance and banking. Merchant banking in particular must play a leading role in mobilizing credit.

In short, we can say that the first and last conditions were satisfied under the Second Empire. But the others were not, because of the strength of French ruralism and traditional employers' attitudes. Yet significant developments in industry made their realization foreseeable.

We turn now from theories of industrialization to what actually happened. The length of the railway network was increased six times and the first Alpine tunnels such as Mont-Cenis were begun. New ports such as Saint-Nazaire were created, and the older ones—Le Havre, Bordeaux, Marseille—were enlarged and rebuilt. Two large steamship companies were founded, as was a powerful modern fleet, which became the second largest in Europe. Ferdinand de Lesseps accomplished the old Napoleonic project of building the Suez Canal. All this, plus free-trade agreements, really constituted a decisive revolution that would mobilize building workers, traders, and merchandise, facilitating migration and commerce. The Bretons and the wine of Languedoc now came to Paris. Communication was improved as well by the telegraph wires that covered France and connected all the cities by 1870.

The impressive public works, especially in Paris, constituted a second great accomplishment that mobilized both capital and labor. Old neighborhoods were opened up, immense boulevards cut straight through the city, markets and sewers enlarged. Meanwhile great department stores such as the Bon Marché appeared to crush the world of small shops. These embellishments dear to the heart of Napoleon III were also a useful check on Parisian insurrections: henceforth cavalry and artillery could operate freely in the city. Furthermore, the demolition and reconstruction provided attractive business opportunities for the prefect Baron Haussmann and the imperial entourage, along with bankers, architects, and property owners who enriched themselves thanks to loans on generous terms from the Crédit Foncier, founded in 1852. In principle, these loans were supposed to help the provinces and the countryside. Nonetheless, today we congratulate ourselves that these beautiful wide avenues were built: they are a boon to automotive pollution.

Operations of a similar nature were undertaken in the ports, railways, wars, and colonial expeditions. They were all extremely expensive, and the national debt tripled between 1852 and 1870. The increasing wealth of France, which then rivaled Britain as the richest state in the world, is even more remarkable. Several phenomena supported this development. A good, slow, and productive increase in prices, on the order of 35 percent over twenty years, was joined by a greater increase in wages, about 45 percent. Also, there was a new gold rush in California, Canada, and Australia. The world supply of gold quadrupled, and in 1855 alone eight times as much gold was produced as in the entire period between 1810 and 1850. About 40 percent of the California gold appeared on the French market, and with such liquidity businesses and investments prospered.

Furthermore, the mobilization of the countless loaded "wool stockings" began, thanks to a system of traditional private banks such as those established by the Rothschilds and their associates, and the rise of deposit and commercial banks. These institutions appeared quickly after 1852: the Crédit Foncier and Crédit Mobilier, the Comptoir d'Escompte, Crédit Lyonnais (1863), and Société Générale (1864). Their goal was to invest their clients' money in French and foreign businesses that promised high profits. At times they assumed too much risk and suffered financial reverses, causing the ruin of *gogo* investors, as they were already known. The Comptoir d'Escompte admitted having made a net profit of 16.2 percent in 1865; the Société Générale made 24 percent in 1867 after only three years of operation. The Crédit Lyonnais had to wait until 1874 to make its nice profit of 54 percent, but even these records were broken in the early twentieth century, when the Banque de Paris et des Pays-Bas and the Banque de l'Indochine achieved rates of return between 50 percent and 73 percent.

These banks rendered important services to their customers, to industrialists and businessmen, and to themselves.

France then constituted a particularly fertile terrain for financial operations. The national wealth in 1870 has been estimated at 175 to 200 billion gold francs, and these figures are probably low. Thus it is not surprising that when a state loan of 400 million was announced in 1868, the issue attracted 800,000 subscribers offering 15 billion francs, nearly forty times the total requested. The main defect of this pool of wealth was its tendency to remain hidden underneath the mattresses. Often lenders were satisfied with modest rates of return, such as those offered by the state and the savings banks, which had existed on the departmental level since 1818 but became truly national in 1861. In coming closer to the level of the general public, the new banks were able to mobilize the sleeping national wealth. Later they would have the opportunity to mislead savers by offering them astonishing investments such as Russian loans. After 1848 the French people, who had known only petty coinage apart from the gold *écu* and the *louis* (or *napoléon*), gradually became accustomed to notes issued by the Banque de France. The first "small" bills of 100 and 50 francs date from 1848 and 1857. Over the term of the Second Empire, the quantity of banknotes in circulation increased from 250 million to 1.35 billion francs; the gold reserve ratio of the Banque de France rose from 50 percent in the beginning to 80 percent in 1869. In view of such sound financial and economic bases, one wonders even more at the political and military stupidity that caused the fall of the regime.

The undeniable industrial growth of this period has often been exaggerated by overly sympathetic or incompetent historians, and it must be put into perspective. Indeed, French coal production nearly tripled, but in 1870 it was still only one-eighth that of Britain, and only one-third that of Germany and the United States. Industrial power, then measured in thousands of steam-horsepower, rose from 270 in the beginning—roughly the same as that of Germany, but only one-fifth that of Britain—to nearly 1,900 in 1870. Yet by that time Germany had nearly 2,500; Britain 4,000; and the United States 6,000. The same relatively slow growth rates occurred in iron and steel. Nonetheless French production tripled, and the country was no longer obliged to import rails from across the Channel. Finally, in 1861 there were still more than three hundred wood-fired forges moving through the forests as they exhausted their fuel supplies. There were only about one hundred coke furnaces, and by 1862–63 some French manufacturers were asking whether the Bessemer converter was really worthwhile. In any case, the metallurgical industry employed only 250,000 workers, while textiles and clothing had more than 2 million. This is another sign that the industrial revolution was just beginning in France.

The great majority of French people remained peasants. According to the census of 1866, they were 69.5 percent of the population and produced nearly half of the gross national product. Industry contributed only 30 percent, and most of that was from textiles, as in the ancien régime, except that now cotton was the leading fiber. Although there were still day-laborers with large families in poor areas, the peasantry as a whole suffered less than it had in the past. Often they owned land: two million properties were less than 1 hectare. To earn enough income, these small proprietors leased other lands, performed day labor, and worked in cottage industries. Peasants gradually increased their incomes by reducing the amount of fallow lands. They cautiously adopted guano fertilizer and simple machines. In 1862 there were fewer than 9,000 harvesters, hardly any cutting machines, but already almost 100,000 steam-powered threshers, in use until 1930. The greatest progress was made in the advanced northern third of the country, where growing conditions favored sugar beets and potatoes. Indeed, potatoes became as important a staple food as bread. The transport revolution had positive effects on agricultural life, and particularly on the vineyards of the south. Inexpensive wines of strong color and flavor conquered the urban markets and sent older producing areas into decline; these areas were soon hit by disease as well. Consumption of wine doubled under Badinguet, and the cheap wines of

Languedoc were the favorite tipple. The Emperor, who showed an interest in agriculture, developed model farms on his own domains in Sologne and Landes. His neighbors soon followed his example. Departmental schools of agriculture were created, and *comices agricoles* (agricultural fairs) awarded prizes each year for the best harvests and improvement projects. Land reclamation and reforesting were strongly encouraged in Brenne, Sologne, and Landes. There were even attempts to replant mountainsides and irrigate dry areas such as Verdon and the Aix basin. These were important enterprises, but they did not yet constitute an agricultural revolution. That would come later.

A NEW SOCIETY?

The high society of the Parisian boulevards, the Bois de Boulogne, and Saint-Cloud has left behind a reputation for luxury, light-heartedness, and vivacity typified by the devilish melodies of Offenbach. The popular image of the Belle Époque relates only to a small part of high society composed of bankers and women of leisure, ministers and barons of industry, nouveaux riches of doubtful origin, and men of spirit. They eagerly flocked around Princess Mathilde or Prince Jérôme, the Emperor's "leftish" cousin, who also provided an excellent alibi.

In reality, the old aristocracy was legitimist in its politics and kept to its châteaux and salons in the Faubourg Saint-Germain. These were closed to the political world of interlopers who congregated around Morny, Persigny, and Mirès, a banker who began with nothing and finished badly. In the provinces, the more-or-less ennobled aristocracy of commerce and metallurgy was comfortably installed on its lands and forests, and seemed to evolve into a softer and more formal world. In each good city, the solid commercial and *rentier* bourgeoisie held its own highly affected, opulent, overfurbished salons. At the same time they were gathering their *écus* and watching the stock market prices. More discreet but nonetheless aping their betters were the shopkeepers, respectable employees, and serious civil servants who also eyed interest rates while eagerly assuming pretensions to poetry and music. This hierarchy of bourgeois circles great and small has been savagely described by many writers and caricaturists. Prud'homme, Homais, Perrichon, and Pécuchet are folkloric characters of ample girth, speaking their thick prose hesitantly. But there is a grain of truth in the image: these were the holders of French wealth. There was not much new in their style, except perhaps in the bourgeois decor and the growing influence of the Catholic church, which explains the vivacity of some of their reactions.

Badly damaged during the Revolution of 1789, greatly reduced in wealth and numbers, the French Church achieved a remarkable and perhaps excessive revival. During the Restoration, the Church covered France with missions and crosses in expiation of past "crimes." Earlier parish priests had been of more exalted social origin, often semi-bourgeois. Now the Church began recruiting the young priests it needed to regain its influence in the pious countryside of the west. Regular orders also returned in force, even the Jesuits. During the reign of Napoleon III, the empress and the regime encouraged a huge increase in the number of nuns, which quadrupled to nearly 140,000 in 1870. The number of monks rose eightfold from 3,000 to 24,000. Also, as a result of gifts and legacies, the lands and income of the Church had been largely reconstituted, while the state—that is, the taxpayers—paid the priests handsomely. Aided by the great fear among property owners after the working-class republican riots under the July Monarchy and in 1848, the Church expanded beyond its traditional clientele of aristocrats and rural women. Now it encompassed part of the bourgeoisie that had once flirted with Voltairean ideas but was horrified by the "reds." Rather curiously, this French Church that had been so strongly Gallican became almost entirely ultramontane. It admired the papacy that resisted civil power and the revolutions of 1831 and 1848, thus recovering all the prestige lost by the feeble pontiffs of the eighteenth century. The vigorous Pius IX, momentarily tempted to make liberal reforms in his territories in central Italy, was disgusted by revolutionary outrages and the attempt to establish a Roman republic. He became the uncontested champion of resistance to every new idea. Accordingly, in 1864 he published the *Syllabus of Errors*—a list of all insanities he rejected out of hand: reason, Protestantism, freedom of speech, tolerance, divorce, socialism, Christian pacifism, ecclesiastical poverty, progress, and modern civilization. In passing, he affirmed that every state should profess Catholicism and use no other methods for educating its youth. These affirmations make certain strong reactions quite understandable. Shortly afterward, in the first council that had been called in three centuries, the pope proclaimed his infallibility in matters of faith.

Church and faithful, strongly royalist in their sentiments, rallied their full electoral power massively behind the prince-president when he proposed the Falloux Law of 1850, which practically gave them control of the University of France. Napoleon I had made the university a state monopoly, designed to do its service; the Falloux Law greatly facilitated the multiplication of so-called free schools (those outside the university). In fact these "free schools" were almost all Catholic. Almost anyone was allowed to open one, and any monk or nun could teach there, as in the public schools—practically without any diplomas. The teachers and professors who remained in the public sector fell under the joint control of the appointed mayors and prefects, and the bishop and priests. As for the rare girls who went to school, nuns were given almost exclusive charge of imparting to them knowledge that was subject to no examinations whatsoever. The young Abbé Duplanloup, on the threshold of a brilliant career, praised the virtues of this law "of liberty" in an enthusiastic essay dedicated to the pope and the bishops.

Nevertheless, relations between the powerful, suspicious Catholic party and the government were troubled by the emperor's aid to Italian unification in 1859, the threats against the temporal power of the pope, and the efforts of Minister Victor Duruy (1863–67) to expand free public education and even increase the number of girls' schools. But the empress was watchful, a French army guarded the master in Rome, and Duruy was dismissed.

Even this brief summary helps us understand the violent and hostile anticlericalism shared by many liberals and all republicans and socialists. Clericalism, in their opinion, meant the intervention of a rich and powerful Church in civil and political life. One round of excesses engendered others, and these problems weighed heavily on French political life from 1850 to 1914. Under the Second Empire, they had little effect on rural people, who were faithful, docile, or indifferent; but they did cause agitation in the cities, where people were more divided and more outspoken.

These urban populations, enlarged by the migration of younger sons and laborers from the countryside beginning in the 1840s, began to diversify and divide in various ways. The older vertical separation of classes with the well-to-do on the first floor and the poor just under the roof gave way to a horizontal separation by neighborhood. In 1860 the boundaries of Paris had been extended to include ten adjacent communes from Passy to Vaugirard, Belleville, and Montmartre. The fashionable western districts were more and more distinguishable from the east and the old suburbs, which quickly became proletarian domains; the old Center and Marais remained the citadel of skilled craftsmen. At Lyon, poor wretches perched on the Croix-Rousse; at Lille they stagnated in cellars; and at Nantes they huddled along the banks of the river. Even worse than the crowding, promiscuity, and lack of hygiene were the meager wages, the absence of all except vaguely charitable aid for large families and the unemployed, the incredibly long working day—ten to fourteen hours—and the systematic exploitation of women and children, who were paid half or a quarter of what men got. We should also mention the merciless discipline of the workshops, the prohibition of any form of workers' association after 1791, the required workpass that could be checked by employers and the police, and article 1781 of the Civil Code, which stated that the master would be "believed on his affirmation" in disputes over wages.

Napoleon III was aware of this situation, and supported welfare institutions such as orphanages, nurseries, and aid for victims of accidents. He suppressed article 1781, and granted the right to strike in 1864, although strikes had to remain nonviolent and could not interfere with the freedom to work. The Emperor also authorized several cooperatives and moderate unions, and encouraged the first adult education programs and pension plans for workers. He even sent the engraver Tolain and several other artisans to visit the exhibition in London in 1862. They returned to London in 1864, laid the foundations of an International Workingmen's Association, asked for profound reforms in the "Manifesto of the Sixty," and then threw themselves into republican demonstrations and plots. Violent strikes took place in 1869 and 1870. In vain the disillusioned Emperor ordered the French section of the First International dissolved. The workers' movement began harshly and once again frightened several bourgeois. Yet it was still not very dangerous.

In reality, the Second Empire melted away all by itself, with an ease that showed that it had no solid foundations. It died of war and incompetence.

FROM GLORY TO DISASTER: THE SECOND EMPIRE AND THE WORLD

As the heir of the Great Emperor and the Revolution—he mingled the two in his mind—Louis-Napoleon desired simultaneously to extend the frontiers of his country and to protect European "nationalities" and the right of popular self-determination. He wanted to defend Catholicism everywhere, but he also dreamed of protecting the Moslems—he imagined an Arabic kingdom in Algeria. He wanted to raise the French flag in Sénégal, Indochina, and Oceania. And on occasion he wanted to play the magnificent role of arbiter for the world: he hoped to realize it by calling for a congress at Paris in 1856 on the subject of the Black Sea, the Danube, and the straits. At the same time this lover of glory could not stand the sight of blood. The spectacle of the battlefield of Solferino in 1859 pushed him to conclude an immediate peace with Austria at Villafranca, infuriating his Piedmontese allies, whom he had promised to accompany all the way to the Adriatic. Furthermore, he chose his generals badly. They were brave and brilliant men, but of limited intelligence, as they proved in the final episode of empire.

In Crimea, where nearly 100,000 French soldiers died of cold and fever before Sebastopol, Napoleon had intervened as the ally of the British against the Russians. They had pretended to protect the Christians of the Ottoman Empire, when they really wanted only to weaken it further and penetrate to the Mediterranean Sea. The victory, the Congress of Paris, and the aftermath allowed the Emperor to support limited autonomy for the Rumanian provinces and cut a figure as a brilliant arbiter. Then in 1860 he ran to the rescue of the Christians of Lebanon, who were already threatened with annihilation by the Moslems of that country.

Up to this point, his policies were successful; powerful and prosperous France was calm. Then came two series of blunders that are difficult to explain.

The first concerns Mexico. In this great state torn apart by civil war, European countries had invested considerable sums. Badly administered, Mexico suddenly decided not to pay its debts and to tax foreigners who lived there. As the United States was in the throes of its own civil war, a fleet of British, Spanish, and French creditors landed troops in Mexico to claim their due in 1861. After having obtained some satisfaction, the first two groups left, but the French stayed behind. Napoleon III dreamed of creating a Catholic and liberal Latin empire on the southern flank of the great Anglo-Saxon Protestant republic. To lead this new empire he had chosen the Austrian Archduke Maximilian, a brave and generous man. Despite furious guerrilla attacks and the defeat at Puebla in 1862, Maximilian maintained himself in power as long as the French army was there and the American Civil War continued. But when peace came to the United States and the Prussian problem arose in Europe, the rather badly commanded French re-embarked. What was left of Maximilian's forces was crushed by the resisters of Juarez, who were actively supported by the United States. Maximilian faced a firing squad in 1867, and all that remained of the Mexican Catholic dream was military and financial defeat—the object of ridicule.

Napoleon I and the treaties of 1815 had reshaped the old Germanic Confederation, reducing it from nearly three hundred petty states to about thirty, under the leadership of Austria. The land of Germany as a whole was rich and well populated, supplied with solid banks, a good network of railways, and a metallurgical industry already symbolized by Krupp. From the Rhine to the Baltic, the various pieces of Prussia dominated north Germany, especially since the Prussians had already established a customs union (*Zollverein*) with most of their neighbors in 1836. Apart from the still powerful states of Saxony, Baden, Württemberg, and Bavaria, the south continued to be dominated by Austria. The king of Prussia and his prime minister, Bismarck, who had been in office since 1862, desired to reduce Austrian power to its own territory and take over the leadership of Germany themselves. To achieve this end, a large, disciplined, and well-equipped army was organized in a few years by Moltke and Roon. It was first tested against Denmark in 1864, in the struggle over the duchies of Schleswig and Holstein. Two years later, with the inept complicity of Napoleon III, Bismarck arranged to have the Austrian emperor and several southern princes declare war on Prussia. The conflict was settled in less than a month: at Sadowa, in July 1866, Austria was crushed and excluded from the new Germany. Bismarck was now free to reorganize to his heart's content. This he did with the agreement of Napoleon III, who asked only that the states south of the Main River would keep some independence, since Prussia had joined all the others under its rule. Thoughtful Frenchmen were concerned at this turn of events; as for the emperor, he asked Bismarck to give him as compensation either Luxembourg or two or three cities. The Prussian did not even answer; he bided his time.

The historic moment came in 1870 with the candidacy for the Spanish throne of a Hohenzollern relation of the king of Prussia. After French protests, the candidacy was withdrawn. The French ambassador then asked for guarantees for the future. King Wilhelm responded evasively, though courteously; however, a slight manipulation of the text of the "Ems Dispatch" by Bismarck made it sound insulting. At Paris the Empress, soldiers, deputies, and journalists were fired with patriotic enthusiasm: this affront had to be avenged. On July 19, the French declared war on Prussia. Within six weeks, this war destroyed the Second Empire.

The Debacle: *August 6 to September 2, 1870*

On August 6, France lost Alsace and the northern part of Lorraine simultaneously. Two weeks later, Marshal Achille Bazaine, who could not retreat in good order to Verdun, allowed himself to be besieged and eventually captured at Metz. He surrendered with 180,000 soldiers, including three marshals and 1,600 cannons. During this time, MacMahon and the Emperor collected 130,000 men from the camp at Châlons in order to lead them toward Sedan, where they hoped to find Bazaine. The Prussians and their allies completely encircled them, and the Emperor surrendered with his remaining 100,000 men to avoid a massacre. Held prisoner in a fortress, he was later sent to England, where he died three years later. The English arranged to liquidate the dynasty by sending his son to get himself killed by the Zulus in 1879. Eugénie survived them for almost half a century.

The capture of the Emperor left France without a government. Parisian crowds invaded the legislature and forced a vote of dissolution. As usual the parade then went to the Hôtel de Ville, where Parisian deputies proclaimed a Republic on September 4. They formed a provisional government and decided to continue the war. Not a single Bonapartist came to the defense of the fallen regime.

Why did the Second Empire collapse so easily? A few words will suffice to explain its fate. The German armies had 500,000 men, almost twice as many as the French; the new Krupp artillery outgunned the old French copper cannons. Finally, the advantage in organization and military intelligence lay with the adversary. The French mobilization took place in wild disarray, and no one dreamed of using the railways. Brave generals knew only how to make war in Africa. One of them, who became a minister, proudly declared that he "did not lack a single button on his leggings" while there was general disorder. Among the politicians, patriotic enthusiasm hardly exceeded incompetence and ignorance: one of them accepted this war "with a light heart." As for Bazaine, it seems that out of hostility toward the newly born Republic he did not even try to break out of Metz. Convicted as a traitor in 1873, he was condemned to death, then simply put in prison, from which he escaped; his case would have been handled better by a psychiatrist, if any had existed.

It is not impossible that Napoleon III had felt this sad end coming on, but he was only the shadow of his former self, lacking his half-brother the duc de Morny. And he could not resist the lamentable initiatives of the Empress.

On September 4, 1870, however, the war was not over. The new regime was courageously trying to continue this uneven struggle.

Chapter Seventeen

FROM
DEBACLE
TO REVENGE:
1870–1914

As the historian approaches his own era, his vision changes. Family stories, distorted memories of youth, passions, and the skepticism of his maturity are always present. A heroic effort of reading, taking a distanced view, and intellectual honesty can help in the quest for the only imaginable goal, trying to unravel and understand the essential points and things as they appear. There is no assurance, however, that the task will be made easier by mountains of books that try to bring the past to life, whether they be learned, passionate, or romantic. Even less helpful is rapid journalism or that gathering of raw materials known as instant history. Fortunately the short half-century between 1870 and 1914 does not present insurmountable problems of knowledge or understanding.

THE SOMBER YEARS

By September 15, 1870, the provisional government of September 4 had quickly contacted Bismarck, who immediately demanded Alsace-Lorraine. Consequently the government decided in a burst of patriotic fervor to continue the war. By September 19, Paris was besieged. Léon Gambetta had left for

Tours to reorganize the army: he recruited and equipped 600,000 men, and planned to save Paris with this First Army of the Loire, which would come to the aid of the city's garrison. But the defection of Marshal Bazaine, who preferred surrender to resistance, neutralized the first victories by freeing the German regiments that had besieged him in Metz. Despite the valiant efforts and passing successes of the armies of the north, the east, the Loire, and Paris, the defeat was complete by January 1871, and the capital was in agitation. Bismarck sat in the throne room of Versailles. In order to consult the nation the provisional government obtained a three-week armistice from him, but at the price of surrendering Paris, delivering fortresses to the enemy, disarming a large part of the French army, and paying 200 million gold francs to the conquerors. During this period, hasty elections would decide whether the French people wanted to continue the war. As exalted patriots, the republicans desired it; as champions of peace—and it is doubtful if there was any other solution—the royalists won two-thirds of the seats in the elected assembly. The Bonapartists had only a mere handful. The peace treaty was signed at Frankfurt several months later. It decreed that France pay the Germans a war indemnity of 5 billion francs, by which Bismarck may have hoped to ruin the French economy. There would also be partial occupation of the country for three years, the third such occupation since 1814. Most painful of all was the cessation of all Alsace (except Belfort) and the northern part of Lorraine, the wealthy German-speaking mining regions. Residents of the annexed areas could choose to emigrate, but at the cost of leaving almost all their possessions behind. Fewer than 4 percent did, and many of them became colonists in Algeria. This amputation of territory provoked hard feelings among the French for forty-three years: the national will and patriotic propaganda never ceased to demand the restitution of the "stolen" provinces and called for revenge on the Prussians.

But of course Prussia was not the only German state involved. After negotiations with the petty kings and princes of the region south of the Main River, Bismarck benefited from their military help and obtained their agreement to the proclamation of Wilhelm I as Emperor of Germany in the Hall of Mirrors of the Palace of Versailles on January 18, 1871. After so many humiliations at the hands of Louis XIV and Napoleon I, the Germans took great relish in this ceremony, which took place only 150 years after the coronation of the first king of Prussia at Königsberg. For at least the next twenty years, the German Empire of Wilhelm and Bismarck dominated the economy and diplomacy of continental Europe.

The French defeat also resulted in Italian unification, as the French garrison protecting the remnants of the papal states was recalled, and the king of Italy could finally install himself in Rome. The popes then thought of themselves as prisoners in the Vatican until 1929, when Mussolini conceded to them the present-day Vatican city-state.

Under the watchful eyes of the Germans, between March and May 1871, the defeated, occupied, ransomed, and reduced French people had to suffer a final trial, the Commune of Paris.

Paris was besieged and poorly armed, without enough provisions for the terrible winter. The Parisians believed they had been betrayed by the provinces, by the bourgeois of the provisional government, and by the defeatist and monarchist assembly. Besides, even with the bitter but still exalting memories of 1848, a whole revolutionary tradition lived on in the old neighborhoods of artisans and workers in central Paris, on the Left Bank, and above all on the east side of the city. This extremely lively world was susceptible to ideas and feelings of democracy, socialism, unionism, anarchism, libertarianism, and revolution, all of which were popularized by pamphlets and interminable discussions. While the more prosperous inhabitants of good neighborhoods fled the city under German protection, a crowd containing many women took charge of cannons and munitions. They also shot two generals, one of whom had fired on the insurgents of June 1848. In the midst of much noise, disorder, quarreling, and privation, the insurgents organized elections in order to establish a "revolutionary commune" worthy of the heritage of 1793. This body barely had time to act. Versailles, Bordeaux, the provinces, and

Adolphe Thiers were horrified. Bismarck allowed liberated French prisoners to rearm and help the Versailles army attack the Communards. Paris was the scene of terrible street fighting; many buildings were devastated and burned, and not always by the revolutionaries. At the end of May 1871, several days became infamous as Bloody Week. The number of victims among the forces of "order" was listed at 877, and among the Communards at well over 10,000, some say as many as 30,000. For three years afterward courts-martial held trials of 14,000 survivors. Relatively few were sent to the firing squads, but many were deported to Guiana and New Caledonia. The most prudent had fled in time. By the end of this purge, Paris had apparently lost eighty thousand inhabitants. All socialist and revolutionary movements were annihilated for twenty years: the goal of repression had been attained.

The enormous wealth of France quickly covered the loans floated to pay the 5 billion francs indemnity demanded by Bismarck. German troops were able to evacuate France six months ahead of schedule in September 1873, but they left behind long-lasting unpleasant memories.

THE SLOW EMERGENCE
OF THE THIRD REPUBLIC: 1871–1879

The Republic proclaimed on September 4, 1870, was paradoxically led by an Assembly composed of monarchists. Unfortunately they had two candidates for the throne: the count of Chambord, a grandson of Charles X, and the count of Paris, a grandson of Louis-Philippe. Like a good Bourbon, Chambord thought only of reestablishing the regime of pre-1789 days, despite knowing its difficulties; his younger Orléanist rival would have accepted a moderate constitutional monarchy. The ideal solution would have been for the Orléanist to succeed the Bourbon, who was already in his fifties and had no heirs. But the latter's insistence on the white fleur-de-lis flag instead of the tricolor apparently caused the failure of the Restoration in October 1873. The royalists could hope only to "freeze" the regime while waiting for Chambord to die or change. He lingered on for ten years; in the meantime, the Republic was firmly anchored, but not without difficulty.

Thiers was courageous, efficient, and authoritarian. He understood that a moderate republic would probably be the least offensive form of government, and he said so. Consequently, the monarchists in the Assembly conspired in May 1873 to force his resignation as chief executive. Their leader, the duc de Broglie, installed himself in the ministry and had Marshal MacMahon elected for a seven-year term to head a fictive republic. This honorable but uninspired soldier was more of an intellectual: he was there to "make the bed" for the monarchy, and he knew it. At the same time a regime of "moral order" was established. Freedom of the press, freedom of speech, and freedom of assembly were restricted; all mayors were appointed by royalists; and giant public ceremonies were organized. There were processions, pilgrimages, and inaugurations of basilicas such as Montmartre by a Church that gladly joined together devotion to the Sacred Heart of Jesus and the white flag. There was also the matter of "reparation" for the crimes of the Communards and making people forget the defeat. But at almost every parliamentary by-election republicans were chosen, as in the municipal elections of 1874. It soon became apparent that only a minority of the French people supported the Catholic and royal cause.

After two or three years of hesitation, it was necessary to establish at least a basic constitution. A series of laws passed in 1875 settled the matter: one of them contained an amendment by Henri-Alexandre Wallon that used the word "republic," and it was passed by a majority of one vote. The government that was created had two legislative houses and a president chosen by those houses. The system was truly parliamentary in the sense that every ministry was at the mercy of the majority of each chamber. Deputies to the lower house were elected by universal male suffrage. Senators, one-quarter of whom were "irremovables" who held office for life, were chosen by a restricted electorate largely dominated by the conservative rural vote. There was no requirement that the president of the republic, theoretically the holder of important powers, should be a mere figurehead, but that tradition flowed from MacMahon's behavior in 1876–77.

At the beginning of 1876, the general elections gave two-thirds of the Assembly seats to the republicans. Pressured by his royalist friends and by the senate, MacMahon suddenly decided not to ask a republican to form a government. Instead, he reappointed Broglie, dissolved the Chamber of Deputies, and launched a new electoral campaign that he was ill-suited to lead. In this scheme he clashed with Gambetta and his friends, who emerged triumphant after a hard struggle. The president gave way. He resigned at the beginning of 1879 when the majority had also captured the senate. The republicans finally occupied the Republic. They elected the mild-mannered Jules Grévy to the presidency, finally decided to fix the seat of government in Paris, made July 14 the national holiday, and resigned themselves to giving amnesty to the surviving Communards.

The Republic was getting itself organized.

THE THIRD REPUBLIC INSTALLED IN POWER: 1881–1886

The fundamental laws were passed by majorities of committed republicans, men who were antimonarchist and almost fatally anti-Catholic as well. They were generally moderates, so much so that their conflicts of personalities, political groups, and parties are not very interesting a century later.

"Republican liberties" were quickly and easily established. As of 1881 there was a measured freedom of the press. Shortly afterward, in August 1883, the judicial reorganization law eliminated 600 posts and removed the monarchists who held them. In 1882 and 1884, new municipal laws allowed all councils except Paris to elect mayors and their deputies. After much hesitation, the Assembly cautiously allowed professional associations, provided that they declare themselves, submit their bylaws for approval, and avoid all political activity. Of course it was not easy to enforce these rules, but for all practical purposes the French labor movement grew out of this prudent text.

The decisions then regarded as most important affected education and the Church. A century later, they are often difficult to understand without realizing that the still-powerful Church was almost unanimously opposed to the republican regime. The first liberal Catholics were almost always condemned by the hierarchy as late as 1910. The Church had enjoyed near-total control of education since 1850, and thus had systematically created opponents of the government. In order to defend themselves, the republicans had to go on the offensive.

Completely free public education and compulsory attendance for children from six to thirteen years of age did not really incite public passions. But other policies did: the education of girls, the requirement that each *département* should maintain two teachers' colleges, one for boys and the other for girls; the regulation of the religious teaching orders; and above all the secularization of instruction enacted during the tempests of 1882 and 1886. For Jules Ferry, as for the Protestants and Freemasons who surrounded him, secularization meant both absolute respect for freedom of conscience and the exclusion of any religious teaching or influence in the public schools. Thursdays were in principle reserved for religious exercises—but not in the school buildings. Laws regulating the teaching orders raised violent emotions that continued even as late as 1925 to 1930 in the west of France.

These measures, in removing the education of boys and particularly girls from Church control, were intended to give the Republic firm popular support among loyal voters of the future. Furthermore, future teachers were required to follow a quasi-military course of simple, solid, practical, and patriotic instruction. Almost every commune received an intellectual "mentor" of practical and patriotic bent, often a successful counterweight to the parish priest. This institution of the village teacher was so effective that in the summer of 1940, when the Third Republic was barely dead, its Vichy successors immediately struck it down.

THE CRISES OF
THE THIRD REPUBLIC: 1886–1906

The Third Republic was dreary in its choice of presidents and ministers. Gambetta died prematurely in 1882, Ferry was dismissed too soon in 1885, and Clemenceau shone at first only by his witty sayings. The new Republic fell prey to mediocre and almost ritual scandals—the sale of honors, bribery, conflicts of interest, the mixing of business and politics. These scandals were amply exploited by royalists and conservatives, and sometimes by the early socialists as well. Beginning in 1886, General Georges-Ernest Boulanger cut an ambitious and dashing figure as a demagogue who played on the popular desire for revenge against the Germans. For a moment he was the darling of various opponents of the government. But he was a pitiful politician. After having failed to seize power on the night of a triumphal election when he was taken to the Elysée Palace by an excited, antiparliamentary, and chauvinistic crowd, he melted away, fled to Belgium, and committed suicide on his mistress's grave. Boulanger deserved the epitaph that Clemenceau gave him: "Here lies General Boulanger who died as he had lived, as a subaltern." Another version, hardly less cruel, referred to him as a "shop girl."

Except at Paris, public opinion was not highly politicized and not much interested in Pope Leo XIII's attempt at reconciliation with the Republic after 1890. While several "social" Catholics, the nucleus of the Christian Democrats of the future, were elected here and there, neither the hierarchy nor the old aristocracy nor the majority of peasants followed their lead. After the law of 1884 allowing unions, there were "hard" strikes with violent repression and a bloody May Day celebration at Fourmies in 1890. Yet these events were less disturbing than the wave of anarchist attacks that swept through Europe: in France the anarchists went on the rampage around 1892. A bomb was thrown in the Chamber of Deputies in December 1893; President Sadi Carnot, who refused to grant a reprieve to the perpetrator, was assassinated in 1894. In response, the assembly outlawed the advocacy of anarchism and suspended trial by jury, but the repressive laws were not strictly enforced.

The Dreyfus case was a different story, however. It has been said that families were divided by it, though one wonders how many. The essential points of the case are straightforward: in 1894, Captain Alfred Dreyfus, a conscientious and efficient Jewish army officer, was accused of espionage for Germany; he was convicted and sentenced to life imprisonment on Devil's Island. He was completely innocent, and the guilty party was even known to the judges, who nevertheless condemned Dreyfus on the basis of secret forged documents. They refused to admit that they had made a mistake because, they insisted, a military tribunal could not be fooled, and the army was always right. Only after a terrifying public campaign launched by Emile Zola's famous pamphlet *J'Accuse* was there a retrial and rehabilitation of Dreyfus, followed in 1906 by the official declaration of his innocence and restoration of his military rank.

The circumstances of this case were fraught with significance in the passionate atmosphere at the end of the nineteenth century. The accusers, all of whom were anti-republicans, enlisted in an exaggerated nationalist campaign led by Paul Déroulède, the ringing poet of revenge. They asserted that the French army was above all suspicion. Anti-Semitism, another tendency of this group, came to France from afar and still has not disappeared: its champion was the journalist Edouard-Adolphe Drumont, author of *La France Juive* (*Jewish France*). Even his violent tone was exceeded by the polemicist Léon Daudet, a wholehearted nationalist and royalist. At times there were xenophobic rages—attacks on the Italians at Marseille, outbursts against the "foreign invasion." *La Croix* and *Le Pelerin,* the powerful Catholic newspapers of the Assumptionist fathers, sanctimoniously came out in force, forgetting the virtue of charity. In general, the left—fighting in the cause of truth—was opposed by the right—fighting, apparently, in the cause of the army. But did the Dreyfus case really have such great effects on the nation as a whole? From our point of view, it appears more symbolic and premonitory.

The religious and antireligious struggles that followed certainly had as much effect on the "deeper France." These conflicts are almost incomprehensible to foreigners, and they have even become so for most French people today. Most religious leaders and Catholic congregations had voiced their opinions during the anti-Dreyfus agitation, when new elections brought to power more and more radicals, most of them anticlericals and Freemasons. Freemasonry, which had been a religious movement in the eighteenth century, had become atheistic by 1877. From 1899 to 1902, René Waldeck-Rousseau, a solid and temperate republican, served for three years as prime minister; he pursued a policy of "republican defense." Waldeck-Rousseau forbade all political activity in the army and brought to trial several nationalist agitators. In 1901, he enacted a liberal law on associations that is still in force, but a clause specified that religious congregations could be established only if authorized by a specific law. If they did not obtain such authorization, they were forbidden to teach. Waldeck-Rousseau simply wanted to curb those he called "the plotting monks and the business monks." At the time, he estimated the value of real estate owned by the congregations at one billion francs, and hinted that these assets might be seized by the state. Persecution was certainly not his intention.

Yet the elections of 1902 resulted in an even more leftist Chamber of Deputies. The new prime minister, Émile Combes, was a provincial medical doctor as well as a former seminarian and doctor of theology who had converted to ferocious anticlericalism. He applied the law of 1901 harshly: requests for authorization were refused, and congregational schools were closed. In 1904, he outlawed teaching by any member of a religious order; even those officially authorized were to be gradually phased out of teaching as secular replacements became available. These measures were not finally repealed until

1940 and 1942, under the Vichy regime. At the same time Combes proposed this legislation, his government was having incessant conflicts over the choice of bishops with the new pope, Pius X, a sort of reincarnated Pius IX. Finally, Combes broke off relations with the Holy See and proposed the complete separation of Church and state. Thus the Concordat of 1802 was broken. The new statute of separation was approved in late 1905, at the persuasive urging of Aristide Briand, who was then a socialist. This new statute began with two firm declarations: "1. The Republic guarantees the freedom of conscience. . . . 2. The Republic neither recognizes, nor pays salaries to, nor subsidizes any religion whatsoever." In fact, aged priests received a pension equal to three-quarters of their salary, and younger ones obtained a proportional amount. But the law provided that all religious buildings again became the property of the state, which would gladly lease or lend them for "religious exercises" after taking inventory. These inventories nearly caused a popular explosion. The legal formalities were represented as sacrilege in the cities of Paris and Lyon and the ultra-Catholic north and west: crowds of the faithful rioted, and armed force had to be used against them. Shots were even fired. From Rome, Pius X poured oil on the flames by forbidding the organization of "cultural associations" to take charge of the religious monuments. By 1907, the successive French governments had found a *modus vivendi* with the Church as their attention was occupied by other social conflicts and international crises. Religious controversies were revived somewhat after the First World War, then quieted down. We may wonder whether the separation really proved so inconvenient for the Church.

THE RISE OF WORKERS' MOVEMENTS AND SOCIALISM

On the important subject of workers' movements and socialism the events of the 1880s shed little light. The older labor movement regarded socialism with suspicion, and the two forces developed independently. The first unions, whether vertical (in particular trades or crafts) or horizontal (local unions and labor exchanges) had little connection to political parties, which were themselves divided. The influence of Marx on French socialism came rather late, since there were no French translations of his works before 1883 and few readers before 1890–95. Besides, there was never a single socialist movement, despite the founding of the French section of the Workers' International in 1905; there were always four or five socialist groups, not counting anarchists of various tendencies and pure revolutionaries. Of course, these were weak minorities, and there was no French Communist party at all before 1920.

Without going back as far as the corporations of the ancien régime, or to the omnipresent apprenticeship system, we can clearly see that the majority of workers, especially the most specialized craftsmen, always had mutual aid societies with meeting places and information about wages, jobs, employers, and suppliers. These semiclandestine groups were occasionally tolerated. Napoleon III, in granting the right to strike, had started them on the road to legality. But their role in the Paris Commune and the repression that followed forced them into a long silence. The effect of the law of 1884 was to recognize the existing associations, which were not really so discreet because they had held four national congresses from 1876 to 1880, the first at Paris, the last at Marseille. Henceforth, in the face of hostility from employers and toleration from the government, workers' associations developed in great profusion. Powerful national trade unions came of age. The hat makers were the first to organize, in 1879; they were followed by printers in 1881, miners in 1883, and railway workers, the most militant group, in 1890. Others preferred to organize locally, a practical and congenial plan, to set up their own labor exchanges, centers for information, employment, documentation, meetings, and discussion. The first labor exchange was founded at Paris in 1887; five years later, during a congress at Saint-Étienne, fifteen exchanges joined a federation under the enthusiastic leadership of Fernand Pelloutier of Nantes. Yet they were anxious to preserve their local autonomy despite the ambitions of neighbors and comrades. Consequently this movement folded in 1902, and the General Labor Union (CGT), founded at Limoges in 1895, absorbed it into a hierarchical and disciplined structure, nonetheless oriented by its general secretary Victor Griffuelhes in opposition to political socialism and Marxism. The Charter of Amiens (1906) represented the triumph of the old workers' and intellectuals' tradition of anarcho-syndicalism, which sought to destroy the state by direct action—the revolutionary general strike. They hoped to operate on an international basis, and sometimes imagined that they could prevent war and bring about the "great night" of social revolution and popular seizure of power. No doubt these were daydreams, but they were shared by tens of thousands of militants, perhaps 1 percent of the workers, and they drew others to the cause, as a series of harsh strikes showed. The list of disorders was long: Anzin in 1884; Fourmies in 1889 and 1891, where nine people died and sixty were wounded; Courrières in 1906 after the mine disaster that killed 1,100 men; Languedoc in 1907, where disturbances among the vineyard workers were supported by soldiers of the seventeenth regiment. In 1907, there were also strikes by electricians in Paris, miners, postmen, and teachers, resulting in three hundred dismissals, twenty deaths, and six hundred wounded by gunfire. The post office was struck again in 1909, and the railways in 1910. In all cases the government responded harshly: Clemenceau prided himself on the title "Chief Cop of France," while Briand astutely kept busy organizing the railway workers, knowing that every rebellion could lead to a court-martial. The atmosphere of the Belle Époque was marked by diverse or even contradictory moods.

What did these workers want? Basically, higher wages— and gradually they received them—but also a shorter working day and a bit more consideration. Without accepting the picture drawn by Victor Hugo in *Les Misérables* of a working world that had improved little over forty years, we should recall the terms of the "social" laws belatedly voted by the Third Republic.

In 1892, the employment of school-age children was forbidden, though it continued clandestinely and they were paid a mere 10 to 25 percent of adult wages. At the same time the working day was limited to ten hours, but only for miners and women. In 1900, a law required the progressive reduction in the working week to sixty hours. Not until 1906 was a weekly day of rest mandatory: many workshops continued their operations on Sunday morning, until just before the last low mass, in order to clean their shops, matériel, and machines. The same year the CGT dared to demand working days of three eight-hour shifts, and some people spoke of an "English week," with time off on Saturday afternoon. Two laws in 1898 recognized and promised to help mutual aid societies, and tried to place the burden of industrial accidents on employers. The following year saw the establishment of labor inspectors, who had some difficulty doing their work. In 1910, after four years of discussion, the government passed a modest proposal for workers' and peasants' pensions: employers, employees, and the state would share the burden. This proposal had only modest success, as less than one-quarter of the workers agreed to contribute. The idea of pensions found greater support among miners and railway workers, thanks to the technique of withholding from wages, which had been applied to civil servants since 1853. As Jules Guesde said, these reforms were only "crumbs." But they give an idea of the world of the workers before 1914, a world that may seem incredible to our contemporaries. The first great social legislation actually dates from the Popular Front of 1936.

During this earlier time, the Labor Congress in Marseille (1908) declared that "workers have no *patrie*" and that war would bring an "attack on the working class." While such declarations were not heeded, they were nonetheless disturbing to the government and the general staff, which cooperated with the police in preparations to arrest syndicalists, anarchists, and pacifists in case of mobilization. In the enthusiasm for "holy union" in 1914, these measures proved largely unnecessary.

At the same period, there was little to fear from the socialists, who were slowly being absorbed by the political system. As heirs of general intellectual movements with utopian or high philosophical approaches characteristic of the nineteenth century, the socialists after the Paris Commune were seldom divided into fewer than five "parties," or "tendencies." These were rarely Marxist. More often they were Proudhonists, cooperatists, anarchists, revolutionaries, or even reformists. From time to time they would argue among themselves, then bury their differences, as they did in the time of the First International (1864–1876), which was torn apart by quarrels between Marx and Bakunin. By the Second International of 1889, the divided socialists had succeeded in electing about twenty deputies from the old radical strongholds of the north, the center, Paris and Provence. The number rose to 50 in 1893, and more than 100 in 1914. After having condemned Alexandre Millerand as a defector for joining the ministry in 1899, the majority of socialists led by Jules Guesde then supported the "Leftist Bloc" after 1902, and united the leading "families" in 1905. They formed the French Section of the Workers' International (SFIO) or United Socialist Party. Soon the former factional "heads" of the party—Millerand, Briand, Viviani and Guesde—left to accept ministerial portfolios. The pliant Léon Jouhaux came to lead the CGT, and proclaimed the "holy union" when war was declared. As for Jean Jaurès, the great orator of the group, he wanted to reconcile humanism and Marxism, patriotism and pacifism; but in 1914 he did not have the time to choose, because an extreme-right fanatic assassinated him.

From 1914 onward, for more than four years, union members and nonunion workers, socialists and nonsocialists met on the field of battle, in the depths of the trenches or under a simple wooden cross. Forty-three years after the defeat and territorial amputation, the warmly desired opportunity for revenge had arrived. French enthusiasm was great, but certainly less universal than generally claimed.

STEPS TO REVENGE

The Treaty of Frankfurt had hardly been signed when Thiers and the Assembly set about the restoration of finances and the economy, which was accomplished in two years. Already in 1872, over Bismarck's protests, they had established compulsory military service of five years, with a view toward raising the French army to the strength of the German forces. For more than forty years, the patriotic flame was kept burning in newspapers, pictures, posters, poetry, music, and speeches. Gymnastics and pre-military training formed part of the curriculum in primary schools. Future teachers, disciplined by military instructors during their three years at the Ecoles Normales, were called upon to form the reserves of the future army. When they were mobilized, their discipline and courage earned them a death rate of 22 percent, a bitter professional record.

Yet all this training struck an insurmountable obstacle: in 1914 as in 1871, the population of France stood at less than 40 million, while that of Germany exceeded 60 and then 65 million. Furthermore, the German population was younger: 44 percent were under twenty, as opposed to only 34 percent of the French. The French hoped to compensate for their numerical inferiority by prolonging the period of active military service and using young reservists, by finding allies, and by using colonial troops from Algeria and Senegal. As long as Bismarck dominated Europe, until 1890, the French had to suffer frontier incidents and diplomatic isolation. Afterward, they were able to purchase the Russian Alliance of 1894 and achieve the *entente cordiale* with Britain in 1904 through colonial exchanges. The British had understood that the maritime, economic, and commercial power of Germany had become intolerable. France saw Russia as a horde of manpower and a second front, while Britain had a navy that could completely dominate the seas. Successive military laws tried to reinforce the total of available men by requiring 10 years of active service, some of which were spent in garrison duty; then came 15 years in the territorial reserve, making a total of 25 annual cohorts that could be mobilized more-or-less quickly on the eve of war. At the same time, the government reduced the number of draft exemptions. Except for very rare cases such as fatherless orphans and eldest sons in families with more than seven children, the overly numerous dispensations or reductions in service that still existed in 1872 were abolished. The greatest resistance came from those who wanted to exempt priests and seminarians: it took the government eight years, from 1881 to 1889, to overcome the opposition of this group. The unacceptable "replacement" of the rich by hired poor substitutes had been suppressed much earlier.

When the men had thus been found, the administration had to deal with them. Great organizational efforts were required, and resulted in mixed successes. French national wealth remained prodigious: a perfectly stable currency, banknotes convertible into gold, a franc as unquestionably accepted as the pound sterling in international payments. The national fortune probably grew from about 120 billion francs before 1870 to around 300 billion in 1913, but landed wealth then represented about 40 to 50 percent of the total, as compared with 75 percent under the Second Empire. This evolution was normal in a period of industrialization. As for national income, it appears to have doubled, and the contribution of industry and banking increased markedly.

What the French did with their money may appear curious to us. An important, unknown quantity went into savings. Some went into the staid accounts of savings banks: the local banks, with 8.5 million accounts, held 4 billion francs in deposits; while the national savings bank had less than 2 billion francs spread over 6 million accounts. These figures are the stuff dreams were made of: they demonstrate how far "down" comfort had spread through society. At a higher level, the public had long subscribed for French stocks and bonds, more than one billion francs per year from 1892 to 1900; but the domestic rate of interest did not exceed 4 percent. Twice as much was paid abroad, and a large mass of French capital took that route. Well over one billion francs annually went into the famous Russian loans, which would later disappoint more than 1.5 million investors. French capital was used to build railways almost everywhere—in Spain, Austria-Hungary, Syria, and even China. The great merchant banks regularly made profits of 40 percent or more and were represented in Europe, Asia, Africa, and Latin America. In 1872, the value of foreign obligations held in France was 12 billion francs, one-quarter of the total. In 1913 the proportion had risen to 41 percent, and the amount to 50 billion francs; of this total, 28 billion francs were in other European countries, and 14 billion in Russia, where three-quarters were destined to be lost. In this role as banker to the world, the French were surpassed only by the British, who lent almost twice as much, but with this noteworthy difference: half of British foreign investment went to the British Empire, while in France only 5 percent went to the French colonies.

With the exception of some defined commercial interests, French political and economic circles as well as public opinion apparently lacked confidence in the overall worth of the colonies that had been collected by the Third Republic. The government was continuing the work of earlier regimes, but the country was not really interested in its empire until the moment when it was dismembered. We should also note that many of these distant conquests had resulted from chance or personal initiatives: Faidherbe went into Sénégal at the urging of several merchants; Captain Rigault de Genouilly's ship sank in the China Seas; and then two other Frenchmen penetrated the countryside as far as Cambodia. In Tonkin, Dupuis, a merchant, drew attention to the Red River; a minor French consul at Aden bought the Bay of Tadjoura from the Somali tribes, and Djibouti was built there.

The true colonial idea—Algeria excepted—had come from Jules Ferry between 1880 and 1885. This man of integrity, rough and intelligent, wanted to establish France overseas for many reasons: patriotic, commercial, maritime, political, even religious and moral. He was misunderstood and fell from power because of his nonetheless successful intervention in Tonkin. With his few friends, he always faced a substantial anticolonialist party that included Clemenceau. In addition to denouncing the obvious excesses of colonization such as expropriation of the natives' property and forced labor, they thought that money and troops were being senselessly wasted in faraway ventures at a time when all the attention and power of the *patrie* should have been turned toward revenge and the recapture of Alsace-Lorraine.

Responsibility for the colonies as they passed through the stages of semi-annexation, federation, and protectorate was long shared by three ministries. Their administration cost much more than they earned for metropolitan France. Also, disputes over colonies nearly led to wars with Italy in Tunisia in 1881; with Germany in Morocco and the Congo in 1905 and 1911; and above all with Britain, notably in the Fashoda incident of 1898. Except for Algeria, the French colonies were not much visited by the home-loving French except for a few adventurers, missionaries, and members of the elite. Their return in merchandise and above all in soldiers, however, was considerable during the Great War. Afterward, metropolitan France belatedly began to take a more serious role in the distant territories that had been acquired by the tenacity, patriotism, or interest of a handful of soldiers, sailors, merchants, and even idealists.

Economic Preparation for War

Shortly after the war of 1870–71, Minister Charles-Louis Freycinet presented a plan to develop French transportation. Roads and railways were extended and improved; new canals were dug and placed in service; and most of the great ports were modernized and enlarged. But shipping did not make commensurate progress: in 1900, half of the French merchant fleet was still under sail, and yet the total tonnage was ranked fourth in the world. By 1913, France had fallen to sixth place, behind Norway and Japan. French-flag vessels accounted for only one-quarter of the port traffic. Marseille was the greatest French port by far, thanks to the Suez Canal and the colonies. At the same time, an important naval fleet was under construction, but it was far from attaining the perfection of the German fleet or the tonnage of the British, whose protection would prove precious during World War I. Yet the abundant means of communication facilitated the deployment of troops, merchandise, and munitions.

Agriculture, finally embarked on the path of modernization, began to improve the quality of seed and the breeding of livestock. Having increased the use of fertilizer six times over, farms raised their yields as well. French agriculture did suffer crises caused by competition from America, Argentina, and the colonies, but especially significant was an attack of phylloxera—plant-lice—that destroyed the vineyards. The government of Jules Méline was compelled to return to protectionism in 1892. Yet agriculture did feed the country well, and the standard of living rose: the French people henceforth consumed white bread, more sugar, and more meat, and no doubt too much wine. It is generally said that during World War I the French peasants practically fed the soldiers, but we must not forget that many peasants were also soldiers, and that manpower was lacking in the fields. The use of whatever workers happened to be available—women, old men, children, and prisoners—imports, and rationing for the poor solved this problem.

The French had to make great efforts in the industrial sector, especially in iron and steel, which furnished arms and matériel; they knew the Germans held an advantage over them. The loss of Lorraine constituted a grave handicap, which French industry tried to overcome by introducing new processes and techniques. French production of coal had tripled in forty years, but was still insufficient; more had to be imported. Germany was producing five times as much coal as France, and the United States fourteen times as much. Production of iron ore, cast iron, and steel nearly quadrupled; but French steel production was still less than one-third of the German figure and one-sixth of the American. Here also major imports were required.

New industries did appear: the automobile industry took off with the Renault brothers in 1899, and the Michelin rubber company was founded in 1889. The old chemical industry of Saint-Gobain, which started under Colbert, was joined by the new Rhône factories, while the pharmaceutical business of Poulenc (1816) and the dye and fertilizer concern, Kuhlmann (1825), were extended and modernized.

All of these ventures did not suffice to carry France to the top rung of the world industrial ladder. France was regularly surpassed by the superior vigor, resources and organization of Germany as well as by the early advantage and solidity of Britain. Already the United States was learning to dominate the world. And a rejuvenated Japan, which had defeated the old tsarist Russian Empire in 1905, had begun to assert itself.

To sum up, overall French economic conditions were generally favorable on the eve of the war, and Anglo-Saxon help strengthened them.

The Decision to Go to War

Since 1905, two systems of alliances had existed in Europe. The incidents between France and Germany multiplied and took on an aggravated tone, primarily in Morocco. To keep the peace, Prime Minister Joseph Caillaux had to cede to Wilhelm II a bit of the Congo in 1911. In the Ottoman Empire and the states that had broken from it (Serbia, Greece, Rumania, Bulgaria), Russia, and Austria-Hungary were constantly at loggerheads. Great Britain, which had settled its accounts with France, was greatly concerned by the growing power of the German navy and by the involvement of German engineers and merchants in the Turkish Empire and in Asia. In fact, since the turn of the century, after having overcome a depression, all industries and business groups were enjoying full expansion. They learned how to become even richer by making weapons to destroy regions that they would have the advantage of reconstructing afterward. Almost everywhere revolutionaries, pacifists, and socialists tried to prevent or deflect the conflagration that everyone could feel approaching.

When the Archduke Franz Ferdinand, heir to the throne of Austria, was assassinated at Sarajevo in June 1914, the Serbian government was held responsible. The diplomatic machinery forced the first measures toward mobilization almost everywhere in Europe. In France, these measures were published on August 1; the alarm-bell was sounded in the heat of the harvest season. On the August 3, war broke out. The general staffs had learnedly predicted that the war would be short, but it lasted fifty-two months. It was the first time since the Black Death of the fourteenth century that so many millions of people had been called to die.

Chapter Eighteen

FROM THE GREAT WAR TO THE NEAR PRESENT (1914–1987)*

* I would like to thank Marthe Sayn for her assistance in the preparation of this chapter.—P.G.

FRANCE AND THE
FIRST WORLD WAR

In the summer of 1914 a provincial assassination at Sarajevo invoked the double system of alliances and unleashed the "Great War." The principal antagonists were the Central Powers led by Austria-Hungary and Germany on the one hand, and the Triple Entente of France, Britain, and Russia on the other. No doubt the war was earnestly desired by Kaiser Wilhelm II, who sought a crown of glory for himself and his country, the Imperial German Reich. Yet the French people in general did not spurn the war either; they were determined to take revenge for their defeat in 1870–71, and above all to recover Alsace-Lorraine.

Victory was by no means a foregone conclusion. While France in 1914 was a very rich country with great wealth invested abroad (where almost everything would be lost, particularly in Tsarist Russia), its solid agriculture remained traditional, and its industrial power was hardly one-third that of Germany. The French population of 39 million was older and considerably smaller than the 65 million Germans; thus an enormous French military effort was required to compete effectively. Finally, the Triple Entente suffered from at least three significant weaknesses: first, the strength of the Tsarist Russian army was overestimated; second, Britain lacked compulsory military service and its army was less powerful than had been thought, although the Royal Navy was strong; and third, distances made communication among France, Russia, and Britain difficult.

These considerations did not prevent the French politicians, including the Socialists, from proclaiming a "Holy Union" of the nation for war. Soldiers, fired up with the hope of reaching Berlin in less than three months, often went to the front cheerfully with "flowers in the barrels of their rifles." The singing, however, quickly stopped.

France mobilized about one hundred divisions for the expected summer campaign. These troops were supplied with Lebel rifles and 75-mm cannons and were backed by a strong fleet powerfully supported by the British Royal Navy. But heavy artillery was lacking, and the French General Staff had made major blunders in planning.

Generalissimo Joseph Joffre, who had vainly and symbolically launched the French attack on the border of Alsace-Lorraine, was surprised at the German attack through Belgium. This violation of Belgian neutrality brought the previously hesitant British into the war, but the Allies soon faced difficulties in the north as the powerful German forces rolled in like a tidal wave. In a few days the Germans had invaded ten *départements,* about 12 percent of the territory of France. The Germans approached Paris, then attempted a flanking movement to the east. Their great military surge was stopped only by the bloody and courageous Allied victory at the Battle of the Marne (September 6–13, 1914), where the victors brought reinforcements from the Parisian garrison in taxis from the capital. Further north, several British and Belgian divisions also put up stiff resistance against the Germans. There was a "race to the sea" as each side tried to outflank the other, and the French were anxious to secure their supply lines to Britain. But after two months of movement, the Western Front remained stable for three years. Line after line of trenches stretched from the Swiss border to the last bit of free Belgium, defended by King Albert, on the North Sea coast.

For three years, 1915–17, the opposing armies were bogged down. They faced each other across a strip of no-man's-land, buried in their infected trenches amidst the mud, rats, and rotting corpses. From time to time, a commanding officer seeking glory would try for a breakthrough which always proved useless and costly—first tens of thousands, then hundreds of thousands of men were slaughtered. Generals Joffre and Nivelle discovered as much from 1915 to 1917 in Artois, in Champagne, on the Somme, and above all at Verdun, where more than 500,000 men on both sides fell. This war of entrenched positions brought about changes in weapons and tactics. The French army finally adopted the helmet and the blue uniform instead of bright red trousers—machine guns, grenades, and poison gas were also introduced. The first tanks were developed, but they were merely auxiliaries to infantry, the so-called "queens of battle." Military aircraft were first used for reconnaissance and photography, then for minor bombing, though without any great effects. The morale of the combatants was generally high until 1916, but in 1917 mutinies broke out everywhere. These rebellions were due to fatigue, homesickness, and the apparent senselessness of battle. After some harsh sanctions, General Philippe Pétain, the victor at Verdun, intelligently restored discipline and confidence. Pétain won genuine popularity among the soldiers as a humane leader.

Another innovation occurred in 1915, when, in order to "fill the gaps" and to replace entire regiments that had been eliminated, colonial troops were brought to France. They included Algerian troopers, Senegalese sharpshooters, Madagascarans, and Vietnamese. Later the survivors of these units remembered what had been asked of them, and what they had been promised. On the other hand, French forces were fighting outside France in the Dardenelles in order to break the blockade of the Bosphorus Straits which were closed when Turkey entered the war on the side of the Central Powers. At Salonica the French also tried in vain to save the small Serbian army, crushed by the combined forces of Austria-Hungary, Bulgaria, and Turkey.

The balance of powers shifted on another front when Italy, formerly an ally of the Central Powers, received secret promises of territorial compensation and joined the war on the Entente side in 1915. But no substantial change occurred until after the United States entered the war in April 1917, following the torpedoing of several of their vessels by the formidable German submarine fleet—which continued to sink 350,000 tons of shipping per month. From the end of 1917, after the Soviet Revolution in November and the speedy capitulation of the much weakened Russian army, the French and British General Staffs could only hope for salvation in the arrival of matériel, tanks, and troops from America.

The collapse of the Russian front and the American entry into the war forced the German General Staff to try moving again on the Western Front. Concentrating their forces, the Germans attacked four times in the spring of 1918, hoping to pre-empt the American intervention: in June they were only 70 kilometers from Paris. But American troops were arriving at a rate of 200,000 men per month. They contributed greatly to the efforts of the Allied Staff, finally unified under the command of Marshal Ferdinand Foch. Soon the exhausted Germans were pushed out of France and Belgium.

When the disgraced Kaiser Wilhelm II abdicated and fled in early November 1918, a democratic revolution with momentary socialist tendencies brought a new government to power in Germany. This government had the good sense to ask for an armistice on November 11, 1918, before their defeated army was completely destroyed and German territory invaded. Thus, on the Western Front, only northeastern France and Belgium suffered heavy damage from the war, devastation further aggravated by the German troops during their retreat.

After many quarrels among the Allies, the Treaty of Versailles was signed in June 1919. The treaty confirmed the return of Alsace-Lorraine to France, required the near-total disarmament and partial demilitarization of Germany, and insisted on German acceptance of war guilt. The Germans had to pay an unspecified indemnity in the guise of reparations, which promised to be heavy indeed. The majority of the German people saw this treaty as a "dictated peace" and never accepted it. The Americans also stood aside from the European settlement and from the League of Nations, brainchild of President Woodrow Wilson, whose international outlook was at odds with the born-again isolationism of his fellow citizens. Of course Wilson should be held partially responsible as well for refusing to make the necessary political compromises to gain ratification of the treaty by the United States Senate.

While millions of Frenchmen were fighting at the front, life continued behind the lines. Political parties and labor unions had joined the "Holy Union," and the government even included three widely respected Socialists—Jules Guesde, Marcel Sembat, and Albert Thomas. They were supported by the leader of the largest union, CGT, Léon Jouhaux, who had a long and skillful career.

When the war began in 1914, the French government, worried at the speed of the German advance, was evacuated to Bordeaux. For practical purposes all power was held by Marshal Joffre as chief of the General Staff. Joffre promised to be what the French called a "good republican"—neither monarchist, nor pro-clerical, nor anti-Semite. At the beginning of 1915, the parliament returned to Paris and tried to govern the country—and in particular the army. Opposition to Joffre caused the fall of two prime ministers, René Viviani and Aristide Briand, both former Socialists who had become moderates. By 1917 the excessively numerous and quarrelsome French political parties had brought back the traditional ministerial instability. Army mutinies, only partly inspired by Russian propaganda, led members of parliament to seek a negotiated peace in four or five unsuccessful initiatives; they also increased the instability of the regime. Finally, Georges Clemenceau was called to power in November 1917. Clemenceau, aged seventy-six, was an intelligent, energetic authoritarian. He imposed the selection of Generals Foch and Pétain, and gave confidence to the soldiers he visited at the front, thus acquiring great pop-

ularity. When the peace came, Clemenceau showed his negotiating skill in discussions with other Allied leaders—Woodrow
Wilson, David Lloyd-George, and Vittorio Orlando. As a realist,
Clemenceau did not believe in Wilson's League of Nations; as
a French politician, he had to consider the domestic consequences of peace.

After fifty-two months of war, the French economy and
society had changed even more than the political world. In the
fields, workshops, and factories, millions of women replaced
men who had left for the fighting. Women were particularly
numerous in the new munitions and equipment industries
required by the war. Accustomed to receiving wages, women
became independent—or nearly so. Their economic freedom
brought emancipation in their personal appearance, hair styles,
and dress. This liberty surprised and sometimes shocked the
men when they were demobilized.

The length and cost of the war had other, often grave
consequences. Agricultural production fell by more than 15
percent as horses, hay, and grain were requisitioned, and the
amount of arable land was reduced by the fighting. To supply
food and munitions to the armies, efficient new businessmen
arose and quickly made fortunes, often considered scandalous. At the end of the war the unpopularity of the *embusqués,*
those who had escaped mobilization and found safe positions,
was exceeded by that of the *nouveaux riches* and war profiteers. But no sanctions were taken against them because they
had been useful and knew how to find well-placed political
supporters.

The French state was obliged to control all economic activity related to the war. For the first time since Napoleon,
public initiative replaced private enterprise in ordering requisitions, carefully controlling imports, and rationing food for
civilians. Bread and sugar ration-cards made their appearance.

Finally, the war cost a great deal, even more in France than
elsewhere. Taxes were progressively and heavily increased.
The state floated several loans and by skillful propaganda managed to persuade the most patriotic or most naive citizens to
exchange their gold for paper. These issues of government

paper were indeed manifold. Before 1914 France had shared with England the role of banker to the world. After the war its debt had risen enormously—increasing ten times over. This debt was particularly owed to the United States, which had won the war for the Allies and assured its preponderance in world affairs for more than half a century.

We should give special attention to the fall of the franc, a currency whose value in gold had remained stable since 1726 (except during the revolutionary episode). When controls were removed in 1919, it soon became apparent that the franc had lost more than 80 percent of its prewar purchasing power.

The loss of human capital was tragic—one and a half million dead, more than three million wounded, disabled, and gas victims, all of whom were handicapped. There was also a considerable demographic deficit during the wartime years of reduced births and this created smaller generations that had rippling effects for the rest of the century. Henceforth the French population appeared locked in stagnation and decline. France of 1919 was a far cry from the kingdom of Louis XIV and Louis XV, which had shared with England dominance in Europe. Without realizing it, victorious France was destined for a secondary role in world affairs.

FRANCE BETWEEN
THE WARS (1919–1939)

With the recovery of Alsace-Lorraine and the lengthy celebration of victory, France still had to take stock of its dead and its ruins. Twenty percent of the working population had been lost; villages and entire cities were ruined; rich farms, mines, and factories were destroyed or heavily damaged. In the postwar period the nation faced difficult social problems, an uncertain demographic and economic future, unreliable ex-allies, and the old political instability so familiar from before 1914. The euphoria of victory lasted less than a year.

Let us enumerate the problems and attempt to understand

441

them. First of all, the political situation: the constitution of 1875 and its progressive interpretations had left very weak power in the hands of the president of the republic, whose active role was limited to ceremonial representations and inaugurations. While the president did designate the prime minister (or *président du conseil*), the political parties actually decided whether to accept him and whether to keep him in office. The Senate, composed of men over forty chosen by a complicated system of indirect suffrage, was dominated by rural groups. The Chamber of Deputies, elected by universal male suffrage, normally had the upper hand. In general, the legislative branch of government was dominant, and for all practical purposes power was in the hands of political parties, or rather, in the "committees"—executive groups of co-opted worthies.

Changeable and complicated when seen from the outside, the spectrum of French political parties nonetheless remained relatively simple. There was always an old "Right," sitting on the right of the presiding officer in the assembly hall. This group was nationalist, conservative, ultra-Catholic (as the Church was still hostile to the Republic), often royalist, still anti-Semitic after the Dreyfus Affair, and sometimes racist. The Right was wealthy and powerfully represented in the press. After 1930–35, it took on a partly pro-Fascist or pro-Hitler character out of fear of communism. There was also always a "Left," but at its 1920 congress in Tours the old Socialist party, long torn by various tendencies, broke into two distinct factions. One group, faithful to the Soviet Union and the Comintern, became the Communist party, whose allegiance to Moscow has almost always been total. Their principal adversary, despite appearances to the contrary, has been the Socialist party from which they came. Marxism went into a decline among the Socialists, who remained strongly democratic and supported major social reforms and nationalization. They were generally pacifists and were strongly represented in the working class, and among intellectuals and government employees, particularly teachers. While the Communists also had strength among the workers, they were for many years an insignificant political force. By contrast the Socialists did participate briefly in some governments before 1914 and achieved genuine power in the Popular Front government of 1936.

Between these extremes were two large groups of moderates or "centrists." They were divided more by personal quarrels and interests than by ideas. The "center-Right" was patriotic and liberal in the classical sense, moderately republican, Catholic (which then meant much), and attached to monetary stability, order, and private property—not very reformist. Among the "center-Left," the largest and most vocal group were the "Radicals" who really weren't very radical any more. They were somewhat reformist, strongly tied to the world of business, and above all openly anti-clerical—often they were Freemasons and atheists. Somewhere between these two tendencies there was a true center. Despite its vague design and the fact that its adherents were not very numerous, its oscillations caused the rise and fall of ministries. As for the more numerous Radicals, they went back and forth between the Socialists and the centrists, for they had anointed themselves as "the government party." Two of the five electoral campaigns were triumphs for the Right, supported by a good number of Radicals; three elections went to the Left. In the latter cases, the Radicals supported the Socialists, and then abandoned them as soon as they encountered the first difficulties, usually of a financial nature; then they again joined the center-Right. The proverbial instability of French governments resulted from these maneuvers, which might have been thought to be comic if they had not had such serious results. France had forty governments in twenty years—the record for brevity was held by Fernand Bouisson, whose term lasted for three days in June 1935.

The detailed political history of this regime contains nothing exciting, but all the same we should mention several important moments. 1919 saw the election of a right wing majority containing many veterans. This "National Bloc" was violently anti-German and anti-Bolshevik, as well as ultra-Catholic. It sought reconciliation with the pope, the triumphant return to France of the Catholic religious orders, and special favors for Catholic schools. But its government proved incapable of dealing with the financial problems resulting from the war and the discontent caused by inflation. Despite its intransigence toward the British and American ex-allies, as well as toward the Germans, the "National Bloc" lost power in the election of 1924.

On this occasion the majority was won by a "cartel of the Left" that included Radicals and Socialists in a simple electoral alliance, though no Socialist became a minister. The prime minister was Edouard Herriot, an intellectual, an orator, and a skillful worker. He soon faced a double-barreled financial crisis as the country's war debt was accompanied by an outflow of gold and capital organized by the wealthy and the Right. French savers were frightened by talk of a tax on capital, although only the Socialists were preaching the idea. Herriot had to retreat before this "wall of money," and the moderate Right returned to power with the support of a good number of the same Radicals as well as that of the banks. A former president of the republic, Raymond Poincaré, a man of energetic order, re-established what was called "confidence" and thus brought back the gold. He nearly managed to balance the budget before successfully accomplishing the regime's first devaluation: the franc went down by 80 percent, from Fr 25 to Fr 125 against the pound sterling. This move hurt savers but resulted in dramatic growth for French exports. Poincaré easily won the 1928 election and reassured his country during a happy period of prosperity. The budget and the economy were healthy, allowing great public works, the beginnings of social security, and a start on the Maginot Line, a chain of border fortresses. These forts were designed to foil any new German invasion, but the Line was never completed.

This brief period of relative optimism was also due to the fact that France had a mature, balanced economy not much inclined to credit. Consequently it was not struck by the Great Depression until the end of 1931. The devaluation of the pound sterling then drove French products out of markets that they had earlier taken away from the British. As French sales and production sagged, 300,000 men became unemployed, though this was fewer than in other countries. Stores were forced to close, peasants could not sell their produce and went into debt, tax revenues decreased, and discontent grew. In the 1932 election there was a new majority, roughly the same as in 1924.

And the same cycle was repeated. Herriot and the Radicals governed by themselves, capital fled, and financial difficulties were added to the murky economic situation. The devaluation of the dollar created further difficulties for French commerce. Members of parliament were apparently involved in various financial scandals. The result, besides the usual series of governments, was the appearance of paramilitary "leagues." These groups included young nationalists and royalists, known as "camelots of the king"; war veterans, misguided Catholics, masonic braggarts, "atheist Bolsheviks" [sic], and even Jews. There were also young admirers of Mussolini and, later, Hitler. As their excuse, street fighters used the financial scandals which were common enough in France but usually kept quiet. On this occasion some Radical deputies were involved. In short, the unity of the Left was broken once again, and the Radicals renewed the alliance with their friends of the center-Right. All this would have been merely ridiculous if, on February 6, 1934, tens of thousands of demonstrators from the leagues had not converged on the Place de la Concorde and attempted to march on the Chamber of Deputies with the rallying cry, "Down with the thieves!" Enraged gendarmes opened fire on the crowd, leaving fifteen dead and hundreds wounded. Prime Minister Edouard Daladier resigned immediately and was quickly succeeded by others including Pierre Laval, who had once been a Socialist but came to a bad end. At this time, in 1935, Laval governed by decree, issuing unpopular edicts in an attempt to deal with the economic crisis. Civil servants' salaries were reduced by 10 percent, for example. Laval also established a surprising Franco-Russian alliance. The first effect of this agreement was to force French Communists to sing the "Marseillaise" instead of the "Internationale"—a foretaste of their future twists and turns. But these were minor developments as the activity of the right wing pro-Fascist leagues produced powerful left wing counterdemonstrations, often led by the Communists, whom Stalin had advised to defend the republican regime. Indeed, in Paris and other cities, thousands of workers, poor people, the unemployed, civil servants, Socialists, Communists, and even Radicals marched energetically against the "factionists." Thus they paved the way for the triumph of the Popular Front in the elections of 1936.

The Popular Front still evokes vivid memories in France, although the term originated in republican Spain. The Front was the broadest political union thus far and even included the Communists, who took practically no part in the government and were attacking it sharply only a month later. Left wing Radicals were somewhat frightened to be in that company, though they owed their election to it; their support slackened shortly afterward when difficulties arose. And there was a solid mass of Socialists led by Léon Blum who was a fiery orator, a talented intellectual (probably a political weakness), and a scrupulously honest man descended from the great Jewish bourgeoisie of Alsace—which his enemies dared to hold against him. For the first time, three women became ministers in the government.

At least three obstacles stood in the way of the Popular Front. First, there was the inevitable opposition of business interests and banks, who again speculated against this legally elected leftist government. Opposition from the Communist party, however, was unforeseen. Supported by the largest labor union, the CGT, the Communists organized long strikes and peaceful occupation of factories in which more than a million men and women took part. Their goals were to obtain greater social benefits and to annoy the Socialists, which they accomplished. Furthermore, the erstwhile electoral allies were divided by their responses to the civil war launched by General Francisco Franco against the Spanish republic and its Popular Front in July 1936. Franco was openly supported by Hitler and Mussolini. The French Communists, many leftists, and simple democrats wanted to help the Spanish republicans. But out of prudence and because Britain refused any support, Léon Blum with a heavy heart stuck to a policy of nonintervention despite the actions of many other states, including the Soviet

Union, which violated this doctrine. The unfortunate result of the Spanish civil war was the birth of a new Fascist state south of the Pyrenees. The final obstacle to the Popular Front consisted of the habitual back and forth movement of the Radicals, who were somewhat reform minded but timid and ready to make all kinds of alliances. Within a year they had condemned the Blum government. Blum was succeeded by Camille Chautemps, one of the Radical *affairistes;* then came Daladier, who did not hesitate to make a deal with the Right.

In one year the Popular Front government made considerable progress in a country that had remained backward in social legislation. But these achievements were costly: a forty-hour work week, at the same salary as for the previous forty-eight hours; two weeks of paid vacation even for workers, who had never had vacations before; and the introduction of collective bargaining agreements in place of individual contracts. A "Grain Office" modeled on Franklin Roosevelt's New Deal agencies was created, and several nationalizations of aircraft factories and railways were outlined. Shortly afterward, secondary education was made free for all pupils. It had previously been closed to the poor, who could not pay tuition. Finally, in 1938 the government adopted a Family Code to encourage a higher birth rate.

We should emphasize that this government and its successors substantially increased military spending and granted the General Staff all the funds requested, even though they were inadequate. Later special support was given to the navy and the air force, which helped to restore production and employment. The minister of finances under Daladier's government, Paul Reynaud, was a man of character who had the originality to support ideas expressed since 1934 by an unknown army officer, Charles de Gaulle. This underrated theoretician of tank-warfare, armored divisions, and attack aircraft had greater influence among German readers. Other French statesmen of the time vaguely sensed a new war coming on the horizon, but they were engaged in day-to-day politics with such concerns as three additional devaluations of the franc and upheavals caused by new strikes. Besides, they thought the country was safe from danger behind the powerful fortifications of the Maginot Line, which remained unfinished.

During these interwar years whose political evolution we have just summarized, there was feebleness and stagnation, even resignation and decline in the French population, economy, and foreign policy.

The demographic evolution was straightforward. Because of World War I, France had suffered a loss of around 2.5 million people, which was not fully compensated by the return of Alsace-Lorraine and its 1.7 million inhabitants. The mobilization of more than 4 million young men caused the birth rate to fall drastically during the four years of war. The few children born during the war had even fewer children two decades later in their own normal fertile period, 1935–40. For more than a century the French birth rate had been falling regularly. By 1939, it was the lowest in Europe at under 15 per 1000 habitants, compared to nearly 19 per 1000 in 1913. While the French population did increase slightly between the two wars, the increase was primarily due to the immigration of White Russians, Poles, and Italians, and to their children. By 1938, France was reporting more deaths than births each year. Meanwhile, the German population had risen to more than double the French total. As a striking indication, Pierre Miquel noted that the French draft contingent of young soldiers in 1936 numbered 165,000, while the corresponding German contingent was 480,000. In response the worried French government enacted family subsidies, which could only produce their effects in the future.

The French economy was in general decline. Agriculture, which had suffered from shortages of labor, fertilizer, and production in the occupied areas, recovered quickly from the war. But French farming remained locked in ancient family structures and routines. In the face of overproduction and weak exports, prices fell and many small family farms were in decline. In 1939, mechanization was still rare, except on the great plains in the north.

French industry, amputated and partly destroyed by the war, reached only 61 percent of prewar output by 1921. Rapid reconstruction and some improvements brought the production index to its peak of 143 in 1929. Although the worldwide depression caused a setback after 1931, the index returned to 127 in 1938—but that was hardly a striking achievement. French production was less than half of the German figure, and only one-seventh of the American. The example of electrical usage will suffice: France consumed 19 billion kilowatt-hours annually, half as much as Britain, one-third as much as Germany, and only one-tenth as much as the vast United States. By such figures, France was the fifth largest industrial nation in the world in the 1930s, but it had been in second place a century earlier.

In diplomacy, the French did not achieve brilliant results either. At first, victorious France could believe that it had free rein, even though its equally victorious Allies did not want to see it triumph too gloriously. The demanding anti-German policy of the French caused reparations to be set at a very high sum. French forces provisionally occupied the Sarre (which politicians had dreamed of annexing), the left bank of the Rhine, and several bridgeheads. Later they took over the rich Rühr region to insure the uncertain German payments. The Allies had agreed to treat Germany cautiously, but the country was ruined by the enormous economic crisis of 1923. Under the leadership of the "National Bloc," France also practiced a vigorous anti-Bolshevik foreign policy and a corresponding anti-Communist domestic policy. France supported the "White" armies that tried in vain to break part of the old Russian Empire away from the "Reds." The French also helped Poland drive out invading Soviet forces, which had attacked in response to Polish aggression. In 1920–21, Paris sent an expedition commanded by General Maxime Weygand. France remained hostile to the Soviets for four years while more skillful powers such as Germany, interested in the immense Russian market, granted diplomatic recognition to the Soviet Union as early as 1921–22. Not until the "cartel of the Left" came to power in 1924 did France resign itself to this step. In 1934 the French accepted the Stalinist regime as a member of the League of Nations; in 1935 Laval initiated the Franco-Soviet

Pact, which was naturally directed against Nazi Germany. No doubt this latter diplomatic arrangement was a simple formality, but it made the break of 1939 even harder, when Stalin bought time by coming to an understanding with Hitler in the Nazi-Soviet Non-aggression Pact.

Faced with a Germany that was unable to pay anything except quasi-symbolic reparations after its financial ruin in 1923, the French foreign minister Aristide Briand pleaded for moderation and reconciliation. Across the bargaining table he found that the German chancellor Gustav Stresemann took the same approach. After various arrangements with the British and the Italians, including the Locarno Pact in 1925, the dispute was settled. Germany was even admitted to the League of Nations, but the United States still refused to join. However, in 1928 the United States did join sixty other countries in signing the famous Kellogg-Briand Pact, which outlawed war as an instrument of national policy. At the time this pact gave hope only to pacifists, wise men, and simpletons.

When Hitler came to power by legal means in Germany in 1933, the diplomatic landscape was irrevocably altered. It is not clear whether the French immediately understood the importance of this event, or, for that matter, whether any other nation did either. They were busy quarreling among themselves.

The Lausanne and Geneva Conferences of 1931 and 1932 had not succeeded in solving the acutely painful problems of reparations and disarmament. At the outset of the world economic crisis, it was decided to annul the reparations owed by Germany since 1919, of which less than one-quarter had been paid. As a result, the French deputies and their English counterparts decided not to repay their war debts to the United States, which led President Herriot to an honorable resignation. The American reaction was harsh: in the face of what they considered affronts to honor, the Americans locked themselves into lengthy isolationism.

From the end of 1933 onward, Hitler acted with impunity. He withdrew from the League of Nations, made an alliance with the Polish regime of Colonel Beck, and tried to annex

Austria when Chancellor Engelbert Dollfuss was assassinated by local Nazis in July 1934. Only the threat of military response by Mussolini, then hostile to Germany, made him back down for a time. After minor incidents the Germans took more serious actions, all of which were open violations of the Versailles Treaty of 1919—reestablishment of compulsory military service and creation of the Luftwaffe in March 1935; rebuilding of the German navy in accord with the Anglo-German Naval Agreement in June 1935; and above all, remilitarization of the Rhineland in 1936.

Despite this willfully insolent demonstration, a real poker-play on Hitler's part, the German army was then weak and inadequate. But the French prime minister Albert Sarrau responded only with a speech. He did not dare risk mobilizing the army because elections were imminent in May, and the prospect of support from Britain was entirely uncertain. Hitler continued unchallenged with the annexation of Austria in March 1938, followed by the seizure of part of Czechoslovakia after the Munich Conference in September 1938, and of the rest in March 1939. In the summer of 1939, Hitler turned his attention to his erstwhile ally Poland; this time he was able to act with the complicity of the Soviets.

These acts of bravado and aggression should not have surprised readers of *Mein Kampf*. However, French public opinion showed incomprehension and fear. The French were strongly influenced by tales of horror from the last war and were badly informed and politically divided. While some were favorably inclined toward dictatorships that were judged preferable to the Popular Front, others were simply indifferent. At any event, the French people were unwilling to accept a renewal of the hostilities of 1914. The clumsy mobilization of 1939 took place slowly and with disorder, though without serious incident. The country had been profoundly weakened by World War I and had not recovered its former power, much less its pugnacity and confidence. For some time military preparations had been mediocre: French rearmament did not really begin until 1935, and then it was accelerated by the Popular Front and Paul Reynaud, a statesman who became minister of finance and later premier of France. Although the French navy was quite strong and the weaponry acceptable, the French air force was in its infancy but growing rapidly. The General Staff seemed to learn only the lessons of the last war. They believed France was safe behind the Maginot Line and the reputedly impenetrable Ardennes forest. They thought aviation was useful only for secondary missions such as reconnaissance. Tanks were considered only in supporting roles to infantry, and were therefore scattered thinly from the North Sea to the Swiss frontier, even though they were numerous and of good quality. Finally, at the moment when the Nazi-Soviet Non-aggression Pact struck like a bolt of lightning, France had only one ally left: Great Britain. And the British, who had long since given way to Hitler's wishes, most recently during the humiliating Munich Conference, were finally waking up: they were preparing feverishly for the war by building airplanes.

FRANCE AND THE
SECOND WORLD WAR

German troops invaded Poland on September 1, 1939, and Britain and France declared war on Germany on September 3. For more than eight months, between 4 and 5 million French soldiers and thousands of English were massed along the Maginot Line and on the Belgian frontier. They had learned by radio how Poland had been crushed in four weeks by 3,500 German tanks and 70 divisions. There followed a long period of inaction, known as the "phony war," interrupted by rumors of a spring peace and the news that Paul Reynaud, who had reentered the govenment in March 1940, requested the British to place mines in the North Sea. Several detachments of French troops were sent to Narvik in Norway to cut off supplies of iron needed by the enemy. These minor operations led to the rapid German occupation of Denmark and Norway, where they installed a pro-Nazi regime directed by Vidkun Quisling. This local traitor would have imitators elsewhere.

In Poland as in the north, the Germans had used a simple and effective strategy of *blitzkrieg* or lightning-warfare, which consisted of concentrating maximum military power with many tanks and planes on a carefully chosen and narrowly defined space. This strategy should have caused the French and British General Staffs to reflect, but they did nothing of the kind. They were persuaded that everything would happen as it had in 1914, with the enemy attacking through Belgium and marching on Paris by way of the Marne, where he would then be beaten.

Very early on May 10, 1940, while many French generals slept or were away on leave, German panzer divisions simultaneously attacked Holland, Belgium, and Luxembourg. Four days later, the 1,500 armored vehicles of General Heinz Guderian crossed the Meuse without difficulty, near Sedan, where the impenetrable Maginot Line ended. The fortresses were thus taken from the rear. At that moment, the best French and British troops were deployed toward the north to defend Belgium. Guderian's motorized divisions did not head for Paris but instead struck at Amiens and the mouth of the Somme River. He thus cut in two the French armies under General Maurice Gustave Gamelin's command. The French were unable to pierce the enemy lines. All they could do was retreat and evacuate their forces under machine-gun fire at Dunkirk. The pitiful exodus of panic-stricken Belgian and French civilians, mixed with soldiers in disarray and trying to regroup, increased the disorder. France appeared in complete collapse. Despite some courageous but isolated resistance, the Germans had overrun the lower Seine Valley by June 8 and captured Paris on June 14. They were then free to operate anywhere they liked in France.

On June 10, the French government fled, first to Tours, then to Bordeaux. On the same day, Mussolini attacked across the Alps, where his thirty-two divisions did not have much difficulty with the six French divisions in the area. Without taking too many risks, the Italians wanted to share in the booty. By June 12, two old Anglophobes, Marshal Pétain, vice president of the ministry, and General Weygand, chief of the

General Staff, were pleading for an armistice to end the fighting because they thought the French army had been defeated. Others such as Paul Reynaud and the newly promoted General de Gaulle demanded continuation of the struggle, even if it was necessary to do so from the colonies. These leaders wanted to make use of the fine French navy, still intact, which the British would be able to support. They understood that the battle for France had been lost, but the war was not over. This was the theme of de Gaulle's first speech to the French nation, broadcast from London on June 18.

On June 16, however, a discouraged Reynaud handed over power to Pétain, who immediately asked the Germans for an armistice. The armistice was duly signed on June 22 at Rethondes, the same place where the Germans had signed in 1918. A separate armistice with the Italians was signed at Rome on June 24.

These agreements could only be reached in accord with the will of Hitler. Perhaps fearing that France would resume the war at sea or in the colonies, the German dictator made relatively moderate demands, at least in comparison with the terrible conditions he imposed on Holland and Belgium. Alsace-Lorraine was handed back; the north, east, and coastal regions were subject to special regulations; and more than half of France became an occupied zone. The rest of the country, south of the Loire and Burgundy, remained in principle a "free zone." Germany promised to respect the integrity of the French fleet and the colonial empire, and even allowed a small French army to remain in existence. On the other hand, more than 1.5 million captured French soldiers were taken to Germany, and most of them stayed there for five years. Finally, the French had to pay an enormous occupation indemnity of 400 million francs per day, and they granted the Germans numerous economic advantages.

The disaster of May–June 1940 requires explanation. Writers, journalists, and politicians have quarreled about this problem for nearly half a century. The historian Marc Bloch placed the major share of the blame on the extreme mediocrity of an aged and narrow-minded General Staff, but also discerned a "defeat of intelligence and character" among France's leaders and some of her people. These are opinions worthy of respect, but one may question whether any historian is really capable of explaining his own time.

With the armistice signed, Bordeaux occupied by the conqueror, and the French fleet at Mers-el-Kébir sunk by the English on July 3 (to keep it from falling into the hands of the Germans, they said), the government was reinforced in its Anglophobia and moved to Vichy. In this spa town there were many hotels with vacancies. After having assembled 666 members of parliament, Pierre Laval, Pétain's counselor and a skillful negotiator, proposed the delegation of full power to Pétain. Only eighty members, including thirty-seven Socialists, voted against this proposal; the marshal immediately became chief of the "French State," as it was prosaically called. The prudent official motto became "Work, Family, Fatherland," far removed from the former trilogy of "Liberty, Equality, Fraternity." The new chief of state inaugurated a quasi-monarchical regime. His first official act was to adjourn parliament "until new order"; henceforth no elections took place, not even at the village level, and every officeholder was appointed from above, frequently with German blessing. The Third Republic was quite dead, though it had been and remains the longest-lasting regime France has known since 1792.

With the courageous exception of Britain, the entire world recognized Pétain's state. The United States even sent him an ambassador, whose influence could have been favorable, and was not insignificant in any case. De Gaulle never forgave the Americans for this gesture, and made them feel his wrath long afterward. The tenacity of his grudge would constitute one of the fundamental characteristics of the future head of state, whom Pétain condemned to death in absentia, even though he had been godfather to one of de Gaulle's sons.

What were the characteristics of the new regime? How did it evolve? How did the French, as far as we can truly tell, welcome it? Did their opinions toward it change? These are difficult questions to treat dispassionately, yet we propose to do so.

The Vichy regime was a monarchy that did not dare to proclaim itself such, and did not tolerate any electoral system. Its official documents opened with an echo of the past in the words: "We, Philippe Pétain, Marshal of France, Chief of State, decree. . . ." Vichy established a kind of moral order. The family was glorified and divorce forbidden for three years. Work was sacrosanct, with an emphasis on returning to the land and granting preferences to artisans and corporate bodies in the medieval style. Organized religion was venerated as well, since all the bishops and almost all the clergy had paid homage to Pétain. The state's program for youth included dismantling the system of lay schools created by the republic, and immediately suppressing colleges for training teachers, who were accused of all sorts of evils. There was a militarization of adolescents through the creation of "youth workshops," based on the German model. The state also harassed Freemasons and fired civil servants who belonged to masonic organizations. Even without waiting for orders from Germany, the Vichy regime persecuted Jews, who were arrested en masse by the French police, a point often overlooked. And, above all, there was the cult of Marshal Pétain. It was taught in schools where obligatory portraits were hung, and a new hymn, "Marshal, here we are!" was heard in classrooms, at public ceremonies, and during radio broadcasts. There was no freedom of speech, neither free press nor free radio. All public statements were subject to omnipresent double censorship by Vichy and by the Germans. The state was obliged to establish a semblance of wartime organization, specifically, a Ministry of Provisions which pretended to distribute food and merchandise equitably. In fact, the majority of French production was delivered to the Germans and to the profiteers of the regime and the occupation, the collaborators and lords of the black market. Most of them had enough sense to become Gaullists in good time.

The regime first found support among men of the old Right and extreme Right: soldiers of the Action Française, ultra-Catholics and nationalists, anti-Semites, Anglophobes (including many naval officers), politicians and businessmen. They were favorably inclined toward diverse varieties of fascism, often because they were horrified by the supposedly Communist Popular Front. Little by little, under the opportunistic influence of Pierre Laval and Admiral François Darlan, the Vichy regime began its decline. Certain German excesses as well as the Allied invasion of North Africa, followed by the German occupation of all France and the scuttling of the French fleet at Toulon in November 1942, resulted in the loss of support for the regime. At the same time, the horrors of its repression rose to new heights with the mass arrest of Jews organized by the police of Paris, the creation of a French secret police worthy of the Gestapo, and even a legion of French volunteers to fight alongside the Germans on the Russian front. In the face of hatred and indifference of the French people in 1944, Vichy suddenly collapsed. The lamentable epilogue was played out at the old Hohenzollern castle at Sigmaringen, where the German clients had fled at the end of the war, only to be captured by the advancing Allied armies. Brought back to face judgment, the barely conscious ninety-year-old Pétain was condemned to death, but reprieved by his former protégé Charles de Gaulle.

Not all French people experienced the Vichy regime. The residents of Alsace-Lorraine found themselves German again. Prisoners of war, exiles, victims of concentration camps, and slave laborers in Germany had varied experiences as well. Nonetheless the lives and feelings of the general population in Vichy France have been widely discussed, and we should attempt to make sense of the diverse opinions presented.

It is certain that many people warmly received Marshal Pétain, who was still quite lucid though diabetic and aged eighty-four in 1940. He had the reputation of victor of Verdun, and was thought to be a humane general and a grand old man with a consoling voice. Among Pétain's supporters were aging veterans, the political Right, particularly Catholics, members of the Fascistic leagues, and women hoping for the return of their husbands—the prisoners in Germany. All those who took comfort in and celebrated the June armistice responded very badly to the British destruction of the French fleet, no doubt a necessary operation of war. Clear-thinking patriots and men of greater vision were quite rare. Often they were non-Communist men of the Left, since Hitler and Stalin were allies at that time. De Gaulle's appeal had been broadcast in the cities of south-west France, and had often been misunderstood. But in response some fighters went to Britain or laid the foundations of the first small resistance groups. In the beginning they were not enthusiastically in favor of the exiled general, who was dubbed "General Micro." De Gaulle himself first paid little attention to these isolated groups, though later he placed them under his nominal authority. As for the Allies, he often ignored them and gave them little help, especially when the outbreak of fighting between Germany and Russia brought numerous well-organized Communist groups into the resistance. Nevertheless, the "maquis" resistance groups that were hidden in the forests and mountains drew more recruits, especially from those who sought to escape from slave labor in Germany. They were important to the final liberation of France by sabotaging bridges and railways, and obstructing or destroying German units headed for Normandy to fight the Allied invasion. By that time, however, almost everyone in France called himself a member of the resistance, even former supporters of Pétain and black-market profiteers.

While the majority of the French people certainly favored Pétain in the beginning, the reaction against him grew quickly. There were many reasons for this change of sentiment: the famous Hitler-Pétain "handshake" at Montoire in October 1940; Laval's return to power in April 1942, after his temporary removal; and above all the changing fortunes of war. The German occupation of France followed the successful Allied invasion of North Africa in November 1942. The first Allied victories were won by the Russians at Stalingrad and by the British in Egypt and Libya. Finally, the long-awaited arrival of the very popular Americans also played a part in converting French public opinion. Indeed, most French people listened to de Gaulle's broadcasts from London even though they were forbidden.

The French people were preoccupied with the painful dilemma of obtaining the necessities of life. Food, clothing, heating fuel, and other goods were stolen by the Germans or confiscated by the lords of the black market, rich peasants, shopkeepers, profiteers, and collaborators of all types. People were anxious about police raids that swept up the youth for slave labor in Germany, deported Jews to concentration camps, and arrested Freemasons. Arrests were numerous and included members of the resistance, Communists, terrorists, and anyone suspected of anti-German activity. The French were distressed by the prolonged absence of the prisoners of war, and suffered (without too much complaint) high-level bombing that often missed its targets—railway stations, factories, airfields—and injured civilians and their property instead. Despite skillful Pétainist propaganda, material and moral concerns, and the long period of waiting, they hoped for nothing more than liberation. To the French people, liberation seemed unduly delayed, even though events in Italy, North Africa, Russia, and the distant Pacific reassured them of their hopes.

Liberation finally came with the D-Day invasion of Normandy on June 6, 1944, thanks to British and American armies and a small contingent of de Gaulle's Free French forces. There was also an Allied invasion of Provence in August 1944, in which troops from French North Africa played a part that should not be forgotten. The internal resistance, organized and unified by Jean Moulin in May 1943, had prepared the way for these events. Moulin was later betrayed and tortured, but his forces managed to destroy 600 trains and 2,000 locomotives in two months. With some difficulty de Gaulle obtained Allied permission for a French armored unit under General Jean Leclerc to have the honor of liberating Paris, already in insurrection, on August 24. De Gaulle himself arrived immediately afterward to wild acclaim.

Beyond the excitement of liberation, the serious problems of French political life remained. The Americans would have preferred a kind of proconsulate or protectorate for the country they had just liberated, so great was their mistrust of de Gaulle and the highly organized resistance groups, and especially the Communists. To explain the circumstances that brought de Gaulle and his team to power, we should take a brief look backward.

In 1940 several hundred men, later several thousand, had

managed, under difficult circumstances, to join de Gaulle in London. Some were already on the spot; others, notably some courageous Breton sailors, came by sea from the Continent or the colonies. In June of 1940, and only after some hesitation, Winston Churchill's government became the only one in the world to recognize this organization of "Free French." Churchill had understood that the farsighted de Gaulle wanted to lay the foundations for a legitimate French government, the embryonic free republic of the future. Although a monarchist by temperament, the general had intelligently rallied to support the republic. His "Free French" might prevent the French navy and colonial empire from falling into the hands of the Germans. Both Churchill and de Gaulle, who barely tolerated each other but eventually came to have mutual respect, believed that the war would be global and victorious for the Allied side. Thus Churchill tried to seize the French fleet. At Oran, he was able only to sink the ships in the harbor and at Dakar in September he also failed as the governors of the most important French colonies remained loyal to Pétain. At least Churchill was able to collect all the French ships that were found in British ports, but very few sailors joined de Gaulle. Among them there were only four staff officers, including Admiral Emile-Henri-Desiré Muselier, who had retired in 1939 after disagreements with Darlan. Indeed, there were more civilians than military personnel around de Gaulle; but by the end of 1940 the general had organized a small force of 7,000 men, and two years later he had ten times as many.

Meanwhile, a small group of colonies, including French Polynesia, had come round to de Gaulle's side. Under the leadership of the Guyanese governor Felix Eboué, Equatorial Africa became a good base for the British navy and the starting point for Free French military operations. A column captured the oasis of Koufra in March 1941, then crossed the Sahara Desert to support the British. Fierce fighting by the French against Rommel's Afrika Korps at Bir-Hakeim even allowed the British to retreat in good order until June 1942, when General Bernard Montgomery's victory at El Alamein launched the counteroffensive that reconquered Tunisia. At the beginning of 1941 Churchill recognized a newly created "Council for Defense of the Empire," and de Gaulle traveled to the French colonies of Cameroun and the Congo (Brazzaville). It was there that the idea was first developed of transforming the colonial empire into a French commonwealth or union.

The situation in North Africa was greatly changed by the Allied invasion in November 1942. No one had informed de Gaulle of the plans. President Franklin Roosevelt did not care for the imperious chief of "Free France," but the invasion nonetheless helped de Gaulle. Almost all the former colonies henceforth escaped from Pétain's influence. Furthermore, a providential assassination had rid de Gaulle of Admiral Darlan, who had switched to the Allied side. Shady intrigues also eliminated de Gaulle's rival Henri Giraud, a courageous general lacking in political skill who had warmly supported the Americans. Finally, de Gaulle decided to deliver a speech with a democratic and even "social" character appealing to men of the Left, in particular Socialists but also Communists acting with Stalin's approval. Thus in Algeria the general prefigured his provisional government of liberation. While de Gaulle and France were waiting, Tunisia was freed with difficulty from the Germans who had come from Libya. And in North Africa, the Free French army recruited Europeans as well as Arabs and participated actively in the Italian campaign, especially at the terrible battle of Monte Cassino. These forces landed in Provence in August 1944.

The internal resistance forces, which were at first scattered about and almost insignificant, grew over time with the help of the Communists, and those who were escaping from the increasingly pro-German Vichy regime. Young people who were avoiding the call to forced labor in Germany also became part of the growing resistance. These movements adopted a more formal structure, joined in federations, and finally accepted de Gaulle's unified command. After having given valuable aid to the Allied victory by attacking convoys and enemy transport units, these heroes found themselves covered with glory during the summer of 1944. By that time their ranks had swollen with dubious elements, but, nevertheless, with the exception of a few holdouts such as Saint-Malo, Saint-Nazaire, Royan, and Colmar, the whole of France was liberated. Pétain and the last faithful Vichy supporters were spirited away to Germany by their defeated friends.

The French army was expanded to include former resistance fighters and those who had been recalled to duty. It then took part in the liquidation of the Reich, penetrating even as far as Hitler's former redoubt at Berchtesgaden. But the establishment of a new French government presented problems. In June, de Gaulle had transformed his Committee of National Liberation into a Provisional Government of the French Republic (GPRF), which awaited recognition by the Allies, finally granted in October. He also appointed some "commissioners of the republic" to prepare a list of former prefects and mayors of the principal cities.

But the country was not liberated all at once, and regional authorities, often under Communist control, tried to establish themselves. There were brutal episodes of revenge and spontaneous "popular" tribunals, which judged guilty collaborators; perhaps 10,000 were executed. To put the matter into perspective, it should be noted that repression was much harsher in other countries. Rather rapidly, however, legal tribunals replaced the others, and resistance forces were integrated into the army or dissolved. The Gaullist forces and their sympathizers gradually prevailed. Unruly incidents became rare and disappeared by the beginning of 1945.

The government still required reconstruction, as did the suffering country. This was the considerable and often disparaged work of the Fourth Republic.

THE FOURTH REPUBLIC
(1944–46 TO MAY 1958)

This brief regime of less than twelve years was and remains not much loved. André Siegfried said that the Fourth Republic did not govern France, but "simply administered." Yet the

Fourth Republic had a considerable task: it reconstructed a country that had suffered a severe test, assured its economic recovery, and quickly enacted such useful reforms as female suffrage, social security, and numerous nationalizations. The republic did strike hard obstacles in colonial problems, which it could not solve. And in foreign policy, despite Communist and Gaullist opposition, the Fourth Republic knew only how to seek shelter under the American umbrella.

The gestation of this new republic was particularly painful. It took more than two years to establish. Grave problems arose during the liberation in August 1944. France had lost nearly 1.5 million inhabitants, more than 500,000 through the rising number of deaths over the number of births. More civilians than soldiers were lost, and one-third of them were women killed either in the camps or by inaccurate bombing.

The return of the prisoners of war and the expanded provisions of the Family Code of 1938 brought about a baby boom that lasted longer than expected. In the post-war period there were 800,000 births per year, as opposed to 600,000 before 1939. Furthermore, vast reconstruction projects called for the building of roads, bridges, railways, ports, factories, and cities. This led to an increase of jobs and resulted in a substantial influx of immigrants from Mediterranean and North African countries, many of whom were eventually naturalized. At the same time progress in medicine and hygiene prolonged life expectancy by ten years for women and five years for men. These factors resulted in a rise in total population from 40 million to nearly 50 million.

All this manpower, however, did not suffice to reconstruct and modernize the country. Matériel and machines costing a great deal of money were also needed. After the Germans had drained the economy and forced large quantities of paper-money to be issued, inflation was enormously high. Rationing and the black-market persisted after the war. The government tried taking large loans and implementing several devaluations of the currency which fell at an alarming rate on the foreign exchanges. From 1939 to 1958, the franc lost more than 90 percent of its value. Finally, in 1959, it was necessary to make the old franc into the centime, 1/100th of the new franc. American financial aid under the Marshall Plan was a decisive factor in restoring the economy.

To sum up, while France did not recover its pre-1914 power, the country made lively progress toward modernization, and the standard of living rose without interruption, at least as rapidly as output, until the first oil price-shock of 1973. The Fifth Republic has taken great pride in this satisfying economic and social progress, but it was really the Fourth Republic that set it in motion.

Political and colonial affairs were conducted with much less brilliance. In September of 1944, the former provisional government created by de Gaulle was quickly transformed into a "government of national unity" containing men of the resistance such as Georges Bidault and Pierre Mendès-France, respectable former members of parliament including J. M. Jeanneney, and representatives of all political parties old and new—even two Communists.

De Gaulle had always enjoyed good relations with Stalin, who was far away and appreciated his resistance to the Anglo-Americans. In December 1944, the general visited Moscow and signed a twenty-year alliance with the Russians. To design the new French republic, de Gaulle established a Consultative Assembly and packed it with his supporters. Under its leadership women received the vote, and a complex procedure for popular referendum was enacted. New laws governed the press and nationalized key industries—Renault, civil aviation, large banks, oil, gas, and electric utilities. During the winter of 1944–45, while the war continued and the more savage excesses of purification ended, some former collaborators were sent to the tribunals, though financiers and big businessmen were excused. Meanwhile, political parties were reconstituted.

The former right wing groups were tainted by their frequent submissiveness to Vichy and to the Germans, and they had to wait several years before reasserting themselves. The three old parties who had formed the Popular Front reappeared with their surviving leaders and others who rose from the ranks of the resistance. The Communists had grown the largest, the Socialists believed they would become so, and the Radicals had shrunk considerably. Two significant new parties were founded: the MRP (*Mouvement Républican Populaire*) or Christian Democrats, which long played an important role and attracted support from the old Right; and the UDSR (*Union Démocratique et Socialiste de la Résistance*), a center-Left group blessed with the strong personalities of such men as René Pleven and François Mitterand, non-Communist members of the resistance.

De Gaulle had to discuss and negotiate constantly with these major parties and smaller groups. Quickly irritated by quarrels and intrigues that he regarded as base and unworthy, he suddenly resigned on January 20, 1946. No doubt he thought he would soon be recalled, but he had to wait for twelve years and force his moment of destiny when it came.

In the meantime, by way of three successive referendums, the French electorate had definitively buried the Third Republic, which had already been suspended at Vichy in July 1940. The people rejected a first constitution in May 1946, but accepted a second in October. The new constitution reduced to nonentity the president of the republic and the assembly of rural notables known as the Senate. Three-quarters of the Constituent Assembly that drafted this text consisted of deputies from the three largest political parties—the Communists, the Christian Democrats of the MRP, and the Socialists.

Under the banner of "tripartism" these three parties governed together for several months, but in May 1947, Prime Minister Paul Ramadier, a Socialist, dismissed the five Communist ministers from his cabinet because their party opposed the government's policies on Indochina, the Marshall Plan, and economic measures. Meanwhile de Gaulle, who had condemned the constitution and the "regime of parties," created a political party of his own, the RPR (*Rassemblement du Peuple Français*—Assemblage of the French People). His party quickly gained great popularity but its strength did not last: this attempt by the general to return to power was premature.

While de Gaulle waited, a vague political coalition called the "third force" (neither Communists nor Gaullists) governed for seven years under eight prime ministers. The coalition remained attached to the North Atlantic Treaty Organization (NATO) which was founded in 1949 and sketched the outlines of a united Europe, the work of Robert Schuman and Jean Monnet: on these two points it was attacked by both Gaullists and Communists. In the election of 1951, what remained of the third force and its opposition was divided among six parties, each of which had about a hundred deputies. From this mixture there arose governments of the center-Right—without Socialists—or center-Left—with Socialists. In the face of insoluble difficulties in internal and colonial policies, several figures emerged. Antoine Pinay, a provincial moderate whose economic policy temporarily succeeded in 1952, saw his government flounder on the problem of Indochina and the first disputes about the European Defense Community, which sought to create a military entity other than the United States or the Soviet Union. Shortly afterward he was succeeded by Joseph Laniel, an authoritarian man of the Right, who was vigorously pushed along by the journalistic pen of François Mauriac. Laniel practiced unpopular cost-cutting policies, had to face strikes in France and revolts in Tunisia and Morocco, and finally melted away after the incredible disaster of Dien Bien Phu in June 1954, when the French army was caught in a trap in Indochina. Six months earlier, he had hoped to become president of the republic but failed after thirteen ballots. The honest and popular moderate René Coty was finally elected.

Finally, in June 1954, Pierre Mendès-France came to power. He was the only truly remarkable statesman of the period, and was able to resolve the Indochinese problem by the Geneva Accords of 1954. Mendès-France promised autonomy to Tunisia, a territory long in upheaval. He liquidated the European Defense Community project, and he had the unfortunate task of attacking the French plague of alcoholism, thereby coming into conflict with many vested interests. He also tried vainly for constitutional reform and fell from power at the beginning of the Algerian revolt because he had dared to send a Gaullist negotiator, Jacques Soustelle, to Algiers. A coalition of the Right, Christian Democrats, and Communists led to his dismissal.

His successor, Edgar Faure, was a politician of rare skill. Faure promised autonomy to Morocco and tried to revive the French economy, but was hindered by the terrible war in Algeria. New elections produced a slightly more leftist assembly and brought to office a center-Left ministry led by Guy Mollet. This government lasted almost sixteen months, breaking records for longevity in the Fourth Republic. As a good but moderate Socialist, Mollet passed several pieces of social legislation, including a third week of paid holidays for workers, an increase in wages, and a social welfare fund for elderly people. Despite Communist and Gaullist opposition, he favored the construction of a united Europe. But Mollet also encountered the obstacle of decolonization and was very badly received in Algeria in February 1956. His government was faced with two very serious events: the failure of the Anglo-French military expedition to the Suez in November 1956, after President Gamel Abdel Nasser of Egypt had nationalized the canal, and the expedition of a contingent of young draftees to fight in Algeria, a measure poorly appreciated in France. The French people did not understand the politics of Algeria, to which we shall return.

After Mollet's fall in May 1957, France endured semi-paralysis and then the the final agony of the Fourth Republic, whose fate was closely linked to Algerian affairs. While its economic and social policies were significant, and its European program quite effective with the signing of the Treaty of Rome which created the Common Market in 1957, the republic's foreign policy brought it back to near total submission to the Western Bloc. President Charles de Gaulle would change all that.

The great drama was summed up in colonial problems. In 1939, France still held the second-largest colonial empire in the world. Aside from the Polynesian islands, the French Antilles, French Guyana, several cities in India, and the massive island of Madagascar and its dependencies, the bulk of the empire consisted of Indochina and immense African territories stretching from the Mediterranean to the Congo. Celebrated during the Colonial Exposition of Paris in 1931, the empire contained almost 70 million inhabitants spread over 10 million square kilometers, including the Sahara Desert. Except for Algeria, which had been settled progressively since 1830 by a million Europeans of various nationalities, the French presence in the empire was weak. The point of the French Empire was not primarily settlement but exploitation of the colonies—which were administered rather roughly at times.

Even before 1914, difficulties had already begun to appear in Tunisia with the beginnings of the "Destorien" movement, which sought autonomy or at least serious reform. In Indochina there remained the effects of the Japanese victory over the Russians in 1905, which proved that Europeans were not invincible. Nevertheless, the colonies had presented no problems about participating in World War I, and they suffered considerable losses in support of the mother country.

After 1919, however, the doctrine of popular self-determination, an old revolutionary principle taken up by President Woodrow Wilson, spread quickly. In Tunisia, the Destour asked for a constitution, and in response the French created in 1922 a mixed "Grand Council," from which all political discussion was excluded. This was the first example of vaguely consultative institutions granted by France without any true desire for effectiveness. In Morocco, which had been more recently conquered, a serious revolt led by Abd-el-Krim was repressed with difficulty in the Rif between 1923 and 1926. In the South, the Berber tribes long resisted French rule. Also serious, though far away, were rising demands for independence in Indochina in 1919. The creation of another ineffective "Grand Council" in 1928 had no effect on the first clandestine party led by Ho Chi Minh, who organized mutinies among the Annamite troops from 1930 onward.

With the crushing defeat of France in 1940, most of the unoccupied colonies remained loyal to Pétain. But the occupation of Indochina by the Japanese, Madagascar by the British, and Morocco and Algeria by the Allied armies brought a new urgency to French colonial problems. This coincided with the general awakening of nationalism, the rise of Moslem fundamentalism, and the reserve of the British and even the Americans toward the French colonial empire. President Roosevelt was hostile to the return of the French to Indochina. Communist propaganda and conflicts born of the cold war also aggravated the problems, especially in Indochina.

Here we must make several painful remarks. On one hand, metropolitan France rarely appreciated the worth of the colonies. Very little capital was invested in them, and the burden of their defense was borne grudgingly by sending young soldiers from the mother country. On the other hand, while French economic development in the colonies was often remarkable, with the construction of roads, dams, railways, mines, and agricultural projects such as the vineyards of Algeria and the peanut plantations of Sénégal, as well as the creation of schools and even universities, colonial peoples frequently perceived the French as greedy and contemptuous masters who thought only of their profits. In response to demands for reform and independence movements, the French created institutions lacking genuine power. All too often they refused to hold dialogues with talented local elites—Asian, Arab, African, or Madagascaran—even though they were French-speaking. Still worse, the French sometimes organized entirely fraudulent elections, as in Algeria.

In a few years all was lost. After inglorious fighting, France withdrew from Indochina in 1954. Morocco and Tunisia were set free in 1956 following some lackluster political moves, including deposing a Moroccan sultan who had to be recalled later, and imprisoning Habib Bourguiba after negotiations. Bourguiba then enjoyed a triumphal return as well as independence for his country, which he has continued to rule for thirty years with the help of his entourage.

Black Africa was easily incorporated into the French Union, a sort of Commonwealth outlined in the Constitution of 1946. Independence evolved fairly peacefully except in Madagascar, where in March 1947, a violent revolt was brutally crushed leaving thousands of victims. Moderate independence movements were anxious not to lose French economic aid. They were directed by remarkable leaders such as Léopold Senghor of Sénégal and Félix Houphouët-Boigny of the Ivory Coast. Successive steps toward autonomy led to a very sheltered independence between 1958 and 1960.

The situation in Algeria was more complex, more serious, and more easily misunderstood. Algeria was a large and rich country inhabited by North Africans and by a million colonials of European origin. They called themselves French and were known as *pieds noirs* (black feet) because they wore shoes, formerly unknown among the natives. By turns polite and harsh, these colonials dominated the apparently submissive Moslem population, who were not always hostile. The presence of numerous Jews also presented political problems. In this complex country, peace had not always prevailed, particularly not among the Kabyles or toward the Jews. Since the Algerians had played an important role in World War II, fighting even more than the continental French, they thought France would grant them certain rights. The growth of nationalist and religious feelings, the idea that Algerian land had been stolen by the French, and the existence of an active educated elite gave rise to two distinct movements after 1945. The first, led by Ferhat Abbas, favored profound reforms that had once been promised by the Popular Front. The second, openly pro-independence and very religious, was led by Messali Hadj. When the government ordered his arrest, major riots broke out at Sétif and in Kabylia and severe repression brought nine years of relative calm between 1945 and 1954.

During this time the clandestine movement for independence was renewed, restructured, and radicalized. It was directed from Cairo by young men such as Ben Bella, and received strong support from Egypt and other Arab countries. The movement was regarded with indifference by the Soviet Union, and perhaps also by the United States. On November 1, 1954, armed insurrection broke out all over Algeria with a violence never seen before involving massacres, killings, tortures, attacks on children, and urban bombing. All this lasted with varying intensity for many years. The repression quickly grew to equal the dimensions of the aggression. Jacques Soustelle and Georges Catroux, two liberal Gaullist emissaries sent by Paris to present reforms and restore order, were very badly received by the rich colonials, the hard core of *pieds noir* resistance. They left disappointed and were followed in February 1956 by Guy Mollet, who was pelted with tomatoes, and Robert Lacoste, Mollet's appointee as minister-resident in Algeria. While the guerrillas extended and reinforced their activities with the help of Arab countries, it seemed that the *pieds noirs* and the soldiers stationed in Algeria wanted to settle their own affairs through violence. They felt misunderstood and poorly supported by metropolitan France. The principal result was that in 1956 the French Chamber of Deputies voted—with Communist support—to send a contingent of troops and planned to mobilize several units of reserve draftees. In essence this was a war against hardened adversaries who used guerrilla tactics, just as the Vietnamese had done. In October 1956, the hijacking of a Moroccan airplane carrying Ben Bella and other leaders of the National Liberation Front (FLN) led to a terrible wave of massacres of Europeans under the most horrifying conditions. General Jacques Massu and his paratroopers restored order, cleaned up Algiers, and kicked most of the FLN out of Algeria, provoking a serious incident with Tunisia in 1957. The French army, in particular the paratroopers, joined its adversaries in the practice of torture.

These overwhelming tragic facts deeply divided French public opinion, even within families. Some demonstrated in favor of keeping Algeria under French rule, while others openly helped the FLN. In this poisoned climate, one group of mediocre politicians resigned and succeeded another amid rumors and foolish intrigues.

In the end, the selection of Premier Pierre Pflimlin, a liberal Christian Democrat who voluntarily negotiated with the Moslem rebels, provoked the fury of the French colonials in Algeria. They revolted against their own government and prepared for unilateral secession on May 13, 1958. On the same day, General Raoul Salan acted on wise advice and made an appeal to de Gaulle, whose long "crossing of the desert" (in

471

André Malraux's words) was over. De Gaulle and his supporters maneuvered with subtlety to recover power.

Paratroop units ready to rebel left Algiers for Corsica. No
doubt others were preparing to move in France itself, where
hardly anyone understood what was happening. Be that as it
may, it was certainly thanks to the professional army, the paratroopers, Salan, and the colonials in Algeria, helped by relative
indifference in metropolitan France, that the Fourth Republic
died. Almost no one mourned its passing. Indeed, its demise
was necessary to get out of an apparently deadlocked situation.

THE FIFTH REPUBLIC:
THE GAULLIST PHASE (1958–1969)

After a series of complicated schemes and subtle negotiations,
the man President Coty called "the most illustrious Frenchman" (among the living, of course) was made premier on May
29, 1958, invested by the National Assembly two days later, and
given all powers for six months. He did not fail to exercise
them to the fullest.

De Gaulle faced three grave problems: first, to establish a
new constitution, since he detested the preceding one—this
was accomplished by Michel Debré; second, to restore the
faltering economy—this was attempted anew by Pinay and the
economist Jacques Rueff; and finally, the most serious of all, to
liquidate the Algerian situation—this de Gaulle did himself
with a mixture of seduction, patience, trickery, and perfidy,
which finally succeeded.

The Constitution of 1958, cut to his measure, was written
quickly and approved in September by a referendum. De
Gaulle liked this system, and at that moment the voters followed him almost blindly. The essential point was the considerable strengthening of powers of the president of the republic.
He can appoint and dismiss the prime minister; he can require

the two legislative chambers to deliberate very quickly; he can dissolve the National Assembly; and, according to article sixteen of the constitution, he can call referendums and assume full power in case of emergency or grave danger. An increasingly important Constitutional Council, appointed by the president of the republic and the presiding officers of the two chambers, ruled on the constitutionality of laws.

At the lower level, a new electoral system was introduced. Proportional representation, which was a more equitable system but led to fragmentation of political parties and shifting majorities, was replaced by a two-round system of majority voting for a single representative from each district. Naturally there was a redistricting that strongly favored the president's party. He was thus practically assured of obtaining the majority of legislative seats with only a minority of the votes—between 35 and 40 percent. Furthermore, new legislative elections took place quickly, giving the desired result—a Gaullist majority. In December 1958, de Gaulle had himself named president of the republic by a curious "electoral college" of 80,000 "notables" that he had chosen to his liking. In a well-known book, a talented opponent denounced what he saw as the "permanent coup d'état" of this regime. The author was François Mitterand.

During this time, the economic team of Pinay and Rueff cut state spending, practically balanced the budget, reduced customs duties in preparation for the Common Market, and devalued the franc by 100 to 1, as we have already noted. Many older French people still have difficulty reckoning in "new" francs and continue to think in anciens. Agriculture was rapidly becoming mechanized and modernized, and farmers assumed debts to accomplish these ends. French industry also made some progress, but certainly not enough. The commercial balance of trade remained in surplus until 1963, while economic growth, already considerable, took off at a rate of 5 percent per annum. But prices shot upward also, inflation reappeared, and the young minister of finances, Valéry Giscard, soon had to order a stabilization program, a partial success.

On balance all these measures appeared well and good, and the economist Jean Fourastie could include this period in his "thirty glorious years" of growth from 1945 to 1975.

The Algerian affair was much more serious and charged with passion. The "ultras" and military officers, especially the paratroopers, were determined to defeat the rebellion at any cost; in this goal they were supported by the majority of the *pieds noirs*. On their side was an army of courageous young soldiers, nonetheless devoid of illusions and not as set on the possible secession dreamed of by their leaders. Yet across the Mediterranean, France was misinformed, indifferent, and desirous of peace. There was even a leftist camp that favored the rebels and gave them support, as well as a powerful and violent extreme rightist group that demonstrated constantly for "French Algeria."

And what was President de Gaulle's position? On his first trip to Algeria during June 4–7, 1958, he made his famous statement, "I have understood you!" which appeared to promise total support to the partisans of French Algeria. Indeed they had made a substantial contribution to his return to power. This apparently total support had led to an intensification of the revolt as well as of the repression. By October 1958, however, de Gaulle was saying that negotiations with the rebels were possible. He launched the expression "peace of the brave" and shocked his more extreme supporters. They were even more outraged on September 16, 1959, when he dared to propose "autodetermination" for all Algerians, including Moslems.

This initiative inevitably gathered strength and provoked violent dissatisfaction among the extreme Right in France and even more so among the entire military and civilian establishment in Algeria. In January of 1960, there was a week of rioting with barricades in the streets of Algiers. A year later there was an attempted military putsch by "a quarter of retired generals" (as de Gaulle called them). The coup was foiled by the refusal of the units—the soldiers themselves—to participate, and by the obvious hostility of the immense majority of the people of metropolitan France. In the face of these defeats, the disappointed activists formed a "secret army organization" (OAS) which agitated using terrorist tactics in Algeria and in France itself. On August 22, 1962, they nearly succeeded in assassinating de Gaulle during the "Petit-Clamart" attack in suburban Paris. Harshly repressed, this clandestine opposition faded away slowly. We must recognize that there were reasons for its existence, for de Gaulle had clearly violated the promises he had made to the army and the colonials in Algeria in May–June, 1958, a fact that was never forgotten.

The general evidently thought that the restoration of French rule in Algeria was impossible, and that decolonization was as unavoidable for France as for the other European colonial powers—Britian, Belgium, Spain, The Netherlands, and Portugal. The Fourth Republic had carefully prepared for the transition to independence in Black Africa, where the process was peaceful, but Algeria was different.

To gain support for his position amid these tragic and badly misunderstood forces, de Gaulle adroitly had recourse to his well-established techniques of referendums and elections. In April 1961, a plebiscite approved the principle of autodetermination for the Algerians by a 75 percent yes-vote. A year later a second vote ratified by 90 percent the Evian peace agreements made in April 1962. These agreements gave complete independence to Algeria and planned for the repatriation to France of the *pieds noirs* and the *harkis,* Moslems who had helped the French fight the FLN, if they wanted to come. Almost all of them did.

For some time, the wealthy colonials had been placing their goods and capital safely in metropolitan France or in Switzerland and for them, emigration was fairly easy. However, the numerous ordinary people, either of modest means or impoverished, suffered the miseries and vexations of exile. The French of France did not always welcome *pieds noirs* and were even less hospitable to *harkis,* who were often abused. However, hundreds of thousands of repatriated people, some of whose families had lived in Algeria for four or five generations, generally managed to land on their feet. They were hard workers, closely-linked to each other, and filled with initiative; fortunately they arrived in France during a period of great prosperity.

While the last desperados of the OAS tried to survive, de Gaulle reinforced his power by holding a referendum to decide (by a 62 percent yes-vote) that the president of the republic would henceforth be elected by universal suffrage. He also staged the election of a new National Assembly devoted to himself. The Algerian affair thus began to burrow into the memory of many French people who had experienced it in contradictory ways and would not forget it easily.

Having thus settled the most difficult matter, and feeling that his authority was well established over a people preoccupied by the increase in its rate of economic growth and standard of living (which nearly rose to the level of the United States), de Gaulle began to show his mistrustful patriotism in various areas of foreign policy.

Skeptical about European unity, he refused to participate in any supra-national body, and blocked Great Britain's entry into the EEC, for it was a country which he regarded as the "Trojan horse of the Americans." De Gaulle insisted on keeping his distance from the United States, whose leadership of the west he refused to acknowledge, just as he refused to acknowledge "Russia's" (as he always called the Soviet Union) leadership in the east. He refused to integrate the modest French nuclear "force of dissuasion" into any international body, and he also refused to sign the Atmospheric Test Ban Treaty of Moscow in 1963. De Gaulle recognized the People's Republic of China in 1964 and even invited Chinese students to attend French universities. In 1966, he decided to withdraw French forces from NATO and asked American forces stationed in France to leave. Diplomatic tolerance was exceeded in Montreal in 1967, when the general suddenly cried, "Vive le Québec libre!" ("Long live free Quebec!"). He was obliged to return to France because he had rudely shocked the Canadian government and the whole Anglo-American world. This so-called "politics of grandeur" was reminiscent of the shady nationalism of Charles Maurras, one of his teachers. It divided thoughtful French people, who soon demonstrated their views at both ends of the political spectrum.

The first effective election by universal suffrage for the presidency of the republic was held in December of 1965. For the first time, television played a large role, as did public opinion polls—although they were gloriously wrong. De Gaulle received only 44 percent of the vote, compared to 16 percent for a strongly pro-European centrist, Jacques Chaban-Delmas, and a surprising 32 percent for the Socialist François Mitterand. Mitterand benefited from a momentary electoral alliance between the Socialists and Communists. Without a clear majority, de Gaulle had to resign himself to a runoff, which gave him only 54 percent. This sign of relative disaffection or fatigue coincided with a less brilliant economic situation, strikes, and unemployment. Jacques Chirac, then a young undersecretary of state, created a National Employment Agency (ANPE), which still exists today. Another indicator of change was the reinforcement of the Socialist party under Mitterand's influence. The alliance of the Left functioned again during the legislative elections of 1967, when the Gaullists barely won a majority. Only the votes from several overseas territories, often a bit "arranged," settled this decision.

The following year, 1968, was more serious and, in the end, decisive. Beginning at the University of Nanterre in March and at the Sorbonne in May, there was a powerful outbreak of student agitation. It spread to several provincial cities, in particular Lyon. There were immense demonstrations, anti-Gaullist and anti-racist slogans, and street battles with paving stones and tear gas—although no one was killed (the Parisian police were particularly well commanded). During the particularly chaotic month of May, leftist political parties and unions, who had at first understood nothing, changed course by lending their support to the agitation and attempting to control and make use of the largely spontaneous movement.

The origin of these agitations could be attributed to a certain "malaise" or dissatisfaction within of the young people of France. They were bored and restless and sought independence. This disaffection was comparable to that which was felt earlier by student movements in the United States, Germany, and Japan. There was also the powerful influence of those schools of thought which were not well known among the general public and established political forces—young Trotskyites and anarchists in particular, Maoists less commonly, and idealists and romantics who dreamed of the old barricades of 1848 and the Paris Commune of 1871. In the beginning they knew how to expound skillfully an unfamiliar literature and imagery, curiously influenced by surrealism. It should be strongly emphasized that the Communist party had nothing to do with starting this movement. Indeed, the party was against it at first, although later it tried to direct and take advantage of the situation.

In the face of these nights on the barricades and days of demonstrations and enormous strikes, the French government and its chief appeared disconcerted. De Gaulle left on a visit to Rumania! The disarray was so great that on May 27–28 professional politicians thought of a palace coup with perhaps Mendès-France or Mitterand as substitute leader. While Prime Minister Georges Pompidou finessed and played for time, de Gaulle suddenly vanished on May 29. Later it became known that he had gone to visit the commander of French troops stationed in Germany, in order to assure himself of their loyalty (which was total). Then, on the following day, in a brief, skillful, and energetic speech broadcast from Paris, the general again took the reins of power. He dissolved the National Assembly and ordered new elections, which would keep the French people busy. Immediately afterward fervent Gaullists who had seldom been seen in the preceding weeks invaded the Champs-Elysées to proclaim their enthusiasm. The students and mingled bands of hoodlums no longer frightened respectable people and no longer burned their automobiles, a sacrilegious gesture that had caused most Parisians to shun the May demonstrations in Paris. Provincial France had neither understood nor accepted the agitation.

Predictably, the voters were seized by a great retrospective fear and elected a fabulous majority, in which three out of four deputies were Gaullists or their close sympathizers.

Nevertheless, it was necessary to negotiate with the millions of strikers and their unions. The Grenelle agreements gave them considerable wage increases of more than 10 percent, family and old-age benefits, a reduction in the working week, and other rather costly measures. The political situation presented further problems, and grave financial difficulties resulted, including a weakening of the franc. De Gaulle rejected any devaluation, even though the situation already required it. No doubt hoping to recover some of the authority that seemed to be flowing away from him, he thought of a new referendum on regionalization, a subject that inspired no passions in anyone. One might also ask whether, at age seventy-eight, with his task accomplished, the general was looking for a decent way out. Some of his former partisans, strong centralizers or strongly ambitious personalities (such as Giscard), gave him only lukewarm support, and naturally the entire Left was hostile to him. He obtained barely 47 percent approval and resigned immediately on April 28, 1969, emptying the Elysée Palace of all his papers. In November of 1970 he died in isolation.

With de Gaulle's death, a page in the history of France had turned. The strong personality of the man, simultaneously harsh and seductive, subtle and stubborn, perfectly honest in material matters though not in politics, had dominated three decades of the nation's life. At times de Gaulle seemed to identify himself with the nation, when he was not imagining that he spoke for her. He was also one of the greatest actors of his time and had a remarkable mastery of the French language.

THE POST-DE GAULLE ERA
(1969–1987)

First came the epigones: Georges Pompidou, a good bourgeois from Auvergne and a calm spirit who came from the

Ecole Normale Supérieure and the Banque Rothschild. In 1969 Pompidou was elected easily thanks to the division among his opponents but he died in 1974 without having had time to finish his chosen task of disfiguring Paris. Next came Valery Giscard, a brilliant and still young technocrat, descended from bourgeois businessmen of modest origins. In the 1920s Giscard's father found it necessary to obtain permission from the Council of State to add "d'Estaing" to his name, in honor of a family extinct since 1794. Giscard himself had dreams of surprising France by becoming a second John F. Kennedy (among others) and by deviating slightly from the old Gaullist policies. He won a difficult electoral victory over François Mitterand in 1974, then lost a close race for re-election to Mitterand in 1981, no doubt because he had tired the French public with his obsessive presence on television, and some overly spectacular scandals including an affair involving diamonds reportedly received from the Central African Emperor Bokassa I.

In the last analysis, the marked difference in the personalities of these two presidents of the republic was less significant than the overall evolution of French society.

One new event had consequences that will appear gradually: French demography changed suddenly. Beginning in 1965–70, the number of births began to decline, and soon generations were not being replaced at a normal rate, though the problem has been less acute in France than in Germany. The aging of the French population was thus accentuated and threatens to cause serious problems in the twenty-first century, when a large group of senior citizens may form a larger proportion of the reduced population and place a heavy burden on younger working people. For the moment the reduction in the French birth rate has been halted by more fecund immigrant families of Spanish, Portuguese, and Arab origin. Simultaneously, life expectancy has still been rising and is now one of the highest in the world, especially for women, who have a lower rate of alcoholism than men and are more robust. As a sign of high-quality medical care and advanced hygiene, French infant mortality has fallen nearly as far as rates in Holland and

Scandinavia, the lowest in the world. And as for the rapid fall in the number of marriages, it is more a social than a demographic phenomenon.

Economic changes are both slower and more profound. The primary agricultural sector employs many fewer people, although its productivity and production have greatly increased. Consequently there have been crop surpluses, depressed sales, and violent peasant protests despite the strongly protectionist official policies of low taxes and numerous subsidies. Industrial efforts have been supported by the state and the leading banks (Suez, Paribas, Rothschild), as well as by a sudden influx of foreign capital. The effect has been greatest in the newest high-technology sectors of the economy, where France has gained some success. But the older textile and metallurgical industries have been left behind: they face great difficulties in renewing their plants, and seem destined for slow decline. As in all other industrialized nations, the French tertiary sector has expanded with growth in services and the rise of managers trained in engineering, of varying quality. Working women have also become more numerous, but women rarely rise to higher management. One particular feature of the French economy is the expansion and rising cost of social benefits: salaries, paid vacations, health and unemployment insurance, and retirement plans. On the whole, production, consumption, and the standard of living grew rapidly and substantially at least until 1975. But the gap between rich and poor in France has increased, even though dire poverty is rare except among recent immigrants and the unemployed.

The almost chronic fragility of the French economy is seen in the budget deficit, the frequent external deficits in trade and on current account, and the poor health of the national currency which is subject to frequent devaluations. Under Giscard the annual rate of inflation regularly exceeded 10 percent, but some of it must be attributed to the OPEC increase in oil prices in 1973.

Contrary to their illustrious predecessor, the two post-Gaullist presidents adopted an openly pro-European policy. In the Common Market they accepted the entry of Great Brtain,

Ireland, Denmark, and Greece—and they prepared for Spain and Portugal as well. They also accepted, though with reservations, the election by universal suffrage of a European Parliament. This Parliament had little power, but its presiding officer was a highly respected Frenchwoman, Simone Weil. And finally, relations with the United States were much improved, especially under Giscard.

Traditionalist France changed little by little. Thus after having accepted votes for women in 1945, France lowered the age of majority and granted the vote to eighteen-year-olds in 1974. After some ferocious debates and thanks to the authority of Simone Weil, parliament established the right to abortion, legalized contraceptive advertising, and simplified the costly and antiquated procedure for divorce. Divorce by mutual consent was no longer impossible. We should perhaps note that with the exception of a few regions, there was a relative decline in religious attendance, particularly in Catholic churches. But like so many other phenomena, this one is not specifically French, and may be a sign that national differences are fading away, at least in some areas.

On the eve of the presidential elections of 1981, new problems were added to old French shortcomings. Two great oil price-shocks had launched a world economic crisis. The French economy had to bear the burden of accentuated obsolescence in some industries, the high cost of social benefits, and subsidies to farmers and factory-owners in difficulty. Furthermore, France suffered the injustices of the income tax system, frequently denounced but never corrected—enormous frauds were perpetrated by those with non-earned income. The state also had to contend with the increased cost of nuclear armed forces, certain prestigious creations such as the Concorde aircraft, and the overly numerous nuclear power plants. No wonder there was a lack of confidence in the franc and galloping inflation until 1983. There also arose the problem of a rapidly growing number of unemployed, a situation that was exacerbated by the problem of jobless immigrants and rising racism. All this was the legacy of Jacques Chirac and Raymond Barre, successive prime ministers under President Giscard.

The turning point of 1981 seemed to bring to a close Gaullism and anti-Gaullism. The unexpected popular enthusiasm quickly cooled—aside from the nation's problems there was the fury of the defeated parties and the rancor unleashed by the powerful press they controlled. François Mitterand, a skillful moderate Socialist, was installed as president of the republic and he dissolved the National Assembly. One month later, he received in the newly elected body an absolute majority of deputies from his own party—never seen before. Also, there had never been a comparable decline of the Communist vote, which fell from more than 25 percent of the total in 1945 to 15 percent in 1981, and even further to 9 percent in the legislative elections of 1986.

We lack a proper perspective to evaluate these five years of Socialist government, but surely they consisted of two phases. In the first phase, when Pierre Mauroy was prime minister and four Communists sat in the cabinet, many costly reforms were enacted. The franc, government finances, and even the economy appeared to suffer—at least one could think so. Then followed a strong reaction after a ministerial shuffle in which the Communists disappeared. This reaction was translated into prudent measures that largely corrected the preceding situation, further ameliorated by falling oil prices. For the first time in many years the rate of inflation fell below 10 percent, and then later as low as 5 percent. But the number of unemployed people continued to increase while French industry, except for a few shining sectors, fell into ruin.

After a hard campaign, the legislative elections of March 1986 gave a narrow majority to the oppostion led by Jacques Chirac. But Mitterand, in accordance with the constitution, would remain president for two more years. Thus began an unprecedented situation of uneasy cohabitation between a leftist president and a rightist prime minister. In principle, it should last until 1988. But who knows?

INDEX

ABOUT
THE AUTHOR

PIERRE GOUBERT has been recognized for more than twenty-five years as one of the foremost French historians of our time. His ground-breaking social and economic study of the Beauvaisis in 1960 inspired a generation of students and researchers. His second book was translated in 1970 as *Louis XIV and Twenty Million Frenchmen*. It is still in print and widely read, as is his 1973 work, *The Ancien Régime*. His most recent book to appear in English is *The French Peasantry*, published in 1986.

Upon retirement from the Sorbonne in 1978, and the Ecole Pratique des Hautes Etudes, he has summarized his vast research and wide reading, his perceptive insights and personal interpretations in *The Course of French History*.

ABOUT THE
TRANSLATOR

MAARTEN ULTEE is a Professor of European History at the University of Alabama. He received his doctorate from Johns Hopkins University in 1975, and subsequently published his original research under the title *The Abbey of St. Germain-des-Pres in the Seventeenth Century* with the Yale University Press in 1981. Over the years, he has published numerous papers and served as general editor of *Adapting to Conditions: War and Society in the Eighteenth Century*.